Managing the Global
Supply Chain

This book is dedicated to our wives, Nancy and Vibeke

Philip B. Schary & Tage Skjøtt-Larsen

Managing the Global Supply Chain

2. Edition

Copenhagen Business School Presss

© *Copenhagen Business School Press*, 2001
Set in Plantin and printed by AKA-Print, Denmark
Cover designed by Kontrapunkt
Book designed by Jørn Ekstrøm
2. edition, 2. impression 2002

ISBN 87-630-0081-4

Distribution:

Scandinavia
DBK, Siljangade 2-8, P.O. Box 1731
DK-2300 Copenhagen S, Denmark
phone: +45 3269 7788, fax: +45 3269 7789

North America
Copenhagen Business School Press
Books International Inc.
P.O. Box 605
Herndon, VA 20172-0605, USA
phone: +1 703 661 1500, fax: +1 703 661 1501

Rest of the World
Marston Book Services, P.O. Box 269
Abingdon, Oxfordshire, OX14 4YN, UK
phone: +44 (0) 1235 465500, fax: +44 (0) 1235 465555
E-mail Direct Customers: direct.order@marston.co.uk
E-mail Booksellers: trade.order@marston.co.uk

Overview of Contents

Contents

Preface

The supply chain is a revolutionary concept embedded in a traditional guise. Commercial activities have been the impetus for empires. Supply relationships have paralleled the development of industrialization. Historically, practices and conventions were created out of the necessity to find ways to make a process work. Many have stayed with us. Others have been modified in response to technologies and management practice. Still others have been replaced altogether. The new elements are the need and the ability to coordinate the chain of activities that become the industrial process. The supply chain is driven by competition, but in new forms that extend beyond any individual enterprise. It is now a management concept with a broad sweep, with tangible implications for the marketplace.

This book represents an attempt to describe the complete supply chain, a task that is ultimately unrealistic. The book began as a course in international logistics. The difference in perspective between Europe and North America led us to the supply chain as an effort to find a useful common denominator that would provide a more general basis for management action. The first edition was reasonably well received. However, it soon became evident that we were dealing with a system that was undergoing rapid evolution, in directions that were not evident at the time of writing.

Much has changed about the concept and practice of the supply chain since we wrote the first edition. Rather than merely try to update the book, we recognized that it was necessary to rethink the entire process. The advent of the Internet, NAFTA, the euro and the World Trade Organization were still in the future. Third-party logistics providers, subcontract manufacturing, e-procurement, e-marketplaces and virtual supply chains had yet to develop. Mass customization, enterprise resource planning, advanced planning and scheduling tools, collaborate planning and network management, while in use, had yet to become major influences.

Decisions flow from the customer, determining products and services, extending back into the chain beyond the immediate partners to the network of suppliers. This has projected customer preferences into the production process. The flow has enlarged the scope of the supply chain to include product design, development of production processes and now moves towards direct distribution. At the same time, outsourcing and direct distribution are changing business institutions. What was once a set of stable relationships is becoming a set of fluid networks linked electronically and subject to rapid change.

The global sweep of the supply chains has become evident in global products, produced in the global production system and sold in the global marketplace. The spread of technology and supply chain is equally global. It has brought greater product variety and lower prices. At the same time, it has invoked social criticism of trade practices, working conditions and environmental practices. Whether the balance is for the good or not is beyond the scope of this book.

This second edition is therefore a completely reconsidered and rewritten presentation. Some themes remain: the triad of activity, process and organization and the importance of interorganizational relationships. Some of the operating practices that were present before are still in vogue. Some themes that were not strongly evident before have come into prominence: the primacy of the customer, outsourcing, the substitution of information for product flow and the enlargement of the concept to embrace reverse logistics.

The task has been made both more stimulating and more burdening by the explosion of interest in the general topic. Supply chain management appears in public discussion, advertising and academic curricula. The general awareness of the topic has risen significantly. The supply chain becomes a new way of doing business, possibly to replace the older enterprise-centered orientation of the past. The burden is that there is so much more to include in a general discussion, recognizing that every supply chain is unique and that the approach of each industry to the task is different. Both practitioners and academics are showing a stronger interest in the topic, resulting in a flood of material in journals, conferences and workshops.

Supply chain management as a field is searching for a set of constructs that can explain and guide the underlying development process. It would be premature to say that we have found them.

The ferment is intense. One reader commented that, in our first edition, we were proposing a new theoretical base. It would be fairer to say that we are moving closer, but we have not arrived. For one of us, the stimulus of the chase has been enough to pull him out of retirement. For the other still in professional life, there is a huge inventory of future research.

As we describe our general approach to the topic, we wish to thank many of our colleagues who listened to our ideas and offered alternatives. In particular, we acknowledge the contributions of Ashok Chandrashekar of IBM Corporation, Herbert Kotzab of Copenhagen Business School and Thomas Skjøtt-Larsen of PricewaterhouseCoopers, who wrote sections in their areas of expertise. We also recognize the contribution through debating the issues with colleagues in Europe and the United States.

Our hope is that this edition will stimulate more discussion, even though it will make the job of encompassing the field even more difficult.

Philip Schary
College of Business
Oregon State University, Corvallis Oregon, USA

Tage Skjøtt-Larsen
Department of Operations Management
Copenhagen Business School, Denmark

1. Introduction to the supply chain

»The only way to gain lasting competitive advantage is to leverage your capabilities around the world so that the company as a whole is greater than the sum of its parts. Being an international company – selling globally, having global brands or operations in different countries isn't enough.«
David Whitman, Chief Executive Officer,
Whirlpool Corporation (Maruca 1994)

This statement comes from the head of a major United States appliance manufacturer, now a global enterprise. Capabilities describe the heart of any business enterprise, a complex system with several distinct but interrelated processes and a combination of strategic elements: marketing, product development, manufacturing and distribution and a global orientation. Any one can become a source of competitive advantage; none is sufficient alone. They must come together as a coordinated system, the true source of leverage.

Business is rapidly moving towards new perspectives of closely coordinated, cooperative networks, business ecosystems, competing with other networks (Moore 1996; Best 1990). The focus is on managing processes that engage other firms as partners in managed relationships to perform the activities necessary to fulfill the process. This is being propelled by a realization that any organization cannot be good at all things and by the expanding ease and reach of communication. This perspective is necessary not only for growth but survival in the struggle for global markets. No firm alone can accomplish the complete process of meeting the demands of the market in the face of this intense competition, rapidly changing technologies and evolving customer requirements.

Business operations are essential to strategy. This book is about management of the supply chain, the process of production and distribution that makes other strategic objectives possible. The underlying concept of the supply chain is simple; a linear sequence of operations organized around the flow of materials from source of supply to their final distribution as finished products to ultimate users. Traditionally it includes sources of material resources and the organization of processors, distributors and users. It also involves supporting enterprises to provide transport, communications and other specialized functions. Together, they become a single coordinated entity that transcends organizational boundaries.

The concept of the supply chain is not new. It is possible to trace the historic commodity chains that supplied industry in the past (Gereffi & Korzeniewics 1994). They were organized essentially as a series of individual enterprises, connected through independent buying and selling transactions, bound by the geography of resources and the available technologies. As resource use changed, or as local supply was consumed, the chains shifted in response to the market, guided by prices. These commodity chains, however, were limited by the available technology and organizational development. Management lacked the capability to coordinate operations. The only alternative to the market was vertical integration, the direct ownership of supplier or customer organizations. Formal management structures appeared in place of independence; authority to plan and control was derived through management hierarchy.

The world now faces global competition, focusing on rapid response to customer needs at low cost, accompanied by market access and rapid deployment of technology. A significant shift is taking place from mass production with standardized products and services towards meeting individual customer requirements for both products and services. Change requires new ways of managing the supply process. The arrival of new technologies in information technology and telecommunication plus new organizational forms in transport and logistics open new possibilities. They enable enterprises to reach beyond their own organizational and national boundaries to coordinate operations and management through the entire supply chain, without the investment and problems of direct ownership. They also require cooperation between organizations on an unprecedented scale.

Introduction to the concept

The concept of the supply chain underscores the importance of operations as essential to strategy. The underlying framework is the Value Chain of Michael Porter (1985). Porter described a series of primary processes that add value to the output of the firm: inbound logistics, operations (such as production), outbound logistics, sales and services. Other writers, as Mannheim (1994) and Treacy & Wiersma (1993), expand this framework into three parallel flows:

Product development. This process is the core of the firm, determining what it produces and how it chooses to compete in the marketplace.

Customer relations. This flow encompasses the entire set of activities related to the market: sales, promotion, sales support and market research.

The supply chain. This flow is the entire set of activities involving the organization and flow of material and other resources to produce and deliver the product to the final customer.

These major processes are normally treated separately within the organization, although they come together to serve customers, as shown in Figure 1.1. Product development determines the focus of the firm and its markets. It also defines its customers and their potential relationships to the firm. These relationships influence the direction and intensity of product development. Relationships determine how products are distributed and customer requirements met. Together, product development and customer relations determine the supply requirements for materials, production and the physical links to customers. In turn, the supply chain influences product development through production capabilities, capacity and distribution. The supply chain also conditions customer relations through performance and efficiency.

Realistically, the effects of operations and its effects cannot be separated from other elements of business. Which element is most important is not as relevant a question as their collective impact on markets and profit. Current discussion of the Web emphasizes this

Figure 1.1. The Three Major Processes of Business

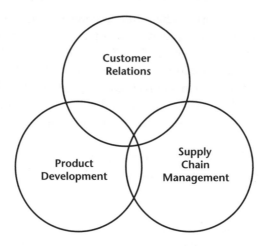

point. Our focus is on design and operation of the supply chain as a management process. However, we must also acknowledge the impact of e-commerce and the interaction of decisions in other areas beyond the supply chain. We must also recognize the scope of the chain, extending beyond organizational boundaries. Finally, the imperative is to manage it as an integral unit for the benefit of its members and the leading organization.

Definition

Commodity chain

Gereffi & Korzeniewics (1994) describe the concept of the commodity chain as a series of independent enterprises and internal organizational units, with individual transactions determined by the market, without overall direction by a single dominant firm. Traditionally, this is still a normal way of doing business for many industries, products and markets. It is sometimes referred to as a distribution channel, even when it also deals with supply and production. Vertical integration was the only alternative; one firm owned and operated the functions that preceded it as internal suppliers or supplying products to internal customers, who then sold products to users. The weaknesses of the commodity chain were 1) that it required firms to duplicate their activities at each stage in the process, principally inventory, and 2) that the system could not respond rapidly to change, other than through the price mechanism. It proved to be inadequate in meeting the demands of a modern, technologically oriented global society.

The supply chain

The supply chain emerged because it provides potential solutions to these problems of duplication and responsiveness. The concept of the supply chain itself is not new. It has embraced a concept of direct, extended coordination of operations across the entire supply process, replacing both the market and vertical integration as the means of managing the flow process. The key is the integration of operations of both internal and external suppliers.

A typical definition to describe the central concept is that of Cooper & Ellram (1993):

An integrative approach to manage the total flow of a distribution channel from the supplier to the ultimate user.

The notion of a distribution channel includes suppliers, manufacturers, distributors and customers, connected by a common process. It also implies a set of supporting links in transport, communications and other facilitators, to connect them to each other.

Integration stresses the coordination of a network of separate operations to achieve common objectives in material and product flow. These objectives include service to the final user and efficiency in the operations of the chain. Product flow extends across both functional boundaries (production, inventory holding and transport) and organizational boundaries (manufacturers, carriers, distributors and customers). It also crosses geographic boundaries to deal with global supply and markets. Boundary crossing involves different domains of decision. Each organization evolves with different practices and values. They have separate management structures and lines of authority. They have different economic characteristics, investment priorities and information systems. They often deal with different technologies. Management integration across boundaries is the major challenge of the supply chain.

Cooper et al. (1997) offer an even broader perspective, defining the scope of the supply chain as »dirt to dirt«. This definition encompasses both the source of raw material to final consumption and then to recycling operations, which returns used material to the material and product flow.

The Customer orientation

All of these perspectives assume that the supply chain anticipates customer demand and that customers receive products off the shelf. The direction of flow in Porter's Value Chain is clearly pointed towards the customer. This is a push orientation; product and materials move towards the final market, driven by forecast demand. A more recent view, one that we adopt here, is that *customers initiate supply chain decisions*, configuring products and initiating orders that pull products through the chain. The supply chain originates with the customer and decisions flow backward through the supply, even influencing the choice of supply chain members.

The developing e-commerce initiatives emphasize this point: decisions at the Web site determine supply chain process (Kalakota & Robinson 1999). A similar approach is the Value Stream, which starts with the customer, specifies the final product and volume, determines activities and then jointly defines the role of partners and their contribution to value (Hines 1996a).

Multiple perspectives

The supply chain is open to different interpretations, depending on the management perspective. Logistics, manufacturing and corporate strategy offer differing views on what constitutes the supply chain. Logistics orients the supply chain towards connecting the firm to its immediate customers and suppliers. Each firm makes independent decisions. The tools of logistics are transportation, inventory and information. Logistics stresses functional (activity) integration such as balancing production capacity against holding finished product inventory within each firm. It does not ordinarily deal with the operating decisions of other firms. In practice, this concept has been stretched by the need to achieve broader goals.

The major contribution of logistics has been the idea of product flow. Materials and other resources enter organizations. They are transformed through production and then are distributed to users.

Figure 1.2. Product Flow in Logistics

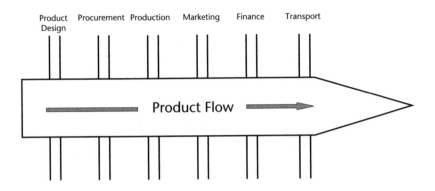

This process crosses functional boundaries, areas of specialized operations. It also influences and, in turn, is influenced by other functional areas, as shown in Figure 1.2.

Logistics interacts with every area of the firm. Figure 1.2 only shows the most frequently cited areas. It raises the question of how to cross the barriers that separate these functional areas from each other. This has been difficult because the historical evolution of business has encouraged the development of these separate functional silos as cost centers without formal consideration of other areas within the firm.

Manufacturing interprets the supply chain as an extended factory, with successive suppliers feeding a final stage of production, followed by distribution. It is less concerned with links to other areas than production but more with internal production processes. There is little direct involvement with distribution or transport except by implication.

The strongest argument is that it provides a focus. Transforming material into products is the core of supply operations. Supply chain decisions about where manufacturing takes place and how it is linked to other stages enlarges the scope of operating decisions beyond the conventional view of the factory. Manufacturing affects both material supply and distribution. In turn, production decisions are shaped by the requirements of other areas of operation.

The corporate strategy discussion often refers to the supply chain in general but in imprecise terms, although it ultimately fo-

Figure 1.3. Logistics and the Supply Chain

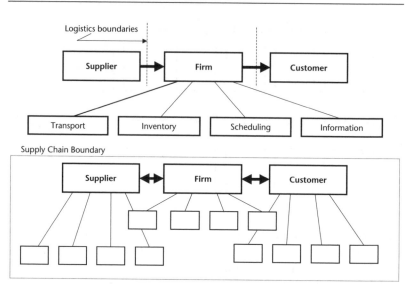

cuses on production. Further, it deals with supply in aggregate more than specific product flows. The contribution of the chain is usually considered to support other areas such as marketing and production rather than to play a central role of coordination. However, recent discussion recognizes that the management of the process is now an important source of competitive advantage. The ability of organizations to establish working interorganizational systems is not easily emulated.

Each view has merit. However, we seek a comprehensive view that recognizes these perspectives as part of a common system. The logistics perspective comes closest to this holistic view. However, it has the limits of organizational boundaries. In Figure 1.3, product and material flow through supplier to manufacturer to customer. Typical logistics decisions are shown for the focal firm. In the logistics concept, control begins and ends with the corporate boundaries. Each firm makes parallel decisions independently, even though they may affect the operations of the other firms in the chain.

The strategic view recognizes the key enabling factor – coordination among organizations. In the supply chain concept, control is extended over the entire chain, including carriers, customers and service providers. The details of what is to be coordinated and how are left to specialists.

The Characteristics of the supply chain

The supply chain takes on characteristics that are not unique in themselves but that, collectively, present new challenges to management. Houlihan (1986) has summarized the essential attributes.

- The supply chain is a complete process for providing goods and services to final users.
- Membership includes all parties, including logistics operations from initial material supplier to final user.
- The scope of supply chain operations includes procurement, production and distribution.
- Management extends across organizational boundaries to include planning and control over operations of other organizational units.
- A common information system accessible to all members makes coordination possible between organizations.
- Member organizations achieve their own individual objectives through the performance of the supply chain as a whole.

The supply chain both extends the logistics concept and creates an organizational system with its own attributes. More than linking operational units together, supply chain management deals with the full scope of supply activities: production, procurement and distribution. By dealing with a more complete definition of product and material flow, it recognizes interdependent behavior among member organizations. Directing this interaction becomes the purpose of supply chain management. It must take charge of all decisions that affect the chain and make decisions for the system as a whole.

The supply chain becomes an organization in its own right, a supra-organization, linking the operations of members. At the same time, supply membership is changeable. Individual member organizations pursue their own objectives. They may also compete for position within the supply chain, shares of profits or even entry into participation. This has important implications for the future of management in general.

The supply chain may also share members with other supply chains. Demands by more than one supply chain on the resources of individual member firms create potential problems for competition between members. It also suggests a locus of power: that the firm with monopolistic demand for its products may ultimately direct the development of the chain.

A case in point has been Intel, with its dominance of the central processing unit semiconductor market. Intel paces the product life cycles of the personal computer industry. However, this leadership position is only possible through continued programs of new product development. As competitors gain relative to Intel, Intel's power declines, but it may then shift to other parts of the supply chain, which offer possibilities for advantage, such as the PC market itself (Moore 1996).

Understanding the supply chain

Understanding the supply chain is prerequisite to managing it. The tasks are three: 1) to develop a framework for analysis, 2) to recognize the systemic nature of the supply chain and 3) identify the processes that are involved. Because supply chains become global in geographic scope, it is also necessary to recognize the implications of an environment with another set of influences, stemming from both factors relating to individual host countries and the phenomenon of the global corporation.

The supply chain presented here is normative, in the sense that we want to establish general understanding of the underlying principles. Actual supply chains vary, affected by their own specific circumstances and evolution.

The framework

Our understanding of the supply chain begins with a static view, freezing the chain at a particular point in time. There are three major components: 1) activities, 2) organizations and 3) processes and

Figure 1.4. The Framework of the Supply Chain

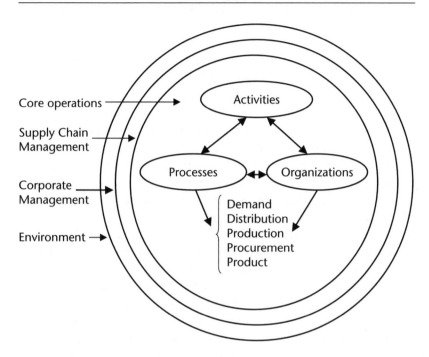

operations.[1] Together they become a »long-linked technology,« a long chain of activities and decisions (Thompson 1967). They are enveloped within an internal supply chain management environment that guides and seeks to buffer the process from outside disturbance. The chain is further linked to a corporate environment that determines strategic objectives for the supply chain. An external environment of industry, technology and local and global political issues, will further modify the impact of these issues. These are shown in Figure 1.4.

Activities become the foundation. The entire process of product flow involves a series of actions and activities that add value and

---

1. Several Scandinavian writers have independently developed a similar approach. The most current version utilizes actors (including organizations), resources and bonds (connections). See Haakansson & Snehota (1995).

change the characteristics of the product flow. They are the building blocks of the system. Organizational units, both internal and external, perform activities. These organizations thus become a reservoir of resources for the supply chain and take responsibility for performance of these actions. The actual operations include individual processes that manage and link activities and also become part of larger sets of coordinated activities. For example, order processing is an activity that is performed jointly by a customer and a supplier. It therefore crosses organizational boundaries and requires previously agreed procedures and possible coordination. It becomes a component activity in an order fulfillment process that, in turn, is part of an overall supply process.

Activities, organizations and processes together become the supply chain system. The supply chain is also a dynamic system. Activities can only be justified within the supply chain as they add value to the overall flow process. They can be reorganized by sequence, augmented, or eliminated as necessary for efficiency or effective performance. They can be shifted between organizations to improve system performance. Organizations as entities can be expanded, contracted, eliminated or created. External organizations within the supply chain can be independent, captive to a larger organization or organizational units. They require motivation and coordination as active members of the supply chain. They are also under competitive pressures both from within the supply chain and from other external competitors. The processes themselves include both actions internal to individual organizations and those that involve more than a single organizational entity. They are changeable as a result of economic pressures, new technology and environmental changes within the global economy.

Together activities, organizations and processes present a static view of the supply chain at a single point in time. A supply chain, however, must also be dynamic in the sense of rapid change. Change can come either through adaptation to a changing environment or through proactive initiatives to gain competitive advantage. Moore (1996, p. 15) conceptualizes the dynamic business system in the term »opportunity environment«. This notion opens possibilities to meet unrecognized customer needs, apply new technologies and respond to potential opportunity in changing public policy. The supply chain must also initiate change to achieve competitive advantage in the market. Strategy involves thinking in terms of entire systems.

Systemic approach

The supply chain is both a network and a system. The network properties involve the sequence of connections among organizational units for product flow and information; the systemic properties are the interdependence of activities, organizations and processes. As one example, transportation transit times influence the amount of inventory held within the system. In the case of global corporations, producing in Asia for delivery to North America and Europe ultimately means that transit times are either long (by surface transport) or costly (by air). These companies produce a limited number of products because each product requires inventory and the longer transit times require more inventory for each product. High inventory costs then often force changes to air transportation or a reduced number of items. This makes the task of marketing more difficult. It becomes harder to match the specific needs of individual customers and market segments. This will also force the production task to adopt fewer and simpler product components that can be combined to build product variety.

The decision to source in Asia to supply Western markets unleashes a chain of events and potential points of disturbance that modify decisions in many areas. While the above example identifies specific influences and consequences of the decision, it can also result in unintended consequences as different elements interact with each other.

The result is that actions in one part of the system affect other parts, in totally different areas; cause and effect become difficult to separate. The objectives of supply chain management are holistic, in that they pertain to the system as a whole rather than to individual members. It is also possible in pursuit of global system optimization to make trade-offs between actions in one area and actions in another.

External elements become the environment of the supply chain. They are essentially one-way influences such as differing issues in technology, competition and even corporate strategy. Changes in public transport policy such as expenditures on highways affect the transport system. Its costs and transit times, in turn, affect other supply chain decisions. In some cases, the environment must be re-defined, such as supply chain actions affecting competitors, who can then retaliate with their own actions. The system can only be defined for a given set of circumstances, but systemic effects will always be present.

The supply chain structure is actually several networks overlaid on each other. One deals with the sequence of processes serving the physical flow of products. This is normally easy to identify and provides an initial step for analyzing the chain. It is generally a serial arrangement in which the order of activities is clearly defined by the requirements of the process. However, it will be governed by a second network of organizations and their interrelationships. Direct interactions between two organizations may be governed by the indirect links to a third member only indirectly connected to the first.

As a case in point, a European food processor dealing with large supermarket organizations as customers commented that these large buyers require processors to buy their packaging materials from certain designated suppliers, to achieve volume order discounts. In this case, the immediate connection determines another connection once removed.

Other networks link processes such as the information links connecting the production schedules of a supplier and an assembler, along with the operations of the connecting transport carrier. Management may exert control over the chain through this network, ensuring that all members receive and are able to take action on common information. There may also be more indirect influences by one organization on others within the supply chain, through market power, political influence or technological dominance.

Supply chain processes

We can visualize the supply chain from several perspectives: manufacturer, retailer or user. In the discussion, which follows, the primary focus is on a complete manufacturing channel, from materials to final user, although few examples match the full scope of these processes. Five operating processes describe the supply chain (McGrath and Hoole 1992):

- *Product*. Product design determines production processes. It also determines logistics requirements for transport, inventory and time for delivery.
- *Production*. Production and related processes add value to product flow. How production takes place also influences inventory, transport and time for delivery.
- *Procurement*. Procurement or purchasing links stages of manufacturing together. In effect, purchasing departments become »managers of outside production.«
- *Distribution*. This provides the link between production and the market. It influences logistics through market requirements for service and efficiency.
- *Demand management*. This includes several related activities related to the market: forecasting, customer order processing, market coordination and sales support activities.

The management tasks

The primary task is to integrate each stage into a larger system. Individual organizations at each stage still manage resources, set objectives and pursue individual objectives. Even within a larger corporate framework, there is a danger from independent decisions. Customers are remote, lead times are long and markets change rapidly. Organizational independence invites conflict.

The concept of supply chain management is shown in Figure 1.5. Coordination is imperative. It becomes a basis for reducing the quantity of physical assets; this, in turn, reduces costs and improve response to change. In a static sense it can improve return on investment, but even more it provides opportunity for strategy.

Coordination becomes the first management task: to make market demands and customer orders visible throughout the chain and direct a concerted effort to supply them. The tools are information systems and organization across normally traditional boundaries.

Figure 1.5. The Management Concept of the Supply Chain

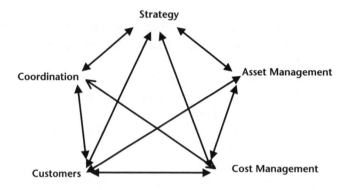

The managers of these traditional organizations may provide the resources, but the direction of operations shifts to lateral management matched to product flow.

A second task is to manage assets across the supply chain, and specifically inventory, to serve customers and reduce costs. Inventory creates costs. It also creates inflexibility because of obsolete inventory that consumes resources and reduces the ability to respond to change. Whereas inventory allows individual organizations to plan their own operations, eliminating it requires coordination in its place.

The concept of the supply chain, however, is more than coordination and managing inventory. It has the potential for strategy, to be valued by customers because it makes their own operations more efficient and profitable. It provides a framework for resource decisions, organizational integration and process design. It becomes a source of competitive advantage through the effectiveness of the entire chain and organizational relations. Building these relationships is difficult but also difficult to emulate. The competitive advantage can be long lasting.

Global issues

The term global supply chain is more than incidental. The interdependence of the world economy has ensured that every supply chain has international connections. Many international dimensions are involved in supply decisions for raw materials, production components or international marketing. Most international operating issues are specific to individual trading relationships. The only practical approach is to list cautions and hazards. On the other hand, presenting a more general framework concerning the supply chain can address the most central issues and then balance possible solutions against international limitations.

The movement towards global business is inevitable. At the same time, many of the processes are closely similar in most countries. Technology knows no boundary. National and regional infrastructures of telecommunications and transport are converging, although at varying rates of progress. Computers and software are becoming ubiquitous. To speak meaningfully of the global supply chain is to deal with a common structure, although with some variation to meet local cultures and economic conditions.

Another set of issues also directly involves the supply chain. These involve the social concerns of the ethics of exploitation of local labor, the power of the global corporation to shift production from wealthy but high-cost countries to lower-cost locations, labor relations and the power to influence local governments. These are beyond the scope of this discussion.

The New corporate environment

The emergence of the supply chain and the global corporation offers parallels changes in manufacturing enterprise. There are five fundamental themes.

The customer orientation. Customer requirements in response and product offerings are supreme. This has led to direct ordering, product and service customization and real-time operations.

The decline of mass production. In many industries manufacturing has moved from mass towards craft production. This reflects the marketplace and market segmentation. Niche marketing encourages unique products and short, flexible production runs. It has been further encouraged by changes to computer-assisted production.

Smaller inventories. Production quantities are smaller, saving inventory holding costs while increasing flexibility in production and distribution. The trend to smaller inventories is reinforced by the concept of lean thinking, which emphasizes reduction of waste and a philosophy of continuous improvement (Womack & Jones 1996).

Development of electronic commerce. The results on the supply chain are significant. Procurement has become more efficient as companies move to Web-based supply networks. Distribution becomes more direct, with less inventory between factory and market. Shorter chains are more responsive and can be more easily switched to different products.

Smaller organizations. Organizations are being reduced by both downsizing and outsourcing, a process noted as »the hollowing out« of the corporation. One outcome is the virtual corporation (Davidow & Malone 1992), a set of quasi-independent operating units pursuing a common goal, coordinated through electronic communication. It emphasizes corporate specialization and core competencies (Quinn & Hilmer 1994), offering their own source of competitive advantage. Other activities are performed by outside organizations. This includes many of the supporting activities of the supply chain itself such as logistics and information services. It has encouraged the development of new forms of enterprise in information system operations and third-party logistics service providers, which perform the entire process of physical movement and distribution to market.

These changes expand the scope and importance of supply chain management. Supplier networks become larger and multi-tiered as suppliers themselves become more specialized, feeding other suppliers, which send their product components to final manufacturing and assemblers for distribution. They place more stress on external coordination. Competition for customers increases the pressure for service and efficiency within the chain. The result is increased pressure for effective management of both internal and external connections.

The concept umbrella

Figure 1.6 portrays the general approach. The supply chain begins with the customer. It moves through five successive stages: distribu-

Figure 1.6. The Global Supply Chain

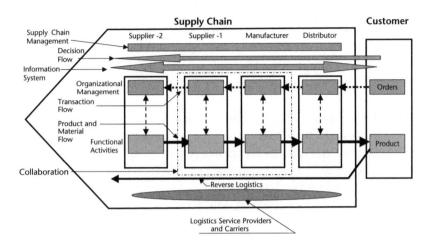

tion, final manufacturing and assembly, first-tier suppliers, second-tier suppliers to basic materials. In reality, the supply chain may be considerably longer. Decisions take this path, determining the choice of structure, partners and processes. Products and materials flow forward, towards the customer. After the product is consumed, product recycling becomes a material flow backward to a point of reuse or renovation. Information flows in both directions: orders and transactions move towards the source of supply. Product movement reporting and shipping transactions move towards the customer. All of this information is potentially available to all participants in the supply chain. Transport provides the physical links between stages through transport carriers and logistics service providers.

The approach of the book

This book follows the patterns established in this chapter. There are four parts: concepts, processes, management and strategy.

Concepts

The first section, Chapters 2 and 3, focus on basic concepts. Chapter 2 deals with the activity structure as the foundation of the supply chain and defining its structure. Activities are the foundation of the supply chain, the tasks necessary to process material to become products and fulfill orders. Chapter 3 deals with the network of organizations and interorganizational relationships. Activities are performed through organizations. Organizations become the building blocks, taking responsibility for investment and performance of activities. However, relationships among organizations are in transition, from market relationships to cooperation and coordination within the context of networks. This chapter introduces two different approaches to understanding organizations: transaction cost analysis leading to interorganizational governance and network relationships that establish the number and nature of organizational connections.

Processes

The next section introduces specific processes. Our emphasis here is not to focus on individual technical issues but on coordination and integration. Consistent with a view that the supply chain is a value-creating system, we begin with customers and customer relationship management. The path is from the customer towards sources of supply.

Chapter 4 develops distribution, the link between customers and production. It includes both traditional institutions in retailing and distribution and new and evolving forms such as e-commerce. It also recognizes the need to conserve resources through the development of the reverse channel, recycling retired products and other consumed materials back to a point where they can be reconverted into useful raw materials and refurbished components.

Chapter 5 embraces both product design and production. Product design influences customer requirements and the needs of the supply chain for organizing production and efficient processing. Production strategy determines manufacturing processes that in turn determine inventory requirements through their degree of flexibility and time for production. It also determines scheduling, in turn influencing capacity, inventory and the ability to meet market demand.

In Chapter 6, procurement links the stages of production from materials and component manufacturers to final assembly. The chapter discusses the changing role of procurement, supplier relations and international factors in supply decisions. Procurement strategy involves selection of critical supply relationships to develop into cooperative partnerships. E-commerce introduces new supply linkages both for on-going relationships and market-related transactions.

Chapter 7 describes the new transport environment of free markets and the addition of value-adding capabilities to the transport relationship. These result in the creation of logistics service providers, which have gone beyond transport to include a variety of services: distribution centers, merging shipments, kitting, light production and information-related tasks such as customer order processing and fulfillment. In a global context, transport options are specific to individual regions, making generalizations difficult and not very meaningful. If there is a geographic emphasis in this discussion, it falls on the European transport industry and its influence on distribution structure.

Management

The fourth section focuses on management issues. There are four topic areas: management; information technology; customer relationship management, a key area for contemporary supply chains; and supply chain modeling, to increase capabilities for management decisions. Chapter 8 describes management organization within the supply chain. We examine new forms of organization made necessary with the expanding scope of the supply chain and with new possibilities made possible by information technology. This chapter also introduces management tools including Activity-Based Management and Activity-Based Costing, the Balanced Scorecard and the Supply Chain Operating Reference Model.

In Chapter 9, a framework is introduced for supply chain information systems. The information system is directly related to decisions and coordinates operations of product flow. How and where it is delivered becomes an important element of management strategy. The evolution in this area has been extremely rapid both in software to perform transactions and to plan and control operations and in hardware, including computers and telecommunications.

In Chapter 10, customer relationships emphasize the role of the buyer or user within the supply chain. Their cooperation is important element in setting the direction for creating value within the chain. Customer relationship management is the interface between the supply chain and the customer. It is concerned with the product configuration to match customer needs and the order process. It begins with customer demands and leads to order entry into distribution and production. This chapter discusses the changes taking place in customer service. It also introduces Distribution Requirements Planning, Efficient Consumer Response and Customer Planning, Forecasting and Replenishment both as concepts and tools for management.

Chapter 11 is a reminder of the global marketplace and the issues involved in managing global supply networks. The visible barriers to global markets are diminishing, but many complex issues remain in managing operations across national boundaries, including the impact of global business strategy on the logistics and management of the supply chain. They include the issues of trade versus local production, the organizational structure of the global enterprise and how global decisions affect the logistics of the supply chain.

Chapter 12 deals with planning models and location. It examines the role of computer modeling for system design decisions, including both simulation and programming models. It also examines geographic location of facilities.

Strategy

The final section is strategy. We deal with strategy at two levels: 1) decisions with long-term effects within the supply chain itself and 2) the interaction of the supply chain with corporate strategy and the search for competitive advantage.

Chapter 13 utilizes the structure-process-relationship paradigm to focus on internal strategic options. These include structural issues such as the decoupling point, where the orientation changes from production and supply to distribution and the customer. We then consider the roles of process, re-engineering, total quality management and time-based management concepts in supply chain strategy. This chapter also develops the application of inter-organizational relations. We also consider the nature of the supply chain as a system.

Chapter 14 deals with the relationship of the supply chain to corporate strategy. After tracing the development of the supply chain as a holistic business concept, we turn to three contemporary views of supply chains. This is followed by the impact of the major technological influence, the Web, which presents possibilities for radical change in business in general.

Our discussion is global; we recognize that supply chain practice is increasingly similar around the world. If there is an emphasis, it is intra-European. Although the general principles of supply chain management apply, each region and country of origin has unique issues. A United States company dealing with the European market brings a different perspective than a European-based firm dealing with the same market. It will differ, in turn, from a European firm operating in the United States. These differences relate more closely to distribution and transport than to manufacturing and procurement. The impact of information technology is global and makes supply chain management into a rapidly changing but increasingly common understanding of concepts and practice.

Summary

Strategy for the global corporation is a quest for competitive advantage. Operations are now being recognized as a source of advantage and profitability. Three fundamental processes determine the course of a business enterprise: product development, customer relations and the supply chain. They are interdependent processes that must be coordinated and directed to successfully carry out strategy for the organization. Our focus on the supply chain emphasizes the flow of physical material and products.

The supply chain is both unique and an extension of the logistics concept. The uniqueness stems from its systemic framework embracing the entire set of supply operations. The logistics concept goes part of the way but is oriented to the actions of a single dominant firm. The key element is integration, not necessarily by ownership but by coordination of operations and decisions.

There are many ways to describe the supply chain, as a supply process. We begin with a three-part framework: activities, organizations and processes. Activities are the foundations, organizations are the building blocks and processes become the mortar to bind the chain together as a system. Processes include product design, production, procurement, distribution and demand management. This, however, is a static interpretation. The supply chain is also a dynamic process. Management must seek adaptation and innovation as part of the quest for competitive advantage in the marketplace.

The issues of the supply chain are necessarily global. Materials and production capacity can be located virtually anywhere in the world. Markets are located wherever they can be found. The central issues of a global supply chain are not necessarily international but are inherent in the structure and operations of the supply chain itself.

CONCEPTS

2. Structure and process

»Why do people call what we are doing reengineering? Our system wasn't engineered in the first place. What we are really doing is reinventing the way we do business.«
(an executive quoted in Bowersox et al. 1999, p. 134)

The supply chain begins with the customer. Logically, customer decisions on products, delivery and other service preferences should ultimately shape the organization of the supply chain and determine its performance requirements. This is a perspective introduced into supply chain management by Hines (1996a) and into e-business, a related area, by Kalakota & Robinson (1999).

Figure 2.1 provides an orientation to the general theme of this chapter. The supply chain is a process that transforms materials into products and delivers them to customers through specific activities. Activities are attached to organizations that manage and support them. Activities more than organizations are the building blocks of the supply chain. While there is a necessary physical order to production and distribution, where they are housed depends on economic and management considerations. The fundamental issue is the conflict between the process of the supply chain and organizational boundaries. Organizations manage and supply resources, but activities must have both coordinated operations and physical links to make the supply chain operate. The management task is to identify necessary operations and select their organizational location to realize the performance of the supply chain as a whole.

Supply chain management must organize and manage a potentially worldwide supply and distribution network that delivers a variety of products and services that respond directly to customers in global markets. Companies gain supply advantage through product development, production and delivery in complex networks on a global scale. These networks extend beyond corporate boundaries

Figure 2.1. Activity Flow and Supply Chain Structure

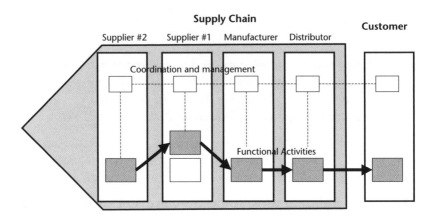

to connect to suppliers, distributors, service providers and customers.

How this network is organized involves strategic decisions that encompass procurement, production, distribution, transport, telecommunication and information systems not only individually but also as integrated systems. We begin with a discussion of Michael Porter's value system. Second, we turn to process engineering as a guiding concept in organizing the supply chain. Third, we turn to the opportunities inherent in the supply chain structure. Because activities are performed through organizations that are responsible for individual performance, the task is to determine where they should be located for optimal performance. Concepts of *functional spin-off* and *net value added* become useful tools in the discussion.

Fourth, the decision must be made whether to internalize or to *outsource*, letting partner organizations manage and perform activities as part of a coordinated effort. The management task is twofold: to design the process to link activities and to coordinate these activities to make the supply process possible. Organizing across organizational boundaries becomes more important as corporations focus on their *core activities*, leaving other less crucial activities for other firms to perform.

The next step involves a strategic issue: *postponement*. The decision involves balancing production in advance of need versus delaying processes for flexibility and reduction of overall costs.

Finally, we briefly consider the impact of e-commerce on supply chain design through the virtual supply chain. Electronic communication does more than connect and coordinate activities. It makes the entire process more fluid and able to be reformed for specific products, markets and customers.

This chapter focuses on supply chain design. The next chapter concerns management across organizational boundaries. Together they provide the orientation of this book. Our premise is that functional activities become the building blocks of the supply chain. They can be outsourced, shifted between organizations, consolidated for the system as a whole or combined into new forms of enterprise. This chapter explores the logic of the supply chain structure, using tools such as transaction cost analysis, functional spin-off, economic value added and postponement.

The Value Chain and the value system

The Value Chain was developed by Porter as a concept to describe a sequence of stages of value-adding activities for product flow within the firm:

Inbound logistics → operations → outbound logistics → sales and marketing → service

This includes both physical product flows (logistics and operations) and marketing (sales and marketing and service), adding value as the flow moves towards the customer. Value results from any activity that makes the final product worth more to the final customer. It can include the production of tangible products, rapid delivery, physical positioning of a product for availability or supporting after-sales support and service. Porter also envisioned a value system in which individual firms and their activities are linked to become a larger chain. This opens possibilities for reconfiguring the Value Chain for greater efficiency through eliminating redundant activities or shifting activities between stages.

Figure 2.2. Activities and Organisations in the Supply Chain

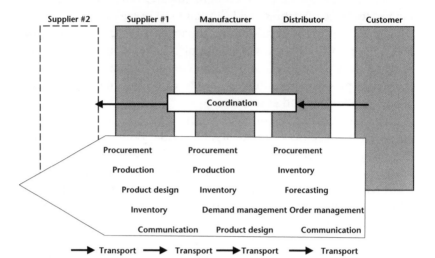

Figure 2.2 describes a conventional supply chain that might be found in Porter's value system. Each stage in the process represents a separate organization, and products are passed between organizations. Each organization is independent of one another. Interfaces between organizations become barriers to coordination and product flow. These barriers also require redundant functions for each stage, such as marketing and procurement to negotiate transfer of ownership and responsibility. Each stage manages its own inventory and production separately. The objective of supply chain management is to eliminate this redundancy by integrating operations, to make the system as a whole more responsive to customers and to reduce the total costs of product flow as far as possible.

The ultimate customer becomes the final judge of value. Each stage incurs costs, but value is created only by the final exchange transaction where the product comes closest to matching the specific needs of customers. Redundant activities, those that add costs but do not add value for customers, should be eliminated. At the same time, activities that add value even at increased cost should be included. As the definition of value changes, the supply chain must respond by reconfiguring activities.

Re-engineering

Any business is a process to deliver a product to a customer. A supply chain is a process involving a sequence of activities. It is both a single unifying process and a series of individual task-oriented processes. Processes link activities in a flow of products and services to deliver a result that matches the requirements of a customer. In so doing, processes cross boundaries that define functions within organizations and organizational boundaries that define corporations. A process is oriented towards a customer, coordinated through one single management.

An early proponent, Michael Hammer (1996, p. xii), has described it as »a complete end-to-end set of activities that together create value for a customer«.

Business process re-engineering becomes the vehicle to organize this flow. It constitutes a radical redesign of business operations, focusing on creating value through the end product of a chain of activities. The driving force behind business process re-engineering has been a search for efficiency and more effective response to customer needs. Organizational processes emerge as a series of activities to accomplish a task, often without any relationship to each other. As the environment of competition and technology changes, these ad hoc processes no longer fit the situation. Some add value, others do not. Hammer actually divides activities into those that add value, those that do not but are necessary to support value-adding activities and waste: activities that do not add or enable value.

Organizations have used process re-engineering to refocus their internal activities towards a common goal. Like all management innovations, it was initially applied indiscriminately without regard for the impact of change on the organization and the cost in human resources. The initial result was a series of failures in implementation. Nevertheless, the concept is still valid and applicable to organizational problems. More to the point, it also applies to the supply chain as the starting-point of supply chain design.

In a supply chain context, the process connects »islands of sub-processes« (Love & Gunasekaran 1997) regardless of whether they are housed in separate organizations or not. The enabler of the supply chain process is the information system. Evans et al. (1995, p.

230) refer to the process as »virtuality business process re-engineering« for electronic coordination of activities. Supply chain business process re-engineering is similar to intraorganizational business process re-engineering as a lateral organization to match the work flow. The common theme is »a specific ordering of work activities … with a beginning, end and clearly defined inputs and outputs: 'a structure for action'« (Davenport 1993, p. 5) but oriented towards a user or customer.

Because supply chain management is a process, the development and management requirements become topics for later parts of this book. They include lateral team organization, leadership, high-level support and especially electronic information and communication. Essentially it is a process for continual change.

The supply chain is re-engineered whenever activities are shifted either in location or organization. Microsoft re-engineered its European supply chain to replace one taking orders from national subsidiaries and delivering from plant to regional warehouse to distributor. The newer model relies on a factory in Ireland for complete stock availability with ordering and delivery directly from the factory to distributors, bypassing the warehouse stage (Collins & Reynolds 1995). In this newer system, distributors carry minimal inventory, shifting it to local dealers.

Hackman Designor, a Finnish company produced culinary items with a complex series of production and distribution units in five countries, expanding from Scandinavia into western Europe. It underwent process redesign in five areas: reorganizing logistics, redesigning information systems, creating a process-oriented organization, establishing a marketing-logistics interface and global coordination combined with local management. The logistics reorganization centralized production and distribution, changing the roles of logistics and sales (Juga 1996). Logistics now coordinates production and sales, whereas sales focuses on customer relations.

Three core processes were identified and developed: 1) meeting customer demands through rapid delivery of broad product lines, 2) improved customer service through more efficient order processing and delivery and 3) faster product development and commercialization.

The structure of the supply chain

In the past, activities defined their organizations. The term »manufacturing« includes multiple activities involving production. Similarly, »distribution« includes activities such as order-processing and inventory. However, these roles are changing. In the supply chain, the activity sequence defines a process of product flow. Management in the supply chain must be concerned not only with individual activities but also with organizing these activities more effectively. Management must have the ability to shift activities between organizations and change their characteristics in search of new sources of advantage and higher financial returns. These shifts in practice are more common than we would expect.

For discussion, we introduce a hypothetical computer manufacturer, Elektra Electronics. Their conventional supply chain is described in symbolic terms in Figure 2.3. The purpose is to recognize that functional activities are modular building blocks that can be combined, reduced in number, or shifted between organizations. The logic behind this approach is the subject of the discussion later in the chapter. We are using generalized designations of activities to avoid encumbering the discussion with detail. However, individual

Figure 2.3. Activity Deployment in the Supply Chain

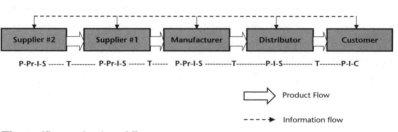

The specific notation is as follows:
P = procurement
Pr= production
I = inventory
S = sales and marketing activities
T = transport
D = distribution
C = consumption

Figure 2.4. Activity Shifting in the Supply Chain

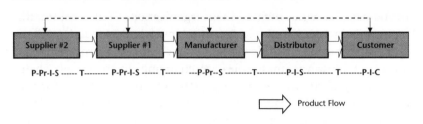

supply chains will use different specific activities to meet their own requirements.

The conventional supply chain includes procurement, inventory and sales activities at each stage and production in three stages, although dealing with different levels of the process. Sales and marketing are included here only to complete the value system. Orders are passed through sales and procurement to become product requests, entering into the production schedules of the manufacturer, who also orders from suppliers. There is a lack of central direction to this process, evident in the redundant activities and the separation of stages. The general tendency is to build inventories based on forecast demand, a push inventory environment.

One objective of supply chain management is to reduce cost by eliminating all unnecessary inventory. Inventory serves two useful purposes: to protect the supply chain against unpredicted demands and to protect intermediate stages against unpredicted delays and other failures. Increasing coordination can eliminate the necessity of inventory. Just-in-time production is one example. In Figure 2.4, inventory is concentrated as finished products at the distributor's level. This places it close to the market, where orders can be filled rapidly. At the same time, orders for inventory replenishment must be filled directly from production, both from manufacturers and their suppliers. This may be possible with stable demands and simple product lines. In most supply chains, there must be adaptations by letting suppliers produce to forecast demands. This is also a push inventory system, but individual interactions between stages may allow suppliers to produce directly to manufacturers' orders.

Figure 2.5. Activity Shifting in the Supply Chain

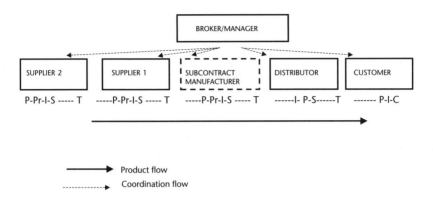

If customers are able to wait for delivery, avoiding inventories altogether may be possible in theory, producing to order all through the supply chain. This is a pull system, where the order pulls the product through the supply chain. Success depends on the speed of production and stable demands.

Another set of design options comes through activity shifting, shown in Figure 2.5. In this case, the »manufacturer« no longer manufactures but subcontracts to companies that specialize in production. The manufacturer now only develops, designs and markets the product. This is what Nike does with athletic shoes, the garment industry with clothing and the electronics industry with both finished products and components. This is essentially the practice of outsourcing.

The practice also works in reverse. Companies that were formerly only transportation companies now offer other services such as inventory management, light production, after-sales services and order processing. These companies, known as third-party logistics providers, take on activities because the combinations are more profitable than transportation. What this suggests is that the institutions that were formerly a set of customary activities are transforming themselves into entirely new combinations for new purposes.

A final set of options has to deal with customized ordering, shown in Figure 2.6. This variant involves the customer in the order process, selecting options and even variations of a basic prod-

Figure 2.6. Customized Order Supply Chain

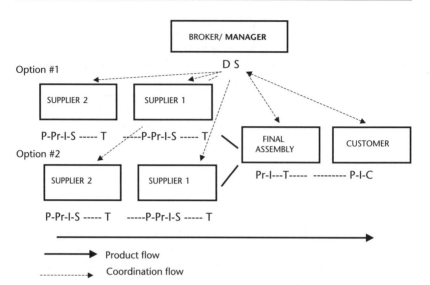

uct. One approach produces component inventories for assembly close to the market, but with suppliers conforming to final customer orders, possibly delivering on short notice. Dell Computer follows this pattern. A second approach avoids final stages of manufacturing, shifting them forward towards the market. This has the advantage of reducing inventory, but it usually depends on modular product design specifically for this purpose. It allows for a wider range of products by combining modules.

Figure 2.6 portrays the customer making a choice that involves selection of supply chains. Customer choice could select components before final assembly that involve completely separate supply chains. Modular products such as computers engage components with their own networks of suppliers.

What are activities?

Specialized activities define a system of product flow. They should only be included within the supply chain if they add value to the final product. Their collective scope extends to all tasks of the supply

chain, from product design to the final customer and return as recyclable material, although their individual tasks are narrowly defined.

As building blocks, activities take on a specific set of characteristics (Bucklin 1960):

- They should be related both to each other and the objectives of
  the supply chain as a system.
- They must be manageable as individual units, capable of standing alone or as part of other organizational units.
- They must be economically significant, adding value and incurring cost.
- They must have economic characteristics that create incentives
  for firms to specialize in them:
  - economies of scale (volume)
  - economies of scope (products)
  - specialization in specific tasks
  - specific operational factors.
- Their specific function should not be duplicated within the supply chain.

Most activities under this definition can be located at any of several
different stages within the supply chain. One option is to assume
their traditional location, such as production within a manufacturing organization. Another is to combine them with other activities
as part of different organizations such as a distribution center operation within a manufacturing organization. An alternative is to outsource activities such as final assembly to another organization,
such as a distributor or wholesaler that could also perform this
function. A third alternative is to create another organization to
perform this operation as a specialized task.

Core competencies and outsourcing

Core competencies drive the enterprise. The concept defines activities that an organization should retain for competitive advantage.
They create opportunity for prices and profit margins that exceed
the market. Other activities would be retained or outsourced de-

pending on the logic of the individual situation and whether the activity earns competitive returns.

Deciding on the core competency of an organization is often difficult. Sources of competitive advantage, including creating brand loyalty, knowledge of unique technologies and skills in management coordination and execution, need to be examined closely. The core is a shifting target; as competition changes and new technologies emerge, new activities become the core and other activities can be shifted to other partners. Long-established activities within an organization often have no advantage that commands a higher price in the market. Many firms would be left with only a few activities, contracting for the rest with outside partners.

Core and outsourcing are complementary concepts. While the core deals with sources of competitive advantage, outsourcing shifts activities that do not add competitive value to other organizations that can perform them at least as efficiently. Outsourced activities release management and capital resources that can be better used to pursue core opportunities. Outsourcing also builds flexibility; non-core suppliers can be changed as markets or supply conditions change. Companies that outsource can concentrate resources on areas that give them advantage, where they can earn higher rates of return.

Outsourcing creates external supply chains. Instead of internalizing activities to manage them within a single organization, they are performed by other organizations, with less direct control over the outcomes. It requires both careful selection of business partners and a need for interorganizational management.

At the same time, other companies annex activities that they can combine with others to build their own competitive advantage, building new institutions. A relatively new industry within the supply chain, third-party logistics providers, combines transportation with warehousing, order processing and even the final stages of manufacturing to create new combinations of service. The objective is to fit the specific needs of supply chain users, while introducing potential advantage for these providers.

The explosion of telecommunications and information technology favors outsourcing. The ease of computer-mediated communication and the development of compatibility standards make it easier to coordinate across organizational boundaries.

Outsourcing is now an interorganizational necessity. One organization cannot be efficient and competitive in every area. Competition between supply chains forces organizations to seek new solutions to what were once intraorganizational issues. Changes in the market are rapid, leaving these organizations with capabilities that do not match market demands, requiring new capabilities under short lead times.

Two examples illustrate the new structure. Hewlett-Packard established a new business unit with only 10 employees to design, produce and market low-cost printer units for computers. Only design and marketing activities are retained within the Hewlett-Packard organization, with production and other parts of marketing, logistics and procurement to be performed by other organizations. The only organization that is visible to customers through the product is Hewlett-Packard. Similarly, Nike designs and markets athletic shoes and clothing. Contract manufacturers perform their production overseas. Other parties also perform logistics activities and distribution.

Scale, scope and specialization

The volume of business may be a critical factor in determining when to outsource. Economies of scale have been widely used to explain why companies outsource activities that would otherwise be retained as a core competency. It is formally used in economics to describe long-term cost curves that decline with volume, as in laying out engineering alternatives for a production plant. Even competitors will sometimes pool resources to gain efficiency through volume production. Economies of scope similarly describe cost reduction that can be achieved as additional products are handled through a single facility.

From a supply chain perspective, activities could also be outsourced if there is not enough volume for efficient operation and other firms offer the possibility of producing at the volumes necessary to achieve these costs. On the other hand, there might be cases where diseconomies of scale with increasing volume would result in rising costs. The solution would be to outsource to firms of smaller scale.

Stigler (1951) proposed that firms might be forced to internalize

Figure 2.7. Functional Spin-off

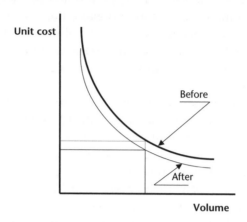

operations at early stages of production where there were no alternative sources, outsource at later stages when specialized producers became available and still later reabsorb these activities under higher volumes of production. Mallen (1973) introduced functional spin-off to describe a response to economies of scale that the firm itself could not realize, shown in Figure 2.7. Firms would use outside firms when it could not achieve economies of scale such as distribution center operation, possibly taking the activity back under efficient conditions, but then a still larger volumes under increasing cost, to spin off again at still higher volumes.

Specialization appears to be another important reason for outsourcing. As an organization gains experience and learns how to make its operations efficient, it gains advantage through its expertise and time advantage over potential competition. Although the advantage may be temporary, it appears to be real in many cases, such as the manufacturing subcontractors in the computer industry. Again, this frees resources for other tasks.

The general management focus is shifting from functional activities to process. Activities were traditionally managed through hierarchy, from the top down. The new orientation is towards the flow process, involving operations directly in making decisions. The change now taking place from traditional to activity-based accounting is only one indicator of the shift in perspective. The supply chain itself is another.

Financial dimensions

The debate about supply chain structure, where and whether to outsource, involves several distinct approaches: cost relationships, economies of scale and scope, value, financial measures, transaction cost analysis and postponement. The fundamental premise of the supply chain is that activities in the physical supply chain follow a logical order, from source of material through successive tiers of supply operations to final production, distribution and delivery to customers. The institutions that take responsibility for these activities will vary and may follow their own paths in component (supply) production. Activities may shift between institutions, as in the example of the third-party logistics providers taking over final stages of assembly and testing. The order of these activities does not normally vary: distribution does not normally precede production, although there is one case in the computer industry where a distributor holds components that are used in final assembly, supplying contract manufacturers.

Cost relationships

The revenues and costs for each organization also describe the supply chain. Cost data provide more readily available information on supply chains than any other source. Revenues can also be estimated directly, if there are intermediate product markets.

The concept of a cost driver is also useful in this analysis. The cost driver is anything that influences cost behavior. Output volume is only one of many possible cost drivers. Shank & Govindarajan (1993, pp. 20-21) divide drivers into structure and execution. Structural drivers include elements that also define activities: scale, scope and experience as well as technology and complexity. Execution drivers relate to operations and include workforce involvement, quality management, plant layout and capacity, product configuration and links between suppliers and customers.

Every activity and firm in the chain has its own set of cost drivers. These drivers not only determine cost behavior for their own activities but may also open up possibilities for adaptation through actions by other partners.

For example, if manufacturing an item costs USD 100 to make internally and an equivalent can be purchased for USD 90, it makes no sense to continue to produce it internally – unless there are other compelling reasons:

- suppliers that have unreliable delivery times, affecting production and delivery schedules to customers or creating a need for additional inventory;
- proprietary processes, with dangers of disclosure and exposure to competitive copying;
- requirement for complex coordination with other schedules; and
- a need for flexibility and short notice for production in a changing market.

In the case of activities that provide competitive advantage, the price created by the advantage provides another basis for evaluation. Suppose that the price of an item at an intermediate stage is USD 130 per unit. USD 130 less the cost of USD 100 to produce it is the profit margin per unit, USD 30. If investment per unit to produce the unit is USD 200, the return on investment is 15%. If this is higher than the returns of other firms producing at this stage, there may be competitive advantage to retaining the stage. Evaluating intermediate stages of production or services, however, can be difficult when there are no market equivalents for comparison.

If investment elsewhere in the supply chain has a higher rate of return and capital is limited, production should be outsourced. If there were no alternative investments in the supply chain that could yield as much profit, then the decision would be to produce internally. However, if other opportunities have higher potential profit, then the activity should be outsourced, in order to make other external investments.

This oversimplified example emphasizes three elements of the outsourcing decision: cost, the value of competitive advantage and return on investment. Direct cost comparisons are the easiest to calculate. However, if the use of an external supplier leads to changes in cost for the supply chain as a whole, these changes must be included. Similarly, if the outsourcing leads to a change in value of the final delivered product, that change must also be reckoned into the calculation. A positive change such as reducing inventory decreases cost, but may also reduce value because the next stage, or the customer has to wait. A reduction in value increases the cost.

Value

Value results from any activity that makes the final product worth more to the final customer. It can include production of a tangible product, rapid and precise delivery, the ability to configure products to customer requirements, physical positioning of a product to be available as needed, or supporting after-sales support and parts service.

The supply chain must be considered as a single integral system, with each stage contributing to a final output objective embracing both a tangible product and the accompanying services in delivery time and support. Each stage must be evaluated on its contribution to the whole. Manufacturing or its equivalent operations are considered to be the most critical element of the supply process, supplemented by suppliers and distributors. This, however, still does not include the firms linking the stages, such as transportation and telecommunications. Nor does it include customers, who often play an important role in interacting with other parts of the supply chain.

More than the performance of individual firms in the supply chain, management must focus on the total operational effectiveness of the chain as a whole. The focus on total profitability for the chain rests on increasing the value of the final output of the chain while reducing the cumulative costs for each stage and the links between. Customer service enhances value and should contribute more to revenue than it does to cost.

Profit for each stage not only measures efficiency but also determines the competitive advantage held by each member of the chain. Each firm must earn profit by processing operations to continue within the chain. Competitive markets for intermediate products or services often determine the firm's profitability. This profitability often determines whether to outsource particular activities to external suppliers or to internalize them within corporate boundaries. In his analysis of supply chain structure, Fine (1998) shows that individual industries tend to internalize through vertical

integration at one stage of their development and fragment by outsourcing at another stage, only to return to vertical integration at
still later stages in their evolution.

Return on investment

This is a simple measure, comparing net profit after tax to the net
depreciated value of the asset. It produces a number that can be
compared with the cost of capital. In a decision-making perspective,
however, asset value would be the cost of replacement. The manager
would ask whether it is worthwhile to continue to invest in the activity or whether capital would be better placed in other activities. The
disadvantage is that this measure does not recognize the size and
therefore the relative importance of the activity in the supply chain.

Economic value added

Economic value added is a parallel approach. It begins with the
premise that each activity and organization in the process should
add value for the customer. The purpose of the supply chain, like
Porter's prototype, the Value Chain, is to create value. One measure of value is the concept of economic value added. The most
common definition of economic value added is that it is operating
profits less the true cost of capital. It is thus the net addition of value after physical resources, labor and capital resources have been
deducted. Economic value added can measure the relative share of
value in the supply chain Kogut 1984). Economic value added is a
measure of total net profit expressed in monetary units, such as US
dollars. It can be compared with return on investment, which is a
ratio of profit to investment. In reality, both measures can be difficult to establish because of asset valuation, the cost of capital and
differences in calculating net operating profit.

Economic value added for the supply chain can be approached
in two different ways depending on the markets in which it operates. Competitive markets usually mean low profit margins, transmitted as pressure to reduce costs. To determine the relative share
of value added for any single activity, Kogut (1984, 1985) suggests

tracing costs, as these should not deviate significantly in proportion to revenues. In some cases, there may be intermediate markets with established prices that will also help. One problem is determining prices and revenues for intermediate stages for which no market price has been established (Shank & Govindarajan 1993). Another is that net profit has two components: volume and net margin. High economic value added could either result from high volume at low margins or less volume at high margins. The most significant stages of the supply chain can be determined preliminarily by the amount of value added. Examining the cost reduction potential and the need for control would follow this.

Associating organizations with general sets of activities such as »production« or »distribution« provides a way to approach the problem of specifying the structure. However, specific activities ultimately need to be organized across the supply chain. There may not be established markets, presenting problems in evaluation. When one organization outsources an activity, to be shifted to another, there should be a way to evaluate the value of the action. Data at this level may be difficult to establish because there may not be a market for the specific activity.

For differentiated markets with higher profit margins, market values for consumer preferences should be linked to the stages that create these values, combining economic value added and customer preference data. The critical question is to link specific activities to the demand characteristics that are important for the future.

Kogut (1984) notes that strategies involve selecting specific activities for their ability to generate downstream profits. Economic value added becomes important in determining which stages in the supply chain should be outsourced, despite the difficulties in comparing companies inherent in supply chain strategy. Stages with low profitability, expressed as return on investment, or low value added become candidates for outsourcing. However, there may also be conflicting measures, as in the case of high economic value added but low return on investment, or low economic value added but high return on investment. The first suggests that returns are competitive and that return on investment could be enhanced and investment reduced through outsourcing. The second indicates by the high return on investment that the firm has competitive advantage and should retain or even expand the activity.

This, however, is a static analysis that is too simplistic for strategic decisions. Kogut (1984, p. 155) suggests that future environments play a key role and that firms should control the links that are critical to their long-term success. As product markets and technologies change, the core competencies may also change. Firms would invest in supply chain activities where they can compete most effectively as »strategic positioning«. Further, activities could be retained to guarantee sources of supply of critical components, even though the firms may not have a distinctive competence in that area. The objectives are thus two-fold: to capture profits and to ensure supply stability.

Taking value added by stage as the only measure, however, is also misleading. The cost of operations and the profits of one partner can be affected by actions of other firms in the chain. The cost components of each stage such as material versus labor costs should be included in any analysis. They may indicate potential opportunity to shift activities, modify operations to reduce costs of partners or to generate new opportunities (Shank & Govindarajan 1993). Actions by suppliers to offer new products, change processes to reduce costs or offer new delivery proposals may change the source of competitive advantage for the entire chain.

Transaction cost analysis

Transaction cost analysis is the most frequently cited theory used to explain outsourcing and vertical (ownership) integration. Coase (1937) originally developed it to explain the reason for the existence of firms, as collections of activities. Williamson (1975, 1985) further developed it further to explain vertical integration by ownership. Transaction cost analysis is relevant both for defining the boundaries of the firm and interorganizational relationships. In this chapter, transaction cost analysis defines boundaries and outsourcing decisions. However, transaction cost analysis also describes organizational relationships and governance, which is the subject of Chapter 3.

In transaction cost analysis, the basic unit is the exchange transaction across a technological interface between two functional areas, such as production and distribution. Transactions can occur within common ownership as in vertical integration (also referred to as hierarchy) or between completely separate organizations, in arm's-length market relationships or in some intermediate non-ownership but integrated point.

In theory, there is a preference is for market solutions in which these firms are free to buy or sell to any organization, unless the cost of the transaction becomes higher than the management cost of internalizing the exchange inside a single organization. In practice, new forms of organization and computer-mediated communication expand the ability to coordinate across market boundaries. Even market-oriented exchanges begin to resemble hierarchical transactions in the amount of complexity of information and direction. This favors outsourcing over internal arrangements.

Barney (1999) argues that firms are now able to secure capabilities and direct activities across organizational boundaries more flexibly through these new organizational styles. The capabilities of potential partners should be considered in deciding the boundaries of the firm. The cost or commitment to develop specialized resources may favor outsourcing, even if highly specific assets are needed. This requires options other than the limiting cases of either hierarchy or the market.

As an example, Barney describes a situation that is not uncommon in global operations and especially in high-tech industries, such as computers, microelectronics and biotechnology. Firm A needs distribution in a foreign country for expanding its market. An already existing firm B may already have a distribution network in place that would serve the first company's needs. Using this network may require high levels of specific investment that could lead to opportunism in the future. However, the cost is high to A to build its own distribution network and it is not possible to acquire the firm that already owns the network. In this case, outsourcing to B and establishing a cooperative relationship may be preferable to any other alternative.

Modern telecommunication reduces direct transaction costs and substitutes in many ways for internalizing activities within the firm. Complex coordination appears to be equally difficult whether inside or outside the firm. Modern management stresses the use of autonomous decision-making units within an organization. The flexibility argument adds further argument to outsourcing. The supply chain appears to be filled with significant arrangements that are not vertical integration or market transactions but involve cooperation between separate parties.

Postponement

Two time-oriented forces operate on the supply chain: speculation and postponement (Pagh & Cooper 1998). *Speculation* is the act of producing and placing inventory close to the market at the earliest possible time to reduce supply chain costs. *Postponement* is the act of delaying »changes in product form or identity until the last possible moment« (Bucklin 1965, p. 68). This means operationally that inventory would not be produced, or that it would be held in a central location. Inventory is the balancing point. Speculative policies are costly in inventory, although they reduce the costs of production and transportation through the volumes that can be considered at one time; long production runs and large shipments. A well-managed speculation policy potentially provides a high level of service. Postponement policies, in contrast, minimize inventory costs but with a higher cost of production in small quantities and high-cost distribution and service also at a high price. The high cost of inventory and the lack of flexibility that heavy inventories create have tended to bias the system towards postponement.

Options in postponement

Between full commitment to speculation or postponement, Pagh & Cooper (1998) outline a continuum involving four distinct strategies: full speculation, manufacturing postponement, logistics postponement and full postponement. The two strategies in the middle blend these opposing forces.

Full speculation. Full speculation positions finished product inventory as close as possible to the market. It generally means multiple stocking points and inventories. Inventory levels control production. The principal disadvantage is the costs of facilities and inventories. Inventory cost includes not only the financial cost but also that of obsolescence, losses and handling. Multiple facilities sometimes mean a loss of control and transshipment costs between facilities. The strategy is useful where there are high service requirements as in health care or spare parts for machines, where immediate support is needed. It has also been useful in the past for international companies pursuing a local emphasis.

Logistics postponement. Logistics postponement consolidates inventory into one central location, a distribution center that serves multiple local markets. It may lose its principal advantage, the short transit times of local delivery, but modern transport can often provide equivalent service. It is still speculation in the sense of holding inventory but is also postponement in avoiding commitment until the customer orders. Inventory drives production orders as before. The advantages lie in the reduction of total inventory, although the central inventory must be larger to accommodate more volume and also to hold any local product variation. The principal disadvantage lies with the longer distance for delivery.

Manufacturing postponement. Manufacturing postponement mixes postponement and speculation. Products are produced to an intermediate form, such as modular components, and assembled, packaged or otherwise completed at a point downstream from manufacturing such as a distribution center or distributor. It provides more flexibility to the logistics system because modules can be used to extend a product line or to match product features to individual customers. Inventory levels of components control production but customer orders control final assembly. The advantages lie in the reduction of finished product inventory, the ability to meet individual customer requirements, product extensions to new markets, economies of scale in the production of components and economies of scope in developing multiple products. Manufacturing postponement as a strategy requires advance planning in product development and the choice of place and partners for final stages of production. The principal disadvantages lie in the time delays for the final stages of production and a potential loss in control over production. Examples include Dell Computer, where customers configure their computers on the Web for later production and the DaimlerChrysler Smart Car, where suppliers provide complete modules to be assembled into a car.

Full postponement. Full postponement delays manufacturing until the order is received. The delay must be considered on a continuum, from the manufacturing postponement above to the production of components as part of the customer order. It represents a shift towards more postponement and less speculation. The reality is that some components are usually produced in advance, although to a level where financial commitments may not be high. Perhaps the major difference lies in the fact that production final assembly takes place at a central point and shipments are direct to the customer. The advantage lies in the lack of reduction in inventory and the complete flexibility to meet new orders. The principal disadvantages are production cost and the time to produce to meet orders. Special purpose high-technology equipment serves as an example.

The factors that determine postponement versus speculation strategy can be divided into product, market demand and supply (Pagh & Cooper 1998). Product factors include the product life cycle, monetary density and value profiles, and product design. Lifecycle requirements vary by stage, with early stages oriented towards customer service and later stages towards cost and risk minimization. Value is associated with reducing inventory, and the profile indicates where value is added. Design involves matching to individual markets. Standard products can be held in inventory; specialized products favor postponement. Market factors are related to service; requirements for short delivery times and high frequency favor speculation policies. Supply includes manufacturing and logistics where economies of scale and scope can reduce costs or where specialized knowledge is necessary.

The virtual supply chain

The conventional view of the supply chain implies stability at least with strategic suppliers and customers. Another form of supply chain is developing rapidly that threatens to change this concept and with it the practice of business itself. This is the virtual supply chain (Chandrashekar & Schary 1999), also called the Value Net (Bovet & Martha 2000) and the Value Web (Andrews & Hahn 1998). Three themes dominate this view: a complete customer orientation, flexibility through temporary connections and instantaneous connection of all parties in the chain. In one sense, most supply chains are virtual in that they are coordinated through electronic communication. The differences are in orientation and organization.

The customer dominates the virtual chain. The chain is organized around the customer order. Bovet & Martha (2000, p. 3) note that »... a value net begins with customers, allows them to self-design products and build to satisfy actual demand«. As the order specifies requirements, a broker or lead firm organizes activities and therefore partners to meet these requirements, the value proposition. The supply chain organization has no permanent structure, as it is formed for one specific task, without necessary permanence. The same chain could be reconstituted for another order, but the customer essentially controls this through the broker's arrangements. The structure of organizational positions within the chain becomes irrelevant. They change rapidly for new orders. Each member in the chain becomes a partner through real-time electronic communication, with joint planning and shared knowledge. Outsourcing is only limited by the core competencies of the lead firm.

The constant element in the virtual supply chain is the sequence of physical activities. Materials become products in a series of stages of supply and production and passed to customers, possibly through a distribution stage. Here the web of connection for information departs from the linear sequence of activities for physical transformation. A case in point is a sequence of manufacturing of computers. Orders are received from a reseller (retailer) by a manufacturer and passed to a distributor holding component parts. These in turn are passed to a contract manufacturer for assembly. The finished product is then shipped to the reseller for delivery to the customer. The organizational path is circular, but the physical path leads from order to components released for assembly to shipment to the customer.

Concluding comments

Supply chains have evolved historically based on established trading relationships. The movement to supply chain management has encouraged re-examination and reorganization of the process. Structure is the starting-point, because it determines what has to be done and which organizations will do it. The orientation is systemic, looking at the process as a whole, crossing functional and organizational boundaries. It lays the foundation for interorganizational relationships and the management of subprocesses in customer relationships, distribution, production and procurement.

The natural tendency is to examine structural change from a cost perspective, as this can be measured. However, there are also pressures from the market for flexibility and response. Using value as a measure is more difficult and more subjective. It depends on the customer's perception of need. If the customers ultimately determine the supply chain, we must be concerned about how they determine these needs and how the supply chain can respond. We now begin to look at potential change from a different viewpoint, at the ability to deliver new products and expanding product lines, perhaps to meet new and changing demands from customers. Supply chain structure becomes part of a larger perspective in corporate strategy.

3. Interorganizational relationships

*»... Relationships are not only a way to acquire resources, but
also a way to develop resources«*
(Haakansson & Snehota 1995, p. 182)

Introduction

Management attention has moved from competition between firms
to competition between supply chains, encompassing all firms from
raw materials supplier to the end customer. The management's capability to establish trust-based and long-term relationships with
customers, suppliers, third-party providers and other strategic partners becomes a crucial competitive parameter. The increased integration and collaboration among companies within the supply
chain increases the complexity of management and control. It requires new management skills in terms of developing interorganizational relationships with strategic partners.

Understanding supply chains is difficult, especially because the
supply chain itself appears to be in continual flux. The key, and the
most vulnerable element, appears to lie with interorganizational
connections. While practice evolves rapidly in response to market
pressures and opportunity from new technology, the most difficult
issues stem from management issues in interorganizational relations. The most stable and promising approach comes from theo-
ries that explain the behavior of organizations, identify and evaluate
the forces acting on their relationships and provide a basis for predicting future behavior. The contrast between practice and theory
is wide, but as one observer reminds us:

»Before we can develop a theory of the firm which will assist our
understanding of how to develop successful external resource
management relationships for business profitability, it is impor-

Figure 3.1. Interorganizational Relationships

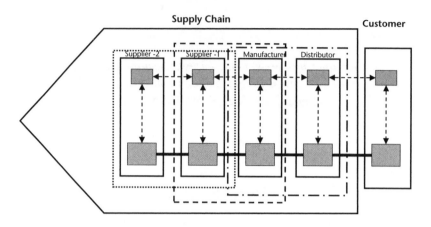

tant to understand that much of the current discussion about concepts in purchasing and supply is based on an atheoretical and unscientific approach to the development of knowledge« (Cox 1996, p. 58).

This chapter presents a theoretical framework for building business relationships within a supply chain. The foundation is transaction cost analysis, which argues for market relationships in relationships between firms. Then, we discuss some inherent weaknesses in transaction cost analysis and present some modifications of its theoretical assumptions to make it more useful in practice. This is followed with a complementary framework – the Scandinavian network approach. This approach describes how industrial networks evolve through time through exchange and adaptation processes. The focus is on relationships among actors in the supply chain. The sections that follow build on this framework: trust, developing collaborative relationships, forms of networks and the portfolio of relationships. A brief discussion at the end suggests the economic value of these relationships.

The issue of trust versus control becomes important in managing supply chain relationships. A high level of confidence allows partners to exchange sensitive information and to rely on informal agreements and incomplete contracts. Conversely, a low level of confidence requires control mechanisms to protect against opportunistic behavior from the other partners. We discuss different perceptions of trust as they fit different types of relationships. We also look at how trust develops over time as a result of positive business exchanges. Finally, we examine different types of industrial networks requiring different control mechanisms for different confidence levels.

Boundaries and governance

Managing the supply chain, its governance, is determined by organizational structure, in turn determined by the boundaries of individual firms within the supply chain. Defining boundaries is therefore the point of departure. Which activities should be performed within the boundary of each firm and which activities should be outsourced? Transaction cost analysis (Williamson 1975, 1985, 1996) presents an economic approach for determining boundaries, emphasizing the role of exchange transactions. Williamson distinguishes among three different governance structures through which firms can manage business exchanges: markets, hierarchies and hybrid organizations. The most efficient governance (organizational) structure is the one that minimizes transaction costs.

Transaction costs are »the costs of running the economic system« (Williamson 1985, p. 18). Transaction costs can be divided into two categories – ex-ante and ex-post costs. Ex-ante costs involve searching for and evaluating business partners and the costs of drafting, negotiating and safeguarding an agreement (contract costs). Ex-post costs include enforcing agreements, negotiation to correct misalignments and mechanisms associated with solving disputes between the parties.

An example illustrates the difference. A firm has to find a new supplier for a specific component. In order to find the right supplier, the firm searches among potential suppliers, evaluates them and selects the most appropriate one. Then, the firm negotiates and creates a contract acceptable to both parties. These are ex-ante costs. After the contract is signed, there may be costs from differing interpretations, enforcement and procedures for conflict resolution to which disputes are referred. These are ex-post costs. However, there is a close relationship between ex-ante and ex-post costs. Careful performance during the search and contracting stages can reduce ex-post costs substantially.

Transaction cost analysis rests on two basic behavioral presumptions about management perception: bounded rationality and the risk of opportunistic behavior.

Bounded rationality may result from insufficient information, limits in management perception or limited capacity for information processing. The actors try to act rationally; however, their intellect or their inability to communicate their knowledge or opinions to others restricts their ability to foresee or to act on potential conflicts. The concept is especially relevant in complex and uncertain environments. In an ex-ante situation with bounded rationality, management may not be able to identify and consider all potential options, future risks and opportunities as the contract is negotiated. In addition, control in the ex-post phase only provides limited capacity to control the results.

This may lead managers to adopt opportunistic behavior. Williamson defines opportunism as »self-interest seeking with guile«. He does not presume that all players act opportunistically but that some players sometimes will behave opportunistically, and it is difficult to predict who will be opportunistic and when it will occur. Williamson further identifies three characteristics related to transactions determine the most efficient governance structure:

- asset specificity
- uncertainty
- frequency.

Asset specificity is considered as the most influential. An asset becomes specific as it relates uniquely to a specific transaction, with a limited value in alternative applications. An example is a car manufacturer, who requires a seat supplier to locate the seat plant close to the car assembly plant. If the contract were not renewed, the seat

Figure 3.2. Governance Structures and Transaction Characteristics

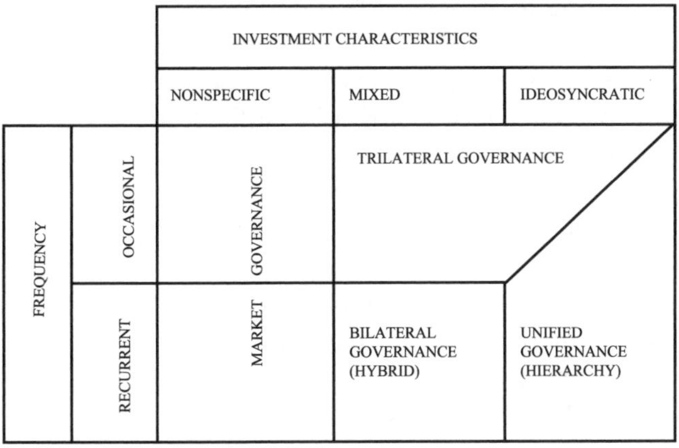

		NONSPECIFIC	MIXED	IDEOSYNCRATIC
		INVESTMENT CHARACTERISTICS		
FREQUENCY	OCCASIONAL	MARKET GOVERNANCE	TRILATERAL GOVERNANCE	
	RECURRENT		BILATERAL GOVERNANCE (HYBRID)	UNIFIED GOVERNANCE (HIERARCHY)

Source: Williamson, 1985, p. 79

supplier would have limited alternative use of the plant and might incur a loss in selling the facility. Williamson identifies several types of assets, such as physical, site, human and dedicated assets that often result in dependence by one party on the agreement and hence a potential cost in the transaction.

Williamson proposes that hierarchy (vertical integration) will be the most efficient governance structure in situations characterized by great uncertainty, high transaction frequency and high asset specificity. This structure favors complex communication, a high volume of communication and absorption of risk from uncertainty and specialized assets. However, in case of lesser asset specificity, He recommends »hybrid« governance structures that mix elements both of markets and hierarchy through different forms of governance. Finally, when asset investments are not specifically tied to specific transactions, the market becomes the most efficient mechanism. Figure 3.2 shows alternative combinations of transaction frequency and asset specificity. This figure presumes that all transactions take place under uncertainty.

Williamson further assumes that transactions often begin in an »ex-ante situation«, where the firm has many potential business partners among which to choose (large numbers bargaining). The bargaining position of the buyer is strongest at that point. A »fundamental transformation« then takes place through selection and negotiation, leading to an »ex-post« situation, where only a few partners are chosen to interact (small numbers bargaining). After having established close relationships with some suppliers and invested in relation-specific assets, it might be difficult and costly to switch to other suppliers.

In a supply chain, the focal firm might have many suppliers to choose between in the beginning, but once a supplier is selected, choice is only available at considerable cost and risk is increased. As protection against opportunistic behavior in such a situation, Williamson recommends that the parties establish appropriate »safeguards« to ensure that the other party does not take advantage of the situation. These safeguards may take on two forms:

- legal ordering
- private agreements.

Legal ordering implies that the parties enter into a formal contract covering as many aspects of the relationship as possible. The latter form presumes that the parties will try to reach a balance of reciprocity. The parties may enter into joint ventures, exchange stocks or make specific investments in the relationship (credible commitments). As a metaphor, Williamson talks about the exchange of »hostages«. An example is a buyer and a supplier, who exchange employees in order to solve problems in relations between the firms. In other contexts, these are referred to as boundary-spanning or liaison positions.

The assumptions and implications of transaction cost analysis have received much criticism among economists and management theorists. The major critical points are (Skjøtt-Larsen 1999) that:

- transaction cost analysis is essentially a static theory;
- the behavioral assumption of opportunistic behavior excludes business relationships based on trust;
- transaction cost analysis focuses solely on cost-efficiency and does not take into consideration the mutual value in the relationship; and
- asset specificity is treated as »sunk costs«.

Static versus dynamic boundaries

Transaction cost analysis implicitly assumes in the long run that only the most efficient governance forms survive, but the theory does not explain how the transition takes place from one form to another. For example, what happens if technology or the competitive environment changes? Noorderhaven (1995) has set up a dynamic model for shifts from one governance structure to another. The model is shown in Figure 3.3. The development of specific human assets often takes place gradually and almost imperceptibly in the relation between two parties. For example, a relationship between a manufacturer and a supplier might develop into a trust relationship over a long period of time, where the partners gradually learn to know each others' preferences and administrative routines. Thus, it is not a question of an abrupt and fundamental transformation, as in the case of investing in physical assets (machines and buildings). The parties are therefore not always aware that safeguards are needed, as the changes take place incrementally.

Supply chain relationships often develop over years of experience. The business exchanges are often based on informal contracts, and the personnel of the organizations involved have acquired in-depth knowledge of one another's procedures, routines and personal preferences. Formal safeguards such as detailed contracts may be unsatisfactory or are often not even available in these situations.

Figure 3.3. Dynamic Model of Governance Structures

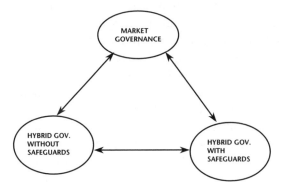

Changes can take place between three principal forms of governance structures: Market mechanism, hybrids with built-in safeguards and hybrids without safeguards. An example of a hybrid structure with safeguards is collaboration between a manufacturer and a component supplier based on a long-term contract with penalty clauses for quality and delivery defaults. A hybrid without safeguards could involve informal collaboration between a manufacturer and a supplier, based on mutual trust.

Noorderhaven makes several propositions about this transition. One is that a rapid build-up of specific assets will lead to a hybrid with safeguards. A slow build-up, on the other hand, will lead to a hybrid without safeguards. An example of a rapid build-up of specific assets is a situation in which a multinational company establishes a pan-European contract with a third-party logistics provider. An example of a slow build-up of asset specificity is the transfer of tacit knowledge between two partners about administrative routines.

A hybrid with safeguards becomes a market transaction if technological development accelerates the depreciation of specialized equipment and replaces it with more flexible equipment, which can be used to produce different types of products.

Is transaction cost theory »bad for practice«?

Ghoshal & Moran (1996) criticize Williamson's assumption of opportunistic behavior as »bad for practice«. They argue that the assumption of opportunism can become a self-fulfilling prophecy, whereby opportunistic behavior will increase with the sanctions and incentives imposed to curtail it, thus creating the need for even stronger and more elaborate sanctions and incentives. An exaggerated emphasis on setting up safeguards against opportunism does not encourage employee initiatives, cooperativeness and motivation. It is rather the reverse, stifling the very elements that could increase the competitive ability of the firm.

Long-term efficiency becomes the deciding criterion. This includes innovation and collective learning. Innovation activities are often characterized by high uncertainty and ambiguity and rely on strong trust and commitment between the partners. Collective learning in a supply chain is only possible if the partners have developed trust-based relationships and are willing to share knowledge and experiences across the supply chain. The original transaction cost approach will only work with stable business environments and stagnating industries. With other words, this approach is only useful in a limited set of business relationships. If the firm is in a dynamic and innovative environment – which most firms are – then it must rely on another paradigm, such as trust-based relationships.

Transaction cost analysis focuses on cost-efficiency

Another point of criticism against transaction cost analysis argues that the efficiency criterion is based on minimizing transaction costs from the perspective of the individual firm and fails to consider the joint value created by the parties cooperating on a long-term basis. Thus, Zajac & Olsen (1993) suggest that, instead of cost minimization by one party alone, the efficiency criterion should be based on maximizing the joint transaction value of a given transaction for the parties involved.

The transaction value includes the transaction costs as a subset of the total costs of interorganizational cooperation. These costs must be compared with the total advantages from the cooperation to achieve an overall assessment of the net result of interorganizational cooperation. Thus, the concept of transaction value is broader than the concept of transaction costs alone and includes the joint value as well as the joint transaction costs associated with interorganizational cooperation. The net joint transaction value is thus the difference between the joint transaction value and the joint transaction costs.

Zajac & Olsen (1993) illustrate the difference between the two concepts by the following example. Firms A and B are transaction partners. Firm B considers whether it should integrate vertically, that is, acquire firm A to minimize the transaction costs connected with the risk of firm A acting opportunistically during the term of the agreement. In the transaction cost scenario, firm B will make the decision based entirely on an assessment of the effect on its own transaction costs and not include the effect on firm A's transaction costs. In the transaction value scenario, the partners will seek to minimize joint transaction costs. However, cooperation between the two firms would also presumably create a joint value that disappears if the cooperation ends.

Dyer (1997) argues that high asset specificity does not necessarily lead to increased transaction costs as Williamson assumes. Williamson's argument is that, as asset specificity increases, more complex contracts and safeguards are required to protect against the risk of opportunism. Thus, transaction costs are presumed to increase with an increase in asset specificity. However, Dyer performed an empirical comparison of supplier-automaker relationships in the United States and Japan and found that the Japanese automakers had lower transaction costs than the United States car manufacturers even though the Japanese manufacturers made higher asset-specific investments in their supplier relationships. Dyer says this is possible because various safeguards employed to control opportunism, have different set-up costs and result in varying transaction costs over different time horizons. For example, the Japanese car manufacturers do not control opportunism through legal contracts as do their United States counterparts but instead rely on self-enforcing safeguards such as relational trust and stock ownership. According to Dyer, these safeguards might have high initial »set-up« costs but, once established, they have relatively low transaction costs.

Asset specificity based on sunk costs

Cox (1997) criticizes transaction cost analysis from a more strategic perspective. His major criticism is that the concept of asset specificity is based on »sunk costs«. Williamson argues that, when assets have been embedded in the firm with a high degree of asset specificity, then the activities related to the transactions should be kept internally in the firm. However, Cox states that this leads to the conclusion that companies are likely to be stuck within a particular operating structure and therefore not able to respond to strategic changes in market expectations or competitive conditions. If firms must respond quickly to changing technology and competitive market pressures, the decisions about internal or external sourcing should not be tied to the sunk costs of past transactions, which would lead to stagnation and myopia.

Specificity should instead be related to whether or not the specific skills, knowledge or assets contribute to the creation of sustainable competitive advantage within the supply chain. The more these skills contribute to maintaining or improving competitive advantage, the higher the value of asset specificity. If they do not now contribute at all or very little, the value of asset specificity is considered to be low.

Thus, asset specificity can be related to competence and revenue. High asset specificity means that skill, knowledge or technology is directly connected to the core competencies of the firm and should therefore be kept internally. In medium asset specificity, the skills, knowledge and technology are linked to complementary competencies. These could be provided by external partners with which the firm collaborates. If the skills and knowledge are of low specificity they are related to residual competencies, which could be required on market terms because they are standardized and the number of suppliers are likely to be large.

Barney (1999) criticizes transaction cost analysis for not considering the relative capabilities of a firm and its exchange partners. In a situation where the firm does not possess all the capabilities itself, it has three ways of gaining access:

- cooperating with firms that possess the capabilities it needs, through market or hybrid exchanges;
- trying to develop the capabilities internally (hierarchy); and
- trying to acquire another firm with these capabilities (hierarchy).

According to transaction cost logic, the choice should depend on the level of transaction-specific investments required. If these investments are high, the firm should either develop the necessary capabilities by itself or acquire another firm that possesses these capabilities: that is, hierarchical governance. However, there are many situations in which it might be too costly or impossible for the firm to develop or acquire the capabilities. This could result from unique historical conditions, path dependence (the sequence of events leading up to the decision) and the time required to create capabilities. In some cases, socially complex capabilities may be too difficult for a single firm to create or acquire. In such situations, the firm might prefer using non-hierarchical governance structures, even if the risk of opportunism is high. Barney (1999) notes that these situations are found in rapidly evolving high-technology industries, such as biotechnology, microelectronics and certain sectors of computer software.

Technology in the guise of e-commerce and other forms of telecommunication present another basis for evaluating transaction cost analysis. The increasing speed and richness of message transmission enables organizations to deal with more complexity in communication with partner organizations. Formal organizations are especially devices for communication through personal contact, bureaucratic procedure and documentation. When these messages can be transmitted electronically between organizations, transaction cost decreases, with incentive to outsource activities that can be performed at least as easily by other organizations. This change does not always lead to market solutions but, in some cases, to integration without the necessity for ownership.

Relationships from a network perspective

Transaction cost analysis is often criticized for focusing entirely on economic issues, failing to include personal and social relations. This argument has especially been used by the Industrial Marketing and Purchasing (IMP) Group; see, for example, Haakansson & Snehota (1995) and Ford (1997). It is a fundamental assumption in the network perspective that the individual firm depends on resources controlled by other firms. The firm gains access to these resources through interaction with other firms.

Industrial networks develop over time. The players, who may be individuals or organizations, invest in relationships with other players, thereby gaining knowledge of their network partners. The network has a built-in tendency to make the relations stronger and more stable over time.

The network perspective is closely associated with supply chain management. Harland (1996, p. S64) discusses the different meanings of supply chain management and defines it as »the management of a network of interconnected businesses involved in the ultimate provision of product and service packages required by end

Figure 3.4. The Network Approach

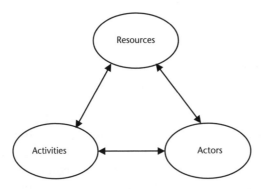

customers«. Instead of considering supply chain management as management of a vertical pipeline of interlinked firms, Harland considers supply chain management as the management of a complex network of organizations involved in exchange processes.

As shown in Figure 3.4 the network approach includes three components and their mutual relationships in the analysis of industrial networks (Haakansson & Snehota 1985):

- activities
- actors
- resources.

Activities are the commercial, technical and administrative functions of individual firms. In a supply chain context, they become the tasks that must be linked together. They would include procurement, product development, in- and outbound transport, production management, inventory control and order processing. They are connected by links between stages. The premise of the supply chain is that activity links become the vehicle to carrying out the supply chain as a whole. These activity links may also connect other links. The supply chain can be considered to be a network of linked functional activities, complex and difficult to map in its entirety.

Actors are both organizations and individuals. We ordinarily consider organizations as our principal focus, although individuals as managers make the decisions that shape the supply chain. Actors become the identity of interest because they hold decision-making power. Actors in the supply chain include suppliers, distributors, customers and transport and logistics service providers and other intermediaries. Actor bonds align organizations into a web of organizational relationships. The supply chain itself depends on the development of these relationships into an organizational Web. They involve mutual identification and commitment, leading to the development of trust.

Resources include the tangible resources of personnel, equipment, financial capacity and production capacity in addition to the intangible resources of knowledge, organizational learning, market image, innovative capabilities and patent rights. Control over resources defines the actors and their activities. Resource ties connect organizational capabilities as combinations of resources for new opportunities. The resource structure determines the structure of the supply chain and becomes its motivating force.

The organization of the supply chain follows a general pattern developed by Haakansson & Snehota (1995). Links serve a functional purpose for individual firms by defining opportunities and constraints through the connections to other organizations and their resources. Relationships among partners (dyads) have the potential to establish teams that combine resources to achieve more than they could individually. The combination can become as Haakansson & Snehota (1995) suggest, a quasi-organization. Links also build networks, with both direct and indirect connections. Firms are affected not only by their own operations and those of partner (dyad) organizations but also by other organizations to which they may be connected only indirectly. Haakansson & Snehota (1995, p. 41) comment that:

>»The network is usually seen as a structure of actors. However, a challenging idea is to set it at a lower level [such as resource ties]. Then the position of all elements (actors, activities, resources and their bonds, links and ties) is given by the existing relations.«

A little later, after discussing the evolution of networks towards new forms, they say that:

»The emergent structure has in any given moment a limiting effect on its actors at the same time as it provides the base for future development.«

A framework for analysis, especially relevant for the supply chain, summarizes this network development in Table 3.1

Following the previous chapter, we start with activities to define the tasks of the supply chain, although actors are the most outwardly visible elements. Activities become an interconnected pattern and the ultimate design for supply chain activities.

We would perceive the firm as structures of organizations, resources and activities. Through actors' bonds, the firm becomes part of a connected Web that enables it to achieve its goals. This Web is the counterpart to the visible supply chain. At the same time, it is bound by the potential opportunities and constraints of the resource network.

The profile of business networks evolves through the interaction of these activity links, resource ties and actor bonds as subnetworks. The resource ties often determine the selection of actors and activity links.

A useful element in developing strategy is mapping the resource structure, to identify potential actors and their capabilities and constraints and then to establish the activity links to enable the system to function.

Activity links are the sequence of actions that link resources and organizations with markets. They reflect the command of resources and knowledge of individual network partners. Activities define the organization through its functions within the network. Activities themselves reflect two opposing forces: economy and effectiveness. Economy involves a search for efficiency, favoring standardization

Table 3.1. Framework for the analysis of network relations

	Company	Relationship	Network
Activities	Activity set	Activity links	Activity pattern
Actors	Organizational structure	Actors' bonds	Web of actors
Resources	Resource collection	Resource ties	Resource constellation

Source: Haakansson & Snehota (1995, p. 45)

and scale economies. Effectiveness, the ability to deliver differentiated performance, matches the requirements of other activities. Activity links between firms in a network develop through two separate, but closely linked types of interaction:

- exchange processes
- adaptation processes.

Exchange processes include exchange of information, goods and services and social processes. Adaptation is a set of social processes covering not only personal relations but also, for example, technical, legal, logistics and administrative elements. Through direct communication, they convey a sense of uniqueness, ultimately resulting in some supply chains as customization to meet individual customer requirements. The parties gradually build up mutual trust through the social exchange processes. In addition to efficiency and adaptation, activities are interrelated through activity links that synchronize their actions. As these links connect to others, they become an activity network connecting resources. They are governed through relationships between organizations.

Resources are defined and gain value only by being used in combination with other resources. Through adaptation, resources are combined within a resource constellation to produce unique outcomes. Resource ties enable the organization to secure resources to which it does not already have access. Ties can become more important than possessing resources per se and can always be expanded to match new opportunities. However, they are also changeable as new situations arise.

Managing resources requires continuing investment and recognition that they can always be further exploited through innovation from experimentation. Further, there may be no optimal allocation, only a search process.

Actor bonds recognize that all firms are integrated into a network context. Individual firms have specific attributes, but they achieve identity in their role in relation to other firms through mutual orientation. By adapting activities, they achieve trust that leads towards commitment. These bonds and perceptions become a basis for future development. Bonds must necessarily be limited because internal resources are limited. Close relations between a buyer and its suppliers only become possible with a few extensively developed links.

Adaptation and trust go hand in hand. Adaptation processes are important for several reasons. First, they strengthen bonds between the parties. If a supplier has adjusted its production process or products to the needs of a particular customer, it becomes more dependent on this customer and vice versa. Second, by adjusting to each other's needs, the parties signal that their mutual relations are stable and lasting and not governed by short-term profit opportunities. Adaptation processes within the network could include mutual modification of products, administrative systems and production processes to achieve more efficient utilization of resources.

Through interaction, the parties in a network develop various kinds of mutual bonds that tend to create long-term relationships between the parties. Haakansson & Johanson (1990) distinguish between:

- technical bonds, attached to the technologies applied by the firms;
- social bonds in the form of personal trust;
- administrative bonds resulting from adjusting administrative routines and systems; and
- legal bonds in the form of contracts between the firms.

Networks are simultaneously both stable and dynamic. New relations are established, and old relations come to an end for various reasons. Some relations are strong, and others are weak, but existing relations also change over time. Thus, a network has a dynamic nature that does not seek an optimal equilibrium but is in constant state of movement and change. In a supply chain, a firm could have loose and changing relations with a large number of potential suppliers but strong, long-term ties with a limited number of key suppliers and key customers.

Any network has a power structure in which individual players have different relative strengths as a basis to act and influence the actions of other players. This power structure combined with the players' contradictory and common interests influence the development of the network. Contradiction is expressed in conflict, such as buyers and sellers negotiating for profit margins. Common interests could be the pursuit of a common vision of a product that is successful in the final market. The power structure also determines the role and position of the individual firm in relation to other firms in the network. The perception of the firm's role and position in the network defines the firm's strategic identity as it is shaped and developed through interaction with other firms. Thus, there is mutual interaction between the strategic identity of a firm, the development of the firm's industrial activities and its relations with other firms in the network.

The existence of any specific network is just one of a large number of possible structures. By establishing new relations, finding new cooperators or making new investments, the firm strives to use the network to create a competitively advantageous position. In a network strategy, a central element is the ability to influence both the direct and indirect players through the direct players. Thus, firms in a supply chain can influence not only suppliers and customers but also their suppliers' suppliers and customers' customers. The network connects players who may also belong to other networks. The performance of a firm depends not only on how efficiently it cooperates with its direct partners but also on how well they cooperate with their own partners.

Hertz (1998) has demonstrated how changes in one relationship can explain sequential, consecutive changes in other relationships. She calls it »domino effects«. When a change occurs in a network, interdependence induces a number of positive and negative effects on organizations throughout the network and in other networks as well. In the transport sector, Deutsche Post recently acquired Danzas, causing disruption of a strategic alliance between Danzas and DFDS Transport, because Danzas also owns the Swedish forwarder ASG, a fierce competitor to DFDS Transport in the Scandinavian transport market. DFDS Transport then acquired another Danish competitor DanTransport to strengthen its position in the Nordic market. Shortly thereafter, a third Danish transport company – DSV/Samson – took over the newly established DFDS Dantransport. The initial acquisition by Deutsche Post thus resulted in a major concentration within Denmark's transport and forwarding market.

Haakansson & Johanson (1990) distinguish between formal and informal networks. This distinction is relevant for the management of supply chains for various reasons. Firstly, formal cooperation between the firms in a network is more visible to the firms involved as well as to external players. Secondly, informal cooperation is based on trust developed through social exchange processes. Informal cooperation develops as a consequence of the parties' mutual interest in cooperation.

In informal cooperation, business transactions come first and the vision of cooperation comes later. In formal cooperation, the visualization comes first, whereas the actual cooperation does not happen until trust between the parties has developed. An example of informal cooperation is a customer-supplier relationship that has gradually developed from repeated transactions into a single sourcing arrangement without a formal contract. Formal cooperation with a third-party logistics provider begins with a contract, which may gradually turn into a trust relationship.

Thirdly, informal cooperation often begins and develops between persons directly involved in operations, whereas formal cooperation often is established at a strategic management level. Formal as well as informal cooperative relations can create »entry barriers« to external players, but also »exit barriers« for the partners involved. According to network theory, a firm's relations with other firms often constitute its most valuable resource. Access to complementary resources in other firms is an important asset. Nelson & Winter (1982) point out that invisible assets (tacit knowledge) play a central role in sustaining the competitiveness of a firm because of causal ambiguity and difficulties in imitating. The invisible assets are often created in and cannot be separated from external relations. If the network is broken, the invisible assets also disappear. This becomes an important reason why network relations become stable over time.

The network perspective assumes that the firm's continuous interaction with other players becomes an important factor in the development of new resources and competencies. The assumption changes the focus from how the firm allocates and structures its internal resources towards how the firm relates its activities and resources to those of other players in the supply chain. The network theory makes an essential contribution to the understanding of the dynamics of interorganizational relations by emphasizing the importance of »personal chemistry« between parties, the build-up of trust through positive long-term cooperative relations and the mutual adjustment of routines and systems.

Different perceptions of trust

The concept of trust is central in understanding how interorganizational relationships develop. At the same time, trust is a diffuse concept, defined in different ways, depending on whether the perspective is psychological, sociological, anthropological or economic. There is no generally accepted definition of the concept of trust.

According to Williamson (1993, p. 484), personal trust is reserved for very special relationships between family, friends and lovers and therefore does not belong in the world of business relations. »Such trust is also the stuff of which tragedy is made. It goes to the essence of the human condition.« Williamson (1985, p. 64) does not deny the existence of trust in business relations, but he states »differential trustworthiness is rarely transparent ex ante. As a consequence, ex ante screening efforts are made and ex post safeguards are created«. Thus, in his view, the concept of trust is based on a view that the other party acts from self-interest by not acting in an opportunistic way.

Sako (1992) identifies three types of trust:

- contractual trust
- competence trust
- goodwill trust.

Contractual trust means that the trade partners can expect that written or oral promises will be kept. This is an important element in all market transactions exemplified by a buyer's reliance on a vendor to deliver on time according to agreements. Competence trust means having confidence in a partner's competence to carry out a specific task, such as the carrier's capability of transporting the goods from A to B without damages or delays.

Goodwill trust is a more diffuse type, reflecting a secure feeling that partners possess a moral commitment to the relationship. It implies that partners are willing to go beyond formal agreements to do whatever is required, such as exceeding the customer's expectations by improving quality or offering preferential treatment or help whenever the need arises. Supply chain management assumes the existence of goodwill trust. The parties are expected to share both gains and risks equitably. It is not an immediate reciprocal relationship but one based on a common vision and long-term reward.

Barney & Hansen (1994) discuss how trustworthiness can be a source of competitive advantage. They define trust as »the mutual confidence that no party to an exchange will exploit another's vulnerabilities«. They also distinguish between trust and trustworthiness. Trust is characteristic of the relation between parties, whereas trustworthiness is a characteristic of the individual partners. A partner is trustworthy when he or she is worthy of other people's trust. Barney & Hansen establish three types of trust:

- weak trust (limited possibilities of opportunism)
- semi-strong trust (trust through regulations)
- strong trust (hard-core trustworthiness).

Situations of weak and semi-strong trust can usually be regulated through the market or adequate economic and social safeguards. In situations requiring strong trust, trustworthy behavior usually rests on values, principles and standards that are internalized in the parties participating in a commercial exchange. Thus, trustworthiness is specified by outside parties in relation to a concrete commercial exchange.

Barney & Hansen's principal thesis is that the vulnerability in strong trust situations with opportunism by the other party that ex-post economic and social governance structures cannot be established. If the parties have sufficiently strong trust in each other, they can establish a competitive advantage over other partners without such a high level of interpersonal trust. Consider a firm contemplating cooperation with a rival firm to develop new, advanced technology; this is associated with great risk but also large potential earnings if they succeed. Firms that develop strong mutual trust with partners have greater opportunities arising from cooperation for competitive advantage than firms that must protect themselves through safeguards. In supply chains where innovation plays a major role, the existence of strong trust is an essential assumption for developing interorganizational relations.

Haugland & Groenhaug (1995) argue that authority (control) and trust represent two different modes of governance mechanisms. Authority means monitoring through rules and procedures. Trust, in contrast, implies monitoring by social norms and personal relationships. The governance of supply chains can be viewed as different combinations of control and trust. According to transaction cost analysis, the actors secure their interests by developing formal structures as safeguards. In the network approach, the actors secure their interests by developing trust relationships. Both governance mechanisms should be pursued simultaneously for generating confidence in supply chain management relationships.

Developing collaborative relationships

Ring & Van de Ven (1994) have developed a model that describes the different phases the parties undergo in developing interorganizational cooperation. The model is shown in Figure 3.5.

Ring & Van de Ven describe a three-phase iterative process:

Figure 3.5. Process Model of Interorganizational Relations

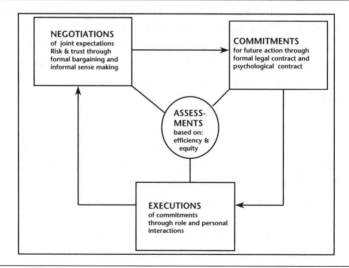

Source: Ring & Van de Ven (1994)

- negotiation
- commitment
- execution.

Each phase is rated regarding both efficiency and equity between parties. The duration depends on the level of uncertainty involved in each particular case, the degree of trust and the role of relationships between the parties.

The Ring & Van de Ven model of cooperation emphasizes the importance of a balance between formal and informal relations. If informal relations are overemphasized, the business relationship risks depend excessively on the relations between the competencies of individuals. If one or more of these individuals should leave the firm, the business relationship risks falling apart. Conversely, focusing on formal contracts that try to allow for any conceivable situation may involve the risk of disintegrating cooperation, as trust within the relations is lacking. The relative weighting between formal and informal relations changes over time. Formal relations weigh in more at the beginning of interorganizational cooperation, but informal relations increase in weight as personal and social relations develop between the parties.

The Ring & Van de Ven model describes how interorganizational relations develop over time and why relations cease to exist. Thus, the model supplements the network perspective, which is largely concerned with the initial development of these relations.

Forms of networks

Management issues led Miles & Snow (1992) to suggest three organizational forms of networks that are especially relevant to the supply chain: the stable network, the internal network and the dynamic network. The form refers to how the network is utilized by the lead firm. All three are specifically relevant to the supply chain. Figure 3.6 shows a stable network.

Stable networks typify many current buyer-seller relationships. The core business is connected to suppliers through unchanging long-term connections. The advantage is that both parties gain experience from close association and working with each other. This

Figure 3.6. Stable Supply Chain Network

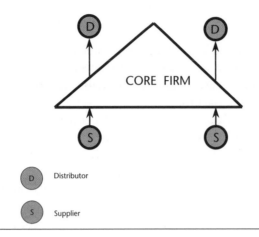

Source: Miles and Snow (1992)

can be invaluable in coordination and informal connection. There are, however, also significant disadvantages. Suppliers become dependent on a dominant customer. The value of their products is not tested in the open market. They have little external incentive to maintain technological competence. The relationship de facto becomes a form of vertical integration in which the customer dictates the output of the supplier. Ownership becomes trivial with only one customer; the supplier becomes a de facto subordinate unit of the buyer. Customers can also specify products and processes so that little scope for innovation is possible. The alternative is for suppliers to sell to other customers in addition to their sales to the lead firm.

The internal network (see Figure 3.7) puts all operations inside the boundary of the lead firm. It can introduce the market into the lead organization itself through internal transfer prices. Each unit produces output in products or services, which it sells to other units in the organization.

The transfer price is an artificial price transferred on the books of the organization but without the exchange of actual money. This price can be established through arbitrary rules such as variable cost-based pricing or through comparable prices in the market. In

Figure 3.7. Internal Supply Chain Network

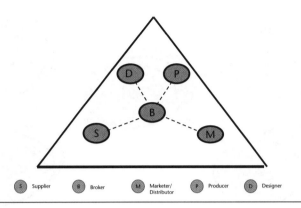

Source: Miles and Snow (1992)

the case of international companies, the price can also be a re-sponse to tax differences. Every unit becomes a separate profit center, also selling to external customers. These units also exercise choice whether to buy internally or from outside vendors. This brings the validation of the market to internal operations while also enhancing internal flexibility.

Transfer pricing directs material and product flows through the network. Their relative autonomy presents potential problems to supply chain management. Operating units have potential opportunities to move in new directions, some of which may extend the corporation into new areas that stretch resources, including management knowledge and experience. Corporations can distort this market by setting buying or selling requirements for intrafirm dealing and by the level of the transfer price. The optimization of product flows is determined by total landed cost. Transfer pricing can guide product flow towards patterns of production and distribution that do not minimize cost for the organization as a whole. In effect, an internal market can become a managed economy isolated from the larger market.

Their autonomy may also allow them to sell services on the outside, which then drive their operations, displacing their internal customers. A logistics manager in a large electronics company in

Figure 3.8. Dynamic Supply Chain Network

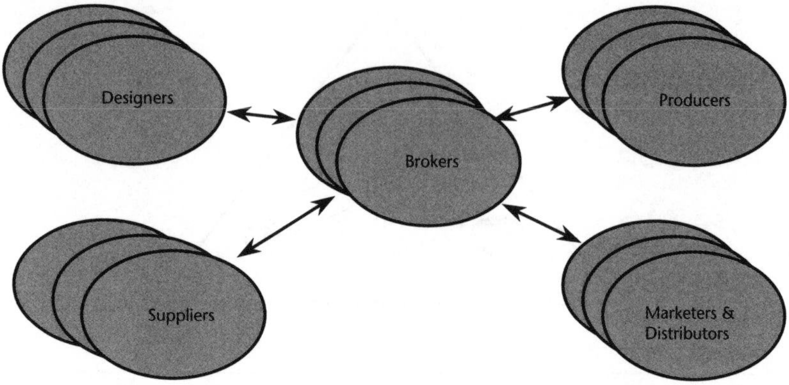

Source: Miles and Snow (1992)

the United States commented that dealing with other divisions inside the company was more difficult than dealing with outside organizations. The internal units had so much interest in their external business that they tended to push their internal customers aside.

Third is the dynamic network (see Figure 3.8). The term »virtual organization« applies more directly here than to any other organizational form. It is a short-lived arrangement, extending usually only for the life of the project, although the structure may remain in place for another project at a later time. It is well suited to organizations with a variety of projects or short production runs, such as publishing, fashion garments or electronics. The company in effect arranges the development and operation of a network but may own few of the resources necessary to bring the project to fruition. It brings the benefit of high flexibility and adaptation to volatile markets or products, which have high degrees of product variability involving large numbers of component combinations.

Networks present some general risks compared with more vertical organizations. The network, in effect, could go too far. It requires continuous supervision to ensure that the network follows the intended direction that it does not become dependent on an external supplier and lose its own competitive advantage.

Managing a portfolio of relationships

A supply chain has many different types of relationships side by side. No single type of relationship will fit all business transactions. According to Gadde & Snehota (2000), developing partnerships with external actors is resource intensive in terms of time and management involvement. Therefore, a firm can only be highly involved with a limited number of external cooperators, regardless of whether they are suppliers, customers or third-party providers. An important role of management is to decide which type of relationship is the most appropriate for a given transaction. For some transactions, arm's-length relationships are the most effective; other transactions require close interpersonal ties. By managing a portfolio of different relationships, the firm can economize on scarce resources.

Bensaou (1999) suggests a simple framework to compare the coordination, information and knowledge-exchange capabilities and their current relationships against the relationship requirements determined by the product and its market. Some relationships might be underdesigned while others might be overdesigned. For example, a firm that invests in building trust through mutual visits, exchange of employees and cross-company teams when the product and markets conditions call for simple market exchanges is overdesigning the relationship. The art is to find the »best fit« for all relationships. This is shown in Figure 3.9.

Figure 3.9. Managing a Portfolio of Relationships

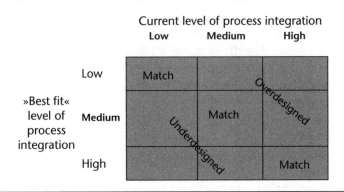

Source: Bensaou (1999)

An analysis of the resources used on different customer or supplier segments will often show the Pareto rule that 80% of the effort is focused on customers or suppliers that only count for about 20% of the revenues or value purchased. Therefore, a more focused and differentiated strategy towards different types of relationships would relieve the organization of the burden of administration for routine transactions and instead concentrate the efforts and resources on developing close relationships with strategically important business partners.

Valuing relationships

Relationships require a new way of valuing organizations in terms of their networks and access to resources. The most valuable capital of a firm lies in its resources and its connections to other firms. A relationship »implies some mutual advantage to parties in continuing to have dealings with each other« (Morgan 1998, p. 47). This advantage is largely intangible, in organizational identity, knowledge-sharing and the capacity to expand or change operations as the market demands. It also goes beyond current exchange to deal with future strategic possibilities.

When we consider the firm as a nexus of relationships, valuation becomes more difficult. Morgan (1998, p. 215) points out that »managing a business is ... in substantial part a process of coordinating relationships with customers, employees, outside suppliers and investors. Corporate managers must align those relationships in a manner that promotes the corporate objectives, particularly the objective of maximizing shareholder values.« Valuation becomes the problem. Potential profit streams can be converted into net present values. Risk can be added to the pot. The problems come in measurement of flexibility, knowledge creation and the development of long-term futures.

Conclusion

The movement of organizations towards network relationships places new challenges on management: 1) to define the core, to establish the boundaries of the firm, 2) to create the most effective governance mechanisms and 3) to develop the most appropriate relationships with external cooperators. The success of the supply chain depends not only on defining these relationships but also on how they are managed and developed over time. The network requires a holistic approach. It recognizes the interdependence not only of immediate partners but also among the entire network of relationships.

Trust relationships are necessary in supply chain management. If partners in a supply chain do not share trust, they will not share information and will not commit themselves to specific investments with a high degree of risk. Establishing trust is essential to collaborative effort in a supply chain. It is a time-consuming process and is based on building positive experience. If the history of the relationship between partners has been characterized by haggling and price reductions, change to a collaborative mode takes time. In the turbulent world of the supply chain, however, formal relationships cannot deal with the full complexity of supply. Devices such as relational contracting may be the only feasible paths, where the details are left for later decision. Once the trust relationship has been established, the collaboration can lead to mutual and innovative benefits.

The strength of the supply chain is in interorganizational relationships. The ability to develop and manage the supply chain is a core competency, apart from product technology or market factors of brand and knowledge. In future supply chains, the ability to assess and establish these relationships will govern the future actions of the corporation.

Illustrative case

Benetton's supply networks[2]

The Benetton family founded Benetton S.p.A., the Italian-based fashion retailer and manufacturer, in 1962. It has become one of

---

2. Material for this case came from www.benetton.com, Harrison (1994), Jarillo & Martinez (1994), Jarillo & Stevenson (1991), Ketelhöhn (1993) and Rovizzi & Thompson (1992).

Europe's largest clothing companies, with sales in 1999 of about USD 2 billion and 7400 employees. The clothing sector includes both casual wear and sportswear, which are produced and distributed from Castrette near Treviso. The industrial complex at Castrette occupies a covered area of over 190,000 m² and can manage total quality control on a production flow of up to 120 million garments using a just-in-time system that operates the production-warehousing-distribution cycle. More than 80 million garments are shipped yearly from a highly automated distribution center directly to 7000 franchised stores in 120 countries.

Benetton only owns a few prime-site stores in major cities such as Milan, New York and Paris. Independent retailers who have signed franchise agreements own the rest. The retailers are selected and supervised by more than 80 regional agents, who again are controlled by seven area managers reporting directly to Benetton's commercial director.

A global information system links stores, sales agents, distribution center, manufacturing, suppliers, subcontractors and carriers.

The structure of Benetton's supply chain is shown in Figure 3.10.

The measurements for all items are kept in a computer-aided design and manufacturing system, so if a store in San Francisco

Figure 3.10. The Benetton Supply Chain

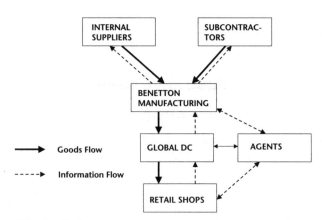

DC: distribution centers

were to run out of a hot-selling pink sweater, the store would call the United States sales agent, who would send a replenishment order to the mainframe computer in Italy. If the sweater is in their automated distribution center, it will be picked by a robot and shipped to the store within 1 week. If the sweater is not in stock, its measurements are transmitted to a knitting machine, and it is produced and bar-coded with a code containing the address of the store and sent to the distribution center. From there it is consolidated with other orders and shipped directly to the store. Benetton can produce and deliver garments anywhere in the world within 10 days of orders being taken. The rapid replenishment cycle enables stores to postpone ordering until the trend of sales is determined.

One »secret« behind Benetton's flexibility and response to changes in the marketplace is its supply chain organization. Benetton outsources most of the production processes to over 500 subcontractors, 90% of whom are located in the Veneto region of northeastern Italy. Benetton supplies raw materials and in-process goods, generates production plans and materials requirements and provides technical and administrative support. Benetton also occasionally takes the investment risk away from the subcontractors by providing them with highly specialized knitting machines with a high risk of obsolescence. The only production processes that remain in-house are grading, marking, dyeing and cutting operations where scale of economies can be realized or that require special skills or technology. Dyeing is one of these processes. It involves complicated chemical processes, and cutting is performed through advanced computer-aided design and manufacturing systems.

Benetton performs most of the design work. Purchasing of raw materials is also centralized to obtain the benefits of buying power and knowledge of commodity markets. The Benetton Group is the largest producer of wool in Patagonia and is able to control the production cycle from »sheep to sweater«. Benetton's own production of wool only supplies 10% of its requirements, but running the sheep ranches enables the firm to improve the technology of wool production and to strengthen its negotiating power with suppliers.

Benetton's production network has surprising similarities to the Toyota system. Benetton has a few family-owned plants, all located within the immediate region of Benetton's headquarters in Treviso. Benetton also owns its own spinning mills. However, most labor-in-

Figure 3.11. Benetton Production System

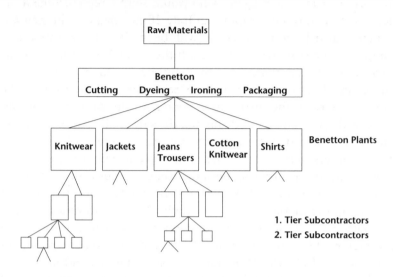

tensive and low-wage work is performed by subcontractors organized in a hierarchical network similar to the supplier structure found with Japanese car manufacturers. The first-tier suppliers are medium-sized subcontractors who work closely with the Benetton plants. These contractors, in turn, manage their own relationships with lower-tier suppliers located in the same industrial regions in southern Italy or in other low-wage regions abroad. Lower-tier subcontractors are typically small, family-owned firms, highly specialized, employing unskilled, non-union workers. The lowest tier consists of small workshops and »cottage industry« workers. This evolving production form is sometimes called »decentralized Fordism«[3] or concentration without centralization (Harrison 1994). The structure of Benetton's production system is shown in Figure 3.11.

These production networks provide Benetton with clear advantages compared with competitors with more traditional in-house production. If demand increases more than expected, the subcon-

---

3. Fordism is used as a term for organizing the production processes by separate departments specializing in different activities. Henry Ford used this principle in his famous plant River Rouge in 1931. This started the age of »mass production« (Taylor & Brunt 2001).

tractors will work overtime and weekends, avoiding the costs and union problems of in-house production. The subcontractors will often have less than 15 employees to save on social security costs. It is also easier to increase or reduce capacity, because these small entrepreneurs are more flexible and often capable of performing a variety of working processes. Benetton also divides orders among a large number of subcontractors to minimize individual risks. Benetton guarantees work for these subcontractors throughout the season. On the other hand, Benetton expects the subcontractors to be willing to carry the set-up costs associated with short-term shifts in the production mix. An additional benefit to Benetton is the effect of continuous improvements in efficiency by the subcontractors.

The subcontractors could run major risks by investing in new machinery. In the past, subcontractors have been stuck with knitting machines that were useless because of changes in fashion trends. Benetton facilitates change of outdated machinery both by buying it and by giving the subcontractors wide margins on some orders, which allow them to re-invest in new machines.

Benetton has a policy of encouraging employees to start and run their own subcontracting units. In return, it requires exclusivity. This clearly imposes problems with decreasing demand because they have no alternative customers. However, many subcontractors are closely interrelated through family or business relationships and share workloads. The relationship between Benetton and its network of subcontractors has been described as an »umbilical cord.« Benetton's plant managers know each subcontractor and his or her family personally. Manufacturing people visit subcontractors frequently and have daily communication with them by phone. This allows them to solve problems quickly and to make adjustments to production plans.

Most competitors within the garment industry have moved the manufacturing to low-cost countries in eastern Europe or East Asia. Benetton still concentrates most of its manufacturing within northern Italy. The company has also set up manufacturing plants outside Italy, such as in France, Scotland, Spain and the United States, primarily to bypass trade barriers in these countries. In the future, Benetton expects rapid increase in sales to Asia and South America. This will move production to joint ventures in countries such as Japan, China, India, Argentina, Brazil, Mexico and Turkey and add complexity to the supply chain.

In 2000, Benetton opened a Web site for Internet sales of clothing (www.theex.it). The Web site is a joint venture between Benetton Group and Accenture. At the time of writing, the Web site is only operative in Italy, Great Britain and Germany. By the end of 2001, Internet sales should be available all over Europe and later in the rest of the world. The assortment offered on the Web site in Europe will be extended to sportswear and sports equipment and other products and services such as holidays and entertainment.

PROCESSES

4. Distribution[4]

»Behind the retail revolution is a distribution revolution.«
Phil Whiteoak, Regional Director of Logistics for a large
food manufacturer in the United Kingdom (Whiteoak 1994)

Distribution links the customer to the supply chain (Figure 4.1). It
is an integral component, influencing both customer loyalty and
the performance of the chain itself. It starts with the final demand
for products and services. As the stage closest to the customer, it
interprets consumption patterns and preferences and transmits orders, defining supply chain activities and motivations, usually involving intermediary institutions. It is also a set of functional activities: order transmission and processing, distribution center operations, inventory holding and control and delivery. In some cases, it
may go even further to include the final stages of manufacturing.

Distribution involves a wide variety of activities. It differs with
every product and market, making generalizations difficult. One division is between consumer and industrial products. Industrial
product distribution is linked to procurement in Chapter 6.

In the traditional marketing channel, distribution is a series of
stages with independent enterprises making separate decisions
about products and inventory, in loose coordination at best to deliver products to a final customer. This system requires heavy investment in inventory for sorting and stock holding for product
availability. The result is high inventory cost and often a lack of responsiveness to changes in the market.

In a supply chain perspective, traditional multi-stage distribution is too inefficient to survive. The fact that the cost of inventory
is too high is only part of the problem. Responsiveness to customer

---

4. Dr. Herbert Kotzab, Copenhagen Business School, contributed to this
chapter.

Figure 4.1. Distribution

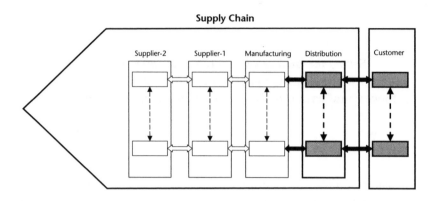

demand has become the key factor rather than product availability. Both are important and respond to a more systemic treatment. The distribution landscape is changing rapidly under pressures from the market, new technologies and competition. At the same time, it presents new opportunities for meeting customer demand through rapid response, customizing orders and now the Internet.

Distribution plays an essential role in the supply chain. Beyond its functional role of product delivery, it makes the supply chain sensitive to the market. If the customer drives the supply chain, distribution translates it into effective product demand, sometimes through forecasts and at other times through direct orders. One of the major changes taking place is the entry of real-time orders directly into the production schedule. Some ordering systems permit or even encourage choices in product features and options that customize production. Another is the coordination of production with demand to reduce inventory requirements. A third is increasing flexibility to take on new products and replace the old. A fourth is a change in the institutions themselves into new forms to meet new demands, such as the change from grocery store to superstore or from traditional stores to home delivery systems.

Public policy now requires distribution to take on an additional task: recovery of consumed and waste materials. This has forced manufacturing and distribution companies to organize reverse logistics processes from the point of consumption to processing stages.

This chapter considers six topics:

- the complexity of distribution
- the new environment of distribution
- the logistics of retail
- international issues in distribution
- e-commerce and the supply chain
- reverse logistics.

While there are many areas of change in consumer product distribution, three have figured most prominently in discussion: food, garments and automobiles. All three have been subject to a series of major technological changes, along with changes in consumer shopping patterns.

The complexity of distribution

The concept of a link between distribution and the supply chain is not universally accepted. Distribution is often considered as a separate entity. However, when distribution is often direct from production to customer or when production schedules are driven by point-of-sale data from major customers, the relationship cannot be ignored.

The realm of post-production processes presents uncertain demands and new intermediaries that specialize in a variety of tasks: inventory holding, sorting and delivery under a wide range of business practices. Governments and trade associations often intervene to protect specific sectors such as retailing and transportation. The very presence of the supply chain threatens intermediaries and the scope of their activities.

Distribution decisions are unique. Production can be selective about location, but distribution must serve markets wherever there are customers. This limits the number of options for locating facilities such as distribution centers. Cost may be secondary to service, but the precise dimensions and levels of service may differ in each market. Competition forces a close link to production.

Events and elements outside the supply chain influence demand: seasonality, sales trends and spikes in demand. The need for product variety also requires close management of inventory. Within the supply chain, flexible production, order sizes and pressures to reduce processing time all influence inventories and production. At some point there must be integration. Several retailers use point-of-sale data to drive production schedules, a demonstration of the need to integrate distribution and manufacturing. Actual sales to the final consumer market become a formal order process.

Complexity arises from the variety of requirements on the system. Increasing concentration of retailers has resulted in a shift in power from manufacturers to fewer retailers as major intermediate customers. Power requires suppliers to adapt to customer operations, including information systems, order quantities, inventory and delivery practices and other characteristics of operations. Supply chain operations must contend with multiple variations by customers.

The supply chain must also adapt to rapid adaptation of technologies not only within the supply chain but also by customers. Not all customers proceed at the same speed, so that there may be several different levels of performance, relating to the specific technology employed.

The strategic framework of marketing imposes specific requirements on distribution. International marketing must make decisions about products and customers in the context of varied markets with the product preferences of individual customers. The requirements for distribution are similarly varied, with specific product preferences, institutions and business practices. There are shorter product life cycles, more frequent promotions, increasing price pressures and changes in the patterns of demand and intermediary practices. The task is to supply the requirements of final customers while protecting the supply chain against too much product variety and variation in local distribution channels. While there are some cases in which marketing strategy has changed to recognize problems that it has created in distribution, how distribution adapts becomes either an advantage or a hindrance.

The new environment

Distribution of consumer goods is undergoing radical transformation. Competition among giants has become intense, with increasing concentration of ownership in fewer chains. New and renovated institutions change the task requirements. Technology, especially in information and telecommunications, has manifested itself in new processes for managing operations. E-commerce is becoming a serious rival to bricks-and-mortar stores. Lean retailing (Abernathy et al. 1999), a combination of information technology, transportation and simplified processing, is becoming a new model for distribution.

The traditional distribution channel involved inventories in the retail store and at local distribution centers, supported by additional inventory held by central distribution centers and possibly at the end of production. This multi-tiering was necessary to ensure product availability for the ultimate consumer, while also protecting local decisions. The result was a system that was slow to respond to changes in demand, produced low levels of service and was often out of stock on high-demand items. Further, it was costly; inventory turnover was low, resulting in high holding costs.

This older system is being replaced by new innovation. The need for more variety, faster service and lower cost forced the change. Supply chain requirements have become more demanding: faster service to customers, faster response to change, more product variety, even customized products, matched to lower costs for lower prices. Inventories are becoming centralized in fewer stock locations, minimizing in-store inventories, eliminating local distribution centers in favor of central distribution centers holding complete inventories and direct distribution from factory to store and, in some cases, to final consumers.

Retail institutions themselves are changing. Consider three categories: food, clothing and automobiles.

Groceries

Food retailing has been moving towards larger units, requiring larger volumes of goods. At the same time, retail power has been projected through private label branding. For distribution, the change occurred in stock control and delivery practice. In the United Kingdom, Tesco's, the largest retailer in Europe, shifted from direct store delivery to central distribution centers with consolidated daily store deliveries. The expansion of private label gave them stronger control over suppliers. Automated ordering processes reduced processing costs and both in-store and distribution center inventories.

The relationship between Wal-Mart, the world's largest retailer, and Procter & Gamble, the world's largest grocery package goods manufacturer, further illustrate some of the change taking place. Point-of-sale data from the cash register has become the basis of ordering replenishment stocks and the basis for production schedules. The manufacturer now manages the retail store shelves for its products as category management. At the same time, delivery is accomplished by delivery from factory to retailer's distribution center for cross-docking and direct delivery to retail stores.

Several initiatives within the grocery industry are now underway. Most notable are vendor-managed inventories and Efficient Consumer Response that we discuss further in Chapter 10 as operational processes in customer relationship management.

Garments

Clothing has normally been sold with long-interval reorder cycles. Department stores would normally order once per season, forecasting demand and building markdowns into the pricing structure to clear away excess inventory. Supply issues only entered into consideration during the initial buy. Lead times were long, not only for retail buyers but also for the entire manufacturing process, making the system unresponsive. Intense competition brought change. Fads and fashion can change rapidly, forcing retailers to seek faster ways to change their own operations.

Some retailers now have set up their own logistics operations to manage inventories and supplier deliveries. Others have contracted with outside operators to perform this service. There was also an initiative instituted by a textile supplier, Quick Response, to compress the time interval through more effective data communication. Again we defer more detailed discussion to Chapter 10.

The need for faster ordering and delivery leads to changes not at the retail level but in manufacturing as well, to shorten production cycles for better response. The movement emphasizes a point that retailers recognize and are taking charge of their own supply chains, managing production and delivery of products to the store.

One often-cited example is a pioneering women's clothing chain, The Limited, again in the United States (Christopher & Peck 1997). Buyers scour women's fashion markets looking for hot items. Samples are sent to headquarters to be converted into production designs and transmitted electronically to Hong Kong to be manufactured in small quantities for market testing. The products are then sent on chartered air freighters to select stores to test market acceptance. Confirmation leads to production orders that are also air freighted to the United States for distribution to the entire chain. The entire cycle takes 5 weeks, producing goods with rapidity, matched to the market.

A wide variety of logistics strategies are possible (Dvorak and van Paasschen 1996). The Limited exemplifies a rapid-to-market approach. Another strategy used by Esprit is to introduce waves of new assortments, using not rapid production cycles but a continuous flow of merchandise. A third strategy is the low-cost approach followed by retailers such as Wal-Mart and KMart. These three strategies do not exhaust the possibilities, or as Dvorak & van Paasschen (1996) noted, »one size doesn't fit all«.

Automobiles

Most automobile dealerships follow a traditional pattern of holding large and costly inventories of cars to meet customer requests for different options and colors. At the end of the model year, the remaining inventory must be discounted to make way for the next year's models. The only major exception to this has been the domestic Japanese dealer practice of displaying only a few cars and taking orders for production, incorporating customer options and colors into the production order (Womack et al. 1990). Cars can be produced and delivered in less than 2 weeks.

Efforts are continuing to reduce the time between order and delivery. A research project called the »three day car project« involving

Bath University, Cardiff Business School and Leicester University and sponsored by CAP Gemini aims to squeeze out some of the excessive stocks in the outbound supply chain.

Ford in the United States has experimented with a regional inventory pool to hold cars with enough variety of colors and options to meet most customer preferences. Dealers can draw on these pool to meet customer requests. This reduces the cost of dealer inventory but it increases the total distribution cost for the manufacturer, although the cost of pooling is less than the cost of equivalent dealer inventories. It also requires the customer to wait for a couple of days for the vehicle.

E-commerce offers another alternative, ordering directly to the production schedule over the Web. The customer can specify options within a limited range. The difficulty is that the customer must wait for delivery. At this time in North America, only Toyota offers this order process, with a limited set of options. The system offers enough advantages that Ford and General Motors intend to make it the normal way to order within a very few years.

These new forms will force changes in the role of dealerships. The argument has been that new vehicle sales are not the major source of profit for dealers. Car service and leasing are more profitable. Who will have the promotional role of selling is not yet clear.

Wholesalers

Wholesalers are being displaced in many consumer markets, although their logistical functions must still be performed. In the food industry, both retailers and manufacturers operate distribution centers to hold, sort and ship to customers. Wholesalers still serve a useful purpose for small stores: buying, holding inventory and delivering to their store sites. In clothing, changes in order patterns have created a need for intermediate collection and sorting points. In the automobile industry, direct shipments to dealers may be replaced by centralized inventory pools that perform the logistical functions that distributors might otherwise perform, or in another scenario, by direct shipment to final customers, almost eliminating finished product inventories altogether. However, in some product groups such as pharmaceuticals, office equipment and sanitary products distributors still play a major role.

Distribution centers

Distribution centers are also changing. Retail distribution centers may still hold inventory for local delivery, but product flow management is emphasized. Cross-docking is information-intensive. Products come in pallets or cases, to be sorted for delivery by store. A collection of optional software programs under the name Warehouse Management Systems provides precise control over inventory, product movement and customer interrogation, down to the level of individual items. Although distribution centers on the surface may appear to be similar to those of 20 years ago, they have changed character.

The logistics of retail

Retail logistics has several relevant facets for this discussion: transportation, information and information. Fast, low-cost transport opens possibilities for rapid replenishment. Rapidly expanding express services create options for delivery, making e-commerce possible. Information adds a degree of control over inventory, order processing and product movement that has not been possible before. These topics are discussed in Chapter 7 on transport and Chapter 9 on information systems.

Integration

The most significant part of the change in distribution is the retailers' new focus on their supply chains. This interest varies by industry, but it is currently strong in groceries and garments. Part of the change is a reported shift in supplier relations from confrontation to collaboration. Most of the discussion comes from the United Kingdom.

There appear to be four stages of integration:

- individual store control
- distribution center control
- headquarters control
- just-in-time delivery.

The pattern shows a movement from local to centralized decisions to supplier integration. It involves establishing relationships with suppliers and service providers, linked to a network of distribution centers by a centrally coordinated transport system. Problems lead towards joint solutions with suppliers, such as shared delivery schedules. This is in marked contrast to a previous tradition of confrontation.

The power in supply chain integration is demonstrated by the experience of a major producer of dairy products that was asked by a major customer to change its foil packaging supplier because the customer was already doing business with another packaging supplier and would able to extract price concessions for larger volume.

Changes in the supply network

Decisions about the distribution center network, including how many distribution centers and their location, are complex because of the number of elements to be considered. The total distribution cost approach provides one answer to the »optimal« number of distribution centers, but it must be used in conjunction with less tangible service variables.

Typically, the following cost components are included in the total distribution cost (Figure 4.2) (Abrahamsson 1993):

- transport costs
- inventory costs
- warehousing costs
- service costs.

Transport costs involve two separate but interrelated systems: 1) a primary system of transport from production facilities to distribution centers and 2) a secondary system of delivery from distribution

Figure 4.2. Total Cost of Distribution

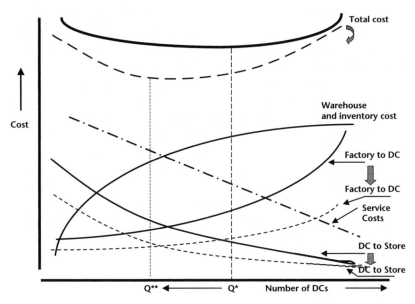

DC: distribution centers

centers to customers. The primary system involves a regional scope, usually with regionally matched carriers. Typically, transport costs from plants to distribution centers are expected to decrease with fewer distribution centers, because there may be system economies in transporting to fewer distribution centers. In contrast, the secondary system would normally be dedicated transport, either contracted or privately owned. Transport costs from distribution centers to customers would increase because having fewer distribution centers increases the distances to customers. The sum of the transport cost curves would be minimized as the two cost elements are balanced.

Changes in the transportation system during the last decade, however, have altered this balance. Establishment of the European Union and deregulation of motor carriage have intensified competition and lowered transport costs. Transport costs from factory to distribution centers and from distribution centers to customers have declined. The effect is to flatten the transport cost curve, reducing the penalties for suboptimal operations and permitting more weight for other grounds. These other elements in the decision include inventory costs, the costs of distribution center inventory and operations, service and the expanding capabilities of telecommunications. The net effect is to pull the optimal solution towards fewer distribution centers (Abrahamsson 1993).

Inventory costs include handling costs and costs of capital tied up in inventory. Inventory has two components: cycle stocks that pass through the distribution center to satisfy demand and safety stocks that serve as insurance, a buffer against unexpected demand or interruptions in supply. Inventory for safety stock and the costs of holding it would decrease as the number of distribution centers contracts. The change in inventory can be approximated through the square root law, which estimates the reduction in safety stock investment (Maister 1976).[5] The law states that safety stock can be reduced by the square root of the number of distribution centers expressed as follows:

$$\frac{S_c}{S_d} = \frac{\sqrt{n_c}}{\sqrt{n_d}}$$

or

$$S_c = S_d \cdot \frac{\sqrt{n_c}}{\sqrt{n_d}}$$

Where S_d and S_c are safety stocks in the two systems, n_d and n_c are the numbers of distribution centers. The subscripts d and c denote decentralized and centralized networks, respectively. For example, moving from a distribution network with ten distribution centers to centralization with only one distribution center would reduce the safety stock requirements by 68%.

The square root law assumes that each individual distribution center serves an exclusive market area, demand varies randomly and safety stock levels are statistically determined. Concentrating inventories in fewer locations aggregates demands, but safety stock

---

5. Cycle stock, which is passed through the system, is considered to be unchanged.

requirements only increase as the square root of variation in demand. The square root law formula can be used under the following assumptions.

- All distribution centers maintain the same level of safety (buffer) stock protection. This assumption is consistent with the practice of many companies that seek to standardize product availability across the market.
- Demands at each distribution center in the decentralized system are not correlated. This assumption is questionable when customers do not accept supplier-defined market territories: when they can get products more easily and cheaply from other distribution centers. International customers with multiple locations may order their total requirements from the most convenient location, taking advantage of price differences.

The formula is a simple rule of thumb to estimate the potential reduction in cost. However, many other variables should be considered as part of the decision, such as access to the full assortment, options of postponing distribution to the latest possible point of time, the ease of phasing products in and out, economies of scale and service requirements.

The cost of distribution center operations includes fixed assets, such as buildings, trucks and sorting equipment, and fixed and variable costs for distribution center personnel, systems administration, heating, electricity, etc. Centralizing distribution centers to one or a few sites would normally introduce economies of scale or networks, with lower building costs or rental costs per unit of space, the ability to take more advantage of automation in distribution center operations, easier coordination and control through the use of advanced information and communication systems and lower costs of damage, pilferage and obsolescence. The cost curve for distribution centers is therefore expected to decrease by reducing the number of distribution centers.

Postponement provides further advantage from centralizing operations. Economies from postponement are better in a centralized system. Final assembly or packaging and labeling for individual customers or commitment to local markets can be delayed until later than in a decentralized system. This problem is especially serious because of the cost of change or repackaging for other markets, when products must be adapted or packaged for specific markets or individual customers. Postponing commitment of stock to individual markets reduces the risks of misallocation from incorrectly estimating demand or misrouting products.

Service considerations involve order cycle time, access to inventory and stock-outs. All of these can result in lost sales to customers. Traditionally, these costs would be higher in a more centralized distribution system. The traditional argument has been that it would take longer to serve the customer because of longer distances. However, this argument is less important now with improved transport service. The question is not geographic distance but elapsed time. Air transport and fast and efficient road transport systems enable delivery to most customers in Europe within 24-48 hours. Although transport costs may be higher, the ability to provide delivery service may increase sales or, conversely, reduce the costs of lost sales. Service costs might well be higher in a decentralized distribution system than with one pan-European distribution center.

A further argument is that the customers get access to the full product assortment. In a two-echelon inventory system, only fast-moving items are normally available at the local level, whereas slow-movers are held at a central stocking point. If customers demand products not stocked locally or out of stock, they must wait for back-order fulfillment and delivery from the central distribution center, which can result in longer lead time.

A more flexible approach could utilize third-party providers for physical stock-keeping and distribution, sharing facilities and networks with other shippers. If the third-party operator has regional distribution centers, it may be possible physically to locate the inventory strategically close to the customer and still manage and control the inventories centrally.

One solution for product groups with relatively low monetary density (low value per unit of weight) is to centralize the safety stock at the factory level with cycle stock located for local distribution. Careful monitoring of stock levels at decentralized locations and supplementing this with expedited shipments from the central stocking point can reduce both safety stocks and transport costs. The Coloplast case in the Appendix illustrates this principle.

Figure 4.2 shows the combined effect of cost curves in transport, inventory, operations and service in relation to the number of distribution centers. The shapes and positions depend on specific circumstances. The total cost curve becomes a simple addition of the individual costs for each configuration of distribution centers. A minimum point will define the optimal configuration. The dashline curves illustrate the potential effects of implementing advanced information technology, communication and transport systems. The result is a shift of this minimal point to the left, showing that a system with fewer distribution centers is »optimal« under changed conditions. This exercise in static comparisons demonstrates the combined effects of these costs at a single point in time. There are also weaknesses, first from the static nature of the analysis, second from the difficulty of estimating the effects of service considerations as »costs«.

International markets

Several issues in international business that influence distribution are unresolved. One is the role of regional or global organizations versus local country control. Parallel to this is whether products should be localized or global. The changes wrought by the European Union point directly to these issues. Finally, we examine the changes taking place in global retailing.

The structure of international distribution

The issues for distribution structure are whether local sales should be served by local or more centralized distribution. Picard (1983) finds the two underlying solutions to be either to decentralize distribution to local subsidiaries with their own distribution centers or to concentrate inventory in regional distribution centers. He further suggests that there are four basic models of product movement (Figure 4.3).

In the classical system, the local subsidiary completely manages its own distribution to customers. There may be a supporting regional supply organization, but the subsidiary or a local distributor holds

Figure 4.3. Basic Patterns of International Distribution

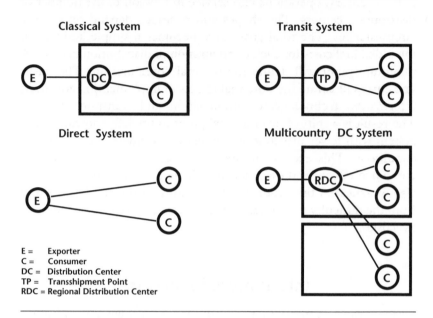

E = Exporter
C = Consumer
DC = Distribution Center
TP = Transshipment Point
RDC = Regional Distribution Center

Source: Pichard (1983)

local inventory and delivers to customers. This system was typical for most multinational companies in Europe up to the mid-1980s.

- In the transit system, the local subsidiary shares responsibility with a higher level in the organization. The parent or regional unit holds inventory and fills orders, which are then processed through the local subsidiary, for local delivery. A recent application of this system is cross-docking, where products are transshipped through a network of terminals belonging to a third-party provider.
- The regional distribution system uses one central distribution center within a region to fill orders and deliver to customers. This system is especially useful within trading blocs such as the European Union or the North American Free Trade Agreement. Many firms in Europe rely on one or a few distribution centers servicing all customers within a time window of 24-72 hours, depending on the location of the customers.

• In the direct system, products move directly from production to customers without using intermediaries or intervening inventory points. Many multinational companies in Europe now use this type of distribution system, a result of low-cost and efficient transportation and communication systems. The upsurge of e-commerce will accelerate the importance of direct delivery to the final customers.

From a supply chain perspective, the central question is the extent of control by local sales organizations over distribution. The classical system gives autonomy and control to local operations, but it also separates important elements of the supply chain. It may lead to multiple inventories and problems of phasing in new products and phasing out old products. It reduces the potential for integrating the supply chain. The other three systems offer more integration but at a cost of additional complexity. In practice, companies often combine systems, by centralizing slow-moving items and placing fast-moving items in distribution points close to the markets.

Global marketing

International marketing managers deal with a changing world. Some product preferences have traditionally varied by individual country, supported by the classical distribution system. Recently, other technologically based, standardized global products reach customers unaltered across national boundaries, supported by transit and direct distribution. More recently, there has been a shift towards regionalism, in which »Euro-products« are developed, modified or packaged for European preferences, as opposed to North American or Asian preferences. However, there are also developing market segments that reach selectively across borders to customers in many countries. In keeping with the dynamics of marketing competition, these segments are constantly emerging, developing and recombined (Halliburton & Hünerberg 1993).

The implications for distribution are strongest in inventory management. Every product is defined by adaptation of specific features or packaging for each market. It becomes a separately managed stock-keeping unit for forecasting, storage and delivery. Products proliferate with national (local) markets, reducing the efficiency of both production and distribution. At the same time, pressure for expanding market segmentation increases their number. On a global scale, the problem becomes so immense that it must be controlled through product line simplification. Further, long lead times for production or transportation require narrower lines for efficiency. The investment in safety stock inventories and the lack of control favors high-volume, stable-demand items. The net effect is that product lines in distribution must be actively managed in parallel to supply chain capacity.

Products are the objects of distribution within a marketing strategy. They can be global, regional or national. Product markets determine the distribution process through competition and the resulting price margins. Pricing is the most locally oriented element of an international marketing strategy, based on local competition and supply costs. Distribution with high revenue margins has greater slack for extra services than with low margins, where competition is intense and emphasis on efficiency is high.

Scale and cross-docking

The changing demand patterns of consumers have favored one-stop shopping. Large retail stores with a wide assortment of both grocery products and other consumer goods have increasing shares of the market, while small and medium-sized stores are in decline. Another trend is the rapid growth of discount stores offering a limited assortment with high turnover rates and low prices.

Economies of scale in retail outlets influence the physical store distribution systems. An increasing number of shipments go directly to the retail stores or are cross-docked at retailers' distribution centers in full pallet loads or even container loads. This allows the suppliers to simplify handling and transportation by utilizing standardized unit load modules. It also furthers the development of transport modules, which can be used as display units in the store itself.

Figure 4.4. The Walmart Approach

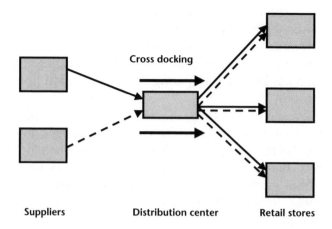

The logistical operations of Wal-Mart in the United States illustrate the impact of efficient high-volume distribution. The replenishment of more than 2000 retail stores in the United States is managed through 18 distribution centers that cross-dock goods, unloading shipments from suppliers, sorting and reloading for store delivery. A typical Wal-Mart distribution center operates 24 hours a day. No cross-docked stock-keeping unit is held longer than 48 hours in the distribution center. Wal-Mart's cross-docking system is illustrated in Figure 4.4.

Goods usually arrive at the distribution center by Wal-Mart's own trucks. All incoming merchandise is bar-coded by the suppliers. The bar-code information is read by scanning equipment, as goods are unloaded. Depending on the quantity of the items, they are placed on conveyor belts, moved directly to the shipping docks or combined with other items in consolidations for shipment to stores. Scanning devices in the shipping area manage the internal routing of each case according to store destinations.

Wal-Mart has gained competitive advantage in both scale and speed as a result of this special replenishment structure. Wal-Mart's logistics costs are 1-2% below the industry average. Wal-Mart replenishes stores twice a week versus the industry average of twice a month.

Separating sales and distribution

Typically, distribution at the local level has been controlled by local sales subsidiaries. Sales departments took in orders, routed them to local distribution centers or warehouses and managed delivery to customers. Many companies have found that managing centralized distribution has required separating the sales function from supply chain activities.

Abrahamsson et al. (1998) studied the change at Atlas Copco Industrial Techniques (Tools). The company managed about 1000 orders per day for about 1000 products, 80% destined for European markets. Before the change, Tools had a policy of serving local markets from local stocks. The lead time was about 2 days if the product was in stock: about 70% of the time. Otherwise, it was about 2 weeks.

The company moved first to direct distribution from one central distribution center. Goods were sent by truck to a local break point in each country. This was a significant improvement, reducing inventories by one third and distribution costs from 15% to 7% of sales. Lead time was reduced from 2 weeks to between 24 and 72 hours. Improvement in sales led to movement and expansion of the distribution center to a more central location with 3300 orders per day and 30,000 stock-keeping units. Orders still came through the sales company to the distribution center that invoiced the sales company, sending a customer invoice to the customer. More details about Tools are given at the end of this chapter.

The second step in centralized sales management is an administrative center. The customer places the order locally, but it is also sent to the distribution center and the administrative center. The distribution center delivers. The administrative center sends the customer invoice to the customer, informing the local sales unit. The customer pays into a local administrative center bank account. The change promotes specialization, economies of scale both at the distribution center and administrative center. The system is transparent. Sales are freed from administrative routine to focus on customers and products.

International Retailing

Domestically owned retail stores currently dominates Europe's retail trade. However, development of information systems and elimination of border inspections and delays will accelerate major changes in internationalizing the retail business. Leading European chains have already developed an international presence in other countries and overseas markets. German chains such as Metro and Tengelmann are expanding in France, Spain, Italy and eastern Europe. The French chain Carrefour is expanding in Spain, Italy, South America and East Asia. UK-based Tesco is invading France and eastern Europe. IKEA has large home furnishing stores across Europe, North America and East Asia. Clothing companies such as Benetton, Laura Ashley and Hennes & Mauritz have extensive systems of their own or franchised stores all over the world. The Danish electronics firm Bang & Olufsen (audio, video and TV) has established dedicated B&O outlets in Europe and North America. United States retail chains such as 7-Eleven and Toys »R« Us are already well established on the European market.

The biggest United States retailer Wal-Mart recently entered the European market through acquisitions of the British discount chain ASDA and a German retail chain. This move can expect to influence the conditions for retailing in Europe in the future and will presumably give supply chain management and efficient response systems a push forward for European suppliers. Also recently, the Dutch retailer Royal Ahold has acquired the Swedish supermarket chain ICA to get entry to the Scandinavian market. Royal Ahold already has a presence in the United States, Brazil, East Asia and several other countries in Europe.

A shifting power structure in the retail trade not only changes market shares but also the structure of the distribution network. The major international retail customers ask for customized logistics solutions across borders. Apart from negotiating frame orders with significant price advantages with suppliers, the most powerful retailers also require information sharing services, such as electronic data interchange, advance shipping notices via the Internet and track and trace capabilities. They typically prefer delivery to their own distribution centers where goods are consolidated with other products for delivery to their retail stores.

Supply chain management is an important support element for key accounts and trade marketing strategies. The development of customized ordering systems, delivery terms, package size and continuous replenishment programs provides benefits for both retailer and supplier. The retailer can reduce in-store inventories, increase inventory turnover rates and generate cash flows from sales even before payment to the supplier is due. Suppliers obtain more predictable information for production and distribution scheduling and often an increased share of the retailer's purchase.

The consequences of this development might well be that the suppliers and manufacturers would reconfigure their European distribution systems around key accounts. Historically, European consumer marketing has been nationally focused with equally fragmented, national distribution systems. With pan-European retailers, suppliers must provide Europe-wide physical distribution. A possible solution might be to focus on serving international key accounts from a distribution center assigned to distribution in Europe. National retailers may continue to be served through traditional national sales subsidiaries, which could also draw on this distribution center, although they would become high-cost competitors and eventually disappear.

From a retail perspective, entry poses unique problems. Dupuis & Prime (1996) emphasize the »prism effect« concept of business distance, a measure of economic, political, legal, geographic and cultural differences. They compared the efforts of French Carrefour to establish hypermarkets in Taiwan and the United States. Taiwan was a successful case; the United States was not.

In Taiwan, they adapted to local conditions of high land prices and changed retail formats, focusing on a narrow range and new products for that market. They were also dealing with a rapidly changing market, requiring rapid adaptation. Personal transport influenced shopping patterns, shifting to motorcycles and then to cars.

The United States experience failed on several grounds. The one-stop shopping pattern of consumers at European hypermarkets did not extend to the United States, which also utilized shopping centers built around clusters of department stores. The scale of the country made competitive strategies difficult to manage. Purchasing and logistics influenced supply relationships. The pilot operations did not reach a size large enough to achieve competitive discounts, and supplier credit terms were much shorter in the United States than they were in France. Logistics were subcontracted, which apparently also created problems.

Locating distribution centers is also different for international retailers. Fernie (1999) notes that, within Europe, new entrants rely on established distribution centers in adjacent markets. As they become established, they build a local supplier base that serves the new market through a local distribution center. The total cost approach may be relevant but requires changes based on local conditions. Land, building, transport and labor costs force a different resolution of the optimal network, along with different customer expectations of service. There is often more reliance on outside contractors for services.

There are several general unresolved issues in international business that influence distribution. One is the role of regional or global organizations versus local country control. Parallel to this is whether products should be localized or global. The changes brought by the European Union point directly to these issues.

The surge in e-commerce

E-commerce makes major changes in the structure and processes of distribution. The Value Chain is oriented towards two market processes: business-to-business (B2B) and business-to-consumer (B2C). B2B is also involved with procurement, and major discussion will be withheld until Chapter 5. Of the two, the B2B model promises the greater immediate potential, but B2C is expanding at a rapid pace as the market develops. The Value Chain involves two closely intertwined processes: 1) demand creation, resulting in customer orders and post-delivery satisfaction and 2) supply and fulfillment. The boundaries between them are unclear, but they interact strongly.

E-commerce usually consists of a Web site combined with a fulfillment system. To the customer, the Web site is the visible part of the process. Demand is created through advertising, branding, recommendations and personal referrals. The site itself plays a role in influencing demand and focusing customer choice. Once the order is in the system, the supply chain becomes paramount. How the order is fulfilled will influence further purchase actions.

Fulfillment involves communication with the customer about the order, delivering the product from a supplier or distribution center to the customer, providing status information en route and any follow-up or post-sale support information. Payment can also be included as part of the fulfillment system, although we do not discuss it here.

The enablers of Internet shopping have been the express package delivery services, fulfillment centers and the development of Web-resident software applications. Express services will be discussed in Chapter 7. Fulfillment centers differ from distribution centers in the order sizes that they experience. Ordinary distribution centers deal with pallet or case unit loads. Fulfillment centers service individual product orders, often with a wide variety of items. The Internet offers scalability, the ability to handle a wide range of volumes, limited only by the physical capacity to handle it. One limiting factor has been software, including installation, data, training and operating costs. By making software Web-resident, it becomes available to enterprises of any size, reducing the cost of installation, replacing it with contract or transaction-based charges.

The structure of e-commerce fulfillment

Fulfillment systems have several different forms. The rapid pace of innovation in both B2B and B2C make this into a partial list, subject to additional configurations as the market develops.

The Dell model. The Dell model takes in customer orders for products directly into production. The name refers to Dell Computer Corporation, until recently selling exclusively on the Web and the largest seller on the Web. The customer order activates the supply chain. Customers can »design« their products from a list of options to be incorporated into a production schedule. The order then initiates a flow of component parts from suppliers to be assembled into a final product, turned over to a logistics service provider, merged with a monitor from another source and delivered to a final customer. The system avoids holding finished product inventory, providing both lower cost and more product variety.

Automobile companies have begun to experiment with variations of this model. Car dealers currently must hold large inventories to meet specific customer preferences. Factories must produce to forecast, also resulting in excess inventories to clean up through heavy discounting at the end of the model year.

Several alternatives are in use for e-commerce fulfillment, as shown in Figure 4.5.

The drop shipment model. The drop shipment model follows a traditional channel pattern; the vendor takes orders, passes them to a manufacturer who then delivers to the customer. While the method of communication is new, the structure of the channel follows a well-worn path. The advantage is the absence of inventory. The disadvantage is the loss of control by the Web site operator.

The Amazon model. The Amazon model refers to the original concept of a virtual bookstore, promoting books and then transmitting orders electronically to the two largest book distributors in the United States. Books would be shipped to Amazon for subsequent delivery to the customer. More recently, Amazon opened its own distribution center to handle books with high sales volume, later

Figure 4.5. E-Commerce Fulfillment Models

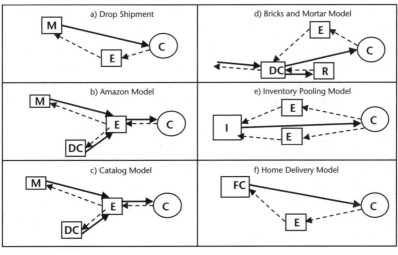

adding more distribution centers to provide better service. The publisher ships books not carried by Amazon or the distributor to Amazon for subsequent delivery to the customer. Amazon thus constitutes a hybrid.

The catalog model. The catalog model is also traditional. Hard copy catalogs have long been used in mail and telephone-order sales systems. This application merely shifts the catalog to electronic media. Orders may either be fulfilled from the vendor's own distribution center or drop-shipped, in a process similar to Amazon's.

The bricks-and-mortar model. The bricks-and-mortar model combines a distribution channel of distribution centers supporting conventional retail stores with a Web site that feeds orders to the same distribution centers. There are potential economies of scale, but these distribution centers may need to accommodate substantial differences in order size: individual product units from broken lots versus pallet loads.

The inventory-pooling model. The inventory-pooling model is especially important where competing customers, such as airlines, use common spare parts. Competitors draw from a common inventory pool controlled by one Web operator, such as MyAircraft.com. The advantage is that a single carrier does not have to carry a complete inventory but can even request a part from a different location.

The home delivery model. The home delivery model is currently subject to experimentation. Consumers place regular orders for grocery items with a Web-based service that routinely delivers directly to their door. One version involved actual shopping in response to a customer Internet order in a retail supermarket and then delivering to a household. This has been replaced by one where orders are filled in a traditional distribution center that also serves bricks-and-mortar stores. Another version substitutes a specifically organized distribution center and delivers to a lock box at the customer's household. Webvan was projecting a national network of specific order fulfillment centers to serve local areas, delivering in pre-designated time windows to customers. However it appears to have encountered less interest than originally planned. The major advantage is customer convenience, although the operators of these services also avoid establishing conventional retail stores. The major detriment is the cost of serving individual households.

Elements shaping e-commerce

The structure of e-commerce fulfillment may be developing, but specific elements will have considerable impact on its future. One is the development of package delivery systems. A second is the emergence of a specialized institution, the fulfillment center; a third is the development of contractual validity on the Web and, finally, Web-resident programs.

Express package delivery has become the most visible part of e-commerce, thanks to FedEx and UPS. They compete almost directly with government-owned postal services. UPS has become the largest transportation company in the world. It also provides Internet services for small businesses. B2C e-commerce requires home delivery, which has turned out to be a costly service. One solution is to establish consumer pick-up locations, which are now being tried experimentally.

The fulfillment center is a specialized distribution center for individual consumer orders. Whereas conventional distribution centers deal in case and pallet load order sizes, the fulfillment center deals in small orders for individual consumers. The parameters are so different that they become separate institutions and do not mix easily. Specialized enterprises have already appeared to perform this fulfillment role.

Establishing customer validity becomes important for consumer confidence and security. Several services are now being offered to perform this task. This should have the effect of reducing transaction costs because the risk element is substantially reduced. Specialized validation services are also beginning to appear as part of other Web sites.

Web-resident software is significant for the development of retailing. Because it resides on application software provider servers rather than at user sites, the cost and delay of software installation is reduced to training and data entry, in addition to licensing and/or transaction fees. The cost of entering into e-commerce is reduced. The connection to suppliers is enhanced because both parties can use the same software.

The implications are interesting. Lower costs reduce the barrier to market entry. We can envision more small, specialized e-commerce channels without being at a disadvantage against larger competitors. The access to common software, accompanied by standardization of data codes and processes would encourage flexibility in forming new supply chains to support marketing efforts.

Reverse logistics

The logical extension of distribution is the return of consumed products and materials. This return flow is the most visible part of the effort to manage the »green footprint« of the supply chain (Van Hoek et al. 1999). It is also identified with the concept of sustainable production, which we discuss in Chapter 14.

Reverse logistics has been defined as »the process of moving product from their typical final destination for the purpose of capturing value, or proper disposal« (Rogers & Tibben-Lembke 1998). A broader definition by Carter & Ellram (1998) includes reducing material quantities upstream in the supply chain to encourage reuse and recycling and reduce the total volume of materials. Reverse logistics is increasingly important, a result of both governmental legislation and consumer environmental awareness. However, it still has a low priority for many companies in the United States. In a survey of logistics managers, Rogers & Tibben-Lembke found that four in ten logistics managers consider reverse logistics relatively unimportant compared with other company issues.

We focus here on the return flow. It follows a variety of channels (Jones 1998). Some of these are shown in Figure 4.6.

- Products return to the point of manufacture for reuse or renewal and return to the market once again as part of a closed-loop system (Figure 4.6a).
- Components are dismantled and returned to suppliers for renewal and market return (Figure 4.6b). A new participant is the dismantler (Dis).
- Consumed products are scrapped and materials passed to a processor for conversion to usable forms (Figure 4.6c). This is an open-loop system in which recycled material enters a commodity market. Prices can vary substantially, determining whether the material is profitable to move and process. The new

Figure 4.6. Reverse Distribution Channels

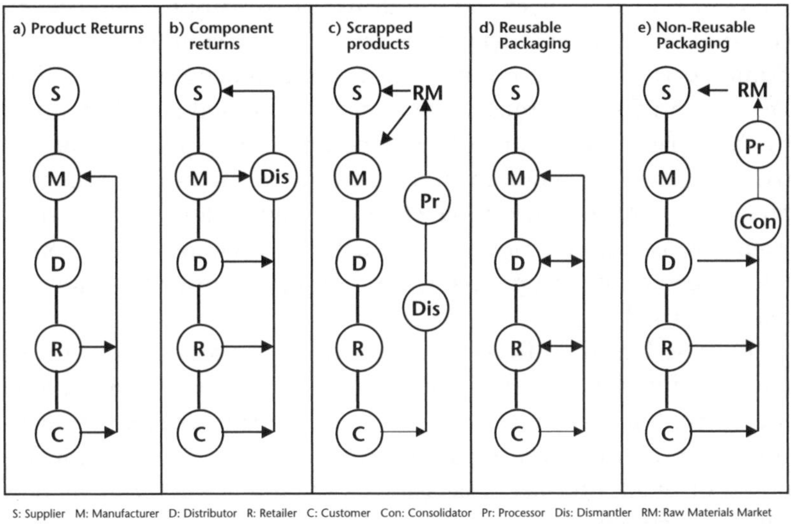

| a) Product Returns | b) Component returns | c) Scrapped products | d) Reusable Packaging | e) Non-Reusable Packaging |

S: Supplier   M: Manufacturer   D: Distributor   R: Retailer   C: Customer   Con: Consolidator   Pr: Processor   Dis: Dismantler   RM: Raw Materials Market

participants are the dismantler, processor (Pr) and the raw materials market (RM).

- Reusable packaging is returned to the previous stage of distribution or production for further use (Figure 4.6d). Reusable containers follow a similar pattern, but the costs of managing a container system become more substantial.
- Nonreusable packaging or other resources includes paper returned for processing and reuse (Figure 4.6e). The new participants are a consolidator (Con) collecting material for shipment to a processor. Similar to other scrapped products, this also becomes an open system in a commodity market.
- Merchandise is returned to the retailer (not shown), because of change in selection, ordering of wrong items by mistake or quality defects. Some of the problems of returns are the loss of control, the costs of repackaging and the potential loss in value of saleable merchandise. The return problems are going to accelerate as more companies turn to e-commerce, where they will deal directly with customers.

Channels for reverse distribution in some cases may be identical to those used for moving goods forward to customers. For example, refillable bottles for beer and soft drinks are distributed and collected through the same distribution system. In the computer industry, printer cartridges are returned to the manufacturer for refilling. Discarded PCs in Europe are sometimes collected and dismantled by third-party logistics providers who are also responsible for distributing new PC equipment to customers. In other industries, however, reverse distribution channels might differ substantially from downstream distribution channels. For example, the automobile industry has set up separate and independent systems for dismantling used cars.

Reverse logistics affects many activities of the logistics process and extends the responsibilities of logistics management beyond the conventional product supply chain. Companies become responsible for their products, even after the customers have bought disposed of them after use. Legislation or voluntary agreements now compel companies in some industries to set up reverse logistics systems to reuse, recycle or properly dispose of products at the end of their useful lives. They are also encouraged to re-engineer the total supply chain to minimize the environmental effects of processes and activities taking place throughout the supply chain. The scope of reverse logistics influences the procurement process, the design of products, the manufacturing process, the choice of transport mode and the interfaces with the final customer. It adds complexity to the supply chain and requires coordination with forward logistics to utilize resources as efficiently as possible.

Recovery of durable products

Throughout Europe, laws are increasingly forcing manufacturers to take responsibility for proper disposal for their own product. The producer-pays principle dictates that the company responsible for an environmental situation should pay for the cost of the clean-up (Rogers & Tibben-Lembke 1998). The policies differ in individual EU countries, but more restrictive take-back laws have been implemented in several countries for product groups such as white goods (kitchen appliances), brown goods (audiovisual equipment), computers, automobiles and batteries.

The European Commission has proposed an »End-of-Life Vehicles« directive that would require car manufacturers to cover the costs of taking back all cars registered after January 1, 2006. According to the proposal, the last owner of a vehicle would receive a certificate of destruction from an authorized dismantler. If the vehicle has negative value, the manufacturer must reimburse the owner for this cost. A number of EU countries have established mandatory or voluntary take-back programs for car manufacturers. In the Netherlands, a national system of government-certified recycling centers has been established. Once a car is registered, the buyer pays a fee, which is refunded when the car has been dismantled. In Sweden, there is mandatory take-back for car manufacturers. The manufacturers are required to set up a network of dismantlers and must accept cars for recycling without charge.

Also, several car manufacturers in Europe and their suppliers have developed programs to recycle used car parts, beginning with the disassembly of used cars. Volkswagen set up dismantling plants at which one worker can strip a car in 20 minutes. They also became the first automaker to guarantee that vehicles would be taken back free of charge at the end of their life cycle. Other car manufacturers in France, Italy and Sweden are also working on recycling programs. Fiat has established a recycling concept called Fiat Auto recycling (F.A.R.E.) in cooperation with a number of Italian recycling companies. The goal is to recycle or incinerate 100% of the car parts. Every car component weighing more than 50 grams is code-marked to recognize the materials and how they should be recycled.

The European Commission is considering similar waste legislation for manufacturers of goods containing electronic components, such as PCs, photocopiers, white goods, videocassette recorders and television sets. Norway has already implemented a voluntary agreement with producers and importers of electronic equipment to take back discarded products and waste materials. The system will be financed by a recycling charge imposed on new electronic products. In the Netherlands, companies that import electrical appliances are required to set up a system to collect and recycle the products. As in Norway, a fee on new products sold to the consumers pays the system (Rogers & Tibben-Lembke 1998).

Returnable containers

Returnable containers do not provide clear advantages over one-way systems. Return transport, cost, maintenance and management can be significant costs. Solutions range from 1) closed loops back to the sender, 2) a central depot as a pool, 3) booking to account for different users 4) and user deposits (Kroon & Vrijens 1995). A model of an operating returnable container organization involved a central agency coordinating an open system where pallets were returned to the agency. The authors observed that this role was unlikely to be assumed by a carrier because of differences in the geographic scope of operations and that it could only succeed where large-scale operations were possible.

Recycling packaging

Packaging materials have high visibility and therefore subjected to both consumer awareness and public policy, manifested in specific legislation. In Europe, the German Packaging Law of 1991 became the most restrictive in the world. Under this law, the product manufacturer or importer to Germany was responsible for taking back not only transportation packaging for protecting goods in transit but also consumer promotional packaging as well. German industry set up a waste collection system called Duales System Deutschland (DSD). Environmentally acceptable packaging was identified by a green dot, which indicated that the package complied with all of the requirements. DSD organized nationwide collection and recycling of consumer sales packaging waste for green dot packaging, for a fee. The first domestic user or importer pays a license fee to DSD that authorizes them to display the green dot on their sales packaging. DSD has been successful in terms of increasing the amount of recycled packaging materials and reducing the consumption of packaging materials in Germany. However, the system has been criticized for being too expensive because of the monopoly situation of DSD. Also, the market for recycled packaging materials has been overflowed, with the result that prices have dropped and large quantities have been exported to other European countries. This has resulted in problems for recycling programs in these countries.

The German packaging waste systems also directly bear on imported products as a potential barrier to entry. Environmentally friendly packaging becomes more competitive than packaging that cannot be reused or recycled. Exporters to Germany must focus carefully on the environmental effects of product packaging, reuse and recyclability.

Due to the consequences of packaging waste legislation in one country on the surrounding countries, the European Commission developed in 1994 a directive on packaging and packaging waste that Member States were to implement in their national legislation by 1996. The directive set up targets for recovery and recycling of packaging. Packaging materials had to be marked and identified to facilitate reuse, recovery and recycling. Systems for return, collection and reuse or recovery of used packaging had to be set up with no discrimination against imported packaged goods. The implementation of the directive has gone slowly in some Member States, but most have largely adopted the principles in their national legislation (Webb 1997).

Returned goods

Today, many retailers invite consumers to return any product at any time, in any condition, for a full refund. This has in some cases led to return rates of 30-50%. The problems of returned goods would only increase as e-commerce and other forms of non-store retailing increase. An article in *The Economist* estimated that returned goods amount to as much as 15% of total sales volume (*The Economist* 1998). However, few companies manage returned goods well. One outstanding company is Office Depot Online, a division of a large office-supply retailer, which is recording returns less than 10%. Office Depot Online is trying to reduce the number of returns by ensuring that customers are not ordering the wrong products by mistake. For example, when a customer is ordering a printer toner cartridge, the customer is automatically asked their printer's brand name to prevent mix-ups. The cosmetics company Estée Lauder has established a reverse logistics program, which has resulted in cost reductions and revenue increases. Estée Lauder has set up a reverse logistics system that automates the process of sorting returned products by scanning expiration data and condition. Based on this information, the company can scrap expired or damaged products and resell products that are still good. In addition, the system is collecting detailed information on why goods are returned.

Managing reverse logistics

Enthusiasm for recycling varies by country. There is no coherent, unified EU policy on recycling of waste materials as yet. Initiatives come from both governments in individual countries and private companies. While the European Commission has succeeded in harmonizing most industrial standards, the lack of harmonization of rules and standards for recycling creates a source of frustration for management and new technical barriers between EU members.

From a management perspective, reverse logistics presents a different kind of challenge to the supply chain. Wu & Dunn (1995) identify four ranked tenets of reverse logistics:

• source reduction and substitution wherever possible
• use of environmentally friendly materials
• reuse of materials in the system such as packaging
• recycling.

Logistics has traditionally taken a role of implementation, while the supply chain requires a comprehensive strategy (Murphy et al. 1995). Van Hoek et al. (1999) cites a three-stage process: reaction, proactivity and value creation, moving from minimal compliance to efforts to minimize costs through product design and recycling effort, to active cost-reduction and revenue programs. In the past, reverse logistics has not been managed as a part of the supply chain (Stock 1998). Even today, apart from efforts required by the EU initiatives, the major emphasis has been on incremental steps such as packaging, not on the process as a whole. Reverse processes begin with material acquisition, continue through logistics operations and terminate with product end-of-life.

Reverse logistics utilizes extensive outsourcing. In the United States, logistics service providers for some corporations perform a variety of tasks. For high-tech industries, the return of repairable units demands special efforts to integrate repair and logistics services (Blumberg 1999). The advantages are reduced inventory and lower transport costs. For the return of durable products, reverse logistics involves the creation of new intermediaries for collection, dismantling and processing. Reusable packaging and materials handling materials such as containers and pallets must be collected and returned. Non-reusable packaging requires intermediaries with collection and processing functions.

Reverse logistics has significant consequences for the total supply chain. Manufacturers must analyze the life cycle of finished products to demonstrate the environmental impact of their products over the entire cycle of production, use and disposal. Products must be engineered for ease of disassembly and recycling. Manufacturers will also have to collaborate with suppliers and subcontractors to deliver recyclable materials and components. Packaging companies must develop materials to minimize weight and that can be reused or recycled without damaging the environment. Even the choice of transport mode and carrier will also be determined in part by the ability of the transport carrier to meet specific environmental standards.

Conclusion

Distribution is integral to the supply chain process linking markets and supply. There are, however, a multitude of processes. The organizations involved in distribution often have differing agendas from other supply chain members, to the point of managing their own supply chains. Distribution is undergoing rapid change in institutions and technology. The push for flexibility and response while minimizing inventory becomes a central theme. There is an evolution from conventional distribution with intermediate inventories to direct distribution through replenishment systems that emphasize information and tight control.

The question has been raised whether distribution may disappear as a distinct entity in the supply chain. E-commerce presents new opportunity to reorganize activities and institutions. Ultimately, customized manufacturing can be visualized delivering products in quantities of one, made individually to match specific customer orders. There are numerous examples where this is already taking place. This bridging of unique demand to flexible supply becomes the ultimate goal.

Illustrative case

Tools[6]

Atlas Copco Industrial Techniques (Tools) is a division of the Swedish Atlas Copco Group. Tools are producing electric and pneumatic hand tools mainly for the automobile, aircraft, household appliances and electro-mechanical industries.

In the early 1980s, Tools had seven manufacturing plants in Europe, each with a warehouse for finished goods. They also had two central distribution centers, one each in Sweden and Finland, and sales subsidiaries in about 50 countries, each with its own independent stock, service and distribution system. In major markets such as Germany, there were also regional warehouses to serve local customers. Thus, there might be up to four echelons of inventory, including distributors' inventory.

The former distribution strategy was designed to be geographically close to the customers, with a complete assortment in the local warehouses. A typical physical distribution channel could look as in Figure 4.7.

Logistics efficiency at that time was not satisfactory. Product availability from sales subsidiaries on average was as low as 70%. The average lead time over all orders from central distribution to customers was about 2 weeks; and the lead time from production to central distribution centers was between 12 and 20 weeks. The

---

6. This case is based on Abrahamsson (1993), Abrahamsson & Brege (1997) and Abrahamsson et al. (1998).

Figure 4.7. Atlas Copco Tools' Former European Distribution System

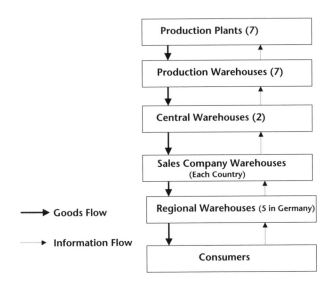

capital tied up in inventories amounted to 30% of annual sales revenue.

The Tools DDD System (Daily Delivery Distribution) was introduced in 1987 with the aim of reducing inventory and increasing delivery performance. New investment included flexible production facilities with short set-up times. Production was concentrated in one plant instead of seven. Traditional hierarchical management was replaced by lateral control at the operating level, with emphasis on a flow orientation. The flexibility of personnel was also increased through training programs. One result was a lead-time reduction in hand tool production to between 2 and 3 weeks.

The next step in the program was to make a dramatic change in distribution, beginning in 1987. Stock holding was centralized in one central distribution center, eliminating all other stock points in the distribution system. In 1992, the distribution center was moved to Belgium, to obtain closer placement to major European markets. From Belgium, 80% of European customers could now be served within 48 hours, and all customers could be served within 72 hours. In the new system, customers' orders to the sales companies were transmitted daily to Tools' head office in Sweden, picked and

Figure 4.8. The Daily Direct Distribution System of Atlas Copco Tools

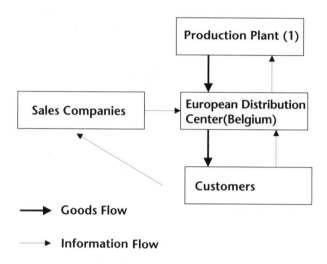

packed at the distribution center and shipped in full truckloads to local break points, from where the goods were transshipped directly to customers in each country. The new distribution system is shown in Figure 4.8.

The effects of centralization can be summarized as follows:

* reduced inventory by one third;
* reduced total distribution costs from 15% to 7% of sales;
* reduced average lead time to customers from 2 weeks to 24-72 hours (depending on market location within Europe);
* product availability increased from 70% to 93%; and
* nearly 50% reduction in warehouse personnel.

Additional benefits have been achieved from information systems integration between order receiving and production planning. In the old system, customer orders followed the distribution channel, passing through several intermediaries before demand became production orders. In the new centralized system, customer orders automatically generated replenishment orders from the central distribution center and were used directly as a basis for production planning. Since 1992, other divisions of the Atlas Copco Group have changed to use the services of the distribution center in Belgium instead of their old distribution channels. This has further decreased the total distribution costs from 7% to about 4% of sales due to economies of scale. Today most logistics activities are coordinated by the distribution center, which acts as the coordinator between production and sales companies.

The separation of physical distribution from the sales and marketing channel has thus improved the cost-efficiency and service performance of the physical distribution of products and at the same time allowed the sales companies to concentrate their own efforts on sales and marketing.

The next step in the reconfiguring process was to centralize sales management at an administrative center, which takes care of orders, invoices and payment. In the new system, the customer orders are simultaneously transmitted to both the distribution center and the administrative center via the integrated information system. The purpose was to allow the local sales organizations to concentrate on customer relationships management and minimize local administration. Another driving force was a pressure to reduce costs and free capital tied up locally. At the same time, the legal status of local sales companies was changed from autonomous companies to branch offices.

5. Production issues for the supply chain[7]

»The more advanced or modern the production process, the longer and more complicated the chain of linkages.«
S. Cohen & J. Syzman (1987, p. 14)

Production is the operational center of the product flow process, as shown in Figure 5.1. It becomes the dividing point of product flow. From this point forward, product flow is determined by actual customer orders or by forecast demand. Behind this point, product components and materials move towards production either in response to customer orders or in quantities determined by forecasts. As both actual and anticipated orders enter the production schedule, the speed of the production process determines how much inventory must be carried downstream towards the market. It also determines the rates at which suppliers must respond. Further, production efficiency and quality along with product design determine the ability of the supply to compete in global markets.

While this chapter is concerned with processes inside the factory, it is important to recognize the position of production within the supply chain. First, the factory is linked to both suppliers and customers. It does not operate either in a vacuum or in a one-way flow. Both customers and suppliers interact with production, changing schedules, modifying products or even influencing design. As we have noted in Chapter 2, companies have been under pressure to outsource major parts or even all of production, so that interorganizational relations and capabilities become important considerations.

---

7. This chapter was written jointly with Ashok Chandrashekar, IBM Corporation.

Figure 5.1. Production

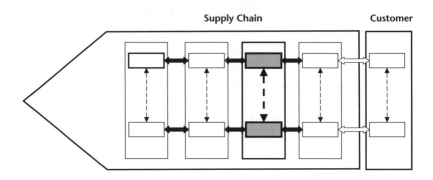

This chapter has four major themes. We begin with the requirements of the supply chain. We then move to the role of product design within the supply chain. Third is the strategic perspective on manufacturing processes, including the options in production technology, production scheduling and planning. The final section considers some of the new emerging technology.

Supply chain requirements

A chain of processes

The global nature of production is important in developing the supply chain. Investment in factories becomes a strategy, of timing and access, where new investment decisions recognize opportunities across the globe. Factories must be located close to markets, sources of technology or low labor cost. Production technologies have been diffused around the world, so that manufacturing in the global marketplace must operate of necessity with comparable efficiency if they are to remain competitive. Plant managers are familiar with current factory technologies, even when modified to meet local conditions. In fact, many new production concepts are introduced in newly built plants in developing countries where no legacies exist from older production systems. General Motors introduced major software programs in its Brazilian plant because the cost of revising older systems to accommodate it was lower than in older, more established operations elsewhere.

A global production system is a network. Logistics becomes important for connecting the production process, both within host countries and externally. The transport system ultimately determines lead times for orders and the ability to respond to change. Some factories are deliberately located in local markets despite higher labor costs to respond quickly to local product demands.

Production may take place in successive or in parallel stages. Semiconductor production often began in the United States, flowed to Malaysia or other points in Southeast Asia for hand assembly and then returned to the United States for finishing. Similarly, garment production often begins with cutting fabrics with computer-controlled laser cutting machines in Europe or North America, sending the pieces to Southeast Asia for labor-intensive assembly, and then return to the United States for sale. The current emphasis in global companies is on regional production to serve local markets. In addition, plants may specialize in specific products, taking responsibility for design, global production and distribution.

Global networks are accompanied by pressures to create local supply sources, both to satisfy employment needs and to transfer technology. Before it started producing automobile engines in the United States, Toyota supplied complete engine assemblies from its plant in Japan to its United States plant in Kentucky to take advantage of economies of scale in production. This also works both ways; United States electronics companies operate in Japan to take advantage of technology. Components are procured locally, but the real motivation is to learn about technological advances.

Plants also vary by factor costs, principally in labor wage costs. The garment industry, with its high commitment to manual work, has pursued low-wage economies across Asia. As one country or region develops higher wages and skills, factories either move or change to automation and even to participation in product development.

Two other factors should be noted: infrastructure and culture. These terms, however, are imprecisely defined in common usage. Infrastructure generally refers to transport, telecommunication and governmental support. The state of transport and telecommunications networks is important, although less so now than in even the recent past. Governments play roles through taxes, incentives and regulation. Governments also influence factory decisions, sometimes forcing higher levels of factory development than the immediate market would dictate.

Culture enters in through workers' attitudes and educational levels and the general business climate. The motivation and capabilities in the labor force play obvious roles in determining the success of production ventures. How factories are received within the local community becomes an important determinant of successful operation.

Production flexibility

Global market demand for both product and volume flexibility at the factory is increasing. Volume flexibility requires the ability to expand capacity, either within a single plant or by adding additional production capacity elsewhere. Demands become unstable coupled with market pressures for faster order response. Customers want products to match their unique requirements.

Product life cycles become shorter, with pressures for inventory reduction and greater demand for product variety. Shorter cycles also require faster recovery of fixed design costs that, in turn, necessitates larger gross profit margins to cover them and lower production costs to enable the margins. Production of individual products takes place in shorter production runs and with more product variety. One purpose is to avoid obsolete inventory in the final market by producing to match demand as closely as possible.

The supply chain imperative is to increase flexibility, to develop faster changeovers and the ability to expand production within the factory. Beyond the factory, the production network must also organize flexible production networks, in conjunction with suppliers. Their factories must adopt similar methods of producing rapidly in response to orders without holding inventory. Even further, the network organization must also provide flexibility in adding partners and production sites, as they are needed to match demands.

The production environment

The evolving production environment has introduced new elements into manufacturing operations. They include the change in orientation from push to pull, real-time interaction with customer orders, wider product ranges with more emphasis on designing modular products, customization, expansion of computer and information technology in production planning, execution and control, quality and new production technologies. We will consider each of these in turn.

- The shift from push to pull changes production scheduling and inventory policy. Instead of producing according to a production plan based on a forecast of demand, production takes in orders as they enter into the system, producing in short production runs. The ability to respond directly to customer orders is becoming a competitive necessity. First, it offers flexibility and the ability to meet customer requests. Second, it reduces and ideally eliminates inventory between factory and customer, other than that in transit. The problem of obsolete inventory is reduced, a necessity in industries with high rates of product development. On the other hand, it now places a burden on suppliers to meet individual product demands. Either the burden of component inventory is moved to suppliers, a cost to them, or they also learn to produce on demand. This shift, however, can only be really successful where production lead and transit times are short, avoiding the necessity for buffer inventories.
- Real-time interaction between customers and production shortens order cycle time, enabling customized orders. Customer orders enter directly into the production schedule. The advantages include matching demand and reducing finished product inventory that does not match customer preferences. The disadvantages are that it means shorter production runs to respond to this changing demand. It takes away the inventory buffers that make it possible to organize longer production runs with their higher efficiency. Again, it places a burden on suppliers to supply component products on demand, requiring either their own buffer inventories or flexible production systems.

- Wider product ranges places demands on production systems for rapid changeovers from one product to another. This was one of the principal strengths in Japanese car production, where production set-ups that formerly took days was reduced to minutes, pioneered by Shigeo Shingo (1987) and Taiichi Ohno (1988), who developed the SMED system (Single Minute Exchange of Dies). Flexibility in changeovers provides one solution. Another is modular products where standardized modules can be combined or added to extend the range of potential products.

- Mass customization was introduced by Pine (1993) to describe adaptation of products to meet individual requirements. Success requires defining potentially feasible product options from which customers can choose. It has been applied successfully in the computer industry where all components are modular, in the garment industry by Levi Strauss to adapt women's jeans to their individual measurements, bicycles also to individual measurement and cars primarily for accessory items and colors.

- Computers and other information technology have become an essential part of the factory. Part of the revolution has been computerized production planning and control systems. Another has involved automation of much of the production process itself. Completely automated factories may not be common and are not usually successful, but »islands of automation« have been useful in supplementing conventional production, especially in hazardous production environments. A third has taken place in linking production to customers, procurement and other areas. The factory is no longer an isolated system but one interconnected to the entire supply chain.

- Quality as a specific focus became important only in the last few years, being closely identified with Japanese car and electronics production. More recently it has been noted in the United States as the six sigma standard in connection with Motorola. There appear to be two aspects to quality: design and production. United States car producers at one time blamed quality problems on the factory, although they have now recognized sources of difficulty in product design. Gradually, as factories around the world improve, quality has become a necessary requirement but not sufficient condition for competitive advantage. Certification for quality management is now a global standard through ISO 9000.

- Zero inventory systems include just-in-time (JIT) and *kanban* (signal card). JIT is a production orientation, to deliver materials directly to the point of use as they are used. Kanban is a signaling system originally using cards to indicate a need to replenish inventory at the user's station in a production system. Now electronic kanban systems provide this coordination. JIT provides flexibility for the using firm under certain conditions, but not necessarily for their suppliers. JIT also enhances quality control; problems in small production batches can be uncovered before they become larger lots and create more serious problems. Both JIT and kanban involve intense coordination between production stages, whether inside the firm or externally between supplier and customer. They provide delivery of components and materials either as a minimal working stock or timed for arrival just before they are used.

  JIT is also a philosophy, more than inventory reduction but of *kaizen*, continuous improvement, worker involvement through quality circles. Because JIT means an abrupt change from established practice, it often becomes the trigger for a variety of other actions for improvement.

- Factory organization has also changed. The culture of production has moved from organizational hierarchy to empowerment of workers in self-managing teams that set their work schedules and methods. The difference is manifested in a change from the authoritarian management practices with their rigid processes to small-group autonomy within the framework of production scheduling. Many efforts have tested the general concept but with only mixed success. The concept of the team has become important, lending a change from production flow from assembly lines to production cells.

Product design for the supply chain

It may be surprising, but product design plays an important role in the supply chain. There is a market role for product design in corporate strategy, but there are also supply issues involved as well. In this section, we consider modular products, concurrent engineering, design for manufacturability, design for logistics, quality and recycling.

Modular products

Modular products give the supply chain flexibility to meet the requirements of a broad product range without the need for specialized production for individual products (Van Hoek & Weken 1998a, b). The definition of a product module also defines the scope of partners within the supply chain: how much partners will participate in the supply chain. Van Hoek & Weken identify three levels of modular production: product, product group and process. Product modules refer to individual products; product group modules mean standardized interchangeable modules across a set of products. Process modularity is the ability to change the process itself, suggesting a means to production flexibility. Modularity presents opportunities for increasing product variety and accelerating product development. It creates more flexible development processes at lower cost, decoupling design tasks to enable module development to proceed on different schedules.

Modularity also defines organizations, specifying roles to be played in the development process (Sanchez 1999). Hsuan (1999) makes the point that supplier-buyer interdependence influences the outcome: more collaboration makes for a higher degree of modular development. Interfaces and constraints should be defined early in the process.

In the computer industry, changes in chip design to incorporate more functions also change the roles of partners in designing circuit boards to adapt to the new chip design. As chips take on more circuitry, there is less need at a given level of product development for other chips to be attached to the motherboard. This may also mean that the overall product sophistication as a personal computer can also change. This in turn shifts the proportions of value added and hence profitability of individual stages.

There is also inventory saving with modular product design. By pooling modules as a group, production is easier because it can be undertaken in longer production runs in advance of demand. Demand for a modular product group can be forecasted far more easily than for individual products, which have erratic demand. For this reason, production of modules is usually more stable than demand for individual products. This also has the effect of reducing finished product inventories, enabling postponement of final assembly. Hewlett-Packard builds inkjet printers in modules, with country-specific power supplies, packaging and manuals added as demand calls (Feitzinger & Lee 1997). Van Hoek & Weken (2000) report on Smart Car, development of a modular automobile by DaimlerChrysler and SMH (Swatch). The car consists of five modules with only seven main suppliers who bring in their modules only when called by the production schedule.[8] Modularization extends production in some cases, to the supplier and into the distribution center such as the case of Hewlett-Packard Inkjet Printers.

There are also distinct disadvantages. The entire product line must be planned with a basic platform with common interfaces for different modules. While it is possible to update modules, basic innovation involving fundamental product change is slowed. Further, modular design may be suboptimal for the performance of individual products in the line. Modularization will inevitably involve compromise, trading off production and inventory efficiency against product performance.

Concurrent engineering

Supply management must be concerned with time to market: the time interval between design concept and market introduction. Automobile companies are extremely aware of the advantages of rapid product introduction. DaimlerChrysler in the United States used to take as long as 5 years to bring a new model to market. In some cases, the elapsed time has been reduced to 24 months, providing the ability to capture changing market tastes through rapid product development. Normal practice meant successive stages of development and design, performed in isolation and then passed to the next stage, described as »throwing the project over the wall«. This has often resulted in limited communication between groups, and

---

8. See Smart Car case at the end of this chapter.

in some cases, product designs that were often difficult to manufacture, with low productivity and poor reliability.

The alternative is to design for manufacturability (Womack et al. 1990), meaning designing products for ease of production as well as functionality. Significant gains in elapsed time and problem solution have come as concurrent engineering where designers and production process engineers work cooperatively on the same design to eliminate problems before they begin. Beyond individual products, Japanese semiconductor manufacturers encourage their capital equipment suppliers to develop processes in advance of the product itself (Methé 1992). Information technology also offers substantial time reduction. Computer-aided design offers the ability to develop and communicate designs without having to commit them to physical models (21st Century Airliner; Schrage 2000).

Design for logistics

Logistics involves both movement and inventory. The location of product assembly affects the cost structure, order cycle time and the ability to respond to change. Modularization enters in through the point of assembly. Product complexity limits the number of possible locations, reflecting skill levels, equipment and product support.

Packaging is directly involved though the types of environments encountered, dimensions and recycling. Environmental considerations such as outdoor exposure or need for refrigeration affect packaging requirements and cost. Dimensions affect materials handling and cost. In many industries, warehouse pallet dimensions and the number of cartons per pallet determines costs. Unfortunately, dimensions differ between countries and industries, such as the difference between Euro-pallet (1200 by 800 mm) and the United States Grocery Industry standard (40 by 48 inches), suggesting a need for more international standards. Physical density is also a problem; it reduces transport efficiency because most vehicles, containers and aircraft tend to be limited more by space than weight. Further, bulky items are more costly to store because they occupy more warehouse space.

Value density is the ratio of product value to weight. The long-term trend has been towards higher value in relation to weight. In fact, even Alan Greenspan, Chairman of the US Federal Reserve Board noted, »While the weight of current economic output is probably only modestly higher than it was a half century ago, value added adjusted for price change has risen well over three-fold« (Coyle 1997, p. viii). Higher value mans that products are more mobile because they can absorb higher transport costs without seriously influencing total costs. This means either longer distances from production to market, or more use of air cargo, or both.

Strategic perspectives on manufacturing processes

Strategic options

The basic choices in production processes are shown in Figure 5.2. Traditionally, these have been determined by the size of the pro-

Figure 5.2. Product Volume and Process

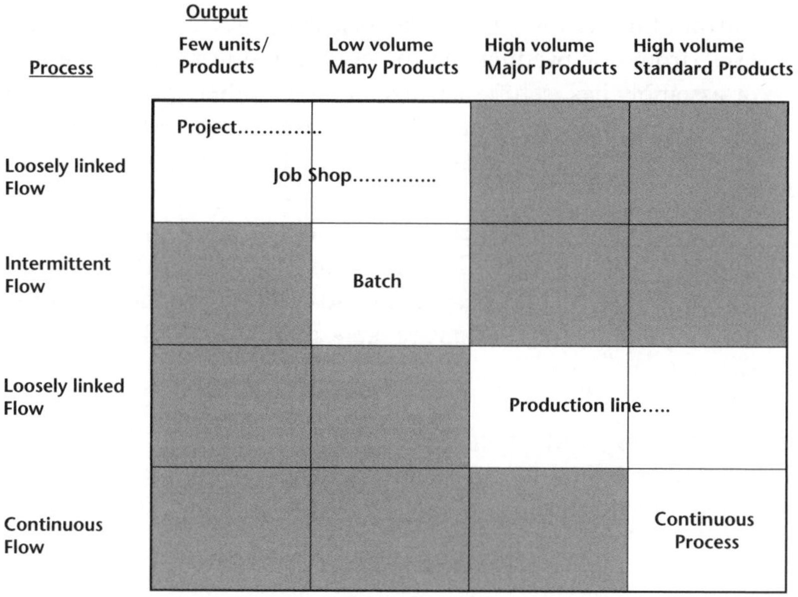

Process	Output Few units/ Products	Low volume Many Products	High volume Major Products	High volume Standard Products
Loosely linked Flow	Project............. Job Shop..............			
Intermittent Flow		Batch		
Loosely linked Flow			Production line.....	
Continuous Flow				Continuous Process

duction run progressing from the scale of a single project through batch production to production lines and continuous flow processes with large volumes.

- *Projects* can be characterized as make-to-order with little standardization. One example is construction of a major building or a unique piece of capital equipment. Suppliers are called in for a specific project with no prospect of continuation on that project, although they may participate on other projects with the same contractor.
- *Job shops* deal with small-order production. They are organized around work centers with specialized activities. The work (production) flows through a series of work centers. Job shops offer flexibility in that they can apply routine operations to several different production sequences at the same time, and their sequences can be changed to meet the specific requirements for each product. The potential disadvantages lie in the scheduling, where conflicts may result in delay in completion, need for movement between work centers and inability of workers to see the results of their output.
- *Batch processing* is similar to job shop operations in that it deals with a variety of operations, where production volume does not warrant full assembly lines. The disadvantages lie in the changeovers from one product run to another, requiring changing dies or assembly jigs, setting up machining or other special processes. Batch processing is probably the most common form of production and is sometimes combined with assembly line operations.
- *Production lines* are associated with standardized products produced in high volumes. *Continuous flow* is characteristic of chemical processes such as petroleum and refinery production. They are normally capital-intensive and therefore involve financial risk.

There are dangers of either over- or underinvestment. Referring to Figure 5.2, a lateral move assumes anticipation of higher volume that may not materialize, a case of overinvestment. On the other hand, if market demand is underestimated, production will be late in shifting to higher volume processes, leading to possible congestion in production and higher operating costs, a case of underinvestment. From a strategic perspective, there appears to be a narrowly balanced efficiency path between product demand and production capacity.

The demands of the supply chain modify this view. First is the problem of product variety. While component volume may justify production lines, final assembly may be done in batches with high service requirements, high inventory costs, in batch or even something approaching job shop scale. Second is customization. Depending on the stage where it takes place, it may require job shop operations throughout the production process despite high volume. Both of these involve short production runs in at least one stage. In turn, this requires flexibility in changeovers not only within the factory but also with suppliers to change over as well. Changing colors on an automobile assembly line requires changeovers not only in the paint shop but also in components such as bumpers and upholstery that are sometimes supplied through external production.

Options in production technology

Technology has influenced production in several ways. Both the Toyota Production System and lean production (Womack & Jones 1996) are contemporary examples of conventional production practice extended through rigid discipline. A Swedish alternative to traditional line assembly and lean production is reflective production emphasizing group responsibility for work sharing, holistic learning and meaningful coherence in work processes (Engström et al. 1996). Another development, not making extensive use of computer technology, is cellular manufacturing. Moving to computer-based information and communication systems, we may consider computer-integrated manufacturing and the flexible manufacturing system, introducing direct computer-controlled production operations. Finally, we will discuss JIT and kanban and their impact on the supply chain.

The Toyota Production System

Many writers have focused on the Toyota Production System (Ohno 1988, Shingo 1987). The most recent to our knowledge are articles by Adler et al. (1999) and Spear & Bowen (1999). Spear & Bowen ask: »Why has it been so difficult to decode the Toyota Production System?« (p. 97). Paradoxically, it is a rigid production system combined with flexible operations. It has been described as a community of scientists, using rigorous methods of formulating and testing problem solutions that are imbedded deep within the organization. It involves four rules:

- All work is highly specified and precisely measured, enabling workers to test changed methods against standards.
- All customer-supplier connections are direct and unambiguous. This refers to both external and worker-to-worker connections including both message clarity and response time.
- The pathways for every product should be direct and simple, including both physical production layouts and services such as requests for help. Products flow to specifically designated machines.
- Improvements should be made using the scientific method at the lowest possible level. There is a precise procedure for learning that is oriented to challenge established methods and assumptions.

Toyota will hold inventory to identify problems, such as separating inventory to protect against process variation and also against fluctuations in demand. This identifies and focuses responsibility on specific actions. More than rules is a common expectation of the ideal production system. It includes defect-free products, delivered immediately in units of one to match a specific request, without production waste within a safe work environment. The creative tension between the actual and the ideal leads to a continuous process for generating problem solutions. The rules apparently become a buffer between improvements in one area affecting work in other areas.

Adler et al. (1999) ask how Toyota could achieve flexibility while it was striving to achieve efficiency. One solution is to create standardized problem-solving for creativity, job enrichment to encourage workers to become more innovative and flexible, switching between routine and non-routine tasks and partitioning to allow workers to refine their own skills (p. 45). Product changeovers present a difficult time for car manufacturing. In the Toyota system at NUMMI, the joint General Motors-Toyota plant in California, suppliers participate in product development instead of at arm's length that is characteristic of United States production systems. Workers participate through a »Pilot Team« to set work routines in advance of production and participate with engineering on final design changes for production. Training and trust create a context to support flexibility in the face of the outwardly appearing bureaucratic structure of production.

Reflective production

In Sweden, an alternative production philosophy to lean production developed in the 1980s at Volvo's production plants in Uddevalla and Kalmar and Saab's assembly plant in Malmö. The production concept is called reflective production, and it deviates from traditional assembly line production at other car manufacturers in the world by focusing on postindustrial societal values such as job satisfaction and job enrichment. The major principles in reflective production are as follows (Engström et al. 1996):

• an assembly process based on holistic learning emphasizing meaningful coherence in work processes;
• parallel organic flows, which ensure overview and self-control; and
• two or four workers belonging to work teams of about ten members who assemble the entire car.

The decline in sales at the beginning of the 1990s forced Volvo and Saab to reduce their production capacity by closing down their smallest assembly plants, including Uddevalla and Malmö. This decision has been interpreted as a failure of the Swedish work reform method compared to the lean production system in Japanese companies (Freyssenet 1998). However, the upsurge in the United

States economy from the mid-1990s has increased the demand for coupés and convertibles and enabled Autonova, a joint venture between Volvo and the British Tom Walkinshaw Racing (TWR) to re-open the Uddevalla plant in 1997. The reopened plant utilizes the basic principles of reflective production. The future will show whether this approach is competitive.

Cellular manufacturing

In this method, production is divided into teams responsible for producing a complete product or component, shown in Figure 5.3. Workstations are arranged in a U-shaped layout so that each team member can see the output of the team. While production tasks are different from each other, workers become multi-skilled, able to take over any specific task in the cell. Production problems are thus

Figure 5.3. Cellular Manufactoring

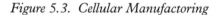

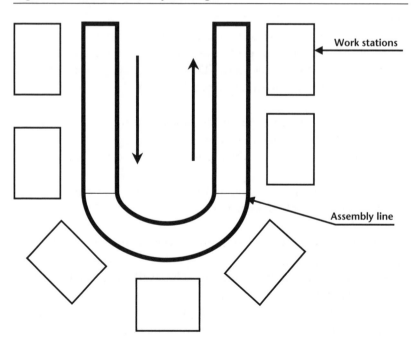

visible to every member of the team who takes on total responsibility for product output. Production control is thus decentralized to the team. Cellular production has been tried in a variety of industries.

One case where cellular production actually improves production lead time is in the garment industry (Abernathy et al. 1999). Typically, garment assembly is a piece-work business, performed either at home or at a factory where each worker receives inventory as work, performs one task and at the end of the day passes the completed work to the next station. It is not hard to visualize a lengthy production process that does not respond well to rapid change. They describe a cellular production line, with responsibility for a complete garment, reducing the time interval to as low as one day. When consumer tastes change rapidly, this would seem to be an improvement. However, they noted that the industry adoption has been slow.

Computer-integrated manufacturing

The computer-integrated manufacturing system describes computer-based software to manage the production process from design to total production (Hill 1994). The defined boundaries sometimes expand to include distribution, reflecting the integration of the entire firm with the production process. It includes computer-aided design, computer-assisted manufacturing and computer numerical control. In addition, there are computer-aided production systems that plan, schedule and control the production process. Computer-aided design accelerates the design process, provides a vehicle for communication and also provides with precise data for tooling and programming of machine tools for factory automation. Computer numerical control involves numerical control of machine tools in factory automation. Computer-aided production systems include 1) a bill of materials that lists assemblies, components and materials for the final product 2) a list of operations to produce each component for the bill of materials, itemized by time requirements for machines, tooling and labor, 3) work centers required with their capacities, 4) customer delivery requirements and 5) components and materials available and the procurement requirements.

Flexible manufacturing systems

These systems deal with operations within the factory, as opposed to computer-aided production systems that are oriented towards management. The flexible manufacturing system is oriented towards group technology, where similar groups of parts are brought together for production, a sort of electronically controlled job shop (Boer 1994). Computer-based numerically controlled tools are now interconnected by automated handling systems. Completely automated factories were greeted with anticipation in the 1980s, but experience has been discouraging, requiring the development of computer protocols so that machines could communicate with each other. They represent a large fixed cost with a scale that may not match the market. Their inflexibility does not support current trends towards flexibility and customization.

Just-in-time and kanban

JIT and kanban are now familiar concepts. The original idea was to bring materials and components to the specific point and time where they would be used, in quantities to match the factory production schedule. This creates immediate advantages to the receiving firm in reduced inventory and factory space, reduced material handling and quality control through smaller lot sizes. There are disadvantages: dependence on precise transit times with potential interruptions and implied stable production. For suppliers, JIT means 1) stable production, 2) inventory-on-hand, shifting the inventory cost from manufacturer to supplier or 3) flexible production processes that can produce on demand. It requires close coordination between manufacturer, carrier and supplier, including telecommunication links.

Intelligent use of JIT requires buffer inventories to account for delays, although not in the quantities required before JIT. From the standpoint of total supply chain costs, it also requires supplier development to improve production processes. The principal value of JIT is more than in reducing inventory. Inventory hides problems. Taking inventory away exposes problems so they can be resolved.

Applying JIT throughout the supply chain would reduce inventory for the entire pipeline. Buffering, however, has advantages where demand or supply conditions are unstable.

In the electronics industry, expanding demand led to shortages and drastically longer lead times for key components (*Wall Street Journal* 2000), leaving some companies unprepared, facing shortages that limit production. The chief financial officer for one Chinese company noted: »Just-in-time has become just-in-trouble.« When suppliers cannot expand, the risk shifts from supplier to buyer.

Production planning

There is a separation between the old and new in production planning with operation in real time. Traditional methods employ materials requirements planning (MRP). MRP itself replaced a system in which factories produced for inventory to meet forecast market demands. This was cumbersome, unable to respond to rapid change and costly in inventory, storage and obsolete stock. The original MRP was purely a production scheduling system. It expanded as an information system to organize procurement, transport, finance and forecasting. Its failing is that it is oriented to the factory alone. However, it serves as a precursor to more comprehensive information systems such as enterprise resource planning (ERP).

The production planning framework

Production planning begins with a framework similar to that in Figure 5.4. A forecast, usually from sales or marketing, drives the business operations plan and the production plan. This becomes an input to the master production schedule. The schedule can be modified by management actions to modify demand, such as allocating production by product. The master production schedule affects distribution through Distribution Requirements Planning, discussed in chapter 10. The master production schedule then leads

Figure 5.4. Production Planning

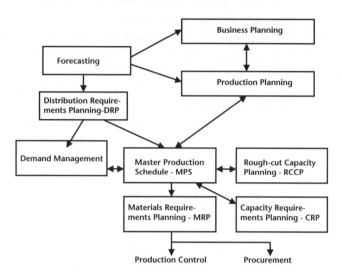

to a first estimate of production capacity to test the feasibility of the proposed master production schedule. After possible modification, the master production schedule is converted into an MRP schedule. This will, in turn, result in revised capacity requirements planning. MRP determines inventory status and release orders for purchasing, scheduling them based on vendor lead times. There is a difficult transition from MRP to production control, where the system often breaks down.

Materials requirements planning

MRP consists of a production schedule and a bill of materials. The underlying logic is that a forecast determines a production schedule, projected on a specific time schedule. Each product has a bill of materials, composed of the product components and materials that enter into this final production schedule. MRP requires three steps: 1) development of the master production schedule, 2), the bill of materials and 3) the master production

Figure 5.5. Materials Requirements Planning (MRP)

Master Production Schedule - Bicycles

Weeks	1	2	3	4	5	6
Requirements	30	–	40	–	50	–

Order quantity = 200 units   Lead time = 3 weeks   Component Plan - Wheels

Projected Requirements	60		80		100	
Scheduled Receipts			200			
On hand, End of Period 100	40	40	160	160	60	60
Planned Order Release				200		

Order Quantity = 300 units   Lead time = 2 weeks   Component Plan - Tires

Projected Requirements				200		
Scheduled Receipts			300			
On hand, End of Period	0	0	0	100	100	100
Planned Order Release		300				300

schedule and the bill of materials together to create input requirements. The number of units in the production schedule combined with the bill of materials determines the number of component units that will be required. The MRP must take into account the lead time and order quantities for these components. It also takes into account bills of materials for component units and their subcomponents in the same manner. It is logical to think of the bill of materials in terms of levels. Products (level 0) are assemblies of components. Each component (level 1) also has assemblies (level 2). Carrying the product materials beyond three or four levels is impractical, as it requires too many data, especially if schedules change.

We demonstrate the process with an oversimplified example in Figure 5.5 on bicycle production. There are three components: frames, wheels and tires. Assembled bicycles are at level 0. Frames and wheels are at the final assembly level (1) and wheels at one level lower at level (2). First we introduce the bill of materials for a single bicycle. Note that we include order information for components.

The production schedule calls for the number of bicycles per week. The production schedule as seen at the start of week 1 therefore calls for 30 frames and 60 wheels in week 1. These wheels require 60 tires. Leaving the frame out for still further simplicity, we concentrate on the wheels and tires. Note that we start the week with 80 wheels on hand. These will take care of week 1. We anticipate delivery of an order for 200 wheels that we placed one week before our start date in time for assembly in week 3. We further anticipate production of 64 bicycles in week 3 and 50 in week 5. In week 3, we have 40 wheels on hand, receive 200 more and use 60 for a net inventory of 160. Again, there is enough on hand to cover week 5, but we anticipate having only 40 on hand at the end of the period. We need to place an order in week 3, to arrive in week 6. The same process will be followed for tires. The tire requirement is driven by the wheel requirement and is in turn by the assembled bicycle production schedule. Note that the lead time for tires is 2 weeks and the order quantity is 300. At this point, the production planner has a view over the entire forecast period.

The documentation needed for MRP can be extensive, recording the production schedule for each component, scheduled receipts, inventory on-hand and the planned order releases.

There is more than one problem however with MRP. First, the production schedule changes, requiring the system to pull in more component inventory, but lead time now becomes a constraint. The feasible schedule now becomes difficult to change. With the data requirements, regeneration of the entire MRP schedule requires massive amounts of computer capacity, although greater power in computers reduces that problem. Second, going below three or four levels becomes cumbersome, leaving lower level subcomponents to be managed through simpler inventory systems. Third, order quantities theoretically could be matched to the requirements of the production schedule, but this may not match schedules or optimal order quantities of suppliers. Even without an environment of constant change, MRP is likely to accumulate inventory on-hand. Changing requirements further compounds the problem. MRP was designed for stand-alone applications on mainframe computers without input in real time. Connection to real-time systems is not a feasible option. Most companies have made extensive changes to make it operate with any success.

New approaches

Production scheduling

Production has moved into a real-time environment, of rapid product changeovers, volume changes and scheduling on the fly as orders come in. This is a result of integration through information technology, discussed in Chapter 9. An important module is the advanced scheduling and planning system. It has become a closely linked component to other process management software, notably ERP that extends beyond production to the whole enterprise. A typical advanced scheduling and planning system program generates a set of possible production schedules through simulation. The advanced scheduling and planning system program selects the one closest to optimal. These schedules may not be truly optimal but are close enough for the scheduling task. The computer then manages the schedule and material flow.

Virtual manufacturing

The key is the computer connection. The unique elements are 1) the ability to make product design mobile, communicating manufacturing requirements for local production anywhere in the world and 2) a vehicle for rapid development through computer-based modeling. Digitally, bits can be substituted for physical products.

Many elements are currently in practice or are waiting for the development of technology. They include solid modeling, collaborative design, rapid prototyping, testing the feasibility of manufacturing, testing factory processes, transmitting product design instantaneously between the factory and the supplier and establishing remote production.

- Solid modeling will ultimately replace the wire diagrams now used in electronically transmitted product modeling. It offers more richness in interpretation. It is only limited by the availability of broadband transmission. The problem will be relieved by extension of fiber-optic cable and wireless transmission.
- Collaborative design takes place now. It is supported by groupware designed for collaboration. It also supports global efforts,

so that one group of engineers and other specialists works on a given project and turns it over to other groups in different time zones for further development. Software is being developed on this cycle, using programmers in the United States and India on the same projects. The Boeing 777 was designed using this approach (Sabbagh 1996). Engineers in Japan were able to communicate and discuss designs directly with engineers in Seattle.

- Rapid prototyping refers to computer modeling of physical and software products. It accelerates the design process to the point of directing the development of the physical model by computer, in some cases creating sintered metal prototypes as output.
- The feasibility of manufacturing can be tested through modeling production processes. This can eliminate some of the problems in the production process.
- Factory process simulation tests can be used to plan factory operations for coordination and product flow issues in advance of implementation.
- Transmitting designs instantaneously to and from suppliers enhances coordination. It becomes vitally important in modular product design and in clarifying and modifying product features.
- Remote production reduces transport costs and increases market response through closer proximity. It becomes possible when drawings and even computer machine instructions can be transmitted in full detail.

Virtual manufacturing changes the factory into a larger system. The organizational arrangements must also change as decisions are diffused not only to the shop floor but to other managers and even external suppliers. The production line is no longer self-contained.

Agile manufacturing

The name agile manufacturing is not a concept in itself but a call for attention to a set of currently available technologies and their application as a change in orientation from mass production to customized manufacturing (Sharp et al. 1999). Agile manufacturing has been labeled the competitive environment of the future (Kidd 1994). Yusuf et al. (1999) describe it as a holistic approach to production more than a collection of technologies. Gunasekaran (1999a) defines it along four dimensions: cooperation, value-based pricing to assess alternatives in costs and product options, organizational change and investment in information. The technologies are not necessarily new in themselves but have been grouped together to respond to the new pressures from the marketplace.

There is little consensus on a precise definition. Desired outputs from production are familiar: cost, flexibility, responsiveness and quality. The inputs are equally familiar: information systems, shifts in decision location, supply chain coordination, real-time ordering, customization and virtual partnerships and rapid prototyping. Ultimately, it stresses the ability to respond rapidly to new challenges.

A model of interdependence is replacing the model of the self-contained factorys with customers, suppliers, marketing and procurement. Procurement and marketing were considered as appendages, one to secure materials and components in the open market, the other to move products out the door to customers. Information was not shared and production was an island unto itself. The new model is one of close integration to match individual customer requirements and serve strategy beyond the boundaries of production. Agile manufacturing is therefore recognition of a need to integrate production operations into the supply chain.

Concluding comments

The emphasis has been on linking production to the supply chain. As production systems become more responsive, there is less value in finished product inventory. Manufacturing itself is dispersing by stages of production. Products may start in one mode such as mass production but become finished products in job shop processes. Information systems and the new capabilities of virtual manufacturing make production possible at more locations, coordinated through the computer. The ideal is to pull products through the system, to manufacture against firm orders. Technology allows us to get closer to it.

Illustrative case

Smart Car began in 1994 as a joint venture between Mercedes-Benz and the Swiss watchmaker Swatch. In 1998 Swatch sold its part and the unit was reorganized as a separate DaimlerChrysler subsidiary.

A Smart Car is a small, plastic-bodied, two-seater city-car – a little more than the half of the length of a Volkswagen Beetle. The average fuel consumption is 3 liters per 100 km. DaimlerChrysler originally forecast a yearly sale of about 200,000 units, but in 1999 only 80,000 units were sold. In 2000, 100,000 units were expected to be sold. The Smart Car is sold in about a dozen countries, including Germany, France, England and Japan. Responsibility for the Smart Car has now been handed over to Mitsubishi Motors Company, DaimlerChrysler's new Japanese partner. A right-hand-drive version, a sporty roadster and a four-seater version are planned in the near future. The workforce at the Hambach plant is about 1400. When the system partners are included, a total of 2500 people are involved in building, designing and marketing the Smart Car.

The Smart Car can be ordered from about 120 Smart Centers throughout Europe or configured and ordered via the Internet and then delivered from the nearest Smart Center. The Smart Centers are high-profile showrooms located in shopping centers or other highly visible places in big cities. From the outside, the characteristic Smart tower is a landmark, which can be seen far away. The Smart Centers have repair shop areas where body parts can be rapidly replaced or new product features be added. When a customer orders a car from a Smart Center, the order is submitted to Hambach. Special features can be added and body parts can be changed in the Smart centers. The order to delivery lead time is 2-3 weeks (Van Hoek & Weken 2000).

The production systems

Smart Ville is the name of the production plant in Hambach in El-zas-Lothringen, France, where the Smart Car is assembled. In Smart Ville seven first-tier suppliers are integrated with the Smart assembly operation. The »integrated« suppliers have co-invested in the production location and are located adjacent to the assembly hall of Mitsubishi Motors Company. The Smart Car consists of five modules: the platform, powertrain, doors and roof, electronics and the cockpit. The modules are pre-assembled on site and synchronized with the production schedule for final assembly. The value added by Mitsubishi Motors Company during production only comprises 10% of the production costs. The assembly time per car is 4.5 hours, and the plastic body panels can be completely replaced in an hour (van Hoek & Weken 2000).

The outsourcing process has gone further than in most other car manufacturing companies. For example, the pressing and painting process has been outsourced to a first-tier supplier. Information systems to plan and control production and logistics operations are run by Andersen Consulting. The buildings and the sites were sold to a property company under a lease-back arrangement.

Smart Car has been a prototype for a new way to organize collaboration between the assembly plant and first-tier suppliers. The investment costs have been estimated to about USD 1.5 billion (Ewing & Johnston 1999). The Smart Car concept is considered as a strategic learning project in the DaimlerChysler Corporation. Other car manufacturers have generally accepted the Smart Car concept as of key importance to future organization of assembly processes. Thus, General Motors has built a plant in Brazil incorporating the ideas of heavy contribution of supplier capital and a small assembly plant.

6. Procurement

*»The arm's length buy-sell transaction, use your clout to beat
up the supplier, is a highly outdated model. We also believe
that to share information is absolutely key, and sometimes
this requires changing a lot of norms and practices in your
company where secrets are sovereign.«*
(Martin J. Garvin, Vice President,
Corporate Management, Dell Computers,
quoted in Mazel 1999)

Introduction

Competition among global companies emphasizes sourcing of materials, products and production capacity around the world. The
search for materials and components and managing the flow becomes an essential part of the international supply chain. It is also
becoming an essential part of corporate strategy as firms emphasize
their core and source other components, processes and services
from outside organizations. This has changed the role of procurement. The traditional role of procurement has been to achieve the
cheapest price and ensure a sufficient flow of materials to production. The conventional wisdom has been to spread purchases
among several suppliers and keep a large supplier base to be sure to
get the best prices at the marketplace.

There is a new perspective on procurement, beyond managing
purchasing transactions, that recognizes that the supply chain is defined by its processes and links to suppliers. One writer describes
procurement as being on the cusp of radical change, changing from
a focus on products to supplier capabilities. Procurement becomes
proactive, designing and managing networks of connections. It involves interorganizational relationships, utilizing the resources of
suppliers, supplier development, cost management and the stages

Figure 6.1. Procurement

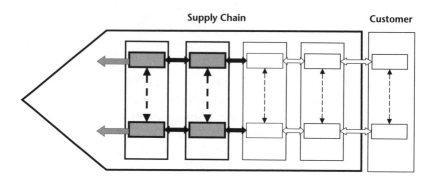

of logistics, connecting and processing. Purchasing management becomes strategic procurement management, shaping the direction of the corporation.

In this chapter we first look at the driving forces behind the new strategic role of procurement. Second, we look at different types of customer-supplier relationships from arm's length to strategic alliances. Third, we use portfolio models as a basis for classifying purchases and purchasing strategy. The underlying assumption is that there is no one-size-fits-all type of relationship. However, within a specific relationship there may be a best fit, depending on the purchasing situation. Fourth, we examine specific procurement issues. One is the use of total cost of ownership as a decision tool to recognize the full cost of buying a particular good or service from a particular supplier. Another is the impending impact of e-procurement on transaction costs and supplier relationships. Finally, we look at trust-based supplier relationships as a source of innovation and competitive advantage.

Procurement is a primary arena for interorganizational relations (figure 6.1). It demonstrates the usefulness of theory from Chapter 3, especially transaction cost analysis and networks. One criterion of supplier commitment is asset specificity, specialized investments that would be difficult to transfer to other uses, including capital equipment and specialized training. These become switching costs, implying the financial risk in commitment by both supplier and customer.

Driving forces behind the strategic importance of procurement

The role of procurement in the modern corporation is changing. Gadde & Haakansson (1994) point to three decision areas in the new strategic procurement context:

- make-or-buy decisions
- organization of the supply-base structure
- customer-supplier relationships.

The decision on whether to buy or to rely on in-house production has always been a major topic in procurement. However, until recently it has not been considered as a strategic issue for top management attention but has been based on short-term cost considerations. The bias has usually been towards internal production. The more recent emphasis on outsourcing has changed management attitudes towards external supply and production whenever the decision can be justified by cost or capacity.

The supply-base structure involves two strategic issues. One is the number of suppliers; the other has to do with their organization. The number of suppliers is related to the classical choice between multiple versus single sourcing. Multiple sourcing is traditional, dealing with suppliers at arm's length through market transactions. Once equivalent products are available, price, quality and delivery become paramount in the decision. Single sourcing and, in some cases, dual sourcing by contrast involves more permanent ties and the development of closer cooperative ties.

The organization of suppliers deals with the variety of ways to organize suppliers, whether as open market relationships, or as networks with tiers, *keiretsu*, with supplier associations or other forms of organization. The customer-supplier relationship has become a strategic issue for two reasons. One is cost rationalization, the other the benefit from utilizing the resources and competencies of suppliers to develop new skills and innovations. Two trends emphasize the differences between market and network relations. One is the development of e-commerce, which allows rapid comparison of supplier offerings. We discuss e-commerce and business-to-business relationships towards the end of this chapter. The other trend, the development of relationships, has been necessitated by the need to collaborate with suppliers and capture their expertise, while reducing company involvement in areas where there is no competitive advantage.

Together, the three decision areas mark a distinct break from past practice of procurement of squeezing profit margins of suppliers for short-term cost reductions. Several factors have influenced this development. The most important are:

• increased outsourcing
• global sourcing
• JIT purchasing
• green supply management
• information technology.

Increased outsourcing

The past decade has seen a strong tendency towards buying more from outside suppliers. In the automotive and electronic industries, typically between 60% and 80% of the product value has been outsourced to suppliers. In the fashion and sports wear industry, outsourcing is even more widespread. Companies such as Nike and Reebok have deliberately planned to retain only design, prototyping and marketing in-house, outsourcing production and distribution. Increased outsourcing changes the role of procurement from largely reactive to proactive activity, searching for and evaluating potential suppliers, establishing contracts and developing long-term relationships.

Global sourcing

The increasing importance of global sourcing demands new skills in purchasing. In the past, being a qualified purchasing manager required good negotiating skills, solid knowledge of the supplier market and practical insights in internal purchasing routines. Depending on the product area, it could require technical knowledge as well. Today, these requirements are still present, but they must be supplemented by cross-cultural knowledge, language proficiency, knowledge of international finance, international logistic and capabilities in information technology and telecommunication. Above all, procurement must be able to establish, develop and manage long-term supplier relationships.

Just-in-time purchasing

The principles of JIT production have also changed the purchasing process from products to production capacity. JIT purchasing provides materials to production just as they are required for use. The fundamental aim is to ensure that production is as close as possible to a continuous process from receipt of raw materials or components to the shipment of finished goods (Gunasekaran 1999b).

JIT purchasing is ideally characterized by a small supplier base of long-term »partners« with the buying company, incorporating production facilities located close to the buyer's plant and frequent deliveries. Supplier relations are built on a high degree of mutual trust and openness. In a study of JIT purchasing practices in the United States, Ansari & Modarress (1992 p. 33) note »the importance of product quality, supplier relationship[s], delivery performance and price, very much in this order.« The objective is to eliminate inbound inspection, establish close relationships for coordination and problem solving, deliver on time in small quantities and arrive at an equitable price. Transportation becomes important, often requiring a carrier commitment to routings and schedules. Many relationships also specify information system requirements such as manual or electronic kanban.

For JIT purchasing to work well in a production environment, demand must be relatively stable with a commitment over a term long enough to cover specific investments. Suppliers must be able to anticipate demands, both through leveling of production orders or through forecasts that allow them to plan their own capacity. Otherwise, JIT will push inventory requirements back on the supplier, with costs that will influence the cost bid for the supply transaction.

Green supply management

Customers have been made aware of the environmental effects of the products they are buying. Purchasing organizations should therefore have a solid knowledge of the supplier market, not only regarding price, quality and technical specifications, but also about environmental issues, such as the origins of materials, production processes used by the supplier, dismantling, recycling and labor force conditions. Commentators on supplier relations note the importance of incorporating environmental aspects into the supplier assessment process (Lamming & Hampson 1996). Life-cycle analysis of products throughout the supply chain should be performed to determine environmental purchasing strategies. An increasing number of companies are being environmentally certified, and the purchasing department has an important role to play in this process. In JIT purchasing, reusable standard containers are used for all parts.

Information technology

During the last decade, developments in information and communication technology have increased the potential to make the procurement process much more efficient. Implementation of automated and e-procurement systems and increased use of electronic data interchange have made transactions with suppliers faster, cheaper and more reliable to replenish materials and components. Bar-coding of individual products, packages and pallet loads has made automatic replenishment systems easier to install and implement, enabling tracking systems to control procurement operations and shipments throughout the supply chain.

The Internet has created further opportunity for electronic exchange both in easier access to ordering and payment and greater transparency of the international supplier market. E-procurement is projected to increase dramatically in the foreseeable future. These developments have given procurement new opportunities to make purchasing more efficient and reliable but have also emphasized the strategic importance of procurement.

Different types of customer-supplier relationships

Sako (1992) and Helper (1993) identified two patterns of relations, arm's-length contractual relations and obligational contractual relations, the extremes of a multidimensional spectrum of possible trading relationships. Arm's-length contractual relations involve a single specific, discrete economic transaction. An explicit contract specifies the tasks and duties of both parties. All business exchanges are performed at arm's length, to avoid undue familiarity and personal ties. Changing trading partners is therefore easy when the contract is terminated.

Obligational contractual relations, in contrast, are more embedded in social relations between trading partners and are also characterized by a sense of mutual trust. Transactions often take place without a prior formal contract. Even when the tasks and duties of each partner are specified in a contract, both parties recognize the incentives to do more than expected by the trading partner. When one partner fails, there is a willingness to seek remedies rather than to shift to other partners.

Comparing supplier relationships in the automobile industry in Japan and the United States, Helper (1993) identified two types of responses to problems arising in a customer-supplier relationship: *exit* and *voice*. These terms, respectively, have the same meaning as arm's-length contractual relations and obligational contractual relations. Exit relations exist when problems are solved by finding new suppliers. Voice relations exist when the customer works jointly with the original supplier to solve the problem.

Any particular relationship can be placed on a continuum between adversarial relationship and close integration. The closer a relationship is to core competencies or investment in highly specific dedicated assets, the more likely that the relationship becomes quasi-integrated.

Cox (1996) proposed a typology:
- adversarial
- preferred supplier
- single sourcing

Figure 6.2. The Range of Supplier Relationships

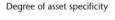

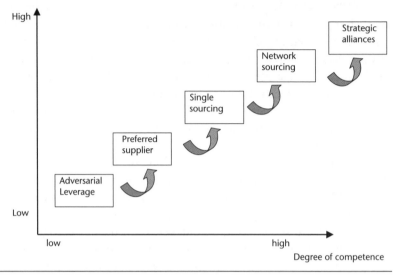

Source: Cox (1996)

- network sourcing
- strategic alliances.

Figure 6.2 places the range of possible supplier relationships in a progression where the horizontal axis represents the type of competencies offered by the supplier and the vertical axis shows the degree of asset specificity.

Adversarial relationships

Adversarial relationships or market relations have long dominated purchasing thinking and practice. Focusing on price comparisons between different suppliers as a major basis for comparison kept supplier-customer relationships at a distance. In this situation the supplier does not retain ownership rights over the goods and services provided. Arm's-length relationships offered flexibility for competitive markets. Today, the arm's-length approach is now subject to criticism because of its focus on short-term cost reductions. However, it has merit under specific conditions: in commodity markets, with multiple suppliers, low asset specificity and little market uncertainty. The market also serves as a control mechanism to ensure competitive prices.

The increasing use of the Internet as a medium for product catalogs has made it possible to compare product specifications and prices across supplier markets. W.W. Grainger, the largest industrial distributor in the United States, for example, offers more than 200,000 different items for maintenance, repair and operations supplies via the Internet. Software such as Ariba and procurement networks such as Commerce One have made searching and purchasing transactions easier. These developments reduce transaction costs for buying products and services. The use of common currencies such as the euro within the European Union or US dollar comparisons in other regions make price comparisons much easier than the multiple currencies of the past. These developments may well encourage more arm's-length procurement in the future.

Preferred suppliers

Preferred suppliers provide goods and services that are of medium asset specificity and can be considered to be complementary to the core competencies of the buying firm. However, the products purchased have relatively low strategic importance for the buyer. Suppliers with equivalent product specifications, quality and price are limited, and the buyer will typically uses a bidding process to evaluate and choose a few suppliers as preferred sources of goods and services. Preferred suppliers have some advantages over market-based suppliers. The contract period is normally longer. The suppliers will be granted preferential relationship for a certain period of time. There will be exchange of planning information, such as forecasts and production plans, making the planning process more reliable and predictable for the supplier while also making supply more reliable for the customer.

Single sourcing

Single sourcing means that the buyer is supplied by a single source for a specified period of time. This type of supplier relationship refers to supply of medium to high levels of asset specificity, with goods and services linked directly to the core competencies of the buying firm. During the last two decades, there has been a debate about the relative merits of single and multiple sourcing. The proponents of single sourcing have argued that there is a need for single sourcing as JIT deliveries are becoming more widespread in many industries.

Bailey & Farmer (1990) have outlined the following advantages of single sourcing:

- The supplier can offer price advantage because of economies of scale.
- Personal relationships can be more easily established, thus making communications more effective.
- The buyer's administrative work is reduced.
- Closer relationships and a reasonable tenure can result in a mutual effort to reduce costs.
- Buyer-tied research can be undertaken.
- Tool and pattern or fixture costs are reduced and long-term tools may be used.
- Transportation costs can be lower and, where pallets are used, common pools can be established.
- Quality control is made easier since there is only one location.
- Scheduling is made easier.

Figure 6.3 shows a single source being used even though two assembly plants are involved. Materials suppliers are linked to one supplier of components, in turn linked to one module producer supplying both assembly plants.

Early studies of Japanese firms suggested that single sourcing was much more common in Japan than in the West. Womack et al. (1990), however, presented contrary evidence. Comparing automotive suppliers in Japan, North America and Europe showed that only 12% of components were single sourced in Japan versus 69% in North America and 33% in Europe. Womack et al. also found in

Figure 6.3. Single Sourcing

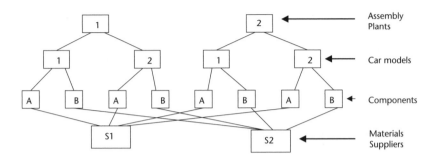

a study of the Japanese transplants in the United States that these assemblers used single sourcing intensively – up to 98% – which could reinforce the impression. A similar pattern was found for Japanese transplants in Europe.

Hines (1995) explains this phenomenon as a consequence of the high degree of vertical integration in the United States automotive industry and the generally adversarial relationships between buyers and suppliers. Therefore, only a few good United States suppliers were available for the Japanese transplants that had to set up their own component plants in North America. Because of economies of scale, they were not able to provide the transplants with multiple sources of supply, so the transplants had to rely on single sourcing. However, in practice Japanese manufacturers use multiple sourcing to a higher degree than commonly thought, but they do it differently than in the West.

Richardson (1993) describes a hybrid between single and multiple sourcing, parallel sourcing, which has contributed to the success of the Japanese auto industry. This system is used when a car manufacturer produces a number of models at different plants using a single source for a component of one model at one assembly plant, while another source is used for the same model at another assembly plant.

Parallel sourcing combines asset specificity and a commitment to long-term single-source relationships and still allows for a high degree of competition among suppliers for future contracts. The principles of parallel sourcing compared with single sourcing are shown in Figure 6.4.

Figure 6.4. Combined Single and Parallel Sourcing

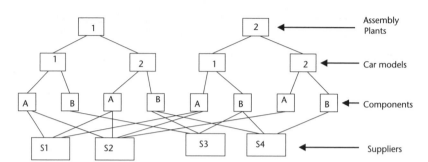

An assembler has two plants producing the same model, and component A is used at both plants. In single sourcing, one supplier will supply both plants with component A. In parallel sourcing, one supplier will supply component A for plant one, and another supplier will supply component A for plant two. Parallel sourcing ensures that two or more suppliers with similar capabilities act as single source suppliers of the same components, but they are guaranteed production for their particular model. The assembler can compare the performance of the two suppliers and keep the competitive pressure for the bidding of the next model cycle. The assembler will also assist the weaker supplier to compete more effectively through exchanges of technical personnel, capital assistance on purchase of new equipment and even taking ideas from the winner to give to the other supplier. At the same time, the winning supplier experiences continuing pressure for improvement, despite its previous success.

When various sourcing strategies are compared, it should be kept in mind that the Japanese auto industry is characterized by large-volume manufacturers producing a variety of models with standardized components. Therefore, the supplier relationship with an assembler becomes important, even when the contract only encompasses one specific component for a single model. Many suppliers are small and medium-sized companies without sufficient production capacity to become sole suppliers for all models and plants.

The risks are clear. From a supplier's perspective, success depends on the demand for the customer's product and the performance of other suppliers in the supply chain. From the buyer's perspective, several sources are an insurance against supplier failures from fire, strikes, quality or delivery problems. In addition, more than one supplier maintains the process of competition.

Some buyers such as Nike and Hewlett-Packard have told suppliers to get additional customers, for even a majority of their business. The advantages are that the supplier is not as dependent on the buyer as they would be if there was only one customer and the supplier has the stimulus of dealing with external markets (Miles & Snow 1992). With a single customer, the supplier becomes a de facto unit of the buyer's organization. The buyer loses some of the advantages of an external supply relationship such as independent product development. The disadvantage is that the supplier gains in independence and power. This converts a dependence relationship into a collaborative one.

Network sourcing

Hines (1994, 1995) used the term network sourcing to characterize the unique supplier network structure of the Japanese subcontracting system. Network sourcing is a combination of many different aspects of the cooperation between major car manufacturers and their suppliers. These include a tiered supply structure, cross-exchange of staff between buyer and supplier, relatively high asset specificity and risk-sharing, early involvement of suppliers in design and innovation, trust relationship, supplier associations (*kyoryoku kai*) and supplier coordination and development. These closely interrelated elements together constitute a complex interorganizational network with a competence that is difficult to imitate and transfer to Western industry.

The Japanese automobile industry has multiple layers or tiers of suppliers. The final assemblers, such as Toyota, Honda, Mazda and Nissan, are at the top of the pyramid. First-tier suppliers provide key components, subassemblies and systems, such as engines, seats, electronic systems, braking systems and steering systems. Typically, there will be about 200 to 300 first-tier suppliers per final assembler.

Second-tier suppliers provide first-tier suppliers with compo-

Figure 6.5. Tier Structure in Supplier Networks

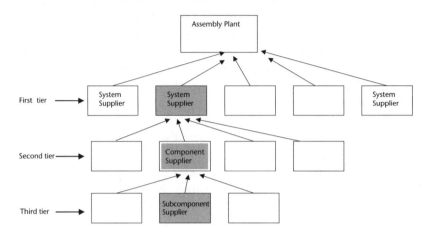

nents or perform specific processes, such as metal forming, painting as well as sub-assemblies. Second-tier suppliers have their own subcontractors to provide them with specialist process capabilities such as plating, casting and machining. Depending on the product and specialization, there may be several layers of subcontractors. The tier structure is illustrated in Figure 6.5.

Embedded in the sourcing network is the institution of *kyoryoku kai* or supplier association. This institution is an evolving form, shifting from a system of supplier dependence towards one of balanced power (Hines 1994). This is a form of external quality circle for suppliers at the same level in the tiering structure. For example, first-tier suppliers form a supplier association where they exchange ideas and cooperate in solving individual or mutual problems. The association includes both non-competing and competing suppliers. Supplier associations are also established at lower levels in the tier structure to diffuse innovations and improvements further into the network tiers. The effect is to raise the skill and sophistication level across the supply network. The success of the concept of the supply network has rested not only on flexible connections but also on diffusing modern production technology throughout the entire network. As a result, participating firms have adopted computer-integrated manufacturing, product quality management programs and modern procurement methods such as value analysis, value engineering and statistical process control.

To the dominant firm, the benefits of the supply network are numerous: flexibility in production to respond to new market requirements; low transaction costs through electronic data interchange and *kanban* systems; and frequent delivery because of close proximity. With stable membership, suppliers can be encouraged to invest heavily in new technology, take part in new product and process development and contribute their own knowledge of production processes. Further, subcontractors advance their own expertise in manufacturing as a balance against the power of the dominant firm. The source of power in the network is diffused away from the customer. Flexible production capacity is distributed across the supplier network. The combined effect is to produce a network with a collective expertise greater than that of any single member.

The question is continually raised about the validity of this supplier network concept outside of Japan. One argument is that Western suppliers would not tolerate the control by parent companies asserted over their suppliers. Also, the parent company wants suppliers to share the increasing costs of research and development and increase the flexibility and efficiency of the production process. Lamming (1993), however, points to a shift of this nature taking place within the European car industry. Further, the United States electronics industry is utterly dependent on the development of new product components and subsystems by suppliers such as Intel and Cisco.

The management role in the supplier network has several dimensions. First, it becomes important to acknowledge the supply relationships of the first-tier supplier. It become crucial to recognize the impact of changes in performance or supply failures in second-tier relationships and cultivates precautionary alternative network links. Second, it becomes important to map the entire supply chain network to recognize where value is added, where capacity may be limited and the complete cost structure (Kulkarni 1996). Cost analysis indicates where functional activities can be reorganized, eliminated, combined or shifted to other partners. It is also important to recognize sources of innovation within the network, both for their direct contribution to new products and impact for changing other components. Third, shifting activities may change the balance of power in the network, when suppliers communicate directly with final customers. The role of the immediate customer is diminished.

The success of the global corporation will depend increasingly on its supply networks as a source of knowledge of technology. Manufacturing location strategy often emphasizes access to new technology through its suppliers, as United States and European companies have pursued Japanese expertise by locating production facilities in Japan. The advantage of the global corporation is the freedom to source components and rationalize production around the world. Most of the motivation has been to seek low costs. Beyond costs, however, is a need to maintain parity in technology with potential competitors. The freedom of the global corporation is limited by the quality of the relationships that it establishes with its suppliers.

Against this is the tradition of arm's-length negotiation with suppliers as adversaries, emphasizing price over quality or service, with the resultant high defect rates, lack of incentive for suppliers to commit to capital expenditures and lack of trust. This relationship will probably hold for much of non core-related procurement, although there have cases where interorganizational teams have developed efficient procurement processes (Banfield 1999).

Strategic alliances

Strategic alliances are voluntary arrangements between firms involving exchange, sharing or co-development of products, technologies, or services (Gulati 1998). Strategic alliances are deeper than normal business relations. They involve complementarities: the matching of skills, knowledge of technologies, resources and activities to complement the partners' own capabilities. In short, they add value. In the vertical context of supply chain management, they appear in both material and component procurement and in services such as third-party logistics, information and transportation services. In a value-adding partnership, each partner performs only part of the process, focusing on one specific activity. The value-adding partnership becomes a long-term arrangement without the necessity for vertical integration by ownership.

Value-adding partnerships are especially useful in international procurement because they provide flexibility and commitment beyond normal contract relationships. Contracts are not easily enforceable across national borders, and cultural patterns often dictate personal relationships in preference to formal contracts. They establish a permanence that might not otherwise be available.

Many examples can be taken from procurement. Research and development is common. Subcontract manufacturing is also used and the supplier's knowledge comes from superior knowledge of production processes. Shipper-carrier and other logistics relationships are frequently used as examples. They are symbiotic in the sense that business operations are complementary; partners become mutually dependent, but the activities can be clearly separated. They have developed because of the synergy between these interrelated roles. In effect, they have resulted in extended organizations, moving away from individual transactions to form quasi-integrated units.

Portfolio approach to supplier relationships

Typically, a firm has to deal with different types of suppliers and needs a model to assist in managing with several kinds of supplier relationships. Portfolio models have primarily been used in strategic decision-making to support resource allocation decisions. We briefly describe two portfolio models that can be used to classify suppliers and serve as a basis for a differentiated supplier strategy.

The Olsen & Ellram portfolio model

Kraljic (1983) developed a portfolio model to be used as a basis for classifying and setting purchasing strategy. His model divides purchasing transactions into four groups based on two dimensions: their strategic importance and the difficulty in managing the purchasing process. Olsen & Ellram (1997) expanded on Kraljic's model to propose an approach to analyze a firm's portfolio of supplier relationships. The first step is to identify important factors related to the two dimensions in the Kraljic model. The first relates to their strategic importance:

- Competence factors describe how close the purchased items are to the core competencies of the firm and their strategic importance. An important question is whether the purchase can improve the knowledge or the technological strength of the buying firm.
- Economic factors include the volume and value of the purchases; the possibilities of getting leverage with the supplier for other buys and the purchased item's contribution to the profitability of the finished products.
- Image factors describe how critical the purchase is to the brand names or perceived image of the firm by customers.

Factors in managing the purchase situation include:

- product characteristics, such as uniqueness and complexity;
- supply market characteristics such as the number and relative market shares of suppliers, their size and power and their shares of the buyer's purchases; and
- risk and uncertainty related to the purchase transaction, such as technological risk and opportunistic behavior by the supplier.

Decision-makers in the firm identify and evaluate the relevant factors for specific transaction categories, assigning weights based on the perceived importance of each factor to the firm's operations. This part of the process is based on individual judgments. However, participants should ultimately agree on their relative rankings, and the factors provide a framework for discussion.

Purchases are then classified into four portfolio categories, illustrated in Figure 6.6:

- leverage
- non-critical
- bottleneck
- strategic.

Figure 6.6. Portfolio Model of Purchases

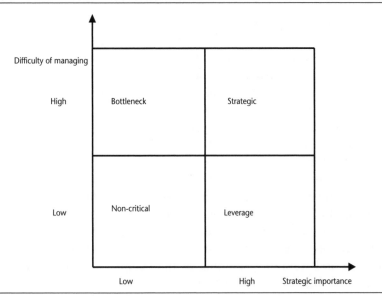

Source: Olsen & Ellram (1997)

Leverage purchases are easy to manage but strategically important to the company. Concentrating purchases at one supplier might enable discounts across product groups or lower administration and transport costs.

Non-critical items are easy to manage and with low strategic importance. Here standardization and consolidation are key words. Purchase administration of these items could also be outsourced to a third-party provider.

Bottleneck items are items that are difficult to manage but have a low strategic importance to the firm. Here the key words are standardization of the purchases to keep the purchasing administration costs down and search for substituting suppliers.

The strategic category encompasses purchases both strategically important to the firm and difficult to manage. This category should get the major emphasis from purchasing management. In this category the firm should consider close supplier relationships, early supplier involvement in product development and similar arrangements to integrate the suppliers in the firm's supply chain.

The Bensaou model

Bensaou (1999) has proposed a framework for managing a portfolio of relationships based on specific investments by both buyers and suppliers, following the transaction cost analysis model. The purpose is to give managers guidance on the most appropriate governance structure under conditions of different financial commitments and on how to manage them with maximal effectiveness. The model is a portfolio of supplier relationships based on the two dimensions of the buyer's and the supplier's specific investments in the relationship.

Examples of buyer-specific investments in a relationship include tangible investments in buildings, tooling and dies committed to the supplier's product or operations or customized products and processes using particular components procured from the supplier. Specific investment also encompasses intangible investments in educating and training personnel of the supplier in product knowledge, administration and business practices.

Supplier-specific investments might include dedicated physical assets such as plants or warehouses and specialized tools and equipment dedicated to the customer's needs. It could also include less tangible research and development projects, specific knowledge about the customer's products and processes, placement of boundary-spanning employees on the customer's premises to solve current problems and intangible investments in human assets, such as training and other methods of skill and knowledge development.

The Bensaou model classifies buyer-supplier relationships into four categories depending on the degrees of specific investments from either party (Figure 6.7):

- market exchange
- captive buyer
- captive supplier
- strategic partnership.

Market exchange relationships are characterized by low specific investments from both the customer and supplier side. The products are highly standardized and typically based on simple, mature technology and well-established manufacturing techniques. Many sup-

Figure 6.7. Portfolio-Model of Relationships

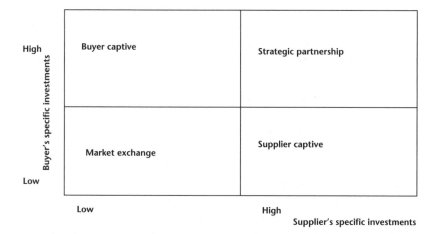

Source: Bensaou (1999)

pliers are capable of delivering these products to a highly competitive supplier market.

Captive buyer relationships involve complex components with some customization, although they are based on well-known, stable technologies. The supplier holds a proprietary technology that provides a monopoly position to the seller. The supply market is highly concentrated, with a few large, well-established suppliers. If the buyer wants to terminate the contract, finding an alternative supplier may be difficult.

Captive suppliers make specific investments to win and keep their customers. Suppliers have limited bargaining power, because of an at least implied threat of switching. Customers have a monopsonistic position derived from their technology or access to the final market. The relationship involves highly complex products based on proprietary technology. However, the supplier market is competitive and the buyer often keeps two or more suppliers, shifting contracts among them to keep their interests.

In strategic partnerships, both parties invest in highly, specific investments in their relationships. To use a term from transaction cost economics, the parties demonstrate »credible commitments« in the relationship. The technical complexity of the buyers' products is high, and suppliers' components are highly customized. The supplier is often involved in the design and development processes. The relationship becomes long-term and based on mutual trust.

Asset specificity in supply relationships must be defined in terms of specific industries. Bensaou & Anderson (1999) examined the United States and Japanese automobile industries to identify sources of credible commitment for buyers adapting to their suppliers: They were able to identify eight constructs:

- the buyer's specific investments for a supplier relationship;
- task features, including both task complexity and architectural interdependence, reflecting the interface between the component and the vehicle;
- supplier credentials, including size and market share, serve to indicate confidence in the relationship;
- environmental uncertainty, relating to both predictability of volume and potential changes in the component;
- thinness in the supply market, reflecting the number of potentially competing suppliers and standardization of resources;
- relational safeguards such as the number of different components from this supplier and the age of the relationship;
- supplier trustworthiness based on its market reputation; and
- the institutional context, which would differ between Japan and the United States.

Investment in specific assets by automobile assemblers (buyers) involves the risk of opportunism by suppliers, which is perceived differently in Japan and the United States. Bensaou & Anderson (1999, pp. 476-478) note: »a significant challenge for European and U.S. carmakers will be to duplicate a Japanese style of dependence on suppliers without having to divert expensive resources to an expensive governance structure to protect themselves from opportunism«.

Bensaou (1999) separately questioned the general assumption that Japanese firms manage supplier relations primarily through strategic partnerships. Based on empirical data on supplier relationships in the United States and Japan across a representative set of components and technologies, he found that this assumption was not justified. On the contrary, he found that the percentage of strategic partnerships in Japan was lower than in the United States (19% versus 25%). He also found that the captive supplier relationships were relatively more important in Japan (35%) than in the United States (15%), whereas the captive buyer relationships were significantly higher in the United States (35%) compared with Japan (8%). Japanese companies appear to be better able to persuade their suppliers to invest in specific assets than are their United States counterparts.

Bensaou concluded that firms could not manage with only one design for all relationships. He recommends managers to follow a two-step approach: first, to identify the type of relationship that matches the competitive conditions surrounding the product or service exchanged and second, to design the appropriate management model for each type of relationship.

Strategic partnership with suppliers

Strategic partnerships are normally established only with suppliers contributing processes, components or systems critical to the customer's Value Chain or that constitute an important part of product value. Strategic partnerships are limited to key suppliers. As an example, in 1998 about 90% of Dell Computer's annual purchases worth USD 12 billion went to just 25 suppliers. Dell earmarks key suppliers and their technology with their products well before product introduction. In many cases, suppliers participate actively in a »virtual lab« for product development. Sharing technical information and collaboration in research and development allows Dell to lead in product transitions and providing an advantage in time-to-market (Mazel 1999).

The Danish audio, video and TV manufacturer, Bang and Olufsen[9] (B&O), developed a cooperative relationship with a plastic molding manufacturer, Kaiserplast. Kaiserplast produces all plastic molded components in B&O's production. Kaiserplast invested in special equipment and, in return, is the sole plastics moldings supplier to B&O. Kaiserplast has on-line access to B&O's sales forecasts and production plans. They are also responsible for replenishment of B&O's stock following prespecified inventory management

---

9. See B&O case in the Appendix.

procedures. In addition, Kaiserplast participates with B&O in new product development.

A special variation is systems suppliers who develop, produce, test and deliver subsystems included in the final assembly of finished products according to specification of requirements. The systems supplier is responsible for selecting and managing component suppliers and maintaining technological development within the systems area (Hines 1996b). Systems suppliers are especially prominent within the aircraft and automobile industries. The concept of modular production in the car industry has encouraged this development. Volkswagen built a factory in cooperation with its suppliers who were to build subsystems that they would even assemble and install on the vehicle on the production line. The concept ultimately failed, but General Motors is currently pursuing a similar but slightly less ambitious plan, also in Brazil. The concept is being applied in other industries where the finished product is composed of a large number of components and services, such as power plants, trains and ships.

Managing sourcing relationships

A recent approach to managing strategic sourcing relations examines both the external relationship and the internal organization under the names of »balanced sourcing« (Laseter 1998) or »strategic sourcing« (Banfield 1999). Like other approaches, it abandons the adversarial relationships of the past in favor of stronger supplier participation. However, it goes beyond partnership to take a proactive position in order to take full advantage of the supplier's capabilities, seeking mutual improvements on both sides. The new elements are 1) the addition of the customer's own capabilities through organizational change including cross-functional teams, 2) autonomy of the buying organization, 3) involving the entire organization beyond the procurement function and 4) upgrading the procurement function. It requires flexibility based on trust between partners and sharing information. It also projects new roles such as bringing partners into new product development.

Two topics bear emphasis: supplier development and supplier participation in new product development. Much has been written about the first. It comprises a mixture of activities from technical assistance, training, exchanges of personnel to specific investments on the supplier's premises. Krause et al. (1998, p. 40) define it as:

>»... any set of activities undertaken by a buying firm to identify, measure and improve supplier performance and facilitate the continuous improvement of the overall value of goods and services supplied to the buying company's business unit.«

The emphasis in current writing appears to be on process more than on the direction of development *per se*. Krause et al. differentiate between »reactive« and »strategic« approaches. Reactive suggests ad hoc efforts to remedy specific problems, while strategic identifies key commodities and suppliers, to anticipate problem areas. The first ultimately leads towards the second. The key element in a successful development process appears to be communication, formal evaluation, training and supplier award programs.

JIT purchasing emphasizes close relationships. De Toni & Nassimbeni (2000) divide development into two sets of practices. Operational practices include product and process development, production planning and scheduling and delivery synchronized to production requirements. Supplier development practices include selection and monitoring, assistance and training, contractual incentives and supplier organizational integration. Investigation led to identification of three types of links between supplier and buyer: logistics, quality and design. The logistics link involving delivery and production planning; shared forecasts and packaging dominated the quality (information exchange and certification) and design (involvement in product design) links.

Involving suppliers in new product development is a difficult process but sometimes necessary and advantageous (Handfield & Nichols 1999). When suppliers have needed technologies, there is often little choice. Suppliers can be integrated at any point between idea generation and full-scale production, although early stages influence a major share of the product cost. Decisions appear at three levels: the system or core product, subsystem and component. The tendency is to internalize value-adding activities, outsourcing commodity elements, although there are sometimes paths of parallel and complementary development that involve both supplier and customer. There are issues of risk and rates of technological change that should be recognized but go beyond the discussion here.

Another alternative in Saab Automobile established procurement for a set of specific subsystems, placing responsibility on a single supplier (Brandes 1995). The system manager is responsible both for designing and procuring for a particular system such as seating or exhaust. This is important when the final product has a high proportion of value added from purchased components.

Supplier relationships and innovation

Innovation involves investment in highly specific assets – both human and physical. From a transaction cost perspective, innovation should therefore take place in-house or through quasi-vertical integration, where the buyer has ownership of specialized equipment and knowledge. However, transaction cost economics is inadequate to deal with innovation, because transaction cost analysis assumes efficient resource allocation that, in turn, assumes known opportunities. But uncertain environments and outcomes characterize innovation. The solution is not in classical contracts that specify outcomes but entering into agreements that share risk and reward.

Sako (1996) suggests that the buyer can enhance the suppliers' incentive to create their own product and process innovation by rewarding the suppliers' innovative contributions. This would mean giving the suppliers a fair proportion of the gain from innovation. McMillan (1990) refers to the practice of Japanese manufacturing, where the buyer specify a target price and a time path of price reduction targets, which remain unchanged whether suppliers enhance their efficiency or not. The supplier can then capture 100% of the gain from increasing their operating efficiency.

Another method is the joint analysis of costs using established value analyses and value engineering methods, sharing efficiency gains equally. This contrasts with traditional Western bargaining patterns, where the buyer dictates both prices and equal shares of additional cost savings at the same time. The famous »Spanish Inquisitor« José Ignatio Lopez, who managed strategic procurement while he was at General Motors and later Volkswagen, was an exponent of this approach. Lopez and his »purchasing warriors« managed to reduce General Motors' bottom line by USD 1 billion over the course of 2 years in the early 1990s (Laseter 1998, p. 25).

As for product innovation, the buyer would be willing to involve suppliers in the design and development process, only with trust present. Chapter 3 mentioned three types of trust: contractual, competence and goodwill trust. Trust in all these meanings becomes a necessary prerequisite for supplier relations involving joint product development.

Clark & Fujimoto (1991) classified parts in the car industry into supplier-proprietary, black box (jointly developed) and detailed controlled (customer developed and controlled) types. They found that the ratios of the three types were 8 : 62 : 30 in Japan, 3 : 16 : 81 in the United States and 7 : 39 : 54 in Europe. The relatively high proportion of black box parts in Japan indicates the high level of trust prevailing in their supplier relations. By contrast, the high level of detailed controlled parts in the United States reflects low trust and therefore a high degree of vertical integration.

Prahalad & Hamel (1990) argue that a firm's core competence is a source of value creation and establishing competitive advantage and therefore should be retained in-house. The implication for supplier relationships and innovation is that analysis of resources and capabilities that create core competencies is essential to determine what processes to outsource. Then, the firm can engage in subcontracting, which is conducive to innovation only if both parties have organizations can take advantage of learning opportunities.

The guiding principles in both transaction cost analysis and strategic management for the use of subcontracting are clear: subcontract out processes and components where only small costs can be saved and the processes do not undermine the firm's core competence. However, Sako (1996) comments, »these principles may protect the innovative capability of the buyer firm, but it may be protected because of, at the expense of, or regardless of, the innovative capability of the supplier firm«.

An alternative would forge partnerships and strategic alliances with innovative suppliers. The prerequisites are the presence of mutual trust, a capacity to learn and a reward for innovative contribution. However, the firm has still to define and identify what competencies will be core in the future.

Total cost of ownership

Suitable suppliers have often been traditionally evaluated and selected solely on price. However, the supplier with the lowest price is not necessarily the most attractive when all the additional costs incurred by the purchase transaction in the customer's organization are taken into account. Total cost of ownership is a purchasing concept to recognize the true cost of buying a particular good or service from a particular supplier (Ellram 1995; Ellram & Siferd 1993; Ellram & Maltz 1995). Total cost of ownership requires that the buying firm determine which costs are most important in the acquisition, possession, use and subsequent disposition of a good or service. It recognizes that the purchase price represents only a portion of the total cost of acquiring an item (LaLonde & Pohlen 1996). The choice of supplier affects costs of ordering, transport, inventory, receiving, quality inspections and disposal after use. These costs are often hidden as overhead costs. The total cost of ownership calculates the total acquisition costs related

Figure 6.8. Total Cost of Ownership

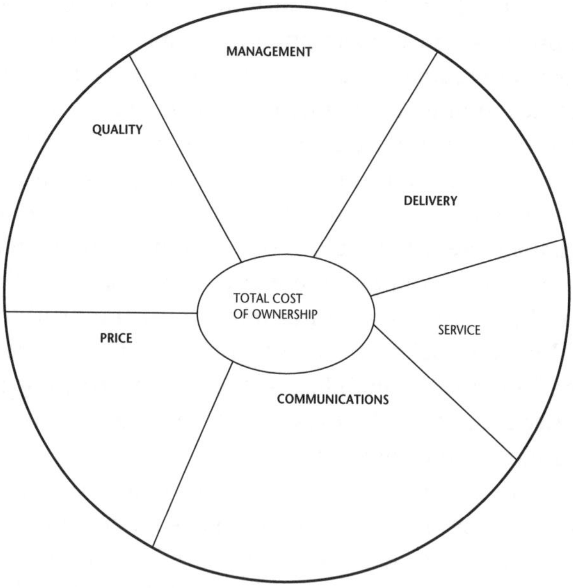

Source: Ellram & Maltz (1995)

to a specific purchase transaction. The concept is illustrated in Figure 6.8.

Recent developments in management accounting, such as activity-based costing have made it possible to assign costs to individual suppliers. Activity-based costing is covered in Chapter 8.

Vendor-managed purchasing

Vendor-Managed Inventory is an efficient replenishment practice designed to enable the supplier to respond directly to actual demand without the distortion and delay of decisions in the customer's purchasing organization (Holmström 1998). Vendor-Managed Inventory is also a part of consumer marketing through the concept of Efficient Consumer Response, which is covered in Chapter 10.

Vendor-managed purchasing is an extension of Vendor-Managed Inventory. In vendor-managed purchasing, the vendor's organization and the customer's purchasing organization are very closely integrated (Christiansen 2000). This is shown in Figure 6.9.

In Figure 6.9, A is a manufacturing company and B is the supplier. Company A use vendor B as the sole supplier of a particular category of goods, typically standard items like »nuts and bolts« or maintenance, repair and operations items. Production planning and automated inventory replenishment rules at A automatically generate orders for items that are then transmitted to B. B then fills these orders, ensures quality and ships to A. The goods are delivered directly to production areas without a need to perform incoming quality inspections.

The vendor has on-line access to company A's production plans and sales forecasts and therefore knows the requirements of the different items for future production. Based on this knowledge, the vendor can order the items from its suppliers and manage documentation, transport and payments. The customer's benefits are cost savings on purchasing administration, inventory management and quality control. The vendor's benefits come from economies of scale in purchasing and economies of specialization in knowing the supply market. Thus, the purchasing organization of company A can be relieved of administration of routine purchasing decisions to concentrate on more strategic procurement.

Figure 6.9. Vendor-managed Purchasing

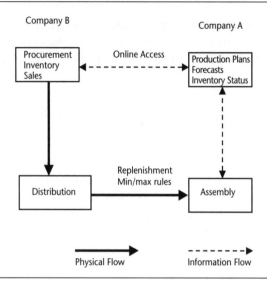

Source: Christiansen (2000)

Growth in e-procurement and e-marketplaces[10]

Electronic procurement has increased dramatically since the late 1990s. E-procurement uses the Internet and intranet technologies to automate the process of procuring maintenance, repair and operations products or indirect products and services. E-procurement is an internal marketplace between the company and its suppliers, enabling the company to do business interactively and in real time and thereby reducing the purchasing order cycle (from product search to payment) significantly.

The first wave of e-procurement projects has been initiated by large corporations who wish to gain control of their maintenance, repair and operations spend and realize significant process optimization. Companies such as Philips, Schlumberger, Swissair, Lloyds, Ford, Anheuser Busch, Bell South and Carlsberg have been first

---

10. Thomas Skjøtt-Larsen, Management Consultant at PricewaterhouseCoopers, contributed to this section.

movers in this market and have gained important insight into the dynamics of the new economy.

Most of the projects have been pilot projects with a limited number of users, subsidiaries and suppliers. Within these environments, supplier catalogs have been converted to uniform buyer-specific catalogs (enabling benchmarking across suppliers). These catalogs are accessible to end users through a Web browser and impeded in Web-based software applications with a user-friendly interface. This enables end users with limited training to carry out the majority of the transactions within the purchase order cycle, allowing the procurement department to focus on the strategic aspects of procurement. Most of the work by procurement is done up front selecting and negotiating with the suppliers and facilitating the process from paper-based catalogs to electronic catalogs. The principles of e-procurement are shown in Figure 6.10.

Significant challenges have been involved with the first implementations:

- the low level of maturity of software applications and catalog providers;

Figure 6.10. E-procurement

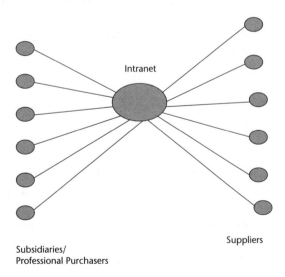

- adoption by suppliers – how to successfully get the suppliers participating;
- adoption by end users – how to ensure that the end users use the system;
- resistance from autonomous subsidiaries being »dictated« technology, processes and suppliers; and
- adapting the organization and creating new roles (such as content manager) necessary to support an e-procurement environment.

In some cases the challenges have prevented the projects from moving from the pilot phase to full-scale implementation, causing disappointing business benefits. However, in general e-procurement has resulted in substantial savings.

Implications of e-procurement

E-procurement will strongly affect future buyer-seller relationships. The greatest savings are expected in the procurement of maintenance, repair and operations products, because many organizations have overlooked this area in the past. The purchasers of maintenance, repair and operations products, such as paper, copiers, PCs, gifts and office supplies, are often not professionals. The number of transactions is high, and a high proportion of many companies' revenues and time is spent on indirect purchases.

E-procurement has several potential benefits. A report from PricewaterhouseCoopers (2000) classifies the benefits in three groups (Table 6.1):

- compliance
- leverage
- process efficiency.

Compliance with purchasing contracts eliminates »maverick« buying, in which individuals buy non-catalog items based on personal preferences and random knowledge. Instead, purchasing is concentrated on contracted products to obtain discounts, priority status, delivery and other benefits. Through compliance with preferred suppliers, the company can use its purchasing power as leverage to

Table 6.1. Benefits of e-procurement

Compliance	Leverage	Process efficiency
• Increased use of pre-ferred suppliers • Reduced off-contract spending • Reduced processing errors **Leads to:** • More goods purchased at best price	• Consolidated details of actual amount spent with each supplier • Consolidated detail of actual amount spent in each product category **Leads to:** • Full purchasing power is leveraged • Appropriate product cat-egories targeted for pre-ferred supplier contracts	• Reduced administration burden • Removal of paper pro-cesses **Leads to:** • Reduced error rates • Reduced processing time • Reduced fax and phone usage • Reduced on-site inven-tory **Enabling:** • Dedicated e-procure-ment staff to focus on value-adding activities such as contract negotia-tion

Source: PricewaterhouseCoopers (2000, p. 120)

negotiate improved discounts and service terms. E-procurement in-creases efficiency in the procurement organization and relieves it of the burden of routine purchases to concentrate on developing sup-plier relationships and contract negotiations.

From e-procurement to e-marketplaces

An e-marketplace or e-hub can been defined as an Internet-based solution that links businesses interested in buying and selling relat-ed goods or services from one another. The main differences to e-procurement are (Lipis et al. 2000):

- There are many buyers and suppliers involved.
- There is an independent third party administering the market-place.
- A marketplace has to take into account the interests of both buy-ers and sellers in its governance.

Figure 6.11 shows the theoretical model of an e-marketplace.
E-marketplaces offer a number of service propositions:

- connectivity – the infrastructure is normally based on open
  standards (such as XML) allowing any legacy system to integrate;
- transactions – enabling companies to carry out purchasing-relat-
  ed processes such as product search, raising requisitions and
  purchase orders, goods receipt and payment;
- value-adding services – in addition to the basic purchase order
  cycle, most e-markets offer more advanced services such as logistics, financial services, auctions and tax; and
- catalog updates and content management – providing structures
  for product categorization, loading and maintaining content.

Many of the service offerings are based on the principle of economies of scale in which a third party carries out activities on behalf
of a large number of buyers and sellers. Catalog updates comprise a
good example of an activity that can be carried out much more efficiently through a marketplace.

Auctions are another example of a service provided on the marketplace. Offerings are sold to the highest bidder and price compar-

Figure 6.11. E-marketplace

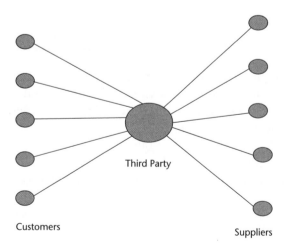

Customers

Third Party

Suppliers

Figure 6.12. Classification of e-commerce Sites

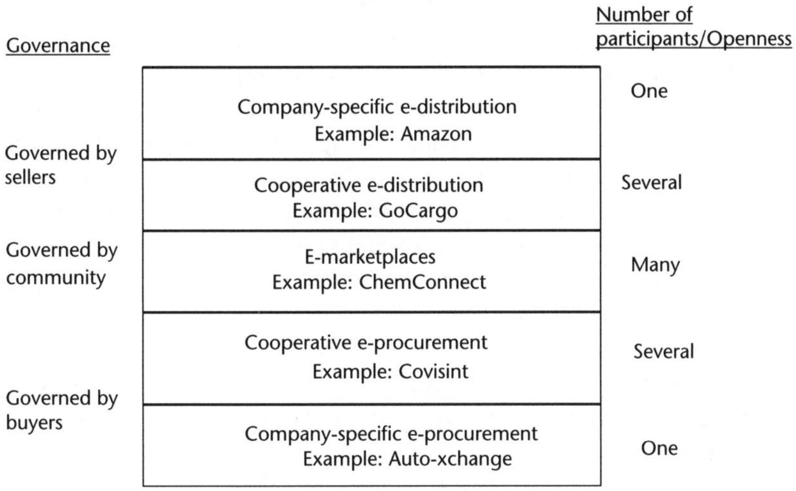

Governance		Number of participants/Openness
	Company-specific e-distribution Example: Amazon	One
Governed by sellers	Cooperative e-distribution Example: GoCargo	Several
Governed by community	E-marketplaces Example: ChemConnect	Many
	Cooperative e-procurement Example: Covisint	Several
Governed by buyers	Company-specific e-procurement Example: Auto-xchange	One

Source: Adapted from Lipis et. al. (2000)

isons are easily made, as long as the offers are standard commodities. There can also be reverse auctions where buyers make offers that suppliers are free to accept or not. The auction has the effect of eliminating long-term pricing dominance. However, it also has negative competitive implications if suppliers face a single buyer in a vertically integrated market, or vice versa. These issues have yet to be resolved.

Figure 6.12 classifies different types of e-commerce sites by governance and access. One distinction in governance is control, related to the numbers of participants and their orientation towards sellers, buyers or a community marketplace, the structure of the sites. Governance could be associated with sellers, buyers or the community. Access determines how open sites are for participants. Some e-commerce sites are open for every member within an industry, whereas others are only open to limited numbers of participants.

E-marketplaces would be open to many sellers and buyers. E-marketplaces serve as brokers. They do not take physical possession of goods or services being traded, but only facilitate their exchange by matching demand and supply. E-marketplaces include industrial products or services, ranging from raw materials to logistics services to human resources. Some e-marketplaces are vertical exchanges that are industry- or commodity-specific, tending to focus on high-volume raw materials or components for production. Other e-marketplaces are horizontal exchanges that cover a broad spectrum of products, some indirectly related to production such as maintenance, repair and operations supplies. Examples of e-marketplaces are ChemConnect and e-Chemicals for chemical products; GoCargo and Freightquote for logistics services and Freemarkets and Suppliermarket for industrial goods.

B2B hubs have been classified by Kaplan & Sawhney (2000, pp. 98-99) into:

- maintenance, repair and operations hubs: horizontal markets that offer catalogs from many potential suppliers to a wide range of buyers;
- yield managers: horizontal markets for short-term sourcing of resources, such as CapacityWeb.com, which matches buyers with short-term production requirements with contract and other manufacturers with momentary excess capacity;
- exchanges: vertical markets for short-term sourcing of commodity production inputs, to match immediate needs against production offerings; and
- catalog hubs: vertical (single industry) markets for systematic sourcing of production inputs.

Several buyers collectively sponsoring a common site becomes cooperative e-procurement. One example of a powerful cooperative e-procurement site is Covisint, an automobile Internet exchange being formed by the three big carmakers in the United States – GM, Ford and DaimlerChrysler. Later Renault, Nissan, Toyota, Mazda, Honda and Mitsubishi Motors have joined Covisint.

Conclusion

The role of procurement has changed dramatically during the last decade. From being a routine competence in the past, it has now become a strategic issue. Relationships between buyer and supplier have shifted from arm's length to close collaboration with key suppliers. Many companies have adopted a differentiated approach to individual procurement situations. Information technology and outsourcing to third parties have relieved the heavy workload of administering routine purchases. The emerging e-marketplaces have opened up new opportunities in procurement. First, purchases of maintenance, repair and operations products can be rationalized and made more cost-efficient. Second, using e-marketplaces and cooperative e-procurement sites can leverage purchases of raw materials and components for production. Powerful buyers such as the auto manufacturers and the aerospace industry can set up their own supply chain networks on the Internet to streamline their purchasing with suppliers. Exchange, auction and reverse auction sites enable supply and demand to be met in a more efficient way in the electronic marketplace. Until now, we have only seen the tip of this iceberg.

At the other end of the spectrum, strategic sourcing is becoming collaborative. Suppliers contribute their technology and innovative expertise to processes, components and subsystems that become part of the final product. The buying organization can become more focused on its own core, and the final output becomes more a joint venture. The boundaries between vendor or supplier and customer become less important than the ability to manage the process.

Illustrative case

Chrysler's supplier relationships[11]

About 15 years ago, the Big Three automobile manufacturers in the United States were organized into vertically, oriented, functional departments. The relationships to suppliers were arm's-length contractual relationships based on tough price bargaining. During the 1970s and 1980s, competition from European and Japanese small and medium-sized cars threatened traditional production methods of building cars in the United States. During the late 1980s Chrysler threw out their old system and created »platform

---

11. Adapted from Stallkamp (2000).

teams,« cross-functional, interdisciplinary teams of people dedicated to each major type of vehicle. At the same time Chrysler built a new World Headquarters and a Chrysler Technology Center outside Detroit. Today, all designers, engineers, procurement professionals, manufacturing, marketing and finance people and representatives from outside suppliers are located at the Chrysler Technology Center.

In 1989, Chrysler launched a new supplier approach consisting of four elements:

- the SCORE program
- target costing
- the extended enterprise
- the centralized supply concept.

The SCORE Program

The objectives of the SCORE (supplier cost-reduction effort) program were to reduce costs and waste without reducing the suppliers' profit margins. All suppliers were expected to come up with proposals that would result in cost savings (but not margins) of 5% of their annual sales to Chrysler. A voluntary sharing of savings was established with each supplier, but half the cost savings would be passed to Chrysler.

The SCORE program proved to be a very effective innovation and communications program between Chrysler and its suppliers. The annual savings was more than USD 1 billion after 4 years and exceeded USD 1.5 billion for the 1998 model year.

Target costing

Target costing starts by estimating what the customer is willing to pay and then converts sales revenue into cost targets. From a total cost target, costs are broken down into systems and components. Target costing follows a procedure of three steps. First, a reference vehicle cost is calculated. This is the actual cost of a current Chrysler car plus costs that would be added at a future vehicle due to added features and higher costs. Second, potential savings obtained through competitive bidding are calculated. Third, a team of people from Chrysler and the suppliers try to find additional cost savings by re-engineering and improving manufacturing processes until the total costs are reduced to the target costing level. The principle in target costing is shown in Figure 6.13.

An example of the target costing process was a headliner used inside Dodge Intrepid and Chrysler Concorde. The previous price was USD 130 per headliner, and the expected price for the new version was USD 140. A team effort between Chrysler and a key supplier established a target cost for the next version at USD 116. At the end, the supplier came up with a new price of USD 104, or USD 36 below what Chrysler might have been expected to pay under the old system.

The extended enterprise

The extended enterprise was an effort to streamline Chrysler's supply chain by establishing a closer link to suppliers. One objective

Figure 6.13. Target Costing Process

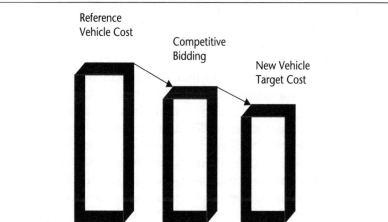

Source: Stallkamp (1998)

was to pass responsibility as far as possible down the supply chain. The governing vision was to persuade each supplier to become part of a team working for the final customer, no matter how small or where the supplier was positioned in the supply chain. Many functions that had been traditionally separate organizations were integrated. This was to establish the role of supply to manage the flow of materials and information to build cars that satisfied customers,. For example, supply coordinated engineering changes with assembly plants, scheduled the plants and managed the transportation of finished cars to the dealers as an integral process.

The centralized supply concept

Chrysler realized a need for a »total systems« approach to accomplish the complex task of getting materials from suppliers to production workstations. They started by reducing the quantity of materials on the shop floor waiting to be used in the assembly process. The material lot sizes were reduced by about 50% by sequencing and delivering parts more efficiently, and Chrysler was able to reduce inventory at the shop floor by 77%. Next step was to invite suppliers to participate in so-called lean production workshops with the purpose of sitting together and »leaning« the total materials flow from supplier to assembly line. By doing this, Chrysler was able to further reduce inventory, free up floor space, improve materials handling and develop models for lean production that could be used elsewhere.

An example from Chrysler's minivan plant in Windsor, Ontario, could illustrate the approach. Two suppliers, the Becker Group and Textron, were producing body components for Dodge and Plymouth minivans assembled at Windsor. Before the change, four individual supplier plants shipped components separately to Windsor – at different times, using different containers and by different carriers. After the change, three plants now ship to the fourth, which then organizes the sequence of components for JIT delivery to Chrysler's plant. Deliveries in small lots take place frequently, using the same carrier and container system. Chrysler pays the supplier to perform consolidation and sequencing, but gains in reduced floor space requirements, elimination of double handling, reduced inventory costs, scrap and packaging. The net effect for Chrysler was about USD 0.5 million from just one lean production workshop.

7. Transport and logistics services in Europe

»The great paradox is that, at their core, Internet retailers are logistics companies. Take away their Web sites, and they look a lot like third-party logistics providers«
(Forsyth, 2000a).

Introduction

The global supply chain relies on the effective use of transportation networks (Figure 7.1). They vary substantially, depending on the region, country or function. Both intercontinental and regional transport become important in the global context of business. Materials supplied in one country can be moved across the globe for processing, returned for assembly and then delivered to many individual country markets for distribution. Each transport link is also a unique market, with its own options determined by its own regulations, business practices and industry characteristics. Transoceanic transport options differ from those within Europe, which again differ from those available in North America. Transoceanic product movements utilize bulk movement, container and air transport; about 35% of United States export and import traffic by value but less than 0.5% by weight travels by air. Transport inside Europe uses motor carriage heavily, railways much less and air selectively. North America uses rail and air transport much more.

This chapter emphasizes the transport and logistics services available within Europe. The options and their impact on supply chains are sufficiently unique to require different management practices. We begin with structural changes in the logistics systems in Europe that have increased the importance of fast and efficient transport systems. We then look at transport policy within the European Union, where the most significant contribution has been

Figure 7.1. Transport

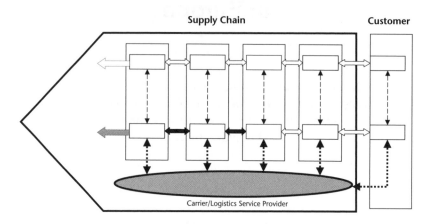

deregulation of the transport market and the removal of barriers between Member States. The major part of the chapter discusses the market for transport and logistics services. The major development has been the increasing presence of third-party logistics providers. Here, we identify different types of third-party logistics providers and present various steps in developing third-party relationships. Finally, we look at the future of the transport and logistics industry in Europe and examine new developments within the transport and third-party industries.

Structural changes in supply chains

Major changes in both European supply chains and logistics systems highlight the importance of solving the transportation problems at a regional rather than at a national level. Changes in production methods such as just-in-time production and flexible production specialization have created a need for flexible, fast, individually tailored transportation systems with reduced shipment sizes and increased shipment frequency to reflect coordinated supplier-customer operations. Both production and distribution have simultaneously shifted from primarily national supply to international sourcing, production and distribution, increasing requirements for efficient international transport systems. The shift from standard-ized mass production to small-scale production of customized high-value products involves smaller shipments, a market that favors road and air over rail and sea transport. Specialized production feeds other production facilities, sometimes located at considerable distances. Distribution has become centralized, relying on fast, flexible transport to substitute for purely localized distribution sys-tems.

Realizing the single market in the European Union has included deregulating transport, removvng customs clearance and abolishing technical trade barriers. Eliminating these obstacles has resulted in large increases in regional intra-European goods movements. Be-yond removing obstacles, growing environmental awareness among people and public authorities changes the focus. A limitation on solving capacity problems through new investment in motorways and airports constrains the free movement of goods. One result is pressure to reduce the volume of road transport and encourage the use of the more environmentally friendly modes of rail, inland wa-terways and combined transport.

Infrastructure investment

Transportation infrastructure in Europe reflects the historical dif-ferences among European countries in geography, demography, communications systems, political and economic systems and cul-tural backgrounds. The current infrastructure is still oriented more towards serving national needs than international goods transport. This is especially true for railways and inland waterways. There is vital concern in the European Union about whether the transporta-tion infrastructure will support the logistics requirements of busi-ness or whether it will impede the free movement of goods and services. Since the early 1980s, road transport of goods has in-creased by about 45%, measured in ton-kilometers. The share of freight transport by road has increased in the past 30 years from about 50% of surface transport to more than 75%. The railway share has decreased to only 15%. Inland waterways and pipelines are responsible for the remaining 10%. Air freight has increased in market share for high-valued products but is still negligible in terms of ton-kilometers. Domestic goods transport still amounts to about 95% of total intra-EU freight, which explains the persisting focus on national transportation infrastructures. However, in the past 5 years, the volume of regional intra-EU transport has been growing by nearly 5% per year, and there are no signs that this growth rate will slow in the future. The combination of increasing passenger vehicles and freight transport, environmental concerns and inadequate investment in infrastructure places pressure on the highway network. It has caused severe congestion problems around some core industrial areas in Europe: the Rhine-Ruhr Area, Greater London, Madrid, Milan, Frankfurt and Munich. Regulation under current policies will further restrict transit truck traffic through Switzerland and Austria.

There is a conflict between national interests in reducing the environmental effects of the increased goods transport and the EU policy of free movement of goods across Europe. In Switzerland, a referendum in 1994 concluded that foreign trucks in transit should be transferred to railways within the next 10 years. Besides, Switzerland is only allowing foreign trucks in transit with a maximum weight of 28 tons, compared with 40 to 56 tons gross weight in other European countries. Austria has implemented an eco-point system to encourage international truck operators to use more environmentally friendly trucks in transit through Austria. There are restrictions on the number of eco-points allocated to each operator.

The significance of these trends lies in the relationship between demand and the capacity of the highway system. Highway capacity in crucial sectors will soon be utilized in full. In Germany the expression *Verkehrsinfarkt* (traffic congestion) has been used to characterize the current traffic situation, which has resulted in increasing congestion costs from time delays, increasing fuel consumption and pollution.

With the near completion of the single market and with gradual deregulation of the transport market, the European Union has focused attention on common transborder infrastructure, notably the Trans-European Networks program, which was included in the Maastricht Treaty of 1992. The program takes into account the need to link island, landlocked and peripheral regions with the central regions of the European Union. Trans-European Networks projects have included investments in high-speed passenger rail networks in Europe, the Channel Tunnel between England and France, the Öresund link between Denmark and Sweden and the Storebaelt link across a major waterway in Denmark, several new motorways and inland waterway connections. Thus far, the huge investments in Trans-European Networks projects on freight transport in Europe have had limited impact. Most of these investments have improved high-speed train service for passengers but not the capacity for rail freight transport services.

Deregulation of the European transport market

The year 1993 was a milestone in transport policy within the European Union: the deregulation of intra-Union transport started. However, it has taken most of a decade to fulfill the vision. Cabotage, carrying goods in domestic commerce by a foreign carrier, has gradually been deregulated since 1993. Cabotage means that a carrier from one country is allowed to perform domestic transport in another country. For example, a French forwarder can pick up cargo between Munich and Basel on a backhaul trip from Stuttgart. Cabotage has led to increased competition between the international transport and forwarding companies, and the freight rates have been reduced on major traffic routes.

Railways are still state-owned and -operated in most countries in Europe. However, in several countries both passenger and freight transport will be privatized and access to perform railroad services liberalized. The competitive position of rail movement of goods differs by country. Railways in Sweden and Germany have relatively high market shares (in ton-kilometers), although for different reasons. In Sweden, this is the result of a combination of long distances and heavy bulk goods (such as timber, pulp, steel, heavy equipment, cars and large appliances). In Germany, the market share has been maintained until recently through subsidies along with restrictions on road transport. In Denmark, England, Benelux and southern Europe, railways have only 10-20% of the transport market.

In 1993 the European Commission proposed a directive aiming to separate the infrastructure (such as tracks, signals, bridges, roadbeds and tunnels) from train operations. This directive opened up access for private firms to establish railway companies, using the public infrastructure for private train operation. The railway companies themselves should be free to take only the part of the traffic they considered being profitable. For unprofitable traffic, special public service contracts were to be negotiated with state, regional and local governments.

In practice, there have been many obstacles to Europe-wide liberalization of access to tracks. Differences in electrical systems, security systems, signal systems and educational systems in individual European countries continue to maintain entry barriers to private train operators.

The process of changing the European railway systems into a single, commercially viable transport system able to compete with road transport will require great investment and total reorganization of the state-controlled railways. In addition, to be fully competitive, new services must be developed and tailored to individual customer requirements; they must provide on-line freight information systems, improve intermodal service across Europe and expand door-to-door service with competitive transit times and high reliability. In addition, European railways can only offer single-stack container train service, whereas railroads in the United States offer double-stack with considerable reduction in costs. This hinders the European railways in being competitive with road transport.

The EU is supporting the development of a system of key rail freight routes running across Europe on which operators will be able to compete for customers: Trans-European Rail Freight Freeways. For example, such routes have established from Scandinavia to Italy and from England to Hungary.

Intermodal transport in Europe is increasing, as road congestion is increasing and more restrictions and taxes are put on road transport. Intermodal transport encompasses several types of rail freight systems, such as ISO containers, swap bodies and piggyback trailers.

ISO containers are boxes standardized according to ISO standards, typically 20 feet (6.1 meters) or 40 feet (12.2 meters) long, used in deep-sea shipping and international transport. ISO containers can be transferred between ships, trains and trucks. Large container ships often arrive at large European ports, such as Rotterdam, Bremen and Antwerp, from which the containers are loaded on feeder ships, trains or trucks to the next or final destination.

A swap body is a demountable body that can be transferred between train and truck. When it is demounted, the legs support it. Swap bodies are mostly used in national or international transport within Europe.

Piggyback trailers are semitrailers with lifting points for transfer between road and rail. A piggyback trailer on a rail wagon is also called a *Huckepack* in German. A variant is *rollende Landstrasse* (rolling highway), where the entire truck is put on a rail car. Piggyback trailers offer high flexibility between rail and road, such as for freight in transit through Switzerland or Austria to avoid restrictions on truck transport.

The increasing privatization of the formerly state-run rail freight companies may result in a renaissance for intermodal transport. The United States rail operator Wisconsin Central has acquired a major share of rail freight operation in the United Kingdom. CSX Intermodal has formed a joint intermodal company, NDX, together with Dutch Railways and German Railways (Gallop 1998). A group of Danish road hauliers has taken over the former state-owned rail company for general cargo in Denmark. In 2001 the remaining part of the Danish Railways' goods transport division (full loads) was taken over by Railion, a joint venture between the German Railways and the Dutch Railways. Several large multinational companies are increasing their use of intermodal transport between their plants and distribution centers in Europe. Examples include Ford, Phillips, Sony and Unilever.

The transport and logistics service industry in Europe

The market for transport and logistics services in Europe has changed dramatically in the 1990s. Shippers now reconfigure production and distribution systems on a pan-European basis. They increasingly outsource warehousing, transportation and other logistics-related activities. The upsurge of e-commerce has increased the demand for direct, fast, low-cost and reliable shipments to customers.

The deregulation and liberalization of the transport market in Europe has changed the competitive environment. New competitors and combinations of previously traditional firms have entered the market: global express companies, postal companies and United States logistics companies. Mergers and acquisitions are taking place at a speed and with geographic coverage never seen before. Strategic alliances among leading transport and forwarding companies have been established to provide pan-European coverage and a wide range of transport and logistics services. Some established strategic alliances have dissolved because of their acquisitions that turned former partners into competitors. Expansion of logistics concepts have also changed the scope of competition as carriers have sought competitive advantage in annexing non-transport services.

Third-party logistics

Since the early 1990s, there has been a pronounced change in arrangements between shippers and logistics providers. A United States writer observes that third-party logistics now dominates the European transport market (Foster 1999b). The industry itself has undergone a wave of acquisitions, mergers and strategic alliances (Hastings 1999). While the initial driving forces were to reduce costs and release capital for other purposes, they now have a more strategic scope: to increase market coverage, improve the level of service or increase flexibility to meet the changing requirements of customers.

Cooperation between parties has become long term in nature, mutually binding and often combined with changes in both organization and information systems on both sides. Solutions are tailored to specific requirements and now often include value-adding services such as final assembly, packaging, quality control and information services. This broader, more flexible cooperative arrangement is termed third-party logistics.

What is third-party logistics?

Third-party logistics is difficult to define because it is still in evolution. Definitions reflect the stage of third-party cooperation. Researchers and consultants in this area most often develop concepts as the practice itself evolves. Some examples may illustrate the broad scope of definitions.

• Lieb & Randall (1996) suggested in a comparison of the use of third-party logistics services by large United States manufacturers between 1991 and 1995 that the concept
»... involves outsourcing logistics activities that have traditionally been performed within an organization. The functions performed by the third-party can encompass the entire logistics process or, more commonly, selected activities within that process«.

According to this definition, third-party logistics includes any form of outsourcing of logistics activities previously performed in-house. If a company with a private fleet changes to common carriers, this would, according to the above definition, be an example of third-party logistics. The same applies to a company that outsources its warehouse operations to a public warehouse.

• Berglund et al. (1999) define third-party logistics as:
»Activities carried out by a logistics service provider on behalf of a shipper and consisting of at least management and execution of transportation and warehousing (if warehousing is part of the process)«.

Other activities include information services, value-added activities, call centers and invoicing and payment services. In this definition, management support is required besides the operational activities. Management support can range from simple inventory management to advanced consultancy about realigning supply chain management.

• Bagchi & Virum (1998a, b) distinguish between simple outsourcing of logistics activities and logistics alliances. According to their definition, a logistics alliance means:

»A long-term formal or informal relationship between a shipper and a logistics provider to render all or a considerable number of logistics activities for the shipper. The shipper and the logistics provider see themselves as long-term partners in these arrangements. Although these alliances may start with a narrow range of activities, there is a potential for a much broader set of value-added services, including simple fabrication, assemblies, repackaging, and supply chain integration.«

In contrast to the first two definitions, which emphasize the performance of functional activities, the last definition stresses the duration of the relationship between the shipper and logistics service provider as well as the potentially wide range of logistics services included in the arrangement.

Figure 7.2 classifies various types of relationship between shipper and logistics service provider according to the degree of integration and the degree of specific investments in the relationship (asset specificity).

Market transactions in the lower left corner involve no specific assets or integration between the parties. The transactions can involve single or continuing purchases of logistics services, but the relationship is typically at arm's length. Agreements are short term

Figure 7.2. Relationships between Shippers and Logistics Service Providers

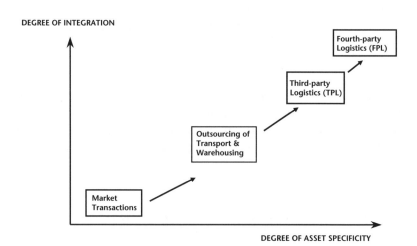

and often informal, carrying no commitment beyond the specific transaction. Usually the transactions involve single activities such as transport. Price is a strong element in competition, although special service requirements may also influence the choice.

Outsourcing operational logistics activities in the second stage would usually include transport and warehousing. The degrees of asset specificity and integration are relatively low. The shipper would maintain management and control internally, outsourcing physical operations to a service provider. The service provider would adapt standard solutions to the shipper's requirements. The agreement would normally be a short-term contract. The price and cost savings are decisive factors in choosing the service provider.

Third-party logistics is the third stage in the development of the relationship and demonstrates commitment by both shipper and service provider. The operations of both parties are integrated in interfaces between information systems and interorganizational teams. Cooperation is based on mutual trust and open information interchange. Asset specificity is also relatively high. The logistics provider may invest in dedicated facilities and other tangible assets and also in the less-tangible personnel training. Agreements are more formalized and binding than for simple outsourcing. Services become tailored to the requirements of the individual client. Sometimes the service provider assumes responsibility fully or partly for the personnel, equipment and warehouse operations of the client.

Fourth-party logistics (defined later) involves the highest degree of collaboration, both in the scope of services and strategic importance (Day 2000). In fourth-party logistics agreements, the logistics service provider offers a broad range of management and logistics services, covering not only traditional operational activities such as warehousing, transportation and value-adding services but also managing and optimizing the client's supply chain, information technology competencies and global coverage. Clients often name a lead provider that will secure and provide a complete package of logistics services. Fourth-party logistics will often be established as a joint venture or a long-term contract between the parties. The collaboration involves high-level system integration and interorganizational teams at various management levels. Also, asset specificity will normally be high, both in physical assets such as dedicated warehouses, specialized handling equipment and human assets involving activities such as the exchange of personnel and specialized training.

The following discussion focuses on third and fourth-party logistics. The emphasis is on third-party logistics, the dominant type of relationship currently employed between a client company and a logistics service provider. Fourth-party logistics is still in its infancy, and it is too early to say how widespread this form of collaboration will become in the future.

Typology of third-party logistics providers

Berglund et al. (1999) have identified three waves of entrants into the third-party logistics market:

- asset-based logistics providers
- network logistics providers
- skill-based logistics providers.

Asset-based logistics providers represent the first wave, originating in the early 1980s. They were typically operators of owned or leased logistics services assets, such as trucks, airplanes, warehouses, terminals and containers; they offer third-party logistics services as a natural extension of their core businesses. For example, a transport and forwarding company may provide dedicated trucks, transport management, distribution centers and information services to a shipper. A distribution center operator may offer inventory management, final assembly services and order administration in addition to basic warehousing. Declining margins and a tougher competitive environment in the traditional transport market have been the main drivers for these companies to enter the third-party logistics market. Some of these providers have used the additional logistical services and third-party logistics arrangements to secure volume for their basic services. Others have entered the third-party logistics market because of higher profit margins and customer loyalty. Asset-based logistics providers in Europe include Exel Logistics, Nedlloyd, Danzas, Frans Maas, BTL-Schenker, Maersk Logistics and DFDS DanTransport, to name a few from a growing list. Well-known asset-based third-party logistics providers in the United

States include GATX Logistics, Schneider Logistics, Ryder Integrated Logistics and Fritz Companies.

Network logistics providers date back to the early 1990s. These third-party logistics providers started as couriers and express parcel companies and built up global transportation and communication networks to be able to expedite express shipments fast and reliable. Supplementary information services typically include electronic proof-of-delivery and track-and-trace options from sender to receiver. They include such familiar names as DHL, UPS Worldwide Logistics, TNT and FedEx. Recently, these players have moved into the time-sensitive and high-value-density third-party logistics market, such as electronics, spare parts, fashion goods and pharmaceuticals, and are competing with the traditional asset-based logistics providers in these high-margin markets. As the largest transportation company in the world, UPS also offers a broad range of services from shipment tracking, shipper-accessible information services and specialized logistic services to e-commerce and financing services for overseas manufacturing (Violino 2000; Barron 2000; Patel 2000).

Skill-based logistics providers are a third wave of third-party logistics providers, starting at the end of the 1990s. They typically do not own physical logistics assets but provide consultancy and financial services, information technology and management skills to the clients. These new players are often subsidiaries or joint ventures. They may merge with players from the previous waves or use them as subcontractors. An example of an information-based logistics provider is GeoLogistics, which is a merger among three traditional third-party logistics providers, Bekins, LEP and Matrix, and an investment company. A consultancy group has been added to develop concepts, information systems and implementation plans to improve client's supply chains. Another example is the strategic alliance between Ryder Integrated Logistics (providing basic logistics services), IBM Global Services (providing software) and Accenture (providing management consulting). Ultimately, fourth-party services could take over complete responsibility for supply chain operations for clients, who would set the performance parameters but delegate the actual operations.

Figure 7.3 classifies the different types of logistics and management services available according to the availability of competence in supply chain management and customization of logistics solu-

Figure 7.3. Typology of Logistics Services

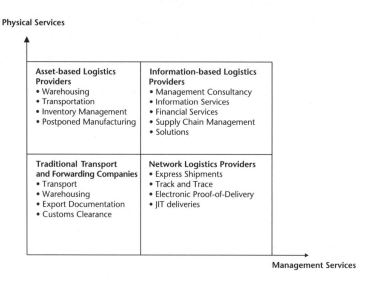

tions. Traditional market-based solutions offer only basic physical and management services. Asset-based providers may perform extensive services but leave control with the client management. With some exceptions, network providers are becoming more oriented towards management services but limited physical operations. Skill-based or fourth-party providers are becoming more comprehensive, offering both management and operations capabilities.

Forces behind third-party logistics

Several forces are driving the development of third-party logistics. In a global environment, logistics and supply chain activities become more complex, expensive and capital intensive. By outsourcing logistics activities, many companies can reduce their logistics costs and/or improve their customer service performance. This parallels the trend to outsourcing in manufacturing. These companies concentrate their resources on the most vital parts of their business, performing other activities via third-party specialists.

The benefits of outsourcing logistic services to third-party logistics providers include:

- the conversion of fixed costs to variable costs
- economics of scale and scope
- creation of a leaner and more flexible organization
- faster access to new markets and distribution channels
- reconfiguration of European logistics systems.

The conversion of fixed costs to variable costs. By outsourcing transport and warehouse operations, a company can free capital investment in transport equipment, warehouse buildings and materials handling equipment and thereby transform fixed costs to variable costs and transfer the financial risk to the third party. If the demand for capacity is uncertain or fluctuating, the shipper can more easily adjust costs to the scale of activity.

Economics of scale and scope. The third-party logistics company can use its assets to serve multiple clients and product groups with complementary demand patterns and thereby utilize assets better. In addition, third-party logistics operators often have knowledge and experience in international logistics exceeding that of the client. The cost savings may partly be passed on to the shipper.

A leaner organization. The shipper may be able to simplify and streamline routine logistics operations such as documentation, distribution planning, inventory control and personnel administration. This also facilitates implementation of electronic data interchange, bar coding and exchange of employees between organizations. Dealing with one or a few third-party operators on a long-term basis is more efficient than working with a number of independent haulage companies through individual transactions.

Faster access to new markets and distribution channels. For example, on-line retailers or e-tailers typically outsource the logistics part of their business to third-party logistics operators. Instead of having to invest in bricks and mortar in different part of the world, the Internet retailers can utilize the global network of third-party logistics operators. This allows the many new e-commerce sites to get instant access to the global marketplace without having to tie up capital in fixed assets.

Reconfiguration of European logistics systems. Some companies are using third-party logistics as a transition from a decentralized to a centralized distribution system in Europe. Until recently, many international companies in Europe had a decentralized structure, with sales subsidiaries in every EU country. Many of these companies have moved from a logistics system with one warehouse in each country to one or two European distribution centers. Examples include Atlas Copco Industrial Techniques, Nike, Philips Electronics, Mattel, Reebok and Xerox. Expansion of logistics services to a pan-European scale has been a strong enabling factor.

Developing a third-party logistics partnership

Outsourcing decisions are both difficult and stressful. Preparing for an outsourcing decision must be thorough. Evaluating and selecting an appropriate third-party logistics partner requires management resources, establishing trust relationships and common information systems and joint standard operating procedures. The most critical resource is time. Case studies and interviews in-depth with both third-party logistics providers and clients (Bagchi & Skjøtt-Larsen 1995, Skjøtt-Larsen 2000) have developed a general guideline for the third-party logistics buying process (Table 7.1). Similar conceptual decision models can be found in Bagchi & Virum (1998a), Sink & Langley (1997) and Magill (2000). The stages include:

* establishing objectives and selection criteria
* evaluating and selecting a third-party logistics provider
* making a contract between the partners
* implementing the partnership
* making continuous improvements
* renegotiating.

Although these stages are sequential, they can also overlap in time. Outsourcing decisions are not simple linear processes but are active search-and-learning, iterative processes, returning to previous stages as necessary.

Outsourcing logistics activities has a number of strategic and organizational consequences that have to be balanced between costs and service benefits. Prior analysis of the current logistics system is therefore an essential part of the process.

Many companies do not recognize their own actual logistics

Table 7.1. Stages of development for a third-party logistics relationship

Stage	Activities
Objectives and selection criteria	• Setting objectives for service levels • Measuring actual logistics costs and service performance • Identifying and ranking selection criteria
Evaluation and selection	• Screening of the third-party logistics market (request for information) • References and records • Prequalification (request for quotation) • Hard and soft evaluation criteria • Mutual site visits • Selection of third-party logistics partner
Contract	• Main contract • Operating manuals
Implementation	• Establishing interorganizational teams • Performance measurement and control • Interfaces between information systems • Exchange of personnel • Training
Continuous improvements	• Mutual problem-solving • Creating a win-win situation • Incentive schemes for improvements • Continuous education and training • Developing of personal networks and trust • Frequent meetings
Renegotiating	• Evaluation of the process • Changes in the environment • Extensions or reductions • New tender or renewal of contract

costs. Indirect costs such as capital costs tied up in warehouses and inventory are not usually identified separately in accounting systems. Transport costs can be hidden in the purchase price, when the goods are delivered with free shipment or cost, insurance and freight terms. Comparing costs between third-party logistics solutions and current logistics costs is often difficult. The comparison is further complicated when the outsourcing decision occurs simultaneously with redesign of the supply chain processes.

In these preparations, the company must establish operational service performance criteria for monitoring and evaluation while setting realistic service objectives. It is not unusual for companies to require substantially higher service performance from the third-party logistics provider than from their own operations. Tasks must be specified precisely to match service requirements, competencies required and market coverage.

Evaluation and selection of third-party logistics providers must match the specific requirements of the outsourcing decision. Outsourcing warehousing and related operational activities becomes a relatively simple decision among many possible alternatives. When decisions involve less tangible requirements such as competencies in management skills, advanced information systems and fast, reliable global networks, the number of potential operators diminishes. There might be few alternatives in a global market.

Typically, the shipper will select only the most promising candidates. Evaluation of bidders can be complex, although it may be aided by quantitative tools, such as analytic hierarchy processing to establish weighting of selection criteria (Bagchi 1989). This would be followed by qualitative evaluation with site visits.

The contract will typically have two parts. The first part includes the scope of the assignment, price agreements, service levels, length of the contract and penalty clauses for failure to meet agreed performance measures. The contract can be specific to safeguard against opportunism. This part is often a statement of intent about the scope of collaboration. The second part is a working manual for the contract, typically including detailed description of activities, performance evaluation, coordination and reporting requirements.

Implementation typically takes up to 1 year because of the difficulties in merging two organizations. Transmitting and sharing information both in hard data and more subjective content is the focal point. Information systems must be integrated, including computer systems, software and data coding. In a few cases such as inventory management, the client may rely on the system of the third-party logistics provider, although clients usually prefer to maintain their own. Data links such as electronic data interchange or Web-based systems must be established to allow fast, accurate data transmission about orders, invoices and other documents, as well as inventory status and shipment tracking.

An important part of a third-party logistics arrangement is transferring qualitative information on products and customers.

This type of knowledge is often tacit and informal but must be formalized for the relationship to operate. It includes setting up joint teams across the participating organizations and a key manager appointed by the third-party logistics provider to be responsible for client relationships. However, there should also be multiple levels of contacts with direct communication across organizational boundaries. One useful approach for information transfer is to introduce boundary-spanning personnel. Key client personnel can be assigned to the third-party logistics provider, or the provider can place personnel at the client's premises.

Continuous improvement is an important part of the process. Costs and service requirements during the contract period should become targets for improvement. Incentives should be built into the contract, providing cost-based savings shared among both parties.

Renegotiating typically starts after 2 to 3 years, although the period of the contract might be longer with dedicated investment in distribution centers or vehicles. The current provider normally holds a competitive advantage for renewal based on knowledge of the client's operations. Clients do not change providers unless there are significant differences in projected performance or dissatisfaction with present arrangements. Initializing and implementation costs become high switching costs for the client.

Obstacles in logistics outsourcing

Turning over an internal logistics function to an external third-party provider involves risk. First is the potential risk of loss of control over the flow of products and materials. This risk can be reduced through information systems linked to the third-party operator with a capability to track products at any time and location on their way to the customer.

A second risk is that of the third-party provider going out of business or being taken over by another company with inferior services or geographic coverage. Such disruptive events threaten the entire distribution process between the company and its customers and severely harm the customer service image of the client company. It therefore becomes essential to evaluate financial strength and stability along with the competence of prospective partners before the contract is signed.

Lack of hard cost data on their existing logistics systems may also prevent companies from evaluating logistics activities for outsourcing. Few companies have adequate accounting systems with realistic knowledge of costs within their own logistics operations. The administrative costs of managing and controlling goods flows are often hidden in overhead costs. Return on capital invested in warehouse buildings and transport equipment is seldom included.

Conflicting objectives among different internal organizational units within the shipping organization create resistance to outsourcing. A logistics department may object to a potential threat to its own activities and even its survival. The sales department may fear deterioration of customer service. The finance department may primarily support outsourcing as a tool to release capital in fixed assets.

Finally, interorganizational cooperation itself presents inherent difficulties in the compatibility of corporate cultures, data systems and the level of employee knowledge and skills. In addition, there may be problems with management coordination. Finally, there is an underlying problem of linking two organizations with differing goals. The result may be service failures, especially in the initial phases of organizational learning.

The future of European transport and logistics

The transport industry in Europe, and in the world at large, will undergo dramatic structural changes in the coming years. Many small and medium-sized transport companies will disappear or be acquired by larger companies. Transport companies as a group are moving away from pure transportation services. Logistics service providers assume a prominent place in serving the requirements of global clients. To do this they are growing through mergers, acquisitions and strategic alliances and, to a much lesser degree, through internal growth.

Five types of logistics service providers are likely to emerge in the future:

- lead logistics providers
- fourth-party logistics providers
- pan-European logistics providers
- niche logistics service providers
- e-commerce logistics providers.

Lead logistics providers

A lead logistics provider is an intermediary between a shipper and a number of more specialized logistics service companies or asset-based third-party logistics providers such as carriers, warehousing companies, express companies and regional logistics service providers. Lead logistics providers are not bound by fixed assets but operate independently of geographic scope and functional activities. They design and manage logistics solutions for their clients, subcontracting the execution to specialized carriers and distribution center operators. The advantage for the client company is that it can concentrate on its core business and has one single point of contact with the lead provider as one-stop shopping. The benefits for the lead logistics provider are primarily a broader access to the customer's portfolio of logistics activities, higher customer loyalty and a potentially long-term relationship to the customer. They are also flexible as the lead provider in dealing with customer requirements, calling in subcontractors as needed.

Global companies, largely based in the United States for now, such as Case Corporation, Disney, Ford, Eastman Kodak, Nike, Sun Microsystems, Western Digital and Xerox are using or planning to use lead logistics providers for their pan-European or global logistics. Lead logistics providers include Emery Worldwide's Global Logistics, Exel Logistics GeoLogistics, Menlo Logistics, MSAS Global Logistics (part of Ocean Group), Maersk Logistics and Ryder Integrated Logistics. Logistics service companies based in the United States are entering the European scene on the back of customers they already have in the United States. Menlo Logistics was asked to set up a new European distribution center for Nike Equipment in the Netherlands. Schneider Logistics recently started operations in Europe at the request of its United States-based client, Case Corporation. Schneider Logistics provides logistics management services for Case's eight European manufacturing plants. Other examples are Emery Worldwide, serving Disney products, and GeoLogistics for Western Digital (Magill 2000).

Fourth-party logistics providers

Another new form of strategic partnership between shipper and logistics service provider is fourth-party logistics. According to Magill (2000, p. 146):

> »This form of partnership focuses on management and optimization of the supply chain, extending beyond operational activities to include tactical and strategic activities. It also extends the geographical scope of the partnership to pan-European or global coverage«.

Bade & Mueller (1999) have defined fourth-party logistics as

> »a supply chain integrator who assembles and manages the resources, capabilities, and technologies of its organization with those of complementary service providers to deliver a comprehensive supply chain solution«.

Fourth-party logistics combines the capabilities of management consulting, information technology and logistics services. Gattorna (1998) points out that fourth-party logistics differs from third-party logistics in several respects:

- The fourth-party logistics organization is often a joint venture between a primary client and one or more partners.
- The fourth-party logistics organization acts as a single interface between the client and multiple logistics service providers.
- All or a major part of the client's supply chain are outsourced to the fourth-party logistics organization.

The strategic alliance between Ryder Integrated Logistics, Accenture and IBM Global Services is in effect fourth-party logistics. According to Ryder's Web site (www.ryder.com), »The collective expertise of Ryder, Accenture and IBM will enrich the integrated logistics solutions Ryder already gives. Together, we expect our complementary skills and capabilities will serve our current and future logistics customers with the best solutions available.«

New Holland Logistics is a joint venture between Accenture and New Holland (Foster 1999c). This company offers spare-parts management operation in six countries. Accenture contributes management support and information technology. New Holland contributes depots in six countries, 775 employees, capital investment and operations management responsibilities. The spare-parts management operations include planning, purchasing, inventory, distribution, transportation and customer support.

Exel Logistics Tradeteam, a joint venture between NFC and Bass Breweries, can also be considered as a fourth-party logistics arrangement, although the collaboration is limited to the downstream supply chain.

Pan-European logistics providers

The pan-European logistics provider provides cross-border logistics services on a Europe-wide basis. The provider normally offers a broad range of services, including groupage (shipment consolidation), warehousing, forwarding and value-added services. To control the flow of goods from door to door, providers must build networks of transshipment terminals covering the most important regions of Europe, along with communication systems to link terminals, network sales offices and customers.

International clients increasingly ask for pan-European, single-carrier solutions. However, only a few transport and logistics companies have complete pan-European coverage alone; they must establish strategic alliances or subcontract with other transport companies to complete their coverage. During the last few years, a wave of acquisitions and mergers has altered the competitive situation of the third-party logistics market towards more pan-European competitors. The merger between Schenker and BTL, Deutsche Post's acquisitions of Nedlloyd (ETD), Danzas, ASG, AEI and a major stake in DHL and the Danish DSV Samson's recent purchase of its closest national competitor DFDS DanTransport typify the merger process.

Niche carriers

Some carriers have specialized their operations to specific regions (such as eastern Europe), specific classes of goods (such as frozen foods, computers, furniture, garments or hazardous goods) or specific services (such as express, courier or parcels). These specialists often work in niche areas requiring unique competencies, technologies and equipment. Competition would not be expected to be as intense as in the subcontractor basic carrier market. On the other hand, specialists become more dependent on individual customers or markets, because competence and equipment are not easily transferable to other areas.

JIT-oriented manufacturers and companies that have centralized their European distribution systems to one or a few strategically located sites provide other niches for specialized carrier operations. A carrier offering customized, pan-European logistics solutions, including unique value-added services tailored to individual customers, can establish a niche that will provide it with long-term relationships with shippers. A specialist carrier may often be able to provide services that larger carriers are unable to perform because of the scale of their operations.

Examples of niche logistics providers in Europe are Tibbett & Britten, which has developed particular capabilities and experience in the fast-moving consumer goods industry, and MSAS Global Logistics (formerly Intexo), with special experience in logistics and value-added services for the high-tech and health care industries.

E-commerce logistics providers

The boom in the Internet trade in both business-to-business (B2B) and business-to-consumer (B2C) has created an increasing demand for fast, reliable logistics service of small shipments to global customers. Global express companies such as UPS Worldwide Logistics and FedEx dominate this new business, because they have the infrastructure needed in terms of physical network and information and communication systems. By industry estimates, UPS controls about 80% of the United States business-to-home parcel delivery market and more than 50% of all Internet deliveries in the United States (Forsyth 2000a). In addition, specialists in e-commerce distribution have emerged to serve particular niches defined by product offerings or time. They include grocery delivery services such as Webvan that substitute for bricks-and-mortar stores and immediate delivery services that offer same-day delivery in certain metropolitan areas. Home delivery encounters conflicts with consumer preferences and work schedules, resulting in experimentation in new methods and institutions to hold packages for customer pick-up (Blackman 1999; *The Economist* 2000).

Internet retailers are beginning to realize that logistics capabilities are necessary to attract and keep customers. It is both costly and risky to build up logistics infrastructure. Therefore, many Internet retailers outsource warehouse management and distribution to third-party logistics providers. Other logistics activities such as order fulfillment, inventory replenishment and returns management are often also outsourced to third-party logistics providers.

One of the unexpected consequences of e-commerce is to make brick-and-mortar distribution centers more important, as efficient, specialized operations become key to order fulfillment.

New third-party logistics providers specialized in serving Internet retailers are emerging. For example, 2000 Logistics is a spin-off from the United States-based Internet retailer WorldSpy.com providing credit card processing; picking, packing and shipping; customer service; call center; reverse logistics; and packaging services.

Traditional third-party logistics providers have established business units specifically dedicated for Internet customers. United States-based Airborne set up a new delivery service in 1999 called Airborne@Home with the US Postal Service for home deliveries. The USPS has also formed partnerships with other private carriers, including FedEx, DHL, CTC Distribution Direct, Paxis and Parcel/Direct, to increase volume density in residential distribution. USFreightways Logistics has established USF eLogistics to focus on Internet deliveries, and GATX Logistics is building national warehousing and distribution networks to handle e-tailing business. In Denmark, a joint venture between PostDanmark and the third-party logistics provider DFDS DanTransport established WebLogistics for home delivery. The key issue in home delivery is to generate enough package volume to obtain economies of scale within the distribution system. Therefore, national post offices and parcel consolidators have a competitive advantage in the home delivery market.

Tiering structure of the logistics market

A tier system, similar to the supplier network in the automotive industry, is emerging in the transport industry. Fourth-party logistics or lead logistics providers operate as the first tier for multinational clients, offering one-stop shopping for global logistics solutions. The first tier makes subcontracts with a second tier of asset-based logistics providers, information service providers and regional carriers to perform operational logistics activities in specific regions or business areas. The second tier might further collaborate with small and medium-sized operators in local and niche markets. A future structure is envisioned in Figure 7.4.

Figure 7.4. Organization of Logistics Services

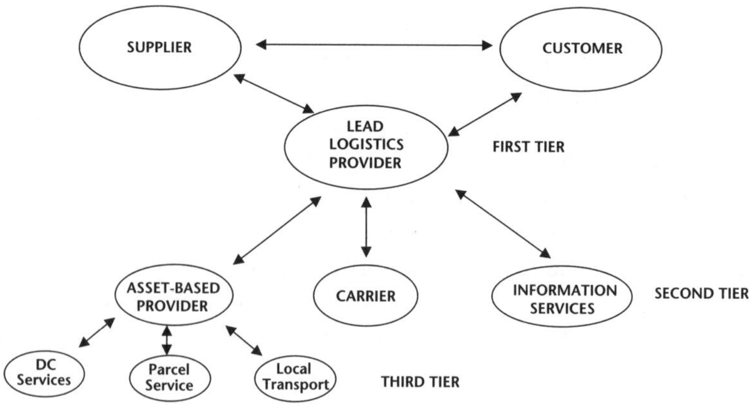

DC: distribution center

Conclusion

The market for transport and logistics services has changed dramatically during the last 5 years. There has been a trend towards broadening the scope of transport and logistics services with wider geographic coverage. There has also been a shift from asset-based to skill- and knowledge-based logistics providers. A wave of mergers and acquisitions has swept through the industry, led by former national postal companies and United States-based logistics companies. Demand has been increasing for pan-European logistics solutions, although a single model cannot be applied to operations in different countries. The logistics industry at large and in Europe in particular is still a collection of diverse markets with differing customer requirements and distribution structures.

Illustrative cases

Grundfos and Maersk Logistics[12]

This case illustrates a partnership between a global logistics provider (Maersk Logistics) and an international industrial firm (Grundfos), both partners with a home base in Denmark. The third-party logistics provider has developed its service base from primarily asset-based logistics services towards more services related to supply chain management. These services cut across the whole supply chain on multiple levels within each stage of the chain. This demonstrates a widened scope of the transport industry in which third-party logistics providers now operate. Further, it illustrates an relationship between companies in which the joint efforts of the parties have been directed not only towards reducing short-term costs but also towards long-term service improvements for the shipper.

---

12. Based on interviews with Corporate Transport Director Karstein Rossavik, Grundfos, and Senior Consultant Anker Noerlund, Maersk Logistics. The interviews were performed by Arni Halldorsson, M.Sc., Copenhagen Business School.

Grundfos Group

The Grundfos Group is one of the world's leading pump manufacturers. The annual net turnover in 1999 was USD 1.1 billion and the number of employees close to 10,000. The company produces about 8 million pumps annually, mostly for export. Grundfos has sales subsidiaries in nearly 40 countries and local distributors in many other countries. The main products are circulation pumps, dive pumps and centrifugal pumps, which are used both by industry and in the consumer market.

The mission of the company is to »successfully develop, produce and sell high-quality pumps and pumping systems world-wide, contributing to a better quality of life and a healthy environment«.

Grundfos has defined five core competencies that support its mission statement:

- integrated product development
- global marketing
- logistics
- quality assurance
- employees/organization.

In 1993 a corporate logistics function was established in Grundfos with the purpose of developing and implementing logistics strategies at the corporate level. An important objective of the corporate logistics function was to establish a bridge between the corporate logistics objectives and the operational level around the world to ensure that the local decisions are performed according to overall strategies.

The logistical vision is that »Grundfos Logistics must contribute to making the customers world-wide assess Grundfos as the best partner to support them in developing their businesses«. The mission of the Group Logistics function is to support the local sales organizations, to get in direct contact with key customers and suppliers and to optimize the total supply chain from supplier to end user.

Grundfos operates production and sales on a global basis. The production is located in various regions, with production plants in Singapore, Taiwan, China, the United States, Denmark, Finland, Switzerland, Italy, France, Hungary, Germany and England in order to be close to the largest markets. The production in Europe is focused, meaning that one group of pumps is primarily produced at one plant and another group of pumps at another plant.

Until the mid-1990s, Grundfos followed the traditional pattern in the European distribution system, in which each national sales subsidiary was responsible for warehousing, inventory control and distribution to its customers. Since then, the distribution system has gradually been centralized to the current four regional distribution centers in Europe, located in England, France, Germany and Denmark. Further, Grundfos has a distribution center in Singapore and two distribution centers in the United States.

Grundfos used to negotiate freight agreements with a large number of carriers covering different parts of the world. Since 1998, for the biggest company in the Grundfos group – the Danish company – they have concentrated the majority of their transport needs on two international carriers, Wilson and Schenker-BTL, and signed a 2-year contract. Wilson takes care of all transport to United States and East Asia, and Schenker-BTL operates in the European market. At the same time, Grundfos has established partnership collaboration with the two carriers to develop customized services.

The philosophy behind this policy is that »the partners should find the services and products that are relevant for us in the various geographical areas«. The two lead logistics providers have made agreements with their subcontractors and control the quality of the services provided by them.

Maersk Logistics

Maersk Logistics is a subsidiary of the A.P. Moller Group, owner of Maersk-Sealand, and the largest container ship operator in the world. Maersk Logistics (formerly Mercantile International) is a third-party logistics provider and has 160 offices in about 55 countries. The strategic objective of Maersk Logistics is to be »the world's most innovative, global integrated logistics provider, delivering business solutions to our customers«.

On the customer market, Maersk Logistics has defined four »target segments«:

- sports and leisure ware
- shoes and apparel
- home improvement stores
- hypermarkets, departments stores and mail order.

In these segments, time to market is a critical competitive parameter. Besides, these customers source many of their products from East Asia, where Maersk has a strong market position.

In general, Maersk Logistics makes use of best practice within supply chain management, which is considered as the core area of the firm. The services include sales administration, supplier negotiations, analyses and business development, freight consolidation, forwarding, project management, warehousing and documentation.

The role of information technology in Maersk Logistics is not only communication but also to analyze and monitor the supply chain from order to delivery. The company has over 10 years of experience with electronic data interchange, sending detailed information directly to the clients' own information systems. This includes information from Maersk Logistics' own operations, vendor bookings, shipping instructions and arrival notices. This offers an opportunity to exploit bar coding already in place at the factory level to provide immediate inventory status with high accuracy. Maersk Logistics' Communication System provides global communication and close coordination between Maersk Logistics' offices and clients.

Partnership between Grundfos and Maersk Logistics

After a Corporate Logistics function was established in 1993, a need for global logistics solutions arose in Grundfos. The company defined global objectives aiming at reducing inventories at the subsidiary level, increasing reliability and compressing delivery times and reducing logistics costs. Further, Corporate Logistics wanted to have transparency in the whole supply chain. They felt that when a shipment was sent from the production plant in Denmark it »disappeared into a black hole« until it was received by the customer. The problem was enhanced by the fact that many actors were involved in the logistics chain, including the shipper, haulage companies, feeder transport, ocean transport, customs clearance, transit transport, local sales subsidiaries and customers.

Grundfos established a partnership agreement with Maersk Logistics. The two partners started a program to measure lead-time performance on each activity in the logistics chain between Grundfos' plant to the customer to eliminate waste time. The two most important elements were a standard operating procedure and the implementation of Maersk Logistics' information management system, called LOG*IT. The standard operating procedure describing specific procedures and a timetable for implementation was documented and signed by both parties. It also defines the tasks and the division of responsibility and serves as motivation for all actors in the supply chain.

Two transport corridors were selected as pilot projects where the partners assumed there was considerable potential for optimizing the operations:

• Denmark to Australia (long lead time and large inventories)
• Denmark to Singapore (distribution center for East Asia).

After the two pilot projects, similar studies were made for other destinations, such as Taiwan, Fresno and Dubai. The following description is based on the pilot study of the Denmark-to-Australia corridor.

Lead-time analysis of the Denmark-to-Australia corridor
The total lead time from Grundfos' plant in Denmark to the customers in Australia was measured at 119 days. The long lead time caused service problems to the customers and required large inventories at the sales subsidiary in Adelaide, Australia. After a preliminary analysis, a target of reducing the lead time from 119 to 64 days was formulated in cooperation with the sales subsidiary in Australia.

The lead time measurements were concentrated on time and place. Maersk Logistics started by measuring in detail how all activities and processes were actually performed. The various actors were asked to report delivery time for their part of the logistics link to Maersk Logistics' database. An essential part of the process was to define a lead time from a total perspective, recognizing the difference between lead time and transit time. The starting-point was a merchandised due date – a fixed point in time when the shipment was to be at a certain place. After the lead-time analysis, Maersk Logistics made a plan for how the flow of materials and information was to be monitored from the production plant to the final destination.

Maersk Logistics' role differed between corridors. In the Australia corridor, they were not involved in the physical handling of the goods. They served as a facilitator, information manager, consultant and controller. They were involved in selecting subcontractors and ensured that subcontractors were capable of communicating information about departure time, arrival time and delays. Maersk Logistics also sent monthly reports to Grundfos, measuring volume in container equivalent units.

After the pilot study, the following actions were taken:

- orders from the sales subsidiary in Australia changed from monthly to weekly;
- orders transmitted via electronic data interchange;
- production planning synchronized with the departure of a container ship from Aarhus, Denmark;
- delivery frequency changed from every 2 weeks to every week to Australia; and
- the time for fumigating protective packaging materials reduced from 1-2 weeks to a few days.

The result achieved in the Australia corridor was a reduction of lead time from 119 days in 1995 to 51 days in 1996, which exceeded the original target of 64 days. In addition, inventory was reduced by 1 month, which saved AUD 3 million. Also, the service level was improved because of shorter and more reliable delivery time. Figure 7.5 shows the components of the total lead time before and after the project.

Seen from a competence perspective, the partnership has been beneficial for both parties. Grundfos was the first export customer to use Maersk Logistics' information technology systems and the first supply chain management customer in Denmark. Maersk Logistics therefore went through a valuable learning process during the project, an experience they can use in future projects. Maersk Logistics not only appeared as a third-party logistics provider but as

Figure 7.5. Total Lead-time Analysis

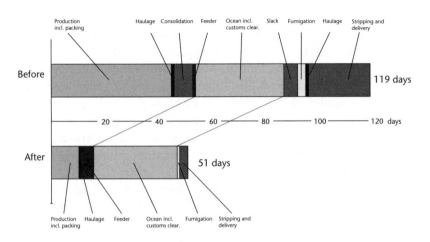

a supplier of systems, experience and knowledge on supply chain management. Grundfos primarily sought to bridge the gap between the current and the desired logistics competencies by developing internal competencies. To proceed with this development, they established a partnership with Maersk Logistics. Through the partnership with Maersk Logistics, Grundfos acquired and built up competence in collecting information from their sales subsidiaries, their SAP platform, their suppliers and their transport partners. Grundfos is now able to conduct measurements on other corridors. As the corporate logistics manager states: »Maersk Logistics helped us to initiate the process, and we learned that our logistics providers should be able to find the services and products that are relevant for us in the various geographical locations.«

Contrary to traditional third-party logistics arrangements, this partnership was not asset-based but skill-based. The starting-point was Maersk Logistics' possession of knowledge and information technology systems, including logistics competencies that complemented those of Grundfos. The partnership aimed at creating the skill of operating on a supply chain level and gaining insight into each component of this chain. Also, Maersk Logistics contributed to the change process and the operation of the selected corridors by several in-house adjustments and initiatives during the 4-year partnership.

Tradeteam – an industry platform for logistics services[13]

Tradeteam was established in 1995 as a joint venture between NFC and Bass Breweries to operate a completely new distribution solution in the United Kingdom brewing and beverage industry. Exel Logistics – a subsidiary of NFC specializing in third-party logistics solutions – managed Tradeteam. Tradeteam provides independent distribution and logistics services to the beverage industry on a national basis, currently supplying over one-third of all on-trade outlets and also delivering to the United Kingdom grocery/retail market in the off-trade.

Until Tradeteam was formed, Bass Brewers was typical of the industry in using its own dedicated delivery infrastructure based on unique systems, delivering only Bass-brewed or -sold product direct to outlets and using dedicated stand-alone regionally based operations. These operations were becoming increasingly inefficient. Bass Brewers realized that it had to reconsider its distribution network not only by integrating it further in the supply chain but also by aligning the logistics process with the best cost levels in the industry.

Tradeteam was formed as a joint venture to accommodate the needs of the rapidly changing beverage marketplace in the United Kingdom. Increasingly, as the ownership of pubs was detached from the brewers, the pub groups that emerged began to act as true retailers. Both beverage manufacturers and retailers found that traditional, dedicated in-house distribution facilities were no longer appropriate to meet trends in market conditions. Additionally, the brewers became less possessive about the ownership and branding of the logistics infrastructure.

The objective for Tradeteam was to access opportunities by capitalizing on Bass's existing network, critical mass and expertise in the brewing industry, while combining this with Exel Logistics' ability to develop practical and innovative solutions, building on its existing supply chain management expertise and its international experience.

The improvement in the logistics network consisted of a change program that focused on the configuration of depots, the staff and

13. Adapted from Magill (2000).

the logistics process. The configuration and structure of depots were upgraded, with several sites closed and two (soon to be three) new purpose-built facilities established in the Midlands and London, which allowed a more efficient logistics operation and significantly reduced stockholding. A new information system was implemented, which consisted of Tradeteam's own order capture and processing system, an independent teleselling and customer service system and the appropriate Exel Logistics systems software, which was linked to a Manugistics software planning system.

The long-term success of Tradeteam depends on the potential of the operation to develop into a distribution network, with other willing brewers and pub retailers participating. Tradeteam was planned as a shared-user network to handle products from more than one brewery or manufacturer and supply a large number of retailers without a conflict of interest. Bass Brewers is now simply the joint financial provider to develop the concept, while Exel Logistics is the managing and operating partner, providing impartiality and confidentiality.

In 1998 Tradeteam signed a 3-year contract with Devonshire Pub Company to provide single weekly centralized distribution service for products from several suppliers, including Bass, Whitbread, Matthew Brown and Carlsberg Tetley, to the Devonshire Pub Company pubs, located across northern England. In 1999 Tradeteam won a 5-year contract to provide centralized distribution service to all Avebury Taverns, with more than 700 pubs. Tradeteam provides a full range of supply chain services to Avebury, including telemarketing, customer service and inventory management and delivering multi-sourced products in consolidated consignments from any of its depots throughout England and Wales. Tradeteam additionally provides logistics services to other customers, including leading brand owner Bulmers and regional brewers Caledonian and Jenning.

Tradeteam is a unique partnership in scope and complexity that exceeds the traditional third-party logistics partnership. Whether it could be called fourth-party logistics is an open question. The delimitation is that it is only focused on the outbound logistics – not the whole supply chain. From a practical perspective, Tradeteam is a fourth-party logistics partnership in essence and clearly an innovative example of a partnership that not only releases benefits across more than one dimension but also creates value not available from each party individually.

Case Corp.'s partnership with three third-party logistics providers[14]

Many multinational companies are using lead logistics providers to coordinate their global logistics activities. The United States-based manufacturer of agricultural and construction equipment, Case Corp., took another direction when it decided to outsource its domestic and international supply chains. The company chose three different third-party logistics providers: Fritz Companies, Schneider Logistics and GATX Logistics, and ordered them to coordinate their activities but to report directly to Case. Before the outsourcing decision, Case had to manage a flow of about 800,000 shipments a year through 16 warehouses and 750 transportation companies all over the world.

The three providers negotiated 5-year contracts. The compensation structure was designed to gradually change over time, starting with fixed management and transaction fees and ending with fees tied to performance incentives. The total logistics process was divided between the three providers. Fritz would perform international freight forwarding and assist with deliveries and consolidation to GATX's warehouses. GATX Logistics did domestic warehousing, including cross-docking and sequencing of parts to the assembly line of Case's plants. Schneider was responsible for trucking in Europe and materials management in the United States. Each had representatives permanently on site at Case facilities to take care of day-to-day problems. The three companies use the Internet to share information electronically.

The arrangement is unusual because Case insisted on keeping control in-house and did not let a lead logistics service provider take responsibility for coordination. The reason was that no single provider seems to possess the breath of services, either functionally or geographically, to meet the needs of a major global client like Case.

---

14. Adapted from MacKenzie (1999).

MANAGEMENT

8. Managing the supply chain

*»In this volatile environment, where instability is the norm,
we're convinced that the last remaining source of truly
sustainable competitive advantage lies in what we've come to
describe as 'organizational capabilities' – the unique ways in
which each organization structures its work and motivates its
people to achieve clearly articulated objectives.«*
(Nadler & Tushman 1998, p. 5)

The supply chain challenges management (Figure 8.1). First, it is
both interfunctional and interorganizational. Second, it is a complex system contending with multiple environments. Third, the
concept itself limits the scope of direct authority relationships.
Fourth, the potential span of management is vast, even to the »dirt
to dirt« description of Cooper et al. (1997). Beyond this, the chain
must be managed to respond rapidly to change in the market and
individual customer requests. In addition, competition and financial concerns press to reduce operating costs and investment in assets. With these varied and conflicting interests, the reality and role
of supply chain management varies with the eye of the beholder.

This chapter is divided into two parts. The first deals with organization and the second with management tools. In the first section, we begin by recognizing the changes in general management.
This sets the stage for the specific problems of supply chain management. We then look at organizational arrangements that offer
partial solutions, but we must recognize that there are no clear answers. In the second section, we examine activity-based management and its counterpart, activity-based costing. This will be followed by discussion of the Balanced Scorecard, benchmarking and
the SCOR model developed by the Supply Chain Council (1997,
no date a, b).

Figure 8.1. Management

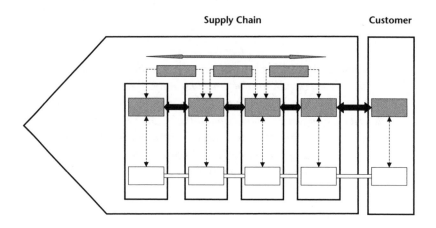

Environments

Supply chain management operates in two prominent and volatile environments: globalization and information technology. The dynamics of the global economy determine the nature of competition, location of production, relative costs and the size of markets. The influence of information technology is even more pervasive, ensuring global communication, automating processes, changing the nature of business and creating new industries as it vanquishes the old. The combination of computers and telecommunications changes the nature of work and connects the world. They enable the supply chain, encouraging close coordination of operations, signaling requirements and commands, transmitting authorizing documents and managing routine processes, in some cases without human intervention. The rapid pace of change makes all management solutions temporary and emphasizes flexibility, rapid response and organizational learning.

The management climate

Changes in general management practice have directly influenced the supply chain. We are in transition from physical to knowledge-intensive products. The nature of work itself emphasizes knowledge. Management faces increasing complexity in both products and processes. New forms of organization and a new orientation must deal with an environment that not only breaks with the past but is itself undergoing change at an accelerating pace.

The contrast is clear in comparing traditional management practice to the new forms that respond to these changes. Traditional management is hierarchical. Top managers make decisions and pass them down a chain of command to operations. The problem is that too many decisions involve specific knowledge beyond the scope of individual managers, with too little time and information for traditional decision processes. In the left-hand side of Figure 8.2, traditional management makes decisions, hopefully with adequate information, sends them through successive management tiers to the level where operations take place. Activity centers do not communicate with each other except to transfer work. Work flows through the organization, but only as a series of separate and disconnected tasks. This is probably one source of the perception of the »functional silo«. Organizations could operate in relative iso-

Figure 8.2. Management Comparison

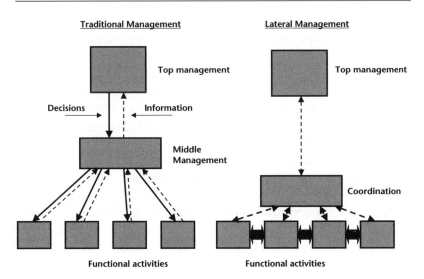

lation, relying on formal documentation processes between operations, levels or from one organizational hierarchy to another. Decisions required successive reviews with slow and unresponsive signals. In the current environment of speed and process, this has proved to be unworkable.

Another concept of decisions made at the point where the work takes place is replacing this traditional concept of management. As products flow through the company, they are handed directly to the next stage: problems are resolved where they occur by the people whose work is directly affected by the decision. Operating units make their own decisions, connecting and negotiating with each other with full authority – across functional activity centers. This is lateral management.

The change places the role of the manager on less certain ground. Operations become part of processes, focused on customers and the delivery of end products, rather than on individual functions. Interfunctional communication and coordination increases as the product flows through the organization. Functional centers do not disappear, but they have a different purpose: to serve as reservoirs of specialized knowledge, supplying knowledgeable people, skills and tangible resources for process-oriented organizations (Drucker 1989).

The combination of competitive pressures and the potential advantages from new technologies have introduced radical change. Telecommunications and information technology (IT) create environments in which managers and workers communicate easily and precisely across distance and time, encouraging collaboration and coordination without regard to organizational position, physical location or time. Information and decisions can move directly through organizations quickly without unnecessary barriers.

The first effect of IT was to eliminate clerical routine; the second automated formerly routine human decisions, with predetermined decision rules. The third gave the organization more flexibility to respond to new demands and constraints. The fourth provides managers with a comprehensive image of the organization through information-based metrics and models for strategic vision and control. IT has encouraged and made feasible a management climate that has literally enabled the supply chain.

Management in the supply chain

The supply chain extends the revolution, outsourcing activities to other organizations. Individual firms reduce their focus to core activities, relying on outside organizations for other operations. By itself, this change alone would create complex situations, beginning with needs for interorganizational communication, coordination and management. The market adds additional pressures for faster and flexible response. At the same time, customers demand variety, customized solutions and the ability to match small market segments, even to product markets for individual customers. These new conditions force organizational change, integration and above all new roles for management.

Supply chain management is unique. Visualize a series of operations connected in a sequence, some contained within the lead firm, others performed by outside parties. The sequence itself is subject to change. The member organizations have a common stake in the success of the system, but they are also independent entities, some captive in serving only a single firm, but other firms with more autonomy dealing with other customers and suppliers. Within the structure of the supply chain, each firm faces its own unique environment: technology, competition, customer base, internal organization and culture. Members of a supply chain are also part of a system that competes with other systems, in the arena defined by the final market and the context of the system as a whole. In addition, individual members within the system may not have stable and enduring positions but depend for their tenure on the characteristics of their own industries and markets.

Comparison with general management

The new role of management in the supply chain management presents a unique challenge. General management addresses problems of structure, leadership, decision-making, human resources and control. Supply chain management also deals with these areas, but it differs because of the scope and nature of the supply chain. Supply chain structure focuses on activities and process more than organizational ownership. It emphasizes establishing and managing connections. Changing direction may require changing organizational partners. Direction comes from leadership, relying on vision and motivation rather than authority.

The supply chain requires trust between organizations, which permeates down to operations and reward through profit-sharing by organizations. Control is possible normally only at the interfaces between organizations where relationships are established. Normally, there may be little involvement with the internal responsibilities of partner organizations, although there have certainly been exceptions. Human resource issues in particular are managed through partners. In brief, supply chain management may design the system, select partners and monitor performance; it can only operate through other organizations.

The other distinction is orientation. Organizations acting independently build slack, buffers of extra resources of inventory or processing time into the system to protect their own operations. The supply chain manager must look at the overall system as an integral unit. Global objectives are achieved through coordination and use of trade-offs to shift activities within a systemic framework. Buffers are costly targets for reduction. The inherent conflict in system objectives of efficiency and response can only be managed through persuasion and contract.

Management in the supply chain

Supply chain management establishes strategic direction, designs the activity and organizational structures and processes to integrate operations, selects and negotiates with potential partners and monitors operations. Designing the management structure for the system is one element of strategy. Another is managing integration of operations as joint processes across organizational boundaries. There appear to be four basic alternatives: 1) functional organizations, 2) market-based organizations, 3) centralized power through integration and 4) decentralized relationships, a federated organization. Conjecturally in Figure 8.3, every supply chain management solution becomes a balance between the internal complexity of the task and the power of external influences. This figure borrows a

Figure 8.3. Organizations and Environment

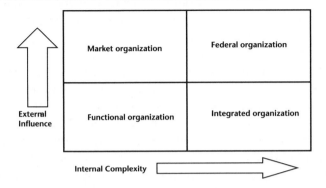

framework from Nohria & Ghoshal (1997), who were describing headquarters-subsidiary relationships in multinational companies (see chapter 11).

The situation of little external influence and simple operations, the functional organization, presents few problems but would also appear to be a rare combination – a simple, completely self-contained entity. This type can only exist as small-scale units under relatively isolated conditions.

The market-based organization links independent firms only by their contractual terms. Internal complexity is low, but the external influences are strong, reinforcing freedom of action through arm's-length transactions for contracting participants. Every organization is a separate entity, making its own decisions. To preserve this autonomy, each organization must hold redundant resources such as inventory and excess capacity, leading to inefficient operations across the supply chain. Changing direction within the supply chain is also inefficient because it means negotiating new contracts and possibly changing partners.

The fully integrated supply chain deals with a high level of internal complexity. The ability to achieve integration depends on an absence of external pressures such as competition. The imbalance may be established through management actions to buffer the system. However, integrated control and decisions usually deal with problems of limited scope. Within its domain, and under specific conditions, full integration is possible. There are limits to the extent of control over activities that can be economically included.

The ultimate level of integration emanates from one source. It would tend to be inflexible and vulnerable to major change. It therefore appears to be an unrealistic solution to the supply chain management problem.

The federated organization is probably the most frequently encountered. It describes loosely aligned organizations that are influenced by their environment but must also participate in complex supply chains. This is perhaps the only way to balance high levels of both internal complexity and external influence. Individual supply chain members cooperate in the process, taking their own power from their particular expertise, market position or franchise, but share decisions to make the process work. Central direction comes from motivation and leadership. There are separate points of decision, which increases the management and communication requirements for coordination.

There may be possible combinations such as integrating closely with a few select customers and suppliers, dealing with others on the basis of power-sharing and negotiating with the remainder through formal contracts. The dangers of extreme integration isolating members from competition can be countered by the stimulus of competition. At the same time, the federated relationships can be developed to allow for coordination of operations.

The federated organization is the situation that Hines (1994), a student of supplier relationships in the Japanese car industry, describes. The *keiretsu* relationships of complete dependence by suppliers on major assemblers are weakening and being replaced by relationships based on stronger supplier power, the *kyoryoku kai* or supplier associations. It also appears in discussion of the European car industry. Further, both General Motors and Ford in the United States have separated themselves from their formerly internal parts networks in favor of more open competition.

Organizational solutions

The organizational structure of the supply chain reflects general management needs for information and interaction. Mintzberg & van der Heyden (1999) set the tone by mapping the functioning organization, which is not the same as the organization chart. Hubs

Figure 8.4. Organizational Design

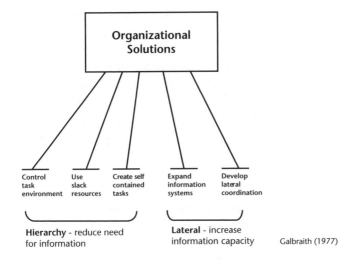

Control task environment	Use slack resources	Create self contained tasks	Expand information systems	Develop lateral coordination

Hierarchy - reduce need for information

Lateral - increase information capacity

Galbraith (1977)

and webs develop as a flexible response to particular problems or tasks. Hubs are informal centers »where people, things and information move« (p. 89), connected by webs of connections.

Galbraith (1977) examined several alternative solutions to the organizational problem that under some circumstances can be applied to the supply chain (Figure 8.4). Solutions can be divided into hierarchical and lateral. Hierarchical solutions reduce the need for information by isolating operations. Lateral solutions are more information-intensive. The hierarchical solutions all go against the precepts of the supply chain. They simplify the organization but increase the cost of supply chain operations and make it less responsive to change. The task environment cannot be controlled when orders come in real time or other elements are changing rapidly. Slack resources, such as inventory and excess capacity, are counter to the objective of minimizing costs. Self-contained tasks are not feasible in the context of product flow.

In contrast, lateral coordination and information systems enhance information capacity. These measures reinforce supply chain strategy by reducing the need for slack resources and the isolation of individual task performance. Lateral coordination supplements routine data generated by the information system. It can take place through either face-to-face contact through teams and liaison positions, or by use of groupware and devices to create shared space for collaboration through the information system. Lateral solutions become the only realistic way to manage the supply chain.

Computer-based lateral management has many possible forms. The potential for meetings independent of location or even time fosters connectivity by people in separate organizations and locations. The computer provides visual display in a variety of ways that extends collaborative perception of the issues under discussion. As Schrage (1995, p. 188) notes, »... successful technology reframes human experience«.

Lateral organizations

Lateral organizations include several different variations: teams, matrix organizations, heterarchy and high-performance work systems. Galbraith (1994, p. 8) defines lateral organizations as »a mechanism for decentralizing management decisions to be resolved across organizational units«. Lateral organizations have been linked to empowerment, in which workers make decisions that affect their own operations. They are associated with operations and are especially relevant to the supply chain. Processes cross organizational boundaries but must still be precisely coordinated. The extent of vision distinguishes the task and level of management.

This can involve both internal decisions and coordination with other units. The concept includes interfunctional, interorganizational and global unit relationships.

The complexity of technology forces more lateral organization to place decisions close to operations. Gupta et al. (1997) found that decentralized (lateral) management was important in making operations of advanced manufacturing technology successful, a point relevant to supply chain operations as well. It increases the speed and capacity for decision-making and places decisions where the experience is most relevant. High-level managers may still focus on long-term strategy, but management and coordination of operations shifts to the locus of action.

Lateral organization can be both formal and informal. Informal groups provide voluntary connections among individuals and have stronger performance than do formal organizations (Joyce et al. 1997). They heighten perception of conflict, provide insights into other organizational perspectives and increase the number of viewpoints. They can be spurred through co-location, such as placing two organizations in the same building, interdepartmental or inter-unit rotation, or provide them with a variety of experience. They can also supplement formal lateral organizations: teams or matrix forms. Authority becomes less one of position and more of competence and access to information.

Disadvantages include potential conflict, time, needs for coordination and for participants: the higher costs of the lack of identification, stress and uncertainty. They place a heavier burden on management for goal orientation and motivation.

Teams

Teams can be formed around problem-solving or process. Some teams may have ongoing responsibility for process management, while others can be formed for temporary assignments and reformed as necessary for other tasks. Management can formally appoint them but they can also arise spontaneously for concerted problem-solving efforts. Within the supply chain, management authorization is prerequisite, because teams involve relationships between organizations. Requirements for successful team performance include specific objectives and the areas and skills matched to the specific task.

Teams can be organized hierarchically; one level can focus on operations, another on relations between companies and higher levels on strategic direction. In effect, they preserve a vertical decision structure while still allowing group participation.

Team interaction can be transformed through technology. Michael Shrage (1995) points to computer-based media such as groupware and visual devices to create electronic space for direct and simultaneous collaboration. This approach lends itself to both structured tasks such as scheduling and planning and less structured tasks such as new product design and process development.

Matrix organizations

Matrix organizations are the most formal structure in lateral management. This is a team with an appointed leader and members assigned from relevant organizational units and functional areas. It can be effective in communicating viewpoints and by placing members in proximity to each other. It may often be the only way to resolve organizational issues, especially when commitment is necessary across functional or organizational boundaries.

Matrix organizations are not efficient in making decisions. They absorb time and induce conflict between functional areas and for individual members. They are subject to continual ambiguity. On one hand, the matrix committee has a task, but the individuals come from areas that must make commitments, resulting in a dual structure of one subordinate but two bosses: a task leader and a functional manager.

They have the advantage of bring conflicting areas together. Nadler & Tushman (1998, p. 99) note:

>»A matrix organization structurally improves coordination by balancing the power between competing aspects of the organization and by installing systems and roles designed to achieve multiple objectives simultaneously.«

Heterarchy
This is in effect a super-matrix proposed by Hedlund (1994) for multinational corporations who have country or regional management in addition to the task and functional management of other matrix organizations. In comparison to matrix organizations, they are multidimensional to deal with several different organizational issues (Figure 8.5). He views them as temporary task forces to be formed for specific projects and then dissolved. Heterarchy suggests a form of organizational solution for the supply chain. The application could deal with the combination of process, function and organization.

High-performance work systems
High-performance work systems can be defined as »loosely coupled self-managed units that are responsible for producing complete products or processes« (Nadler & Tushman 1998, p. 147). This appears to be a set of general rules for team efforts, similar to business process re-engineering, but they describe high-performance work systems as a more comprehensive management system. High-per-

Figure 8.5. Heterarchy

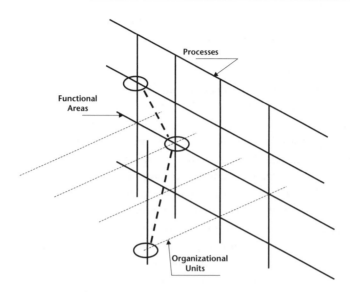

formance work systems are designed for lateral processes but appear to emphasize human factors more than business process re-engineering. This is a general concept and not a packaged solution. A high-performance work system was implemented in one case in a production setting but has a more general application. There are several guiding principles:

- The design begins by focusing on the customer to determine organization and processes.
- Tasks are designed for loosely coupled self-managed operating units completely responsible for products or processes.
- Work is guided by clear direction, goals and performance measures.
- Variance should be detected and controlled at the source.
- Social and technical systems should be closely linked.
- Information should flow directly to the people who need it.
- Work assignments should be flexible and enriched for motivation.
- Teams and individuals should be empowered for self-direction.

- Management structure, processes and culture must support the system design.
- The organization and its work units must be able to reconfigure to meet changing conditions.

The locus of power

Where is the center of power within the supply chain? First, it is a question of centralization in a decentralized operating environment. Nevertheless, the chain requires guidance. Second, the purpose of management guidance is to serve the strategic interests of the dominant party: manufacturer, major supplier, distributor or retailer. The basis of power stems from market share, dominance in value added within the chain, a particular expertise or intellectual property in the form of key products and processes. It may be delegated to other firms by outsourcing activities outside their own core competencies. Even the complexity of decision-making within the chain places a limit on centralized decisions.

Power is important for control over the flow of transactions but also for the information system. The supply chain operates on the basis of immediate access to information and visibility of operations across all activities within the chain. This requires cooperation for system compatibility, to develop acceptable process and procedures, common databases and data coding to integrate operations. Extending power across borders also limits the extent of supply chain management. It normally excludes internal operations of partners, except when situations arise when they threaten to disrupt the supply chain process.

Leadership

Leadership gives direction. The first step is visioning: »the systematic development of an organizational consensus regarding the key inputs to the [supply chain] planning process, as well as the identification of alternative ... strategies« (O'Laughlin et al. 1993, p. 279). Visioning begins with general business strategy and progresses towards the supply chain. Second, it incorporates service requirements for each market. Third, it considers external forces: trade barriers, transportation, social legislation, financial issues and information systems.

Leadership in the supply chain faces a scope beyond the organization, delegation of decisions to operating units, negotiation with outside parties and accommodation to continuous change. It calls for integrators to (Lawrence & Lorsch 1967, p. 150):

- contribute through knowledge and leadership rather than authority;
- maintain balanced perspectives towards both diverse functions and organizations;
- be rewarded for their management of the entire process, more than as individuals; and
- have the capacity to resolve interfunctional and interorganizational conflict.

The organizational nature of the supply chain tends to be a federation rather than a permanently integrated unit. Individual units specialize in transport or production. While the need to coordinate may be high, the initial links may have low coordination. As relationships develop and the balance of management power shifts towards the lead firm, it may be possible to integrate them into a more closely knit network. One task of leadership is to develop a tighter network with close coordination.

Virtual supply chains

Supply chains are networks. They can be formed for long-term relations where suppliers and customers operate with stability in expectation of continuing operations. Others operate for single products or even single units. Hedberg et al. (1997, p. 195) observe that »... with the emergence of modern technology, a new way has opened up to connect and coordinate 'islands of enterprise'. Transaction costs have declined so sharply that new forms of organization have become possible.«

A virtual supply chain is usually organized around a central organization, where the »broker« pulls other organizations into a supply network for the purpose of serving one customer with a specific order for one product in limited quantities (Chandrashekar &

Schary 1999). After the order is finished, the specific supply chain becomes dormant until a similar order reappears. Pre-arrangement allows the network to adapt to changing demands with extreme flexibility; potential partners are pulled into the supply chain for specific tasks. These pre-arrangements require establishing trust in business relations and competence among partners, that profits will be distributed equitably and assume that there will be sufficient business. They also must ensure information system compatibility that will allow the system to respond to individual orders.

The role of management in the supply chain

The role of managers in the supply chain is consistent with the new climate of management. Operating decisions are made at their point of impact. Managers at high levels provide strategic vision, resources and support, but the people involved with the problem take responsibility and act on their own judgment. The four areas in which the supply chain manager can make the greatest impact are 1) establishing the organizational architecture, the structure of formal relationships, 2) advancing integration, mechanisms for connecting and coordinating operations, 3) securing resources and 4) fostering a learning environment.

Directing the supply chain appears to involve seven specific tasks:

- establishing overall strategy, objectives and direction in the context of corporate strategy;
- specifying the structure of organization and processes to provide products and services to meet market requirements;
- developing common information and operating systems;
- establishing interorganizational relations to integrate operations;
- ensuring available resources, through ownership and outsourced contractual relations;
- fostering a climate for continuous improvement and innovation; and
- monitoring the supply chain environment to meet changing conditions.

Strategic vision, organization and common information are the foundation. Common strategy sets direction. The process structure determines task assignments, communication requirements and organizational responsibility. A unified information system connecting stages and participants encourages integration across the chain. Interfunctional and interorganizational participation involves negotiation. Monitoring and anticipating resource needs requires tracking both physical and intangible assets and personnel. Finally, establishing a learning environment fosters continuing improvement. This atmosphere must extend to interorganizational relations. The multiple environments experienced by chain members require continuous monitoring and adaptation, while recognizing a systemic perspective.

The content of management

Supply chains are important for corporations because they are central to other elements of strategy. They require a broad strategic view of supply and the supply system. Management decisions must be linked to the product line, customers, production, distribution and information systems. How well supply chains perform determines success in other areas of strategy. The professional knowledge of the logistics manager includes inventory management, transportation and related processes. The professional knowledge of the supply chain manager now must also encompass managing systems, interorganizational relationships, information and strategic issues. These last factors may ultimately become more important than applied knowledge in specific functional areas.

Systems design
Supply chain management emphasizes more than disciplines. The supply chain is a complex, closely coupled system with sometimes unintended connections and behaviors. Operations are interdependent but are also vulnerable to actions by individual members. Failure in one area can bring the entire system to a halt. The supply chain manager must recognize systemic characteristics in designing organization and information system architectures to buffer the most critical parts of the system from unanticipated disturbances.

Buffering could include inventory at critical points but also human intervention to review data, to prevent instability in the system from exceeding the supply capacity.

Interorganizational relationships
Supply chains link organizations as systems. Application of information systems and product flow depends on integrating operations beyond corporate boundaries. Establishing strong cooperative interorganizational relations underlies data flow and the structure of activities. Relationships rely on motivation, confidence, trust and open communication. Trust becomes a building block for technical agreement on operations and information systems.

The core of the supply chain is interorganizational integration. Savage (1990, p. xii) emphasizes its importance:

> »Integration is essential if companies are to become more responsive and agile in dealing with the complexity of ever-changing global markets ... And both integration and networking are preconditions if we wish to manage our multiple strategic alliances with suppliers, partners and customers.«

Information systems
Managing the physical transformation, movement of material and product to delivery of a product to a customer are the objects. Control comes through the flow of transactions, reporting systems and software that automate and support management decisions. This is also supported through collaborative computer-based communication that allows participants of different functional activities and organizations to participate jointly in problem solutions and coordinate operations. Sales force automation expands the potential for product customization, collaborative forecasting and direct interrogation of the entire supply chain. Production scheduling can activate different supply chains automatically. Electronic procurement can select partners and carry out transactions. Management now has the potential to make supplier schedules and inventory positions visible across the chain.

Managing information becomes a crucial part of the process, changing as technology evolves. Changes in technology also change perceptions in communication and in turn change management itself. These do more than extend logistics, but create a paradigm shift in the content of management in this area.

Strategy

The supply chain perspective is strategic. It is becoming the core of corporate operations. It has been characterized as a resource-based strategy where the quality of execution potentially provides differential advantage. Pasternack & Viscio (1998, p. 13) describe the current situation:

>»Competition is now based more on capabilities than assets. Firms compete, not by acquiring market share, but by doing things consistently better than the competition, driving the marketplace, and creating more business space for themselves.«

The supply chain, driven by information, is becoming oriented towards knowledge: the understandings that managers use to make decisions. Strategy in the supply chain deals with capabilities linked to decisions based on knowledge. It includes two types of knowledge: explicit knowledge, written documentation and software, available to everyone, whether competitors or collaborators, and implicit knowledge, organizational knowledge, undocumented and unwritten, inherent in the organization.

Organizational learning uses knowledge for competitive advantage (Bartlett & Ghoshal 1996). Organizational change is continuous. The learning process becomes a constant striving for improvement. The management task is to create a supporting climate for learning. The ultimate strategy is to manage the learning process for superior organizational performance.

Managing the learning process is difficult, because it requires organizational change. Pasternack & Viscio (1998) describe it as »the four unnatural acts«: sharing thoughts, using ideas of others, collaborating and improving. It becomes even more difficult across organizational boundaries, where organizational objectives may differ and organizational cultures resist change. Even technical solutions are not easily transferred. Nevertheless, supply chains that overcome the difficulties will gain strategic advantage.

Tools of supply chain management

Control over the supply chain as a process is still being developed. Discussion centers on a few approaches with promise for establishing metrics for the chain as a whole. These include activity-based accounting, benchmarking, the Balanced Scorecard and the Supply Chain Operating Reference (SCOR) Model developed under the sponsorship of the Supply Chain Council (1997, no date a, b).

Activity-based accounting

Processes in the supply chain are series of activities linked together to serve customer requirements. The rise of customer power emphasizes processes, often hidden from management in organizational and functional units, with accounting systems that do not show costs of individual activities, let alone the driving forces behind these costs. The pursuit of more precise activity costs has led to activity-based accounting and activity-based management to identify and utilize these costs along with non-cost metrics to identify opportunities (Cokins 1996). Conventional accounting systems are of little help; they hide more than they help. Activity-based costing offers a more useful approach: a logical framework to trace the specific costs of serving individual customers (or groups of customers) and activities and the total set of costs of providing individual products and services. It fits a process orientation through its capacity to provide end-to-end costing.

Cost accounting systems serve four purposes: 1) to determine the costs of processes and products, 2) to track the changes in costs over time, 3) to allocate costs for financial statements and 4) to evaluate alternative decisions (Johnson & Kaplan 1987). Conventional cost accounting was developed in labor-intensive factory environments. Costs were distributed to products on the basis of person-hours directly incurred for the production of individual products. Other costs were retained as overhead. This approach has become inadequate to meet the needs of modern industry, when labor costs are a small part of the total cost of a product and other costs enter in a more significant way. Conventional cost accounting fails to meet these purposes even within a single organization, let alone the supply chain, as the most important resources are often classified as overhead costs.

The supply chain adds further difficulty. Comparison among partner organizations is difficult using conventional methods. Each organization has a different set of activities and cost structures. Further, the supply chain as a process is oriented towards a flow of products and materials, adding value through the application of resources to activities in ways that are not always related to the convention of direct person-hours. Approaches using other singular measures such as machine-hours or space utilization are also inadequate to the task. Further, the systemic nature of the supply chain involves trade-offs between functional costs or between costs and service levels where a change in one activity area affects costs and performance in other areas (Pohlen & LaLonde 1994).

Each activity, such as order-processing, product assembly or materials-handling, utilizes different sets of resources and costs change in response to different measures of output, such as the numbers of orders processed, numbers of units assembled or numbers of warehouse pallets handled. Under conventional accounting, this cost behavior is hidden under overhead costs. A partial solution is offered through activity-based accounting.

Financial accounting fails to provide cost control. In response, two other measurement systems have emerged: operational control and activity-based accounting (Cooper & Kaplan 1999). They operate under different procedures, collect different data and perform different roles for mangers. They are incorporated into ERP systems to provide managers with direct measures of operating performance. Operational control provides continual feedback about individual unit performance. It uses highly specific cost data that employees can directly influence or control. Because it reflects daily performance, it will necessarily produce variable results. Activity-based costing plays a more strategic role.

The system

Activity-based accounting is part of a management shift towards managing businesses as a set of processes, called activity-based management. It recognizes a flow process: resources to activities to products. The flow is the core of the system, linking a series of activities and their costs. It is strategic in orientation, relying on statistically determined cost drivers. By following the flow of operations, the development of activity-based costing parallels that of the supply chain. Activity-based costing serves strategy and management decisions. In activity-based costing, all costs become variable but stable. The scope includes the entire Value Chain. Where conventional cost accounting would include inputs at their purchased price, activity-based costing would carry the impact of these inputs to vendors' resources.

Costs originate with the quantity of a specific resource committed to a process activity (or function). They become cost pools within activities, allocated on the basis of the quantities consumed and the related costs such as person-hours times hourly wage rates. Each activity has its own cost characteristics, based on the nature of the activity. These become cost drivers: »any event or transaction that causes the incurrence of cost in an organization« (Garrison & Noreen 1997, p. 82) Costs for individual products are then determined by resource consumption in processing the product.

An activity-based costing system is designed in a series of five steps:

- analyze process by value
- identify activity centers
- assign costs to activity centers
- select cost drivers
- apply to products.

Process value analysis follows a procedure outlined in Chapter 2: identification of value-adding as opposed to non-value-adding activities within material and product flow. This is essentially process engineering, designed to increase efficiency through improved process design.

An activity is any event or transaction that drives a cost. They should have clearly defined boundaries. However, if two adjacent activities have the same cost drivers, it makes little sense to separate them. Boundaries should be clearly identified. The danger is data collection and management in such detail so that the costing system becomes cumbersome to use.

An activity center is any part of a process for which management wants a cost. Activities are combined into activity centers to simplify the reporting process. Materials-handling in a distribution center could involve several different activities that are aggregated into a single activity center. The reporting level depends on the purpose and could focus on individual product units, batch, product category or facility. Assigning costs to activities should recognize only those costs directly incurred by the activity center and that vary with the volume of activity. Costs that influence cost behavior in a facility may not be relevant at a product unit or batch level. This also excludes overhead costs that cannot be assigned to activities or products.

Selecting cost drivers may be the most difficult part of the design process. A cost driver is the event that incurs the cost for the activity. The first step is to find the dominant characteristics that influence the costs of the activity through statistical analysis or, as a last resort, informed judgment. These, however, are limited by the availability of data for measurement. Further, the measurement should reflect resource consumption of the activity. A given activity may have more than one driver, and one advantage of activity-based costing is the ability to include multiple drivers. There may be several layers of cost drivers. The cost assignment path may go from general accounting ledger drivers to intermediate drivers that collect data in a particular functional area followed by a final activity driver that combines cost flows from different sources related to the characteristics of individual activities (Cokins 1996). Assigning costs to products at this point becomes straightforward. As products move through the supply chain, they will pass through a series of activities, incurring costs determined by the individual activity drivers. As products and materials flow through activities, they incur costs on the basis of the activity cost drivers.

A simple example will demonstrate the process (Figure 8.6). This distribution center has two activities: materials-handling and storage. Materials are handled by automated machinery. Storage involves the use of space within the building. In the first stage, the cost of performing the operation as a whole is calculated. For materials-handling, this is based on the costs of operating the materials-handling system. If more than one product is involved, the costs of individual products should be separated, tracing the proportions of use if necessary. For storage, this would be calculated based on floor space occupied. These costs flow through activity centers (cost pools), where they would be combined with other costs related to the activity. These activities are linked by cost drivers to the

Figure 8.6. Activity-based Costing

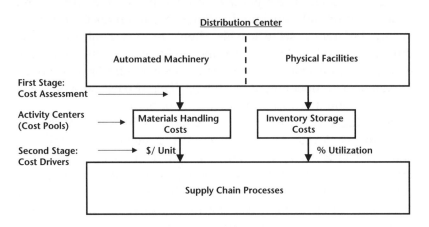

number of units handled for materials handling. The cost of storage is related to the proportion of space utilized. Both costs then flow through to the supply chain process, where the cost per unit handled and the cost of storing are combined and attached to the specific activity. Every activity involves a similar cost measurement procedure. The total cost of the process is the summation of all the individual activity costs. Only the costs that can be separately identified are included. Activity-based costing assigns general overhead costs as far as possible to specific actions based on logical and measurable associations between cost drivers and activity levels.

A further addition is proposed by van Damme & van der Zon (1999) to make activity-based costing into a decision support system: adding factors that influence drivers and tracking the system on a continuing basis for changes in operations. Using a three-tiered set of drivers for resource, process and product, they would incorporate additional factors to allow for critical dimensions. For example, resource drivers would deal with equipment age or vulnerability, process would deal with quality levels and product factors would look at batch size.

For the supply chain there is an additional problem. Cokins (1999, p. 5) notes that activity-based costing as currently practiced has »an inward looking focus« being tied to conventional accounting systems. Members of the supply chain behave as a single organization. They incur costs for each other through their own decisions.

The advantages of activity-based costing for the supply chain are that the costs of every activity can be measured. As long as every partner uses activity-based costing, the costs of these activities can be used to decide on courses of action for the supply chain as a whole. Cokin emphasizes the role of activity-based costing in boundary spanning at the »touch points,« where the impact of a supplier's actions impinges on the customer or vice versa. Management should be concerned with the total costs of actions such as changing delivery frequency for a supplier versus inventory holding costs for the customer.

Activity-based budgeting

Combining operational control with activity-based costing creates a decision tool for future planning: activity-based budgeting. The orientation reverses the activity-based costing process. It begins with final demand, translates into activities and then calls for the appropriate resources. Only resources needed to meet demand are included. Finally, planned use is compared with capacity, based on operational needs.

Computer-based ERP systems incorporate activity-based costing modules capable of providing a profusion of routine operating data. Cooper & Kaplan (1999, pp. 118-119) point to a shift in emphasis in accounting for control, away from periodic financial reporting to information available for immediate use.

The Balanced Scorecard

This approach establishes a framework for measuring organizational performance over multiple dimensions, including both financial and non-financial data (Kaplan & Norton 1996). The Balanced Scorecard links performance directly to strategy, making it especially valuable for supply chain management. It measures only the factors that create competitive advantage. The purpose is to provide a quick view of major activities and performance. There is no »correct« set of measures, although Kaplan & Norton identify four general categories (Figure 8.7):

- financial measures such as economic value added and return on investment;
- customer-related measures, including customer satisfaction and market share;
- internal performance, including quality, response time and cost measures; and
- learning, which stresses measurable aspects of employment skill development, retention and information technology.

The value of the Balanced Scorecard is its contribution to achieving strategic objectives. Formal strategies are in effect a series of cause-and-effect statements: hypotheses linked to a course of action. By measuring performance, it indicates whether the system is achieving the chosen objectives, providing feedback on the performance of policy and decisions. It validates strategic objectives by linking strategy to individual units, activities and resources and separates tactical from strategic information. Through data selection and tracking, it also identifies non-actionable strategic objectives.

Application to the supply chain must stress measures for the system as a whole. Liberatore & Miller (1998 p. 135) state that »the more comprehensive yet concise set of measures the set of measures, the greater the probability that the balanced scorecard will provide an effective monitoring and management tool for a firm«.

Figure 8.7. The Balanced Scorecard Model

For this purpose, measures must be individually determined and should relate to the firm's mission, objectives and strategy. Brewer & Speh (2000) propose that application to supply chain management should include:

Goals
- Waste reduction
  - Eliminate duplication
  - Harmonize systems
  - Maintain quality
- Time compression
  - order cycle
  - cash-to-cash cycle
- Flexible response
  - Product
    * Product form
    * Customer adaptation
  - Orders
    * Quantity
    * Delivery
- Unit cost reduction

Financial benefits
- Profit margins
- Cash flow
- Revenue growth
- Higher returns on assets

Operational improvements to supply chain management
- Process innovation
- Partnership management
- Information flows
- Threats and substitutes
  - End customer benefits: how customers receive benefits
- Product and service quality
- Timeliness
- Flexibility
- Value

The Balanced Scorecard approach is more than a summary of traditional measures in logistics. The Kaplan-Norton model combined with the interfunctional and partnership perspectives of the supply chain led Brewer & Speh to this prototype of measurements for the supply chain:

Customer perspective
- Product/service – number of contact points
- Timeliness – order response time
- Flexibility – flex response
- Customer value ratio (performance : cost)

Business process perspective across the entire supply chain
- Waste reduction – supply chain cost of ownership
- Time cycle efficiency
- Flex response choices and average response time
- Target costs achieved

Innovation and learning
- Innovation – product finalization or postponement
- Partnership management – product category commitment ratio
- Information flows – shared data sets to total data sets – cooperation
- Threats – performance trajectories of competing technologies

Financial perspective
- Profit margin by supply chain partner
- Cash-to-cash cycle
- Revenue growth
- Return on investment on assets

The Balanced Scorecard and activity-based costing have a potential synergy (Liberatore & Miller 1998). The scorecard is broad in approach, whereas activity-based costing is narrowly focused on cost measures, as an alternative to traditional accounting. However, activity-based costing can also monitor progress towards fulfilling strategy. They suggest using analytical hierarchy processing (see Chapter 11 for an explanation of the method) to establish the relative importance of criteria in meeting the strategic goals of the supply chain. The process begins by linking the supply chain mission to the Balanced Scorecard framework. This step uses subjective judgments by management about the ability of each of the four components of the scorecard in meeting the firm's objectives. An analytical hierarchy process is then used to determine the relative weights of individual measures. Key measures are then used to compose an index of overall performance.

Benchmarking

Benchmarking is a management process for comparative measurement and organizational learning, setting internal processes against »best practices« to establish needs and methods for improvement (Spendolini 1992). It seeks common metrics to compare activities across organizations. The underlying concept establishes measures for standardized process performance, focusing on the how these activities are performed, more than the content of the process.

In application, benchmarking appears to have five basic purposes (Spendolini 1992, p. 29):

* strategy – short and long-term planning
* forecasting – predicting trends in specific areas
* new ideas – stimulating new thought about familiar processes
* process comparisons
* setting objectives and targets based on current best practice.

These have been useful in corporate applications where there is clear purpose, systematic data collection and analysis and the focus is specific and not too large. It has been targeted in general towards problem areas of high visibility: critical success factors. These include significant costs, areas of competitive advantage or vulnerability and factors influencing customer satisfaction. The principal benefit from benchmarking is the improvement in processes. It is not intended to encourage imitation of »best practices« but to stimulate new thinking for change.

Benchmarking has several uses. Internally it can be used to track processes over time or compare performance of similar processes in different parts of the organization. Externally it can compare operations against competitors. Finally, it can be used to generate ideas by comparing operations against operations in other supply chains that demonstrate particular expertise or high levels of performance, such as the case of Xerox Corporation comparing its order processes with those of L.L. Bean, a mail-order catalog retailer. It becomes a vehicle for diffusing new innovation across industry.

Descriptions of benchmarking procedure differ. Benchmarking in general should be a continuous process, tracking performance. It should also have a precisely defined focus. Although it normally would have a continuing measurement role, a single exercise may serve to investigate problems.

In a supply chain context, a narrow focus presents both conflict and opportunity. Narrowing the focus conflicts with the systemic character of the supply chain. Measurements emphasize the performance of individual components, without relating to the chain as a whole. This introduces a danger of sub-optimizing components at the expense of the system. The opportunity stems from its role as a tool to fix local, narrowly defined problems. Benchmarking involves reactive learning more than proactive leadership. Its major value is the ability to look beyond organizational boundaries as a search for industry current best practice.

Bagchi (1996) explored the use of benchmarking in logistics (and by implication in supply chains). He began by selecting a target process, assessing, moving to data collection and analysis and leading to process re-engineering. He noted three types of benchmarking:

- previous performance
- »best practices« across industry as a cooperative venture
- »best practices« across competitors.

Gilmour (1999) reported on a study of benchmarking supply chains in six Australian firms. Respondents were given questionnaires asking them to rate their own organizations using a numerical scale about current and future levels of sophistication. Differences were compared between companies as well as between present and future positions. Each supply chain was divided into 11 capabilities:

Process capabilities
- Customer dialogue-driven supply chain
- Efficient distribution
- Demand-driven sales planning
- Lean manufacturing
- Supplier partnering
- Integrated supply chain management

Technology capabilities
- Integrated information systems
- Advanced information technologies

Organizational capabilities
- Integrated performance measurement
- Teamwork
- Aligned organizational structure

Five dimensions identified the level of management sophistication: 1) strategy and organization, 2) business process and information, 3) planning, 4) product flow and 5) measurement. As an example, supplier partnering included under strategy and organization: supplier selection, purchasing strategy, purchasing organization and information sharing. Business process and information used transaction automation and the need for direct purchasing authorization. Planning used planning and product development. Product flow included the point and timeliness of delivery.

The use of logistics benchmarking has been correlated with firm size and benchmarking (Daugherty et al. 1994). It is also linked to both internal and supplier performance, formal organizations and the adoption of technology. Firm size is important because benchmarking involves commitment of resources for the study. Managers who monitored logistics processes closely were more inclined to use benchmarking to develop formal organization and procedures and to adopt new software.

The SCOR model software

The Supply Chain Council (1997, no date a, b) developed the Supply Chain Operations Reference (SCOR) model as a form of benchmarking specifically applicable to supply chain management. The last version at the time of writing is the Process Reference Model (SCOR 4.0), intended 1) to provide a standard cross-industry language for supply chain management, 2) to allow for external benchmarking, 3) to establish a basis for analyzing supply chain structure across organizational boundaries and 4) to compare the current state of a process with a future target. The SCOR model is shown in Figure 8.8.

The model is based on an overview of four management processes:

- PLAN balances supply and demand, leading to a course of action
    Demand and supply planning
    Managing planning processes
- SOURCE procures goods and services to meet demands
    Sourcing of material
    Managing procurement processes
- MAKE transforms goods and services into finished products
    Production
    Managing production
- DELIVER provides products to meet demand
    Order management
    Warehouse management
    Transportation management
    Manage the delivery process

SCOR 3.0 contains three levels of process detail:

- top level – defines the scope and content for the specific supply chain;
- configuration level – designs the chain using choices from 17 core processes: this is the primary use of SCOR; and
- process element level – applies detailed information on each process, such as process definitions, inputs and outputs and system capabilities required.

A process is composed of process elements that are, in turn, composed of tasks, major categories of activities. Tasks are in turn a set of activities standardized for comparison between supply chains. For example, the source processes procure materials and services to meet demand. These, in turn, become process categories that identify the characteristics of the process, such as whether the component is standard or unique. At the configuration level, these categories become the basis for selecting processes such as procuring or manufacturing materials. At the element level, processes are further divided into elements such as scheduling deliveries, receiving and verifying and transferring to inventory.

The scope includes customer orders, material transactions and aggregate demand. It compares present and projected individual processes using quantitative measures of similar companies and establishes internal targets based on best performance. It also links management practices and software solutions to those practices. SCOR includes all customer interactions from second-tier supplier to customer order fulfillment and aggregate demand.

The SCOR model depicts supply chain activities for a single firm but can create an interorganizational configuration. The primary use is »to describe, measure and evaluate supply chain configurations« (Supply Chain Council 1997, p. 14). Every supply chain links source, make and delivery processes through nodes of planning. Supply chain configurations are described by »threads« that link specific processes in the chain of organizations, such as supplier (sources, produces and delivers) to assembler (sources, makes-to-stock, delivers) to distributor (sources and delivers) to retailer (sources and delivers).

Figure 8.8. The SCOR Model

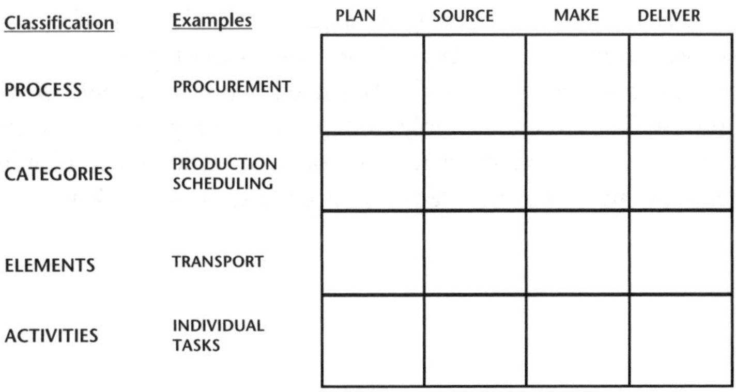

The SCOR method involves four steps: 1) analyzing the basis of competition, 2) configuring the supply chain both internally and inter-company, 3) aligning performance levels, practices and systems and 4) implementing supply chain processes and systems. These are specific procedures resulting in performance metrics at two levels and numerical scoring of performance relative to the competition.

Concluding comments

Management takes place in a rapidly changing environment of empowerment, emphasis on process, rather than functionalism, electronic connectivity and outsourcing of non-critical activities. The rules and organizational structure are uncertain, because the traditional measures are no longer relevant.

Managing the supply chain is itself a pioneering effort. It involves complex systems, interorganizational ties and self-managing entities. At the same time, it must be integrated as a single unit capable of accepting and meeting customer requirements in competition with other supply chains. Organization is ill defined, with ad hoc teams formed around specific problems. The span of the supply chain itself exceeds the bounds of normal management. The enabling element in the supply chain is the information system, extending communication and automating many elements of the transaction and order fulfillment processes.

Managers in this environment must combine technical, business and general knowledge, persuasiveness and breadth of vision and personality that gains satisfaction through the achievements of others. The focus on process leads to managing specific sets of activities across organizational boundaries. The tools to assist in this task, activity-based costing accounting, the Balanced Scorecard, benchmarking and the SCOR model, are only now gaining acceptance on a broad scale. In the end, however, as it is in more conventional organizations, managing is an art form more than a precise scientific endeavor.

9. The information system for the supply chain

»Information has economic value if it leads to the satisfaction of human desires. A small portion of that is final goods, which derive their value from supply and demand. By far the larger portion is intermediate goods that derive their value substantially from the value of the goods and services to which they lead.«
(Dertouzos 1997, p. 236)

Introduction

Information technology (IT) both enables and dominates the supply chain (Figure 9.1). It has changed business operations through the flow of information, control over operations remote in distance and across organizational boundaries and by automation of processes. IT is also shaping the future development of the supply chain through the Web, offering fast, easy connection with complex communication potential. It is no longer a search for efficiency alone but an enabler of new opportunity. No business can ignore the power of IT to transform operations and strategy.

The most important contribution is to bring visibility to the entire supply chain. It enlarges the scope of management and allows managers to make informed operational decisions in a variety of areas where information was previously lacking. It becomes a vehicle for monitoring and controlling operations without regard to geographic location. It also allows supply chain partners to coordinate operations using common data. The term system is used here to identify the information system, recognizing that there is a larger context for the term that embraces the supply chain itself.

Figure 9.1. The Information System

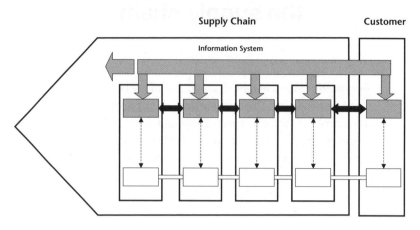

Information technology can automate processes such as documentation and internal operation routines. Orders can be processed and result in complete fulfillment of orders without human intervention. Automation, however, has limits. There are inherent dangers of supply chains going out of control from data errors and incomplete decision rules when they are left to their own devices and not subject to human supervision (Wilding 1998). Small data errors become amplified and potentially create havoc over time.

The information system becomes the glue of the supply chain. Visibility through operating data coordinates operations, either through automated tasks or management surveillance. They can provide managers with overall direction for strategic decisions, to match market requirements with resource allocations to optimize the system. IT is the basis for developing the supply chain as the extended enterprise (Tapscott 1995). The concept of the supply chain as a network of separate organizations becomes the foundation for redefining the concept of the enterprise as we enter the age of the network economy.

One software vendor identified five levels of development of supply chain management (Fox 1998):

- stage 1: fundamental processes: automation of existing tasks;
- stage 2: cross-functional teams: concentration on customer-related processes and specifically order fulfillment;

- stage 3: the integrated enterprise: emphasis on efficiency and operational flexibility within the organization;
- stage 4: the extended supply chain: developing relations with key customers through service differentiation; and
- stage 5: the supply chain community: establishing scope and direction for the chain as a single integrated community.

The promise and the danger come from the rapidity of the changes now taking place. Much of the description of the supply chain information system is transitory. The transition from stand-alone applications to direct interfunctional and interorganizational communication created the supply chain. The movement to real-time operation has forced functional integration to execute operations. The transition from relatively fixed to flexible networks will change from permanent to more temporary structures.

This chapter focuses on several distinct areas:

- the operations process
- the concept
- the system hardware
- the system software
- communication
- automatic identification
- the organization problem.

The operations process

Supply chain operations are activated by a series of transactions that trigger the movement of products and materials. Some observers in IT divide the supply chain into supply management and demand management (Figure 9.2). Supply management covers the flow of material and products from production back to sources of supply. Demand management encompasses the span from customer order to production. The critical link is the production schedule. Supply chain operations begin with a customer order. In many industries and product lines, the order is actually point-of-sale barcode data scanned at a retail checkout counter or inventory stock location, aggregated by the retailer customer and transmitted to its

Figure 9.2. Information Systems and the Supply Chain

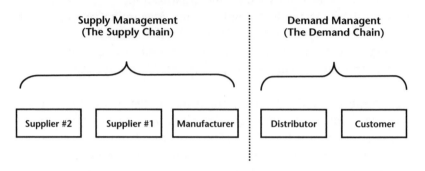

supplier. In other cases, orders come directly as orders from the sales force or as electronic commerce from Web sites. Sales provide data that become orders either transmitted to a distribution center for order fulfillment or directly to a production-scheduling unit or serve as input data to forecasts by customers, users or the supply chain itself and become a basis for the production schedule. In the case of the distribution center, inventories are replenished by production based on forecasts.

Production scheduling determines when orders will be fulfilled using one of several approaches. Feasible solutions include MRP or priority-based, chronologically based or optimized schedules randomly generated by computer. Setting a production schedule becomes a basis for automatically released orders to major first-tier suppliers, who then release orders to their own (second-tier) suppliers. With non-critical or standard items, the system monitors inventory and dispatch electronic agents to business-to-business exchanges to procure items in a process similar to auctions or to vendor catalogs.

Complete customer orders ready to ship release electronic advance shipping notices to customers, notifying carriers, producing electronic bills of lading and other documentation. The carrier's data system tracks the shipment to the point of delivery. Electronic proof of delivery triggers the billing and payment systems, using automated payment systems to transfer funds electronically.

The transaction system is supplemented by other electronic data and information systems. Transaction data held in the system create records of performance for later analysis and planning as part of decision support systems. This support is provided through database query, modeling and optimization tools. In addition, drawings and other technical data can also be transmitted between partners. Joint discussions can also be facilitated by groupware and e-mail, allowing dialogue and simultaneous access to common databases. Ultimately negotiation can also take place through the information system, culminating in transfer and acceptance of legal documents that obligate partners to perform agreed services and other actions.

These elements of the information system are now in place, although they are not universal and not always in the same supply chain. Other elements such as the transport market should also be included. The current interest is on transaction systems, with management and decision support falling in behind. The ability to implement and utilize these systems has become a major management challenge.

The concept

The essential role of the supply chain information system is to bind the entire chain together as a single integrated unit. The underlying framework is shown in Figure 9.3. It has both an intra-firm dimension that is largely vertical and hierarchical and interfunctional and inter-firm dimensions that are horizontal, following the transaction flow. The intra-firm system is highly developed, following a traditional management orientation. The inter-firm system is emerging slowly, restrained not by technology as much as by relationships among organizations in the supply chain.

The intra-firm information system

In a hierarchical orientation, top management deals with strategy and strategic direction. From this follows planning to implement strategy and the specific decisions necessary to direct operations. The work of the organization comes from execution, functional activities performing the tasks determined through the flow of transactions. Transactions flow horizontally across functional and organizational boundaries from customers, external partners and suppli-

Figure 9.3. The Concept of the Information System

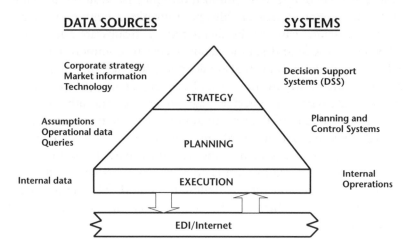

DATA SOURCES

Corporate strategy
Market information
Technology

STRATEGY

Assumptions
Operational data
Queries

PLANNING

Internal data

EXECUTION

EDI/Internet

SYSTEMS

Decision Support
Systems (DSS)

Planning and
Control Systems

Internal
Oprerations

ers. At a higher level, functional activities must be coordinated between organizations and intraorganizational units. High levels become involved with joint planning and strategy, negotiating the terms of partnership and participation.

The source of activity is the transaction flow. There has been a migration from paper (hard copy) documentation to electronic, computer-compatible data. The entire information system is vulnerable to data problems. There are potential problems of compatibility in the form of data and computer formats, although these barriers are being overcome more easily now. In terms of information systems, execution involves internal operations systems such as vehicle scheduling, warehouse management or production scheduling. These operations may involve automated processing, with precise decision rules, flagging of deviations and the ability to manage exceptions manually. Although they may have external connections for guiding delivery and production priorities and schedules, their principal focus is on the utilization of internal resources. In the course of operations, they generate data that can be reported and stored for use at higher levels.

The role of coordination is to synchronize operations between separate functional activities, to supervise ongoing processes and to balance capacity. As the first level above operations, it is closely linked to transaction flow. Planning is involved both in operations and strategy. In operations, it uses data from operations to project activity levels and to anticipate facility capacity and process requirements. It includes optimization and forecasting. Planning also establishes monitoring and control systems. It also provides a reporting function to inform management of the state of operations. At a strategy level, it also deals with capacity, process and optimization, although at a more aggregated level. At this level, it also becomes more oriented to external data.

Both execution and planning deal with established processes. In contrast, the need for strategy also calls for less predefined activities. It includes environmental scanning, the development of alternative scenarios for the supply chain and reaction to new situations. The key is to make tools and data easily available to management for data access and analysis. The decision support system is designed to promote this ease of use, characterized by the contingent question: »What if?«.

The data sources also show this difference. Internal operations use and generate data relating to specific activities. This becomes input to local operations planning. Higher levels of planning may also use this data, although usually in more aggregated form. At a strategic level, outside sources of data are corporate planning, external product and supply markets. These data would be selective, project-oriented and gathered to meet a specific need.

The inter-firm information system

The central management problem of the supply chain is coordination of operations. In concept, the information system enables this to take place, integrating operations of separate organizations into a unified system capable of responding to customer orders, changes in market and supply conditions and changes in corporate direction. Figure 9.4 displays a framework in simplified form. It includes a first-tier supplier, the lead enterprise and one customer. Each firm includes the framework of the intra-firm information systems discussed above. The central concerns are the connections and co-

Figure 9.4. The Supply Chain Information System

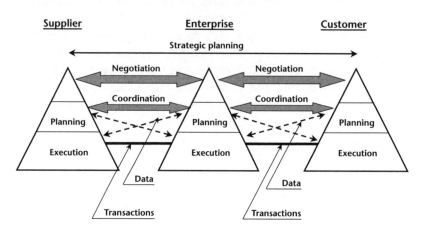

ordination. Transactions between organizations activate the supply chain. Executing operations in these organizations generates performance data which are shared with other operations and planning units. Linking operations requires coordination. This can involve routine data to signal between activities, routine reporting, e-mail, complex messages including visual elements and non-standard multimedia communication.

Establishing or changing the terms of this coordination requires negotiation, again utilizing multimedia. Further, as supply chain strategy becomes a collective activity among partners, there are further demands for multimedia connection. All of this requires broadband connections that require a technical solution within the information system.

The information system involves both hardware and software systems. While we treat them as separate topics, they are closely linked. Advances in hardware such as computers or the connecting links enable software development towards more sophisticated programs. Similarly, the complexity of software influences the development of computer and connecting links.

Elements of the supply chain information system

Visualize the information system as a web of connections. The power of this system should not be understated. The ability to control and make decisions about the supply chain depends on the capabilities of this system. Within this web are three major components: computing power, connecting links and software. These are interrelated, and the driving force is difficult to isolate. The expansion of network communication through broadband capacity increases the power of computer networks which, in turn, is limited by the computing capacity available within the network. These two elements together enable more complex software to be written.

The hardware components

Hardware includes computers and connectors. The governing dimension is communication. The power of the computer in the supply chain comes from its connections. The current hardware architecture for the supply chain information system is a client-server configuration. Clients, PCs serving as local terminals, are connected to a central server by local area networks (LANs) or over a larger geographic area by wide area networks (WANs). Software can reside either within individual PCs or in the servers, to be called as needed for specific tasks.

PCs in networks provide manual input to prescribed forms, documents and messages or manual intervention in computer-based processes. In contrast, increasing volumes of data are entered automatically from transactions, documents and automatic identification flowing directly to servers, to be monitored only for exceptions or trend indicators. Human inputs and interventions at an operating level appear to be becoming less, but communication at higher levels is increasing.

Servers as hubs of the system connect PCs and hold both applications and data. Transaction data flow between servers. They also connect PCs with other hub servers and PCs. In some systems, they are actually two separate units, applications and data servers, connected for immediate access. The emphasis is on connectivity and real-time processing.

The client-server system has proven to be costly when implemented on a large scale (Taylor 1999). It has also been criticized as overly complicated for most users. One solution is to use thin-client systems of servers with terminals that do not hold applications individually but access them from a central server. They offer a chance for substantial cost savings, they can be more specialized to specific uses and are simpler to use. Data can be stored both locally and in a central server. However, they have not been widely accepted in their present form.

The current development of hardware encourages this development of pervasive computing, the diffusion of applications and data across entire networks. There are a large variety of entry devices now, such as hand-held palm top personal data assistant (PDA) devices, mobile computers , vehicle-based computers, screen phones and more in prospect. The problems are the confusion presented by the variety of operating systems available, their lack of compatibility and their ability to connect to the information systems. The danger is that changes will be recorded in these devices and only later will they be able to update the information system.

Software systems

As much as the hardware, software defines the supply chain information system. To date, it has emphasized transactions and operations in real time more than planning and strategy. The collective thrust of development has been towards connecting and integrating operations across the supply chain. This reflects a current management focus, but development is also taking place in strategic areas.

Supply chain software has branched into two orientations. One becomes specialized, focusing on specific tasks. The task is to link them together as a coherent system. The other is more broadly encompassing but immediately becomes complex and difficult to install and use. Compatibility among proprietary software programs becomes a critical problem. Another problem is time; there are problems of data entry into the system. Enterprise resource planning is a case in point.

Enterprise resource planning

The first specific development in software for managing supply chain information took place in ERP systems. These systems manage financial, human and material resource transactions within the boundaries of a single organization. Originally offered as mainframe applications, they are now available for client-server applications on the Internet, typically using Java as the language. Typically offered in process modules, they are oriented towards operating processes rather than particular functional areas, crossing functional and departmental boundaries. Enterprise resource planning systems typically utilize process engineering, matching the work flow across the organization. They parallel the development of lateral organization. Typical modules include accounting, financial payments, human resources, inventory and order processing. At the present time, SAP offers more than 800 separate process modules.

By managing and documenting the execution of transactions on the computer, ERP offers precise control and potential elimination of paper documentation within the organization. Data generated from operations can be held in databases for reporting and analysis. In the past, ERP has been difficult to implement because of the sheer size of the task, initial data requirements and the compatibility with other systems.

SAP has made the largest body of installations, although others such as Baan, J.D. Edwards, Oracle and Peoplesoft also offer ERP software. Their programming complexity is often more difficult to change than the underlying organization. Many companies encountered unexpected costs of installation. One company was even forced into bankruptcy by its installation of an ERP system. The size and rigidity of the program often makes changing organizational structure easier rather than altering the software. It has also been estimated that, for every dollar spent on the application itself, 7 to 20 dollars are required for implementation.

Implementation has its strongest appeal in large organizations, and the costs can run into hundreds of millions of dollars. However, some vendors have developed simpler applications for small and medium-sized companies. SAP now offers Ready-to-Run R/3 for companies with 15 to 200 users. Others such as Baan, IBM and Peoplesoft have offered applications in smaller modules. Peoplesoft and USinternetworking offer ERP for medium-sized companies to run over a national Internet network.

Enterprise resource planning is currently limited to the boundaries of the firm, but the open architecture of many systems permits connections to external applications. Enterprise resource planning is a foundation for managing interfunctional supply chain processes within the firm. By itself, it is inadequate to manage the supply chain beyond organizational boundaries, without supporting applications linked to external partners. Boundaries mean that transaction data do not always reflect immediate inputs from on-line connections. Data are fixed at the time of entry and therefore require updating. As one observer notes, ERP systems alone do not deal with logistics well. These systems normally do not accommodate special orders or customer inventory positions. They does not deal with global logistics problems easily, such as the timing of invoices in relation to customs clearances.

The Internet presents new possibilities for installing ERP with Web-resident applications. Enterprise resource planning programs such as MYSAP are accessible by users where the physical installation has already taken place on the Web. The remaining task is to develop the data to make the program operable. Although this can be a major task, it requires far less time for installation: 4-5 weeks, compared with as long as 2 years (*The Economist* 2000b).

The complexity problem presents another difficulty for corporate strategy. Adoption of standardized ERP programs on a wide scale means that enterprise differentiation through operations is difficult. Information processing becomes similar when ERP systems impose their own logic on organizations (Davenport 1998). The trade-off is therefore between accepting standard ERP and customization.

Customization offers opportunity to deliver unique supply solutions to customers but also comes at a price: the cost of programming and program maintenance. This inflexibility has created problems in organizations with diverse organizational demands, such as multi-product and global corporations.

Some organizations use ERP to improve internal efficiency. Others use it as a lever for organizational change. Enterprise resource planning follows a characteristic of hierarchical management: data accessible at one central point, encouraging centralized control. At the same time, it offers increased accessibility for more members in the organization. By one estimate, about 10-20% of people in using organizations now have access to ERP information, but this is anticipated to grow to between 40-60% within the next 5 years, diffusing decision-making on a large scale. Similarly, ERP enables the firm to interact directly with the market. Managers can observe the state of their operations as a basis for discussion with customers.

Software for supply chain management

Software for supply chain management followed on the development of ERP, specifically to solve the problems of external coordination. It presents a more holistic view of the enterprise imbedded in a network of suppliers and customers. The overriding concept is coordination with customers, suppliers and service providers to create a single integrated transaction system that is interorganizational and interfunctional. These software systems are offered in suites of modules dedicated to specific processes such as order

Figure 9.5. Software in the Supply Chain

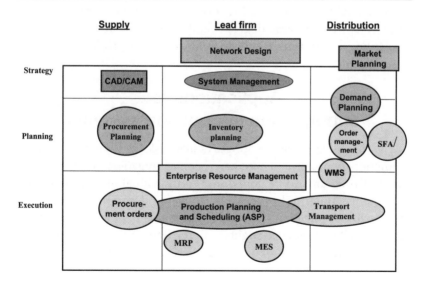

processing, demand management (including joint customer-vendor forecasting), transportation management, purchasing and supplier coordination. A map of supply chain software applications as of 1998 is shown in Figure 9.5.

This software is also linked to sales force automation software, because of the stress on data for forecasting. These modules are also typically offered as additions to ERP, although they are also offered as a separate, linked coordination system. Typical vendors include Baan, i2 Technologies, IMI, Logility, Manugistics, Numetrix and Oracle, some independently and others with alliances to ERP vendors for specific functions and levels of interaction. Further, some offer vertical market, industry-specific supply chain software. Typical examples include Oracle CPG, focusing on consumer products industries, and Baan, supporting such industries such as automotive, chemical and forest products industries. The most interest has come from distribution-oriented demand chain users, rather than the supply chain.

Supply chain management software adds a new element to ERP, the ability to coordinate the flow of products and material between organizations. The stress is on interorganizational collaboration. It allows partners to negotiate forecasts and deliveries based on constraints within the chain. Although ERP systems have been strong on transaction processing and operational management issues, they have generally not emphasized overall supply chain management and strategy to the same degree. Vendors are now adding planning, scheduling and optimization capabilities to their product suites.

Applications for
supply chain information systems

The variety of applications for particular tasks in supply chain management is impressive. There have been aggregations of functions as suites of programs to be configured to individual organizational requirements. What follows here is an overall description of some of the possible applications, recognizing that this is a highly changeable landscape. The sequence begins with the demand chain and leads to the supply chain and supporting services such as transportation.

Distribution management

A typical program is linked to customer orders either directly or through automated sales programs. Some will perform sales allocation and assert control over inventory and shipments through distribution centers. Some will also include warehouse management capabilities, although ERP and supply chain programs may have links to software for warehouse management systems.

Warehouse management systems
Warehouse management systems embrace a variety of modules for distribution center operation in a real-time environment (Trunk 2000; *Modern Materials Handling* 2000). These options include data files on stock locations in the distribution center and inventory management, communications modules for radio frequency contact with pickers, generation of packing slips and advance shipping notices.

Some warehouse management systems handle partial shipments from multiple distribution centers. The Internet makes tighter control over the operation of distribution centers imperative with B2C retailing order fulfillment, direct shipments passing through distribution centers, pressures for inventory reduction and the new culture of the supply chain for customer-specific inventories and mass customization.

Order management

This is often the path into the supply chain for customer orders. Typical modules assume a customer-pull environment, managing contacts with the customer, providing customer service with the ability to manage orders under complexity, from different locations with large numbers of products with differing service requirements. Customer credit, product and proposed shipping dates can be accessed through the order management modules. In addition, customers may have access to some files to trace order status, with possible links to a carrier data system to trace shipments after the order has been shipped.

Demand planning

Supply chain software has become important because of the need to take in customer order data from the point of sale or sales orders directly from the source and to forecast future sales. Typical programs such as CPFR include sales planning, forecasting, customer commitment, order delivery promising and customer demand data from the point of sale or orders. Some may include pricing data as well.

Production planning

The most difficult technical problem for IT in supply chain operations is probably production scheduling. Orders now are processed and scheduled in real time, requiring reformulation of the scheduling process. Materials requirements planning (MRP) and master production scheduling (MPS) preceded ERP. Even MRP II, which as an improved scheduling program offered many data processing capabilities now associated with ERP production planning and scheduling, has not been adequate to the task. MRP was developed in an era of stand-alone computers and programmed in COBOL, a now arcane language. It has not been adaptable to this new environment of on-line processing. New production planning programs under the name advanced planning and scheduling have been developed to replace MRP and master production scheduling within the supply chain (Tadjer 1998).

The original MRP took the material requirements of a production schedule and matched it to a bill of material, generating production schedules and purchase orders. It did not consider production capacity. Information flowed downward from the schedule to the shop floor but not the other way, often leading to unfeasible production schedules. Devices instituted to counter these problems included time fences and rolling production time horizons, requiring additional inventory to respond to service demands.

MRP II integrated order processing, cost accounting, billing, shop floor scheduling and machine utilization and permitted some schedule adjustment. Despite these improvements, it was a sequential system; all the tasks such as master production scheduling and final production scheduling were independent of each other. Both MRP and MRP II assumed infinite production capacity. As stand-alone applications, they are not readily adapted to real-time applications and the rapid changes necessary to deal with interactive demand requirements. Optimizing solutions are often too difficult to achieve. Newer versions of ERP now incorporate advance planning and scheduling modules, however, that include options for MRP and master production scheduling.

Schedulers now often work to an approximate solution, followed by the use of simulation models to evaluate the results. The process is sometimes augmented by visual displays. The current process integrates information from customer orders, purchasing, iterating production scheduling until the user finds a successful schedule.

Enterprise resource planning changes the nature of manufacturing. One typical application automatically builds schedules recognizing constraints such as equipment capacities, shipping loads, material availability and marketing requirements, utilizing an optimizing algorithm. It supports global production optimization, interactive scheduling, rescheduling and what-if planning. The need is for people who understand both operations and IT, with the emphasis on operations. They will need to understand the production cycle, the supply chain with some knowledge of networks and databases.

Procurement

There is divergence in purchasing applications. One approach assumes a pre-existing relationship with major suppliers, emphasizing coordination of operations to ensure that products are delivered as needed. The other assumes procurement of standard items, open markets with an emphasis on search and selection, involving business-to-business (B2B) markets. This process lends itself to automation of procurement through the use of electronic software agents and optimizing choices based on price, delivery costs and related variables. Some applications involve development of large-scale Web-based catalogs of pre-qualified suppliers for non-critical items, using standard protocols and data codes, previously established within the buyer's own network. All of these may operate side by side in the same system to meet differing procurement needs.

Transportation

A trade journal survey as of the year 2000 (Forsyth 2000b) noted 80 transportation and logistics providing widely varying Internet services. These services include software development, B2B freight service exchanges and auctions, contract negotiation and transport and logistics management. Typical software programs route shipments through multiple hubs, pooling points to customers, recognizing constraints from customers, production, material availability, transportation and other sources and also offer optimization. Some also perform consolidation of shipments, load planning and documentation. Others also offer shipment tracking to precise locations.

Collaboration

One purpose of supply chain software is to promote collaboration across organizational boundaries. Collaborative software has developed as a general category utilized for a variety of purposes. Some applications in supply chain management have been developed in customer relationship management, forecasting and transportation management. The next wave will be to align software to underlying business processes. One program allows for free exchange of data in multiple message types between the supplier and customer. It allows partners to share planning data and requirements.

Program suites

The problems of connecting separate software programs into a single coherent unit have led major supply software suppliers to collaborate in teams. IBM, Ariba and i2 Technologies as one group and Oracle and Commerce One as another, for example, offer complete supply chain management software systems. Ariba and i2 also offer their own software solutions. These are more or less complete integrated sets of programs matched to the evolving environment of e-commerce trading. The most information publicly available at the time of writing is i2's Trade Matrix™ (i2 Technologies 2000). It consists of six integrated modules:

- Trade Matrix Design Solution™ provides capability for collaboration both internally and with partners.
- Trade Matrix Buy Solution Solution™ improves procurement efficiency through collaboration with suppliers, aggregating procurement requirements across the enterprise.
- Trade Matrix Plan Solution™ optimizes the company's resources to balance demand with supply.
- Trade Matrix Sell Solution™ manages customer interactions across the supply chain, including marketing, sales, customer collaboration, order processing and order tracking.
- Trade Matrix Service Solution™ increases customer satisfaction and revenues while seeking to minimize investments in resource assets.
- Trade Matrix Fulfill Solution™ responds to customer orders and requests and physically moves the product to customers.

The effect of this collaboration is to move supply chain information systems into a limited number of vendors and, even with individual configurations, with also a slightly less limited number of options.

Web-resident programs

The Web introduces a new dimension to software development. The ease of access using browsers overcomes several barriers that have impaired acceptance of software in the past: ease of access, training, costs of installation and the problem of perpetual obsolescence. Servers become application software providers (ASPs) holding software resident such as ERP, to be configured individually and called as needed for individual transactions.

The cost of implementation and disruption of existing processes has been a major hurdle to the use of supply chain management software in small and medium-sized businesses. Web-resident software makes it more accessible without the fixed costs of installation. Applications can be scaled to meet specific requirements.

The use of Web-resident software supplied on demand reduces this barrier considerably. It also reinforces collaboration between partners if they both have access to the same software, even with restricted data access. It does not eliminate all of the problems related to software use in the supply chain. There is still a problem of data collection and coding. The fixed costs of installation are replaced by transaction or time-based charges, converting a fixed cost into a variable cost. There are still the costs of data collection, training and connection to other systems. Further, the possibilities of gaining competitive advantage by differentiating individual systems are more difficult to achieve when competitors use the same system.

The use of application software provider systems differs for each company. PricewaterhouseCoopers (2000) defines the range of implementation from point solutions, a starting-point for many companies, to cross-functional solutions and end-to-end collaborative electronic planning solutions for the supply chain.

- *Application software provider point solutions* focus on a single planning function, such as production planning or distribution planning, and offer a quick problem resolution.
- *Application software provider cross-functional solutions* link multiple functions. They serve as a catalyst for better integration. One example is demand planning, where the goal is to produce a forecast based on consensus across sales, marketing and finance functions.
- *Application software provider end-to-end supply chain solutions* synchronize all functional areas to the same plan. This normally requires consistent transaction data from an ERP system.
- *Application software provider data integration with supply chain partners* presents an additional level of data sharing. Here the scope of access includes suppliers, customers and other external partners through an extranet.
- *Application software provider collaborative e-planning* is the highest level of access and collaboration. Beyond sharing data about productions plans, forecasts, product changes, promotions, etc., the supply chain participants work together to create a plan incorporating the goals and constraints of all parties. This level of collaboration requires a high degree of inter-firm trust and coordination.

Web-based supply chain information systems will significantly influence the future organization of the supply chain. The ability to connect partners to applications eases the problems of coordination. The ease of connection encourages the development of limited purpose temporary virtual supply chains connected electronically and dissolved when the task is completed. This may encourage a large number of small-scale chains as it removes a major cost barrier.

Communications

The backbone of the supply chain is communication. What distinguishes supply chain management from earlier supply systems is the potential for instantaneous communication, presentation of data, analysis and the ability to react with speed to changing situations. The emphasis in supply chain strategy is on information, to be substituted for products wherever possible. It has the potential to influence the development of organizations in three areas: 1) the physical tasks, 2) internal information handling and 3) interorganizational relationships.

The ability to manage the supply chain depends on 1) the capacity to handle the volume of individual transactions, 2) the speed with which these transactions and their accompanying data can be processed, 3) the visibility of operations to participants and 4) the complexity of communication. Technology provides an increasing ability to handle the requirements of these tasks; information will play an expanding role in supply chain management.

The information system is limited by its bandwidth to handle multimedia messaging with high-speed data transfer. The foundation is the telephone system (telecoms). It has progressed to direct data communication via electronic data interchange and now to the Web. Beyond this lie broadband and wireless services. Each has particular characteristics that define its use.

Telecoms

First came telephone (sometimes referred to as POTS, or plain old telephone service) plus modem connections. It was unsatisfactory because of its lack of speed (up to 56 kilobaud with current modems) and capacity. This led to the second major development in telecommunication, the convergent network, the ability to handle both voice and data. The most prominent offering was the integrated digital service network (ISDN), which can provide transmission speeds of up to 139 megabits per second (Dizard 1997). The cost of leasing lines has been a major deterrent in expanding its use. A variation has been digital subscriber lines offered as a lower-cost substitute. More recent are fiber-optic lines and wireless data transmission. Both will reduce capacity limitations for data networks.

Basic telephone service loses some restrictions with the use of packet switching. Voice, data and video messages can be sent in digital blocks and reconstituted at the receiving end. One publicized application transmits drawings from one location to another, allowing design teams to participate in joint design activity (*Business Week* 1998). A telecommunications channel is used only for the time that the block is being transmitted, allowing other blocks to share the same channel, with much reduced cost.

New developments include the use of fiber-optic cable and wireless transmission (Gilder 2000). They have the potential of almost infinite capacity and hence broader bandwidth for richer, more complex communication. Wireless also offers freedom from a need for specific locations. Electronic collaboration may have been restricted in the past by bandwidth capacity. These developments will certainly open the door to more joint development and planning by parties separated geographically. The freedom from specific location offered by wireless is a new dimension for supply chains. How it will be used cannot be predicted.

Electronic data interchange (EDI)

EDI was originally intended to provide mainframe-to-mainframe computer communication. Computers operated as stand-alone systems, and EDI protocols had to be adapted to each system. The result was individual supplier-to-customer connections, and if there was more than one connection, each one required individual programming support. It was widely adopted and by one estimate accounts for USD 3 trillion in transactions. Smaller firms appear to be more receptive to Web solutions such as XML because of cost and flexibility.

EDI generally utilizes a value-added network (VAN) to carry EDI messages to ensure connectivity between partners. Major firms continue to use it because it offers data security and compatibility with legacy data systems. It is sometimes used in parallel with more current Web-based systems that currently have less security. Many companies use both conventional EDI for security of data and internets for more general use.

One outcome of EDI was the development of standardized messages (transaction sets), based on common standards such as ANSI X.12 for the United States and EDIFACT in international use. These messages include (in the United States):

- advanced shipping notices
- bills of lading
- purchase orders
- invoices
- warehouse shipping orders
- warehouse inventory status reports
- motor carrier shipping documents.

The cost of installing and programming has been high enough to confine it to major corporations and their partners, restricting the number of installations and thereby limiting potential competitors. Large customers made EDI a prerequisite for suppliers. Specific industry initiatives led to the development of EDI-based supply networks such as the UCS (Uniform Communication Standard) with standard messages for procurement transactions. A subsidiary set of standards was developed for public warehouse transactions serving the industry.

EDI is vulnerable to competition from the Web, especially as the security problems of the Web are resolved. Message sets can be transmitted via the Web as well as through conventional EDI. Because these messages have specified legal standing, EDI may survive within a Web-based environment, even though the original carrier arrangements may ultimately disappear.

The Internet

By contrast to EDI, the Web offers much broader adoption and coverage, ease of use and the ability to handle a wide variety of message content. Compatibility problems are eased by using a common protocol, TCP/IP (Plock 1997). Operating costs have been reported to be from 20% to 40% lower and training costs 80% lower. It utilizes browsers, similar to consumer Internet installations. It thus expands the number of potential sites, allowing small and medium-sized companies to become connected. Potential entry is eased, and a single user can handle more than one system with the same procedures. One disadvantage is the public nature of the Internet; security becomes a major problem, although solutions are now being offered. The use of externally managed value-added networks is usually recommended to establish and maintain the network and circumvent the technical problems.

Specific Web-based networks have developed to deal with accessibility. Intranets and extranets are corporate networks, accessible only through the use of passwords or specific identification. Intranets serve as the basic corporate communication system, with a richness of communication modes from text to graphics to voice and video. It extends the reach of the organization and serves as a vehicle for disseminating knowledge, experience and judgments. Extranets serve similar purposes but embrace suppliers, customers and others beyond the corporate boundaries linked to the supply chain.

The Internet has resulted in electronic markets, industry-wide B2B extranets to facilitate the procurement of non-strategic items on a broad scale. These initiatives do not eliminate all the problems with EDI. There must be agreement on standard transaction sets. Reliability must be established through acknowledgment procedures and audit trails (Zuckerman 1995). An additional problem is security and verification of sources to enable transactions to take place, especially in the case of extranets. Transmission and authentication of digital documents concerning contracts, shipping documents and monetary transfers is another problem area but is currently undergoing development.

Development in the past has been hindered by lack of common languages between systems. XML is now being promoted to solve the data interchange problem, XML is a Meta language that identifies data files and tags them so that they can be recovered by different systems. Thus, it promotes collaboration through data sharing, removing the problem of system incompatibility. Some vendors are offering automated translation services between EDI and XML.

RosettaNet, an industry consortium for the high-tech industry, introduced Partner Interface Processes, standardized processes for data transfer between separate computer systems (Souza 2000). Early reports indicated significant savings in processing times for standard procedures such as order status reports, advance shipping notices. The net effect is to reduce barriers to data transfer. RosettaNet is intended to supplement XML for more complete integration.

Automatic identification systems

Automated data collection is essential to the supply chain and takes place through machine-recognizable labeling and identification systems. The two most prominent are bar codes and radio frequency identification. They have been normally used to identify individual items, unit loads, vehicle loads and equipment, but they also enable control over operations beyond the ordinary reach of the computer. More recent developments have applied bar coding to product and shipping documentation and special handling instructions. Automatic identification is passive in that it only supplies data when interrogated by a scanning device or radio frequency transmitter.

Bar codes

Bar codes provide a common information system for the entire supply chain, from retail through manufacturing. Retail products are commonly labeled by the Universal Product Code (UPC) in the United States and the European Article Numbering (EAN) system in Europe. Data identify the manufacturer and the product. The EAN system holds one more digit than the United States system, useful for identifying special characteristics such as pack size or special promotions, but introduces problems of compatibility across the Atlantic. UPC and EAN generate point-of-sale data that are useful in establishing sales trends and setting forecasts and production schedules, even serving as a substitute for replenishment ordering in addition to their initial role of automating part of the sales process.

The next level, distribution coding, introduces its own problems. The shipping container is often scanned by laser beams at a distance, requiring high readability. Codes are also used to designate shelf and pallet locations. The result is a special code, UCC/EAN Code 128, developed jointly in the United States and Europe. The objective is to link to automated warehouse scanning and picking systems.

Manufacturing introduces still a different set of problems. Component parts may have more elaborate coding because they enter into multiple products. They require special codes with additional capacity to encompass more information.

New developments in automatic identification

Two-dimensional bar codes provide the ability to hold extensive information. Linear bar codes such as UPC or EAN or even UCC/EAN 128 are limited in information. Additional information such as documentation, routing or special environment instructions attached to individual items could serve a useful purpose. Two-dimensional bar codes were introduced to solve this problem. One label can carry from 50 to 100 times more data than a conventional bar code. They can also be read under poor lighting conditions. At present, there are at least 14 separate codes.

Radio frequency identification labels have not been widely used in the past, but the technology now presents new opportunities. A radio frequency identification label is fundamentally a transponder, interrogated by a radio transmitter and reflecting back data such as product identification (Kay 2000; Johnson 2000). There are two forms: active and passive. Active radio frequency identification labels are battery-powered labels and can be identified at a distance, such as vehicles passing at high speed. Passive tags must be read from short distances and can be used in distribution center environments. They now have the advantage of being low in cost. They augment control by indicating product location and status. Several labels can be read in a single action. All of this increases productivity by enabling faster and more immediate status reporting by item or vehicle. There has even been discussion about radio frequency identification replacing bar code labels. There is one impediment: a lack of common coding that may possibly be relieved by a prospective ISO standard.

Some radio frequency identification systems have the ability to write changes in labels, giving them more flexibility than standard bar code labels. In these »smart« labels, as an action takes place on an individual item, the label updates the new status on a magnetic strip or embedded microchip, similar to »smart« cards now entering the consumer market.

Smart radio frequency identification tags become an alternative information system, accompanying the objects to which they are attached. They have the advantage of accompanying packages and unit loads beyond the boundaries of the formal computer-based information system, providing new information through the label. The danger is that the formal system becomes uninformed about current status and out-of-date, requiring close to instantaneous, periodic links between the two systems.

The organization problem

Information technology transforms business operations. It automates processes that formerly required specialized intermediaries and human intervention. It compresses time intervals, increasing response to customers and reducing delays. At the same time it is changing the concept of organization, because it frees organization from time and place. It creates the ability to reach beyond corporate boundaries to coordinate operations with supplier networks and customers. In brief, it has becomes the enabler of the supply chain.

E-commerce has the most visible impact on organizational change. It promises the virtual supply chain, an organization of extreme flexibility. While stable, traditional supply chains will not disappear, they will use elements of IT to simplify operations and communicate with both suppliers and customers. One of the most important elements is its influence on interorganizational relations.

As IT technology develops, it offers new forms of relationship. Bressler & Grantham (2000) define three stages in electronic relationships: coordination, cooperation and collaboration. They are determined by two dimensions: complexity and creativity. Today the technology limits the extent to which these relationships can be developed. Text-based information systems limit communication to management of routine and project-oriented operations in which the need for managing complexity can be served by data alone or by simple visual imagery. This is in turn limited by the available bandwidth in electronic communication. Expansion of bandwidth makes possible more complex images and hence more free-form creativity. Bressler & Grantham suggest that the combination of high complexity and high creativity encourages the development of creative teamwork, described by the statement »we can't predict what we are going to produce or how we are going to produce it.« (p. 45) This invites the prospect of virtual teams.

They propose three levels of interorganizational relationship: coordination, cooperation and collaboration. *Coordination* is a form of process control, operating by data. It requires prior agreement on information system compatibility, data coding, data security and the internal processes of partners. However, it does not require awareness of the entire process. *Cooperation*, on the other hand, does. Partners share responsibility over the process and knowledge of the events both before and after the particular stage. It requires a higher level of communication in both frequency and the depth of information. *Collaboration* involves shared understanding and responsibility with a range from supply chain operations to product and technology development. It demands the least amount of predetermined structure. For an electronic organization, it requires the greatest amount of bandwidth capacity. Collaboration is obviously the most difficult to manage, and whether it can be done electronically is problematic.

One emerging form of electronic organization is the virtual Web-based supply chain. It is formed for a specific project task, such as a single product, and then dissolved after production ceases. It requires a broker/manager to provide organization, and a Web community of potential supply chain members (Franke 1999). The concept is supported by B2B market exchanges in which buyers and sellers within a particular industry can establish temporary connections. It may be further supported by application-specific providers (ASPs), who would provide a »neutral ground« for negotiation.

Concluding comments

Discussion of information systems never ends. The continual change in technology opens the door for new possibilities while destroying the old order. The Web-based information system enables the virtual supply chain that changes the assumptions behind more traditional models. Although the potential development and the reality are still far apart, the movement is visible. Organizational arrangements cannot help but change in this environment.

The professional orientation of supply chain management is also changing, from a focus on physical processes such as production, inventory management or transportation to managing information. This requires different technical knowledge. Automation of data collection, analysis and decisions relieves management of an impossible burden. IT also presents a danger of formalized knowledge without a guide: knowledge without a knower (Brown & Duguid 2000). Failure to take advantage of the information revolution presents a danger for the future. At the same time, without a human presence, the ability to manage is lost. The future development of IT and organizations is not predictable. But, as Drucker wrote (1999, p. 54) citing a historical context, in a lay journal:

»The new industries that emerged after the railroad owed little technologically to the steam engine or to the Industrial Revolution in general. They were not its 'children after the flesh – but they were its 'children after the spirit'.«

10. Market relationships

*»The new economic order is a relationship economy
dominated by services in combination with new information
and communication technologies.«*
(Morgan 1998, p. 5)

Supply chain strategy involves customers and relationships (Figure 10.1). The customer is the point of final demand. Relationships infer long-term association and possible active collaboration: the market-driven organization (Day, 2000). Strategy involves several distinct elements: 1) identifying individual customer requirements, 2) developing and supplying products to match them, 3) coordinating the entire order process and 4) capturing orders early and transmitting them directly to production. Advantage comes from responding precisely to customer needs, reducing cost by minimizing inventory in the supply chain.

The new environment of business and technology has created new market relationships. The rapidly developing business of e-commerce creates new opportunity and change from established patterns of business. Ease of communication encourages close relationships with both intermediate and final customers. The final customer becomes a partner.

The underlying theme is to match products and services to individual customer needs. The new combination of technology and organization requires getting as close as possible to the specific requirements and the time of need, but it also enables involving the customer directly in the operations and even the configuration of the supply chain itself.

This relationship has several significant characteristics:

- The convenience of the customer is dominant.
- Operations take place in real time.

Figure 10.1. Customer Relationship Management

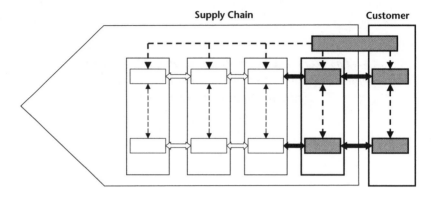

- Customers now order directly from vendors.
- The direct order process captures actual product demand.
- Markets stress time compression in filling orders.
- Customers share market information with the supply chain.
- Customers collaborate in the supply chain decision processes.

This chapter deals with four general topics that currently define market and customer relationships:

- the market-driven supply chain
- the changing nature of market demand
- organizational links to the market
- the role of sales and customers in the supply chain.

The market-driven supply chain

Customers and relationships

The supply chain begins with the customer. The ultimate aim is to deliver products and services to satisfy customers. Customer preferences ultimately determine what is produced and when and how it is delivered (Blackwell 1997). Preferences ultimately result in decisions about structure, organizations and processes.

The new environment of business stresses market relationships – long-term associations potentially involving mutual collaboration between supplier and customer. The climate is more than dealing with individual customers but understanding the direction of markets and their implications for the supply chain. It involves the enterprise in both sensing and responding to markets through strategic actions (Day 1999). The strategic thrust goes beyond the scope of this discussion to formal marketing programs, but it also presents implications and specific direction for the supply chain.

Who is the customer? There are at least three. One is the ultimate consumer, either served through the Web or other direct sales media. The second is the »trade«, a collection of retailers, distributors, other intermediaries between production and the ultimate user. The third category comprises the series of industrial suppliers in the supply chain. Each has special requirements.

Three types of marketing relationships are embedded in the supply chain: order fulfillment processes, product configuration and strategic marketing. Each presents unique requirements.

At a minimum, order processes include standard products and processes. They include forecasting, scheduling issues and delivery. The focus is time-related.

Product configuration allows customers and sometimes the trade to select product options and add modifications to basic product designs.

Strategic marketing involves customer contact for purposes of long-term planning and market analysis.

Table 10.1. Customers and characteristics

Customers	Orders	Configuration	Strategy
Consumers	Direct service Small quantities Market data	Individual options Market data	E-commerce Market data
Trade	Large quantities Concern with process Collaboration Market data	Volume options Market data	Collaboration New structures Process redesign Market data
Suppliers	Focused production Standard products Collaboration	Specific products	Collaboration Capacity and schedule data

The combination of customers and relationships presents different forms of opportunity and requirements for service from the supply chain (Table 10.1).

The consumer-oriented supply chain is a direct retail marketing and delivery system. It deals with small quantities, and service focuses on product inventory and delivery. Transactions produce data that can be utilized directly in the order process. Strategic possibilities include Internet retailing.

The trade-related supply chain is both simpler in operation because it handles larger order quantities and more complex because it places an intermediate step between consumption and production. The simplicity reflects the structure of the traditional marketing channel of manufacturer to wholesaler to retailer, but the lack of direct contact with the final market makes forecasting difficult. Collaboration between trade customers and manufacturers becomes important for production and inventory planning. These relationships generate data useful both within the relationship and for long-term strategy in customer selection and retention.

Trade relationships can be both strategic and transaction-oriented interactions. Strategic relationships deal with negotiation, usually with partial or full visibility of supply chain data and linked production schedules. The scope can involve component and product design, selection, production and delivery schedules. Non-strategic relations involve routine order transactions of standard or limited product and service configurations with limited discretion, and the primary concerns are administrative efficiency, inventory and price.

Customer relationships

Trade customers play an essential role in determining the direction of the supply chain because of their knowledge of markets and product usage (Prahalad et al. 2000). This role has two aspects: placing orders and configuring products and services. For orders, the instant of need should trigger supply operations. Replenishment can respond to point-of-sale data, inventory changes, operating schedules or anticipated consumption. The general concept is for the supply chain to position itself as close to the customer as possible. It requires close observation of customer behavior and processes. Ultimately this is a marketing task, but it determines supply chain operations. One application of this concept is Collaborative Planning, Forecasting and Replenishment, discussed later.

Configuring products at the point of sale not only matches immediate customer requirements but also provides direction for product options and supplier selection. These orders provide immediate information on preferences, production schedules or even supplier selection. Product needs are potentially infinite, but competencies and resources limit production possibilities. Supply chain management limits the range of options in configuration, but marketing must determine which ones customers can choose. We explore this as mass customization.

Push versus pull

The roles of marketing and the supply chain are interconnected. Both are concerned with process and serving the customer as its focus. The supply chain of necessity is becoming a market-driven organization, responding to market pressures. Where the supply chain anticipates customer demand, it is a *push* orientation, placing inventory at the point of sale. This concept is shifting to an orientation where the customer order *pulls* the product through the supply chain.

The push concept produces to a demand forecast to meet projected sales targets. It requires inventory at the point of sale, because of the lead times required to produce and distribute products to the market. A push system is costly because of inventory and the danger of missed sales by not having the right product available. It does not respond rapidly to market changes.

Pull strategies treat orders individually. The supply chain only operates on the basis of orders received. Products are made to order, accompanied by direct coordination with suppliers. It is possible to configure orders to individual customers, to create micro market segments, as small as one individual customer. In theory, it is more responsive, with production matched to individual customer orders. In practice, even the most responsive system must anticipate the general direction of demand and respond by organizing the supply network and capacity, possibly producing components and materials to match a general forecast. The ultimate impact on supply chain structure would be a virtual supply chain of suppliers, assembly and distribution created for a single order.

Mass customization

The underlying theme of relationships between the supply chain and the customer is seeking solutions to customer needs. This involves product development to match individual customer requirements one on one. Instead of using mass production to push standardized products towards a market, it becomes a process of building unique products for individual customers. This extends the supply process beyond standardized customer orders to respond to all customer orders individually. The message of mass customization for many product categories is that there is no longer a standard product but only solutions matched to individual customer requirements (Pine 1993). Customization becomes a necessity for creating localized products in an international orientation (Van Hoek 1998).

The potential for customization ranges from pure standardization to complete individualization. Not all products can be customized, nor can all customer orders be treated in the same way. Customization appears to be a continuum. Lampel & Mintzberg (1996) identify five distinct categories (Figure 10.2):

- *pure standardization*, in which all products are identical and there is little opportunity for differentiation, as in basic foods;
- *segmented standardization*, in which there are options available in different distribution systems, such as cars and personal computers;
- *customized standardization*, which includes performing final assembly operations from modular products;
- *tailored customization*, which broadens the perspective to include alteration of components for final assembly; and
- *pure customization*, which involves the design process to create truly individual products.

Each category involves a different stage in the supply process. The ability to customize ultimately reflects the flexibility inherent in

Figure 10.2. Options in Mass Customization

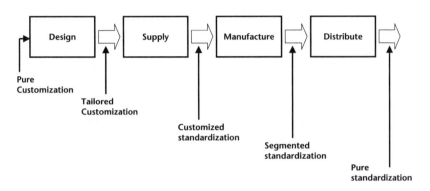

product and service design and the ability to add or combine components or even to reformulate the product. The current wave of home grocery services is essentially segmented standardization, with individual orders varying substantially from each other, sold and delivered through a different process than conventional grocery channels. Personal computers reflect customized standardization, where attaching different component modules can satisfy product preferences. Tailored customization reflects its name, where the customer selects components and materials and orders the assembled unit. Finally, pure customization involves one-of-a-kind products, such as artwork or building construction.

Process design for customization

Product design for customization has implications for management. First is the product architecture. Designing in product modules allows for flexibility in product assembly. Components can be produced in volume and assembled into a variety of final product forms as »mushroom products« (Mather 1992). Basic modules can be produced through mass production but are incomplete until they are attached to other modules. A modular product strategy requires developing a product line of multiple products with compatible components and standard interfaces. This requires close coordination when modules are purchased from outside vendors. The combinations of modules then define products and the product line.

On the other hand, some products are inherently modular: designed to add, subtract or combine components to generate product variation. Personal computers are assembled from standard components, but the specifications, functions and performance differ depending on what the customer has ordered. Customization also requires a product-line strategy. This has two different dimensions. It is either the same basic model with different additional options or different models combining modules to produce different characteristics. This raises operational questions about where assembly will take place and where component inventory will be located.

The basic model suggests doing the final configuration at distribution stages. Different model would pull this operation towards the factory. Further, if product modules will support multiple products, there must be either simultaneous product-line development or compatibility between modules.

Customization becomes an example of a postponement strategy. Avoiding final assembly until the last possible moment reduces inventory costs, provided that there is no question about maintaining quality in this final stage. Postponement also allows for a broader range of customer choice.

Customization increases forecast accuracy. Forecasting components for a product line deals with larger volumes and is inherently more accurate than for finished products that must project demand for specific configurations. This leads to better control, higher levels of service and lower inventory costs because of the reduced need for safety stock.

The degree of customization reflects the organization: how far should the customer order penetrate the system before being served? Standard products without individual customer identity would be filled at the distribution stage. Pure customization is completely identified with one customer. Customization therefore has implications for the information system, production and distribution. Order systems must carry the details of the order to the point where it can be filled. Production must be flexible to adapt to changing product order characteristics. Distribution may require unique handling to deliver to the customer. These become obstacles to further implementation because they require re-engineering of the entire supply chain as a process (Greene 1999).

Customization as strategy

Customization has strategic implications. First, it is the ultimate pull system. Orders are specific and unique requests. Production must be able to match requests on the production line or in the distribution process. Flexible production begins with product design, but it also requires managing the production process to match components to the order and to make rapid changeovers from one product variation to another.

Mass customization necessitates advance planning about the degree of flexibility to build into the system. McCutcheon et al. (1994) point out that customization has a price in a loss of responsiveness. They propose several possible solutions:

- analyze customer expectations;
- alter product design for modularity and ease of manufacture;
- alter production processes to increase flexibility;
- manage demand by controlling the options available, enforcing time fences in production and improving forecasting methods; and
- hold more finished goods inventory.

Managing more finished goods inventory is not usually a desirable choice. Another choice is to develop commonality in product components and to change combinations as orders come in. This usually requires extra production capacity for flexibility supported through agile manufacturing.

Customization in some cases may involve virtual supply chains, organized for one specific product configuration but then dissolved until another specific order comes into the system. In the case of capital equipment, this can amount to single unit quantities. Alcatel in the past built customized digital telephone switches for individual telecommunication companies. Unique supply networks were organized, with individual suppliers designated for each order.

Services can also be customized, apart from the product to which they are attached. This has been called establishing multiple threads through the supply chain. Customers establish relationships with their suppliers in different ways to match previously established internal systems. They may also need to contact and coordinate suppliers. It makes logical sense to adapt delivery, billing, documentation, status reporting services and coordination to meet these needs. There may be as many different pathways (threads) through the supply chain as there are customers.

Mass customization offers advantages in opportunities for learning, both for customer preferences and improved production and supply. It provides a vehicle to experiment and to adapt to changing preferences. At the same time, it offers a way to reduce inventory requirements because customers specify their specific product requirements as firm orders pulled through the system, rather than as items pushed through as speculative inventories.

Nike

Nike iD lets customers design and order footwear on-line. They choose colors and size and add a message on the back of up to eight characters. Orders are transmitted to Nike factories in Asia, where shoes are made and shoes are sent directly to customers. At the time of reporting, there were limits to the system: 400 pairs per day versus 600,000 from daily mass production. The company initially expected to lose money from the system but to develop a market as the integration of 3-D and interactive software improves (*Custom Manufacturing ...* 1999). The principal difficulties have been order cycle times of up to 3 weeks and developing overseas partners to handle these orders.

Vendor-oriented coordination

Supply chains within specific industries have taken steps to develop stronger coordination ties among members. The general thrust has been to shift towards a pull orientation responding to customer orders. A true pull environment where customers wait for custom-ordered products is not usually possible, especially in mass production industries such as consumer package goods. The closest solution is to gain information about demand early, so that supply follows closely on demand.

Three prominent efforts in coordination have been Distribution

Requirements Planning (DRP); Quick Response (QR), developed within the garment industry and later applied to groceries; and Efficient Consumer Response (ECR), a collection of independent initiatives with a common theme of reducing inventory within the grocery industry. Two current outcomes are Vendor-Managed Inventory (VMI), extending the supply chain to the retail store shelf and Collaborative Planning, Forecasting and Replenishment (CPFR), an initiative to provide focused interfunctional communication between supplier and customer.

Distribution Requirements Planning (DRP)

DRP projects inventory and transportation requirements for the movement of products to customers, beginning with projections of actual sales transactions. It is a planning system to communicate and coordinate inventory movement and position by specific location and time. It is also a push system. Products are delivered precisely when and where they are needed on the basis of forecast demand. It becomes a schedule to determine aggregate inventory and transportation requirements by combining individual product (stock-keeping unit) demands by location in specific time periods. It was created as a counterpart to MRP, discussed in Chapter 5. It becomes the basis for precise delivery plans that indicate inventory requirements compared with storage and transport system capacity. Further, it becomes a basis for production planning and scheduling.

The structure of DRP consists of the forecast and a bill of distribution, a set of products and quantities necessary to make up an individual order, similar in concept to a bill of materials found in manufacturing systems based on MRP. This bill changes daily or weekly for each customer. Bills are aggregated by time period to create the distribution plan. The system is governed by the sales forecast by item and time period for each stock location. Movements are projected using the net changes in inventory at each location. By using the forecast to project specific future needs, it provides vision to inventory and production planning. It depends, however, on the reliability of the forecast. As an alternative, it may be possible to ask customers to provide their own future buying

Table 10.2. Distribution Requirements Planning (DRP)

		Time period				
		Week 1	Week 2	Week 3	Week 4	Week 5
Demand forecast		100	160	80	260	120
Customer orders processed		60	20	0	200	0
Inventory at start of week		110	300	140	310	300
Inventory at end of week		50	140	60	50	180
Incoming supply at factory		0	250	0	250	250
Orders to be placed	250	0	250	250	0	0

plans, again in specific product, time and quantity detail. DRP operates as a push system to anticipate demand, with a structure that allows managers to provide resources to match these needs.

Table 10.2 demonstrates the process. Inventory replenishment for one product at one location is planned for period of 5 weeks, based on a weekly sales forecast. Information is provided on minimum order quantity, safety stock and order lead time. The perspective is that of the planner at week 1, looking ahead over the 5-week period. In week 1, actual customer orders of 60 units can be supplied easily from stock on hand, 110 units carried over from the previous week (week 0). Projected demand for week 2 is for 160 units. Actual customer orders have been received for 20 units. A previously ordered supply of 250 units (in week 0) has arrived, making the total inventory available 300 units. This exceeds expected demand so that 140 units are carried over to week 3. We can meet demand in week 3, but looking ahead, we will be short 200 units in week 4. A supply order will be placed for 250 units in week 2 for delivery in week 4. A further supply order will be placed in week 3 for delivery in week 5. This calculation is paralleled by similar ones by stock-keeping unit and location and combined to create a comprehensive plan.

DRP has two major requirements: management and coordination with partners in the distribution process shown in Figure 10.3 (Martin 1994). Successful DRP requires sharing information on scheduling requirements. Buyers must share their future buying plans and changes with their vendors. Management must also rec-

Figure 10.3. Distribution System Planning (DRP)

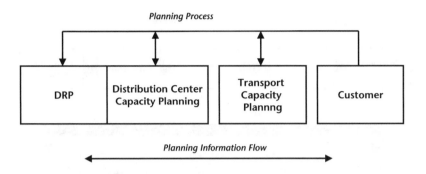

ognize that local and product requirements can be unstable and must be interpreted as they are aggregated. The size of the data problem is immense when the number of stock-keeping units is multiplied by the number of inventory locations.

The advantages are the potential inventory savings and the ability to incorporate special knowledge, including seasonal factors, promotional buying and other special considerations. By using advance knowledge, the inventory system becomes more predictable, reducing the need for non-productive inventory safety stock. The forecast is more accurate when it is based on final sales transactions rather than orders received at the factory. DRP has become accepted practice in consumer goods industries and in some industrial products companies as well. It can be valuable in identifying capacity problems and negotiating delivery terms. However, it is also vulnerable to the accuracy of the forecasting process and to the willingness of partners to share data.

Quick Response

The Quick Response approach focuses on faster communication between members, enabling them to respond better to rapid changes in the retail marketplace. It was initiated in the garment industries to increase the industry response to change in product demand and to reduce total pipeline costs. It utilizes a combination of EDI and standardized bar codes to capture demand by stock-keep-

Figure 10.4. Customer/Supplier Information Flow

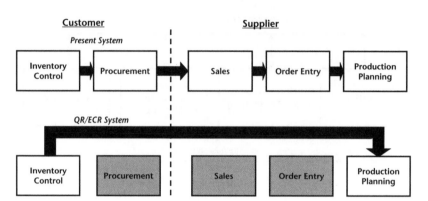

ing unit and transmit it backward through the supply chain, from the retail store through distribution centers to final stages of garment assembly and on to thread suppliers. The Universal Product Code (in the United States) provides point-of-sale data to distributors and manufacturers through EDI connections. Physical operations identify products in shipping containers through UCC Code 128 that can be easily recognized by laser scanners at distribution centers. Manufacturing control uses a standard manufacturing component bar code 039. The major step was sharing of immediately generated data from retail stores throughout the supply chain, even to basic material and thread suppliers.

Effective implementation required change in both manufacturing and retail planning and operations, bypassing traditional steps involving procurement and sales in favor of direct communication from customer inventory to vendor production planning (Figure 10.4). It also forced standardization of EDI and product identification procedures within several trade groups. Spectacular early gains from implementation were reported. Most were the result of replacing a paper document flow and achieving better data within the supply chain. This system involved customers in the supply process through sharing of data. As lead times became shorter, it created incentives on both sides to process orders immediately and reduce inventory, moving towards a JIT-type system in distribution. It also encouraged last-minute ordering. Manufacturers became more dependent on demand forecasts as their inventory buffer protection disappeared (Whiteoak 1994).

In Australia, Quick Response workshops were used to develop common goals and communication standards. They provided a vehicle for individual companies to form supply chain partnerships, supplemented with monitoring and feedback for continued improvement. Their success came from open communication, the role of facilitators and support of upper levels of management (Perry et al. 1999). The net result of Quick Response has been to create a closer partnership in distribution between vendor and customer, and it has become a prototype for other distribution systems.

Efficient Consumer Response (ECR)

The ECR approach was initiated and widely promoted by a consulting firm Kurt Salmon Associates (1993) and has been responsible for several process innovations within the grocery industry. It embraces five separate concepts (Knill 1997):

- *EDI* for paperless, seamless communication among manufacturers, distributors and retailers. At the time when ECR was introduced, conventional EDI using specifically developed protocols was the standard. However, the Internet is an easier vehicle for EDI messages.
- *Category management*, which emphasizes reorganization of merchandising and buying operations to manage similar products as separate business units. It has also meant reduction in the number of stock-keeping units through product line simplification.
- *Continuous replenishment*, using demand-generated reordering and replenishment using point-of-sale data at the retail store.
- *Flow-through distribution*, emphasizing reduction in handling of merchandise by use of cross-docking and direct store delivery, bypassing inventory holding at intermediate warehouses and distribution centers.
- *Partnerships* to share data and supply chain activities to increase supply chain service and reduce costs. The key element is data sharing. This is hindered when partners are not ready technologically or culturally to proceed.

Figure 10.5. Efficient Consumer Response

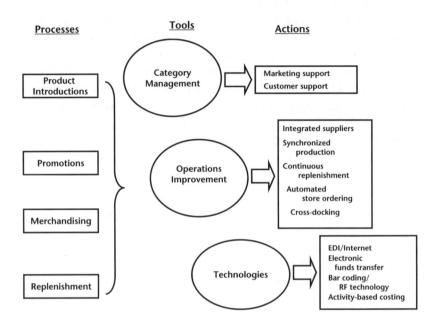

These are encompassed within four processes: product introductions, promotions, merchandising and replenishment, shown in Figure 10.5. These processes rely on three categories of tools: category management, operations improvements and information-based technologies. In turn, they result in a variety of actions to support these concepts and processes.

ECR differs from Quick Response, which focused on communication and bar coding, by encouraging reorganization of other processes in the supply chain: managing replenishment inventory, new product introductions, promotions and product variety. It involves customer collaboration through involvement in retail store and supporting distribution operations. It has reduced replenishment cycles by encouraging sort-and-ship movement to replace more conventional buying and storing and cross-docking where products move from manufacturer to store shelf, stopping only for intermediate sorting before moving to individual retail stores. For many product lines, distribution centers were converted to cross-dock operation. It has also encouraged the development and implementation of warehouse management system software to provide closer real-time control over distribution center operations.

ECR has been criticized for lack of progress. The major weakness is in partnerships between companies. Copacino (1996), for example, emphasizes that ECR is a not a specific program in itself but part of a larger concept of supplier-retailer value creation. He argues for segmenting retailers on the basis of their individual merchandising practices and developing supply chain strategies to match. Other failures include the emphasis on cost reduction and not taking advantage of the potential for revenue enhancement through expanded service opportunities (Horowitz 1996).

To some extent, all five of the components have been adopted, although unevenly. Category management and continuous replenishment have shown the greatest objective success. Perhaps the most significant change resulting from ECR in the United States has been to change the culture of the grocery industry towards co-operative efforts (Toth 1998).

The European experience apparently follows closely on the United States experience (Kotzab 1999). Full implementation of ECR in Europe would reduce total distribution costs by almost 6% by one estimate: 84% of this from operating costs and the rest from inventory reduction.

Poirier & Reiter (1996, p. 46) provide a statement of caution:

»It is critical to remember that ECR is a single process within a larger process and not an end in itself. It is just one tactical step in a closed loop information system designed to facilitate the construction of an effective strategy for the deployment of industry resources toward the eventual aim of better satisfying the demands of a consumer driven marketing system.«

Vendor-Managed Inventory

Vendor-Managed Inventory is one outcome of ECR and follows from continuous replenishment. The major difference is that, in continuous replenishment, the customer takes responsibility for inventory at the point of sale, whereas in Vendor-Managed Inventory the supplier manages the process. In some cases, the vendor is selling on consignment and owns the inventory up to the time that the product is sold to the final customer. In effect, the supply chain »rents« the store shelf from the retailer and manages merchandising and replenishment across the store shelf in response to forecasts. Responsibility and control shift from the retail store to the manufacturer. Because it is based on forecasts, it extends the push system one step further, to the point of sale. It has also been adopted outside of the grocery industry, including garments (Sender 1998) and electrical products distribution (Franza 1998).

Reduced inventory is one of the most compelling arguments for Vendor-Managed Inventory. A simulation study by Hewlett-Packard demonstrated that Vendor-Managed Inventory produced lower inventory costs for both manufacturers and retailers (Waller et al. 1999).

From the manufacturers' or distributors' perspectives, there are both advantages and disadvantages. The advantage is the logistic control that it offers over shipment and inventory. It eliminates fluctuations stemming from retail buying practices. Vendor-Managed Inventory may accompany category management programs that allow the manufacturer to merchandise their products more effectively. The disadvantages are the difficulties in unstable order patterns and the need to prepare shipments for individual retail stores (Cooke 1998). It is most successful when the number of items in the product line is limited and demand is stable. It also fails when retailers either do not want to share point-of-sale data or do not use it themselves.

The criticism of Vendor-Managed Inventory by the major retailers has been that it has not been integrated into their own processes. Retailers conventionally order in fixed quantities. In a Vendor-Managed Inventory system, the supplier makes shipments based on the difference between actual and maximum inventory levels, based on sales data, performing production planning on the basis of forecasts. Point-of-sale data are not always available and are often difficult to interpret. Withdrawals from distribution centers are sometimes used instead, resulting in lagged and distorted data. Deliveries must be precise in time and quantity, as the retailer carries no safety stock. Retailers also complain that they have no visibility into the suppliers' system to identify problem areas.

Vendor-customer collaboration

Customers ultimately configure the supply chain through their product and service choices. Customer interaction appears at two levels: intermediate and final demand. Intermediate levels include retailers and distributors. Final demand focuses on direct ordering and product configuring by the customer. They involve distinctly different processes: one to manage inventories through better coordination and joint forecasting and the other for the customer to place firm, possibly customized orders.

Collaborative Planning, Forecasting and Replenishment

Collaborative Planning, Forecasting and Replenishment stresses operational relationships between customer and vendor. Increasingly, they are oriented to Web-based value chains. The focus is external, linking both supply and demand. However, it changes internal business practices when they are directly linked to external partners (Frook 1998). Collaborative Planning, Forecasting and Replenishment requires more detail compared with aggregate market forecasting by product or region, because it focuses on data for individual key customer accounts.

In one sense, Collaborative Planning, Forecasting and Replenishment seeks to accomplish what earlier initiatives have tried before: standardizing shared data and making it visible between trading partners. It directly addresses the problem of vendors that are forced to operate without knowledge of the market. This often led to erroneous data, resulting in practices such as loading the system with extra inventory to avoid loss of potential sales (*Trading Partners Unite* ... 1998). It requires acceptance of a common data and communication infrastructure that includes specification of 1) data content and format, 2) a communication vehicle to support sharing of data and 3) security procedures.

To date, Collaborative Planning, Forecasting and Replenishment efforts have aimed for one jointly prepared single forecast. The Collaborative Planning, Forecasting and Replenishment process begins with a generic model (VICS 1998a):

- Develop an alignment of functions as a joint process between vendor and customer.
- Create a joint business plan.
- Create a sales forecast.
- Identify exceptions to the sales forecast.
- Collaborate on exception items.
- Create the customer-defined order forecast.

Collaborative Planning, Forecasting and Replenishment requires organizational realignment from functional activities to process (VICS 1998c). First, it is oriented towards a micro-marketing holistic approach to serving specific customers. The objective for both parties is to satisfy final customers (VICS 1998b). It is also cross-functional, including sales, marketing, finance, logistics, production and procurement. The contribution of Collaborative Planning, Forecasting and Replenishment is in linking these functions across organizational boundaries, communicating and supporting joint business planning.

The three levels of responsibility: management, interorganizational operations and internal decision-making, play distinct roles. Management must decide on alternatives to holding inventory, such as additional production capacity, or allocation. The operational issues concern how these joint processes are integrated into internal operations. Internal decisions involve functional teams within partnering organizations to commit their organizations to specific actions.

More than data, Collaborative Planning, Forecasting and Replenishment offers a vehicle for collaborative planning (Figure 10.6). One early experiment between Nabisco as a supplier and Wegman's, a major United States food chain, resulted in a joint business plan with defined objectives and a partnership agreement that identifies improvement goals, collaboration points, the information to be shared and joint performance metrics. The effort resulted in sales growth in the product category and intentions to expand the trial (*Internet-based Supply Chain Collaboration ...* 1998). Another earlier experiment between Wal-Mart (a retailer) and Warner-Lambert (a pharmaceutical manufacturer) was equally successful (Doherty 1998). Despite these early indications, how far Collaborative Planning, Forecasting and Replenishment will succeed in benefiting both sides is still uncertain.

Figure 10.6. Collaborative Planning, Forecasting and Replenishment (CPFR)

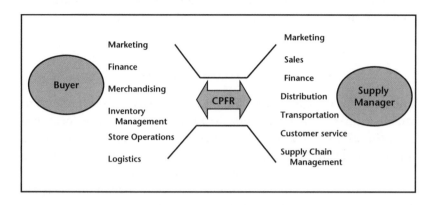

The traditional emphasis in both forecasting and supplier-customer relations has been on historical data and reaction to past events. Collaborative Planning, Forecasting and Replenishment provides faster response through a unifying framework in which supply and demand become visible to both vendor and retailer. Collaborative Planning, Forecasting and Replenishment emphasizes development of common forecasts between vendor and customer, taking into account market factors and supply constraints. However, it requires commitment and trust on both sides. The trading relationship becomes the foundation.

Software development is an enabling factor in the success of Collaborative Planning, Forecasting and Replenishment. The direction lies in linking both customers and enterprise systems together for rapid and free flow of information. One commercial program currently available communicates customer demand and replenishment requirements, notifying users of new promotions or deviations from forecast. It includes store-level sales forecasting and freight consolidation, displayed graphically and adaptable for individual customers.

Sharing data across organizational boundaries presents both compatibility and security problems. The use of XML computer language may overcome this barrier. With more accurate data, dangers of disclosure become greater. Suppliers may deal with several customers at the same time at equal levels of intensity. Customers may similarly deal with several suppliers. The problems are not only from accidental disclosure by individuals but also the security of the computer and communication systems themselves. Security becomes an important element in partnership relations.

Sales force automation

The quest for real-time order data is the objective of most efforts to establish links with customers. Traditionally, the sales force has been the ultimate connection to the customer. This is now being supplemented by direct order systems that allow customers to take their own initiative and place orders directly in the system.

Demand management, however, is now becoming feasible through sales force automation and product configuration programs. These enables sales staff to interact with corporate databases to access supporting information and to the supply chain for coordinating orders and activities. Much of the functionality of this software is intended to make sales staff more productive by placing more information at their fingertips. This includes such features as customer and product information, market analysis and competitor analysis. It makes possible the new concept of one-to-one marketing from suppliers to individual customers (Rogers 1997).

New sales force automation software enables orders to be taken over the Web directly into the supply chain from the customer's office (Vizard & Bull 1998). One advantage is that transcription time and scheduling buffers are eliminated, substituting »hard« data from firm orders for estimates from forecast data, thereby reducing uncertainty of demand.

Customers ordering for themselves and software agent technology further automate the sales process. Software as virtual buying and selling agents can roam the net to find specific products or customers and make offers, without necessary direct human intervention on either side. When they interact, there will be immediate pressure to reduce prices and provide precisely specified service. This will change many products into commodities, placing a premium on operational performance. These developments reduce the requirements for sales service and also reduce the time between requirement and ordering.

Another dimension is order documentation. Automating paperwork can do more than merely free the time of sales staff or reduce transcription errors. It is a relatively small step to interactive communication directly to inventory files or even the production schedule to provide delivery promise dates without leaving the customers' premises. Product configuration on-line is a further development. Product configurators can present predetermined options, »choice boards«, so that customers can make specific decisions for customized product orders (Slywotzky 2000). The configurator makes customers into designers of their own products. In some cases, first-tier and even second-tier suppliers can be accessed to query about special options or expedite production schedules.

Two other developments, the extranet and software agent technology, also change the nature of sales operations. Customers can order directly without human intervention from extranets, with in-store or remote Web connections. They can be guided through menus to choose options, delivery and payment plans, reducing the cost of individual transactions. These orders can then enter directly into production schedules, ensuring accuracy and reducing cycle times.

Conclusion

The front end of the supply chain is the frontier of the supply chain. Market segments become smaller and more precisely defined. The underlying trend is towards one-on-one marketing. This can be translated into more product variety and supply flexibility. Simultaneously, the ability of customers to search the market for lower prices increases pressure for lower costs.

For the supply system, emphasis on the demand chain is beneficial. Real-time order data is the goal, and Collaborative Planning, Forecasting and Replenishment and sales force automation have brought the supply chain much closer. Another is making the system more transparent to the customer. This affects cooperative relations and shifts the power to manage the chain to customers.

Several trends are changing the marketplace: Internet consumer shopping, extranet industrial purchasing, individual product configuration through mass customization, close collaboration between manufacturers and suppliers with intermediate customers such as retailers and automated sales contact. Even in situations that normally require human interpretation, more transactions will be automated.

The field is driven first by changes in technology. The Web offers comprehensive search capabilities, information and convenience. Mass customization requires agile manufacturing, with computer-based design and production control, small production runs and connections in real time. Collaboration requires groupware that permits interactive communication. The monetary volume of sales force automation applications will surpass ERP.

The principal obstacle to this transformation lies with organization of the process. Responding to the market involves design of options for customers, information flow to indicate demand and flexibility in response. Interfunctional coordination is a traditional hurdle. When interorganizational coordination is added, the problem is compounded. Strategy can only be successful when the supply chain can sense the direction of the market as change takes place.

11. Global issues

»At Cisco, anything outside of San Jose is international.
It's just the way we plan, control and ship our product.«
(Linc Holland, Vice President,
External Manufacturing, Cisco Systems,
quoted in Laseter 1998, p. 241)

Almost every supply chain is international to some degree. There are always materials, components or services originating in another country that enter into the final product of the supply chain. The global concept of the supply chain, however, is more than incidental. It deliberately recognizes the necessity to supply markets in multiple national markets, perhaps using overseas production. The global network is an extension of the domestic supply chain. It is more complex, faces a diverse set of environmental conditions and is inherently more difficult to understand and manage. It also deals with a global economy in transition from autonomous countries to an integrated system of producing, trading and consuming, driven by technology and where the vision of the ultimate goal is also changing.

What makes the global supply chain different? In a conceptual sense, very little. In practice, the global dimension presents major challenges:

- supplying a unique value proposition to customers around the world;
- meeting intensifying competition from around the world;
- adapting to multiple national environments with differing cultures, political and economic systems, business practices and infrastructures;
- the global politics of economic and trade relationships;
- the availability and level of infrastructure in transport and telecommunications;

- the complexity of managing an extended network; and
- the impact of geography: time and distance and the location of markets.

This is a typical but not exhaustive list. The problem is illustrated in Figure 11.1. First, the most important differences relate to the customer. The global supply chain must come as close as possible to meeting specific national market requirements through specific products and services matched to individual customer requirements. Second, meeting competition places pressures to seek out the most efficient sources of supply. This drive for efficiency often conflicts with matching customer preferences. Third, the supply chain must adapt simultaneously to multiple constraints posed by the environments in which it operates. All of these are changing rapidly along with the world economy. Fourth, the immutable constraint of distance and transit times affects the dynamic response of the supply chain as a system. The management task is immense: to coordinate a complex system when the sheer scope challenges the ability to control it.

Three elements make the global supply chain possible: changes in global economic policy plus the technological revolutions in transport and telecommunication. The trend to lower tariffs and removal of non-tariff barriers plus the development of regional trading communities such as the European Union encourage international trade and investment. The growth of air cargo, motor carriers and motorways and ocean containers make the physical movement of goods easier than ever before. Finally, telecommunications including computer-to-computer communication make it possible to coordinate operations across the globe. Together they have changed the entire perspective on global markets and supply.

The impact of the change in the global market can be found in this quotation from a recent comment from a McKinsey study: »We are moving from a world where 90% of the competitive advantage was derived from geography to a world where 90% will be non-geographic.« (Bryan et al 1999, p. 7). Their sense of the term geographic is anything that impedes the movement of products, whether physical, cultural or political. The implication for the supply chain is clear: the ability to bring products to world markets and to meet the needs of customers with competitive prices will be crucial in competition.

Figure 11.1. Global Issues

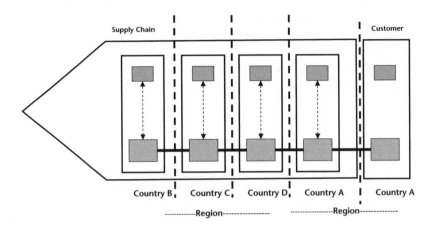

This chapter first discusses the key environmental elements affecting the development of the supply chain. The second section then provides an overview of the direction of trade and investment. The third section examines the international corporation and its evolution towards global integration. At this point, we shift to the supply chain itself, which presents issues both parallel to and different from those of the international corporation. The final section looks at logistics issues in international commerce. With the high turbulence of the international arena, the overriding purpose is not so much to describe current development, except where it contributes to overall understanding, but to present a more durable framework in which to interpret more current events for strategy in the supply chain.

The orientation of the supply chain

There is a distinction between international logistics and the global supply chain. Logistics involves the movement and inventory of products. International logistics and international trade have close parallels. International logistics manages product movement across national or regional boundaries, including transport, inventory, customs barriers, telecommunications and related topics. Part of logistics involves domestic processes within host countries. The other part is international. The global supply chain adds the structure and location of activities and organizations to supply and distribute products to global markets. It determines where logistics take place. Both domestic and international logistics together with the procurement, production and distribution structure become part of the supply chain.

Options

There are many ways to become involved in the global economy: export and import trade, direct foreign investment, alliances and partnerships and other contractual relationships. Export and import trade may involve different modes of transport, inventory and coordinating communication. Direct foreign investment in production or distribution overseas can require both domestic and international movements. Alliances and partnerships bring in outside parties for production or distribution, without direct investment. Licensing gives the right to produce or sell products, either as independent operations or as part of global supply and distribution networks. The global supply chain may include all of these within a single network as components of a process of supply and distribution.

History

The evolution of economic internationalism begins with trade. Investment evolved with trading companies. The patterns of early modern multinational corporate development were established in the period prior to World War I, oriented first towards exploitation of resources and secondarily towards the development of markets. These subsidiary organizations focused on limited tasks and adapting to the environments of their host countries. The same patterns continued between the world wars. Only a few companies began patterns of investment to develop markets on a systematic basis. This pattern continued in after World War II into the 1970s. Investment pursued markets, and international companies set up produc-

Figure 11.2. The Global Corporate Network

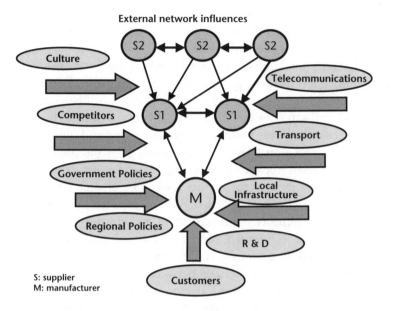

tion to serve local consumption. These are described in Figure 11.2.

Two technologies: transport and telecommunications, combined with the convergence of markets towards global products and changes in trade and political policies, have changed international supply investment decisions (Hasnet 1998). Highway transportation within Europe, air cargo and containers in transoceanic trade provide manufacturing with physical mobility, allowing it to pursue low labor costs in the electronics, software and garment industries and production specialization in the automobile and other manufacturing industries. As ships become larger and more efficient, transport costs have decreased, encouraging more trade in manufactured goods with formerly remote areas.

The growth of air cargo reflects a further impetus. This is partly from expanding services but also from the increasing value of manufactured products relative to their weight. The ratio emphasizes the importance of time over freight costs. The physical volume by air, measured in tonnage, has been extremely small in comparison to ocean transport, dominated by bulk materials. The proportion of trade by value moving by air, however, is significantly larger. For global trade, the proportion was about 32% of value in 1998, reflecting electronic products, component parts for a variety of industries and garments (Forsyth 1999).

Telecommunications and specifically computer-to-computer communication has carried this investment in production one step further: towards close coordination. Expansion of fiber-optic cable networks and satellites has made global communication feasible on a larger scale than ever possible before. Satellites and other forms of wireless transmission free communication from the physical infrastructure of fixed networks, extending networks into countries that had little prior investment in this area. The change has been accompanied by the rapid diffusion of computer technology and computer-to-computer communication around the world. The effect has been to standardize production and distribution processes across national boundaries. Transactions, production schedules and designs can be transmitted between parties regardless of distance, with effects that are still being absorbed. The most dramatic example is probably the development of the Indian software and data-processing industries, to write programs and perform data entry, transmitting their product via satellite and fiber-optic cable without physical transport to North America and Europe.

Regional market arrangements have encouraged the development of regional supply and distribution networks. General tariff reduction through the World Trade Organization and other initiatives removing obstacles to trade provide additional motivation for production specialization and network development within global supply chains. Further stimulus has been provided through direct subsidy and tax deferrals by individual countries seeking investment.

These developments make global supply chains possible. Other resources such as low-cost labor, materials or infrastructure or location in proximity to markets determine the location of production units. Research and development takes place wherever resources, primarily human capital and infrastructure, are available. Telecommunications make it possible to coordinate operations even of external partners. The flow of data enables management of intermediate product and finished product inventory, which is crucial in increasing efficiency, a key element in competing in the glo-

Figure 11.3. Global Evolution

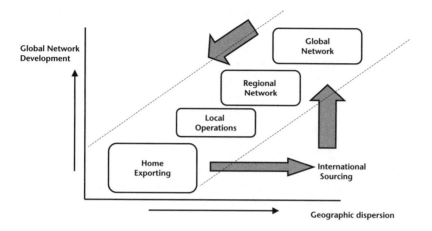

bal marketplace. Products become the responsibility of many organizations and not just the parent organization. At the same time, there is a renewed interest in regionalism for both production and distribution. These influences are shown in Figure 11.3.

Patterns of global supply

In discussing global supply chains, we deal with two patterns: trade and investment. International trade is highly concentrated, both by international companies (companies with a parent company and at least one affiliated company producing in a host country) and by regions of the world. Total global production value, both domestic and international, is larger than global export trade (USD 11 trillion versus USD 7 trillion) (UNCTAD 1999, p. xix). International companies control about 25% of the total global output, one third of which is produced in host countries. Trade within these companies (intra-company) amounts to about one-third of world trade. Production and trade are linked by the need to import goods and services as inputs to production. The combination of intra-company trade and trade with external partners is about two-thirds of total world trade. External trade by foreign affiliates alone amounts to about one-fifth of their sales.

Trade has been dominated by the Triad: Japan, Europe and North America (Ohmae 1985). At one time, they were responsible for almost 80% of the value of world trade, both within and between regions. Regional trading relationships have expanded further through the creation of the European Union and the North American Free Trade Agreement (NAFTA). Latin America and Southeast Asia (including China and India) are now also becoming major sources of global production and trade as their economies develop.

The composition of exports is changing. Between 1990 and 1995, primary products such as minerals grew at an annual rate of 1.4%, low technology 5.6%, medium technology 6.9% and high technology 12%. For developing economies, high-and low-technology export shares are overtaking primary exports, reflecting labor costs.

Investment in international production is only measured imperfectly. International production is defined as »the production of goods and services in countries that is controlled and managed by firms headquartered in other countries« (UNCTAD 1999 p. xvi). Foreign direct investment shows transfers of funds from a parent company to a host country to build facilities or to invest in existing foreign companies. What is not measured are investments from funds raised locally or internationally. Foreign direct investment does not accurately measure the supply chain. When companies such as Cisco and Nike produce and distribute without the benefit of direct ownership, the focus must turn to contractual and other interorganizational relationships. The extent of global supply chain investment is therefore significantly understated.

Foreign direct investment alone shows both growth and dispersion in concentration. UNCTAD has estimated the numbers of parent and affiliated companies (Table 11.1). More than the number of participating parent companies, these figures suggest an even more rapid expansion in the number of affiliates.

The global corporation

International business increasingly involves corporations that span national borders. These corporations follow a shifting orientation

Table 11.1. Growth of international production, 1990 and 1998

Companies	Parent	Affiliates
1990	37,000	170,000
1998	60,000	550,000

Sources: UNCTAD (1993, 1999)

from international, multinational and global organizations to transnational companies. Each has a particular management style and involves a specific logistics commitment. International companies serve overseas markets through exporting. The other three have some production in other countries. The reality is that companies may actually be involved in all stages simultaneously, exporting part of their product lines to supplement those produced locally, supplying local markets from local production or meeting world demand from global production networks. We examine them in further detail here.

International companies
The export orientation of the international company from a home base implies economies of scale or specialization in production that cannot be economically duplicated outside of the home country. Products are intended to cover an entire market. It may be at risk from lower-cost competitors in other countries. Other dangers are that decision-making is removed from the market and that logistics may involve long transit times, customs duties and other barriers to trade. It is also vulnerable to local pressures for production.

Multinational companies
Traditionally, multinational companies have responded with products and production adapted specifically to local markets. Companies such as Nestlé operate as a set of local affiliate companies. Logistics is usually domestic, although there may be some support and cross-border products from other affiliates or the parent company. Decisions are decentralized, and these affiliates seek out local opportunities. From a management perspective, knowledge of markets or processes also tends to be local.

The global corporation

By contrast, the global corporation treats the world as one integrated market. Production may take place from a home base or it may be localized to local markets but becomes identical to that of the parent company. Products are standardized. Knowledge is centralized, and the role of affiliates is to implement the strategies of the parent company. The personal computer industry operates in this mode, essentially relying on global standards to maintain product uniformity. Logistics is also largely localized, although supplementary support from other affiliates and the parent may also create international movements to fill in product lines.

The transnational company

The transnational company combines the market flexibility of the multinational company with organizational flexibility. Ultimately it becomes an integrated network embracing a variety of organizational forms with differentiated roles and responsibilities. The transnational company is described by several writers as a »global-local« or »strategic localization« solution (Mair 1997), meaning that the corporation sets global strategy but adapts to local conditions. The transnational company is basically a knowledge-generating organization, holding a few core competencies but varying the roles of national organizations to meet local requirements. Management decisions are decentralized. Not only production but also product research and development and even entire product divisions can locate anywhere within the network. Supply chains can also specialize by product line and operate independently of each other, although there may be economies of scale and scope in combining. The dominant characteristics of transnational companies are the dense connections of their communication and physical networks and the emphasis on joint development and sharing of knowledge. Logistics provides the physical connection as a combination of local domestic and international operations.

The difference between global corporations and transnational companies stems from the need to adapt to local conditions (Storper 1997). A global corporation assumes that resources and market preferences are essentially similar and that, if labor costs become too high, the company can move its production to other countries. A transnational company, on the other hand, recognizes differences in both resources and local markets. One country may be attractive for production because of a technology base and another because of its proximity to local market preferences.

Interpreting this difference in a supply chain context means that supply chain configurations and their resulting logistics support must be managed as unique systems even within the same corporate umbrella. This makes the task of coordinating operations more difficult than for global companies. Supply chain management also becomes localized, and corporate direction can only be one of general control over a series of separate portfolio operations.

Growth in the dispersion of ownership has slowed. In 1960, 60% of these companies were tied to four countries. By 1990, this proportion had declined to 49%. Nevertheless, the 100 largest non-financial companies in 1998 held 15% of total assets and 22% of sales. There has also been lesser but growing foreign investment by developing economies.

There are also differences between industrialized and developing countries from the perspective of inbound investment. Most current investment in industrialized economies goes to the acquisition of existing firms. In developing countries, it is new plants and equipment. In both cases, it is driven by a search for economies of scale in manufacturing, research and development and management. There are further shifts, from large firms in traditional industries to new entrants, smaller in scale but more oriented to new technologies and from stand-alone affiliates towards incorporation in integrated production networks.

Global production

The classification above implies production networks. Global market pressures place specific requirements on production networks to achieve lower cost, higher quality, more flexibility, rapid delivery and faster product introductions. Shi & Gregory (1998) proposed classifying production networks in two dimensions. One dimension is multi-local versus global. Multi-local or local-for-local production is shown in Figure 11.4. A second is integration and rationalized production, whether production follows a single path of product flow from components to assembly within the same organiza-

Figure 11.4. Local-for-Local Production

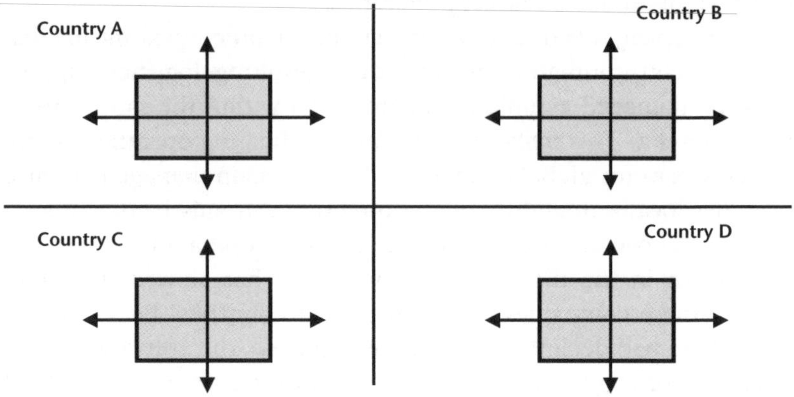

tion, that is, sequential production, or whether the network is horizontal, with parallel production facilities producing different products to supply the global network. These options for organizing production are shown in Figure 11.5.

Several specific factors influence manufacturing locations. One study identified product process, product technology, competitive priorities, the need for market responsiveness and firm-specific characteristics, including the depth of international experience (Du Bois et al. 1993). Products under development were produced closer to research and development facilities, where coordination and control over production were easier and changes could be implemented more easily. Competitive priorities include supply cost, quality, dependability and flexibility. Market responsiveness was especially important in industrial markets where delivery times were important, such as JIT. Local manufacturing was necessary to penetrate some markets, even in the absence of specific tariff rules. Logistics costs related to the ratio of value to weight strongly influenced the decision. Low-value products were produced close to markets; high-value products could be produced at longer distances from the market because they can bear higher transport costs.

Ferdows (2000) proposed another view. The reasons for concentrating production in the home country are declining tariff barriers, the increasing sophistication of both production and product development and the need for world-class suppliers. Against these are the

Figure 11.5. Rationalized Production

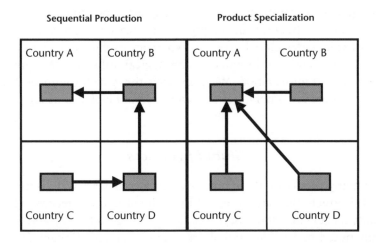

need to establish links to markets, low-cost labor and local research and product development. He suggests six roles for foreign factories:

- *offshore* – oriented to low cost for export;
- *source* – also oriented to low cost but with more responsibility for local procurement;
- *server* – to supply local or regional markets;
- *contributor* – also supplying local markets, but with added responsibilities for product and process development;
- *outpost* – a primary role is to collect information from a locally advanced environment; and
- *lead factory* – creates new technologies, products and processes for the entire company.

Factories migrate through successive roles as they gain capabilities, moving from internal improvements to build competent supplier networks and ultimately to become centers for global products. In the process, they may gain intangible benefits such as learning to improve customer service or new technologies. Ultimately they can strengthen networks through development and exposure to the stimuli of overseas environments, although that was not a specific part of this framework.

The environment of the supply chain

The global environment embraces a long list of possible topics. Even a shorter list affecting the supply chain must be selective in scope. This list includes global products, currency exchange, cultures, political issues and the dominant technological influence, telecommunication and information. We emphasize those with the most direct effect. There are others, but the reader should look elsewhere.

Global products

For many products, the global marketplace has arrived. Standardized products that are accepted by a global market become global products (Levitt 1986). Bryan et al. (1999) at McKinsey and Company noted that in our global transition economy, perhaps 20% of products offered in the world deal with global markets. They forecast that, within 30 years, this will become more than 80%, with increasing levels of competition. Customers see an increasing number of products as essentially similar, used in the same ways to meet similar needs. They become commodities. The driving force behind this convergence is technology. The mantra is reliable, quality products at low prices to gain market share, placing the focus on efficient quality production. This does not apply completely to all products. Some will remain completely local in orientation to meet market needs in individual countries. This appears to be especially true for some but not all food products. Others will be adapted to regional preferences, such as automobiles. However, an increasing number of products will be either standardized or adaptable for national or regional markets with minimal effort, such as electronic goods.

The outlines of strategy in a global market are becoming clear. Standard products around the world evolve towards commodities that are subject to intense competition. Products that can be matched to individual customer preferences become the basis of competitive advantage. This results in the need to organize the supply process to make these individual adaptations. Advantage, however, is short-lived. Pressures to reduce cost are present, but the advantage here is also short-lived. Continuous innovation is the minimum requirement to remain competitive. This, in turn, requires rapid product development and distribution to markets.

Information technology enables customers to follow the law of one price (Bryan et al. 1999). Through the Internet, customers can easily search the market to find prices on comparable products. Selecting the lowest price for commodity-like products destroys profit margins. This forces supply chain managers to search continuously for the lowest-cost source for the product, regardless of where it is produced. Transportation costs provide some protection, although transport cost is diminishing over time as a geographic barrier to competition because of higher value products and the state of competition within the transport industries themselves.

The alternative to global price competition is to create new value in products that meet market needs. The role of the supply chain is to provide flexibility for this innovation process, but at the same time providing advantages of economies of scale and scope in production. Distribution for many of these products must be instantaneous in all markets at the same time because of the need to beat competitors to market. These are conflicting objectives, and how they are resolved determines the success of strategy. Managing the process becomes the core of competitive advantage.

Monetary exchange

One of the principal elements that make the global supply chain different is monetary exchange. It has the power to make a source of supply competitive or unprofitable. In theory, changes in exchange rates can force production to shift, to avoid reducing or eliminating profits, or at the least, to incur the costs of counter-measures such as purchasing monetary instruments.

Global supply networks require flexibility to meet potentially disruptive changes in currency exchange rates. Carter & Vickery (1989, p. 23) observe that, »In the international market place, there is no such thing as a stable market.« Theoretical discussion about flexibility in response to exchange rates is not always fully matched in practice. Some companies such as the Danish enzymes and insulin producer Novo Nordisk specifically invested in plants in major currency regions to hedge against these changes (Stonehill et al.

1982). Empirical observation of actual firm behavior shows that firms do respond by shifting production to countries with a low exchange rate, but this is a difficult step. The cost may be high and the other reasons mentioned above are usually the motivation.

The investment by Japanese car manufacturers in United States production in the early 1980s may have been motivated by a desire to maintain a market presence in the face of the United States quota systems but became advantageous from an exchange perspective when the rise of the yen against the dollar threatened to make cars either high-priced or unprofitable.

Some firms for which all costs are variable and directly linked to specific sites may be able to move to more favorable locations. It may be easier to switch suppliers to other countries where exchange is more favorable, provided that supplier outputs are interchangeable. Short-term contracts would therefore favor flexibility. Direct investment in plant and equipment is not so easily moved. Sunk costs may limit the ability to change locations. At the least, local supply and logistics relationships are disrupted, necessitating establishing new connections. In some cases, fixed costs must be covered, reducing the immediate value of the change. An empirical study indicated that corporations only made modest changes in production location in response to changes in exchange rates (Rangan 1998).

For procurement across currency rate boundaries, a variety of hedging devices are used to cover foreign exchange currency fluctuation: payment in home currencies, buying foreign exchange forward, purchasing futures contracts and individual contractual agreements with suppliers. However, they are only available for some countries and not all currencies. Some macro-strategies have also been useful in reducing risk (Carter & Vickery 1989, p. 20). They include timing purchasing to avoid unfavorable rates, using exchange rate forecasts in source selection or volume purchasing to take advantage of volatile exchange-rate differences. Other procedures using Bayesian methods have also been suggested (Vickery et al. 1992).

These methods have the effect of shifting risk either in time or to outside parties. Some companies such as Hewlett-Packard have operated central clearinghouses to manage currencies within an individual region at a single point at a given period of time. The risk is also reduced in many parts of the world when host countries align their own currencies to a common standard, such as the euro or the US dollar. However, this does not always protect transactions, as the Southeast Asian currency crisis of 1997 demonstrated.

In a longer perspective, shifts in exchange rates cannot be ignored. At the time of writing, Nissan announced that they would be forced to move production from Britain to the European continent because of divergence of value between the pound and the euro (Griffiths et al. 2000). No matter how efficient the facility in question is, the cost differences are sometimes less than the differences in exchange values.

Cultures

Culture can be defined in many ways. A few include education, management practice, national identities, work values and relationships. Education suggests institutions. Host countries may invest in education in the hope of attracting foreign investment. A variety of management questions are associated with cultures. National identities may also be involved in attracting foreign investment, to secure new technologies, identify working interaction or to build a local industrial base. Work values reflect on the motivation of the local labor force. Culture also determines the roles of organizational relationships and contracts and the flexibility of the supply chain to respond to change through changes in partnerships.

Within management practice, several dimensions influence international organizational behavior: language, context, task orientation and time, power and information flow (O'Hara-Devereaux & Johansen 1994).

Together they define management culture:

- *Languages* of course can be a major problem, not only between countries, but also between professional subcultures. Choice of language determines meeting outcomes and negotiation.
- *Low or high context* determines the information requirements for communication. In the case of low context, the explicit message carries the whole burden of communication. High context includes relationships, history and status.

- *Task-related time* is divisible into monochromic or polychronic time. In its simplest terms, monochromic time refers to single task management, while polychronic time is analogous to multi-tasking, carrying forward several activities at the same time.
- *Time orientation* looks either to past experience or to the present and future.
- *Relative power and equality* determine organization structures, individual roles and sensitivity to communication.
- *Information flows* describe the path and media of information within and between organizations and how decisions result in completed actions. Media describes text, graphics and means of presentation.

Social cultures lay the foundation as the primary system of thinking, feeling, behaving and values. On top of these are layered professional and organizational cultures. Organizational cultures are the most adaptable, changeable with the group. They serve a purpose in providing application of operating behaviors and stability. Social cultures change only slowly, emphasizing a need to recognize differing cultural patterns.

In general, North American and northern European social cultures tend to be low context, monocultured, forward-oriented and with low hierarchy in organizations. In contrast, Asian, Latin and southern European cultures stress relationships (high context), are polycultured, respect past experience and history and power relationships. In the supply chain, information technology follows a North American mold, low in context and monochromic. It thus goes against the social cultures of major parts of the world. This suggests a need to build and maintain personal relationships between organizations.

Interorganizational relationships become the glue of the global supply chain. They go beyond market buyer-seller relationships to establish personal connections. Networks of relationships precede and hold primacy over the development of electronic information systems (Yeung 1997). Yeung describes how Hong Kong-based transnational companies use family and other personal connections, relying on personal assessment at government, external network and intra-firm levels to enable overseas expansion. However, a recent article in *The Economist* (2000) points to a shift towards professional management bought in by better access to information and contracts. Personal networks may be a result of specific preconditions and lose their value when those conditions change.

Political levels

There are several aspects to politics in global supply chains. One is protectionism; a second is trade liberalization through the World Trade Organization. Third is the development of regional trade and unification through the European Union, NAFTA, Mercosur and the Association of South East Asian Nations (ASEAN). All of these have drawn criticism because of opposition to transnational companies and global corporations. The attacks have centered on labor rights, losses of jobs, environmental issues, the free movement of capital and the inability of any one country to control the transnational companies.

Despite avowals of commitment to free trade and the free flow of capital, local and national governments play an influential role in the development of the global economy. Emerging market economies often use protectionism through high tariff barriers and direct controls to limit internal competition and encourage locally based technology. They may also seek to attract industry through direct subsidies and special financing arrangements, as the United Kingdom did for several years to encourage transnational companies to locate in Northern Ireland. The Philippine government has been able to attract semiconductor industry investment in competition with other countries in Southeast Asia because it has more university graduates.

The World Trade Organization is an agreement among countries to liberalize trade and investment. It provides a basis to eliminate discrimination and other barriers in trade. It replaces the highly successful General Agreement on Tariffs and Trade that enabled global trade in the years following World War II. Countries that are party to the agreement must pursue lower tariffs, unrestricted flow of capital, enforcement of intellectual property rights.

The underlying trend is to move away from individual country barriers towards regional arrangements that offer no barriers to goods movement between countries within the agreement and higher barriers to those outside. The intent is to build regional self-sufficiency. Allowance has been made in both the United States and the EU for generalized systems of preference that allow less developed countries to sell products within the allowing regions without tariff barriers. This has meant to encourage less-developed countries to attract investment and further their own development.

The supply chain responds to economic incentives of subsidy and tariff protection and disincentives of tariffs as barriers (discussed in more detail later). Exchange rates are of major importance because they change the cost relationships of countries and regions and therefore, in theory, change the movements of the physical products. Capital availability also has a strong influence on location: witness Silicon Valley as an attraction for high-tech industry. At the same time, the high cost of labor has encouraged companies that locate there to establish production somewhere else. Parallel to capital, research and development has proven to be a magnet for particular industries.

The EU is the strongest regional agreement, dismantling barriers to the free movement of labor, capital, goods and services with the Member States that now include 15 countries across Europe. Notable non-members are Norway, Switzerland and countries in eastern Europe. Negotiations have started between the EU and central and eastern European countries about conditions of admission to an enlarged EU, encompassing most countries in Europe. The result has been to establish a common market across national boundaries. The agreement abolishes tariffs and non-tariff barriers and establishes universal technical product standards within the EU. All EU Member States except Denmark, Sweden and the United Kingdom participate in the single European currency, the euro.

The North American Free Trade Agreement (NAFTA) is an arrangement among Canada, Mexico and the United States to develop free trade and industry within the combined area. It has attracted some interest in expanding to other countries in Latin America such as Chile. NAFTA involves tariff reductions and ease of movement of goods and capital across borders. It is not intended to be an exact parallel to the EU. Free movement of labor is not a NAFTA objective. Experienced logistics managers commented that the most substantial gains came not from tariff reductions but from logistics improvements (Ghosh & Cooper 1997).

Mercosur is an effort to increase trade among four countries: Argentina, Brazil, Paraguay and Uruguay. Tariffs within Mercosur are reduced and currencies were to be coordinated. There were two apparent thrusts in developing Mercosur: development of common markets in automobiles and agricultural products. Brazil's sudden devaluation in 1998, however, has reduced the volume of trade substantially. Perhaps the greatest benefit from Mercosur may lie in investment in a neglected transportation system (Vantine & Marra 1997).

ASEAN includes Brunei, Indonesia, Malaysia, the Philippines, Singapore, Thailand and Vietnam. Although one purpose has been to develop complementary manufacturing within Southeast Asia along with a common market for products, most activity within ASEAN has been political. The financial crisis of 1997 and the lack of a common transport network have thus far limited its development. One study indicted that shipping an automobile door from Thailand to China cost more than shipping it to the United States.

Social issues

Social criticism of world trade has directly involved supply chain issues. In January 1999, United Nations Secretary-General Kofi Annan announced a proposed Global Compact for business practice (*The United Nations Global Compact and SA8000* 2000). It involves three areas:

- human rights protection and avoidance of abuses;
- labor practices, including collective bargaining, elimination of forced labor, abolition of child labor and elimination of discrimination; and
- environmental support for precautionary steps, taking environmental responsibility and supporting the development and diffusion of environmentally friendly technologies.

This initiative, known as Social Accountability 8000, is supported through an ongoing program of consultation, training and guidance (*The United Nations Global Compact and SA8000* 2000). SA8000 is modeled after ISO 9000 and ISO 14000 standards. Compliance would be verified through third-party audits by qualified organizations. It has been tested and adopted by several companies with combined 1998 sales of USD 75 billion. The *Financial Times* (Knight 2000, p. 1) observed that it »provides what other initiatives have lacked: a common framework for ethical sourcing for companies of any size and type, anywhere in the world«. Phil Knight of Nike Corporation, the subject of much social activist criticism, pointed out the complexity of complying with these standards: »Nike and thousands of other companies have a monumental task defining what our global responsibility is, and how to act on it, in many host countries. The Global Compact provides a proper framework« (Knight 2000).

Information technology

Information technology (IT) plays a crucial role in operational coordination. As we have noted, it has been a major driver behind the movement to globalization. IT, however, requires standard data and operating practices, requiring uniformity of management practice. Beyond the general problem of supply chain information systems are specific issues related to crossing national borders. The global system includes networks, communications links and software. The problem areas center on access, adoption, data and time. Not all partners or even subsidiaries adopt uniform technology at the same time, limiting the level of communication within the global system to the lowest common standard. Other communication links then become necessary.

Global networks as currently configured are often costly investments in server-client networks of computers feeding local PCs. Both hardware and software must be compatible, and changes must be consistent throughout the system. Web-based networks in prospect with resident software coupled with thin client terminals are a smaller capital investment with reduced software changes (Taylor 1999). With widespread adoption of fiber-optic cable and high-speed lines, data transmission becomes less a problem than even in the recent past. Further advances, especially into wireless modes such as satellite transmission, make access to remote areas easier, even in emerging countries that have not invested in fixed lines. EDI is often used because it provides security. However, the Internet is already available in most areas, is easier to use and offers flexibility of use. Security on the Internet presents problems but will be improved with promising solutions.

Software specifically designed for global supply chain applications appears to focus on international logistics applications. New solutions involve integrated applications that route and manage shipments, link to customs tariffs and currency exchange data, interact with governmental customs and produce documentation.

The major remaining hurdle appears in cross-border data transmission, which is often restricted by governments (Monahan 1998). At the time of writing, there is a conflict between the EU and the United States over protection of personal privacy. The effect is to limit information to United States businesses, as the United States does not offer sufficient protection in European eyes.

For emerging markets, the system problems are more of delayed adoption than of technical or cultural hurdles such as the transition from paper to computer-based systems. Infrastructure is not as much of a hurdle as it was prior to the introduction of wireless and satellite networks. Computer systems and protocols have become standardized. The Internet opens up communication still further, beyond transactions to meet other communications needs (Procknow 1999). However, the problem of extending information systems to foreign suppliers appears to be a daunting problem (*Information Week* 1999).

The differentiated network of the transnational company poses potential problems in system design. In one company, there was a ratio of 400 : 1 in the volume of international-to-local message traffic in individual markets (Bingham & Pezzini 1990). In the past, this would have led to different equipment and network requirements. Current solutions appear to be more scaleable to deal with this disparity.

Curiously, some companies have found it easier to install complex management software such as ERP systems in plants in emerging economies, because new systems do not have to adapt to older legacy systems and their associated practices. The insurmountable barrier is time, the time zone differences around the world. This, however, can be an advantage in programming and engineering design, when different groups around the world can work on a project and then shift the work to others in other time zones as a global product development team. This has the effect of accelerating the development schedule.

Message content in a global setting raises cultural issues. As noted earlier, IT follows a United States model of low context, meaning that the message stands by itself. Reliance on e-mail and the Internet alone for message transmission places a heavy burden on communicating to partners in high-context cultures where gestures and facial expressions also communicate. Transmitting to a different place and time does not have the capabilities of face-to-face contact. O'Hara-Devereaux & Johansen (1994) think that it may be an advantage, allowing the other party to develop their response in their own style. Participants become less influenced by status of the other party. Barriers also may be easier to negotiate. Same-time, same-place communication at the least requires coordination of global schedules and equipment. The technical development of broadband communication may encourage new forms of interaction involving cyberspace and virtual teams. However, it is too early to tell.

There may be difficulties in transmitting data across international borders because of restrictions on disclosure. There are restrictions in the EU concerning data about individuals. Other governments may be sensitive about operational data.

The global supply chain

The global supply chain is more than direct ownership of production and distribution. It is also a network of relationships with both internal and external partners. It requires establishing relationships with organizations operating under completely different political, economic and physical environments. These relations require close coordination despite these differences. The networks themselves become so extended that no manager can hope to achieve close control over more than a limited part of the entire operation.

The transnational company becomes the cornerstone of the supply chain. It is an organizational structure that internalizes markets through transfer pricing mechanisms. It may not own most of the means of production, as Dell, Nike and Cisco demonstrate.

Nevertheless, it is constrained by its environment. It is more than an economic entity engaging in foreign value-adding activities. It is also a collection of sources of comparative advantage and location-bound endowments, operating as an »eclectic paradigm« (Dunning 1993). These can include physical resources, factor markets (labor and capital), research and development, management and technology. The eclectic paradigm can be summarized as ownership, location and internalizing (OLI): a firm will introduce international production if it has:

- ownership-specific advantages;
- location-specific advantages to an overseas site; and
- internalizing these advantages is more profitable than to sell products in open markets or to license them to others.

The supply chain is influenced first by corporate strategy, shaped by products, technology and markets and also by the moves of competing supply chains. It is further influenced by the elements in Porter's Diamond: government policies, factor markets, competition, supporting industries and demand in both home and host country markets (Porter 1990). They determine the climate in which the corporation operates. While Porter uses the Diamond to explain how particular kinds of corporate advantage arise in home countries, it would appear to be useful in explaining how the product divisions of a transnational company become established in other countries as well. One example would be the establishment of new automobile plants by the German companies DaimlerChrysler and BMW in the United States.

Developing countries offer both opportunity and problems, depending on the country. Opportunities come from potential market development and low labor costs. Interestingly, they offer potential for innovative supply chain development, as there is usually no legacy of past business practice (*Emerging Markets Offer Fertile Ground* ... 1999). The problems, however, are usually the lack of infrastructure and exposure to criticism.

Infrastructure can be defined in terms of education, transport and telecommunication. Education for the work force appears to be a crucial issue, especially in dealing with modern technology. Some Southeast Asian countries have invested heavily in educational institutions to attract new investment beyond basic manufacturing. Transport infrastructure consists of highways, carriers, ports and airports and access to major international routes. It can vary from primitive to highly sophisticated operations, depending on social investment and the economic level of the country.

The transnational company and its supply chain are also subject to social criticisms, including their independence of national governments, their ability to influence local economies, their power over local labor markets and environmental considerations (cf. Korten 1995). Environmentalists have accused transnational companies of destroying natural resources and creating pollution or not establishing adequate safeguards in their production processes. Companies with labor-intensive products such as Nike have come under fire by charges of exploiting these labor markets in low-wage host countries (Knight 1998; *Business Week* 1999). At the same time, transnational companies introduce and upgrade necessary skills for host countries to achieve higher levels of development. Both criticisms and programs to aid developing countries influence supply chain decisions.

Structure

The structure of the global supply chain follows the general conceptual framework from Chapter 2, with a few additions. The major differences appear to lie in the tensions between location and operational flexibility (Kogut 1989). Location creates value. The relevant questions are where and for what activities (Kogut 1985)? Location exploits comparative advantage among countries, whether in labor cost for production, research capabilities or proximity to markets (Sweeny 1994). It determines where competitive advantage can be added, when Japanese companies supply key components for United States electronic products, or country comparative advantage provides the lowest costs. Flexibility also incurs a cost from coordinating flows within a global network. As the costs of coordination decline, the supply chain can take on more flexibility and shift production more readily in response to changes in the global economy. Production would be transferred between host countries as factor costs change.

The pursuit of low labor costs, however, creates a dilemma. Seeking the lowest cost can mean a location with long transit times to markets. Long lead times may lead to higher costs of inventory in the market to compensate (Levy 1995). Further, this may also lead to inadequate response to changing demands. The alternative is to locate at higher-cost locations but closer to the market. This has led to solutions such as using Turkey for garment production sites close to western European markets, or Caribbean sites for the United States market or even to maintain plants within the United States for even faster response, even at a slight cost penalty but with substantially reduced transit times.

Flexibility and even customization are also furthered by postponing the final stages of production. Postponing final product assembly allows companies to adapt products to particular markets. Hewlett-Packard designed inkjet printers with modular power supplies to enable them to be configured to European markets at a distribution center within the European market, rather than to complete final assembly at the source and hold additional product inventory (Feitzinger & Lee 1997). One study identified three different stages in which postponement takes place in transnational companies: engineering, final manufacturing and distribution (Van Hoek et al. 1999). The use of postponement increased as products moved towards the customer; engineering design changes in manufacturing were used less than in distribution for final configuration assembly. United States companies in Europe utilized postponement more in final manufacturing and distribution than did their European counterparts. Much depends on the history of a local presence by European companies in the European market. With new plants, there may be scale effects to consider in the postponement process. United States companies, on the other hand, may be encouraged to do more postponement in the field.

The global corporation and the supply chain

Relationships

Global corporations operate integrated international production and distribution networks to satisfy global markets. Their boundaries are not automatically synonymous with the concept of the global supply chain. Some supply chains utilize partners outside their corporate boundaries. Some use external third-party logistics providers. On the other hand, a global corporation can be a member of other supply chains.

Johnson Controls and Lear Seating are global suppliers of automobile seating and interiors, operating in many different countries and drawing on their own chains of suppliers. They are also contractors to major automobile assemblers to supply seats. Similarly, Solectron and Flextronics operate networks of electronic assembly plants around the world as part of the supply chains of other international companies.

International supply chains, whether multi-local or transnational, involve complex and unique relationships with other companies. The variety of relationships creates difficulty in management. Their presence in multiple countries in production and marketing adds to this complexity in the necessity to deal with differences in trade regulation, customs, taxation and other barriers. They extend over long distances, creating problems in supplying markets across the world. Distance also creates difficulties in time and transport cost.

These two factors lead, in turn, to problems in inventory management and response to changing markets. Culture adds a further complication, dealing with differences in business practices, local work force education and skill levels, requiring more personal contact. At the same time, personal contact is more difficult across borders and distance.

Production can be oriented with flexibility to meet uniform global product demands. Ford's production of the same engine design in Kansas City (United States), Wales and Cologne (Germany) allows them to balance production capacity with demand across regional boundaries. Other companies develop networks oriented to regional markets such as the EU. Other companies, not global brand competitors, will produce to meet local market demand on a »local-for-local« basis.

Global production provides the most flexibility and local production the least. Product configuration flexibility does not reflect the factory network as much as it does the inherent product and factory design.

Procurement policies

In the global network, manufacturing eventually requires suppliers in localized networks in order to manage lean production through JIT and similar methods. Japanese car producers in United States and European markets have pursued two differing strategies. One, followed in the United States market, is to encourage suppliers from Japan to establish satellite production in the host countries (Florida & Kenney 1993). Another, in the European market, has been to utilize and strengthen existing European suppliers (Mair 1994).

At the same time, these suppliers often seek outside markets. In some cases, suppliers become significant, independent of the supply chain with which they are connected. The global corporation may even encourage this development, in the interest of reducing their risk in the original chain and also to stimulate new product development (Miles & Snow 1992).

Products

The global corporation benefits from a trend in the marketplace towards homogenization of tastes and preferences. An increasing number of global products can be sold in world markets without substantive functional or aesthetic changes to meet the market requirements of individual countries, although they may still require adaptation to meet local physical requirements such as voltages and standards. Some television set producers have incorporated the three world video standards in the same circuit, requiring only a difference in connections to adapt them to different markets. This allows production to take place with economies of scale any place in the world. It also encourages product specialization by individual production facilities, such as the BMW plant in South Carolina building sports cars, or DaimlerChrysler producing sports-utility vehicles under the Mercedes brand in Alabama.

Not all products can be global (Ohmae 1999). Some must meet significant regional preferences with major adaptation to emerge as regional products. Honda has taken one basic design and created flexible chassis dimensions, plus changes in exterior styling to accommodate differences in taste (*Business Week* 1997). The cars have been adapted to regional orientations, even though the basic design emanates from a single source. Japanese car producers such as Honda, Toyota and Mitsubishi have developed a regional orientation, even to the establishment of research and development centers and production in both the United States and Europe.

Local products persist, especially in foods, although the development of international tastes is also changing perceptions. Traditionally, packaged food and household products producers have been firmly oriented towards local markets. Nestlé is a case in point. Local production and distribution tends to make supply chains also local, and cross-border supply relations are only attractive where regional political alliances have influenced trading patterns.

Distance and time tend to influence three elements in the supply chain. First, they restrict the number of stock-keeping units, forcing simplification of the product line. Recognizing that inventory levels reflect lead times, the cost forces attention to high turnover product lines. A second is the ability to respond rapidly to changes in market demand. This may result in dividing the production sequence by multiple locations, with the stages of final production or assembly being located closer to the market. To some extent, this has taken place in garment production. For the United States market, cloth production can take place in Southeast Asia, with final finishing done in Caribbean locations that are closer to the market. The third is the problem of matching capacity to changes in demand. The accepted solution has been to forecast ahead for longer periods. Nike, for example, will use 6-month forecast periods to set production schedules, recognizing that immediate response is not possible.

Customization to meet local requirements has been one solution, starting with production of »raw« product in one location, to be configured in distribution centers closer to the market. Imbedded language instructions on copy machines, power supplies and automotive accessory items are candidates. Once the product is designed for modular customization, the supply chain question becomes a case of where and when to adapt to local markets (Lee et al. 1993).

Packaging includes two aspects. The first is protection in shipping and storage under potentially poor climatic conditions. Ocean container shipping has reduced these in developed country markets, although they persist in other markets. Second, it must adapt to local markets. Package« issues involve language, size and quantity. Language requirements in the United States market have changed with NAFTA; packaging and instructions now come in English, French and Spanish. »Europacks« are now common in the EU, incorporating as many as six different languages. Other products, such as photographic equipment with wider geographic appeal but smaller markets, often come with even more. Package sizes also differ and are related to materials-handling requirements. They must be matched to different warehouse pallet sizes, Euro pallets versus GMA (United States) pallet sizes, that determine case and smaller package sizes for retail display. Quantity is determined by local practice. United States units are matched to dozens. Countries on metric systems use decimal sizes.

Global management

The global corporation and its supply chain face parallel management problems. Management asserts control over other organizations that often act with varying degrees of autonomy across national borders. This autonomy also spans functional areas, such as marketing, production, procurement and research and development. Further complexity is added with multiple products marketed to multiple national markets. The paradox is that customers are local, with specific product and sales requirements, while competitors are global, competing in individual country and regional markets. Marketing also recognizes that market segments now reach across national boundaries. There is a critical balance between local orientations for operations and global orientations for strategy.

The relationship between headquarters and national subsidiaries presents one of the most unique aspects of global corporate management. Individual national (local) subsidiaries began as sales offices, some later becoming almost self-sufficient in manufacturing in the »local-for-local« concept of the multinational corporation. Under regionalization such as the EU or NAFTA, production and distribution become rationalized across national boundaries (Jarillo & Martinez 1994). One manufacturing plant serves more than one country, reducing local product variety to simplify production followed, in some cases, by customization at distribution centers. Distribution itself also becomes rationalized into fewer facilities. The limitations have been 1) political pressures from the sales force of the subsidiary losing control over product delivery, 2) slow development of regional transportation systems to deliver across borders and 3) local customs barriers, either official or de facto in operation.

Where does this leave the local subsidiary? Logically the local sales force continues, but in many cases, even order processing is taken away. Routine orders are routed to a central office, via EDI or Internet processing. Power shifts to centralized operation, and this is especially true of supply chain operations operating almost completely independently of the subsidiary.

The governing concept of global management is that solutions are unique but that organizational structure must match strategy. The term *differentiated networks* describes this mixture, where individual subsidiaries have unique relationships with headquarters, determined by the environmental complexity and their local resources, shown in Figure 11.6 (Nohria & Ghoshal 1997). When

Figure 11.6. Global Corporate Structure

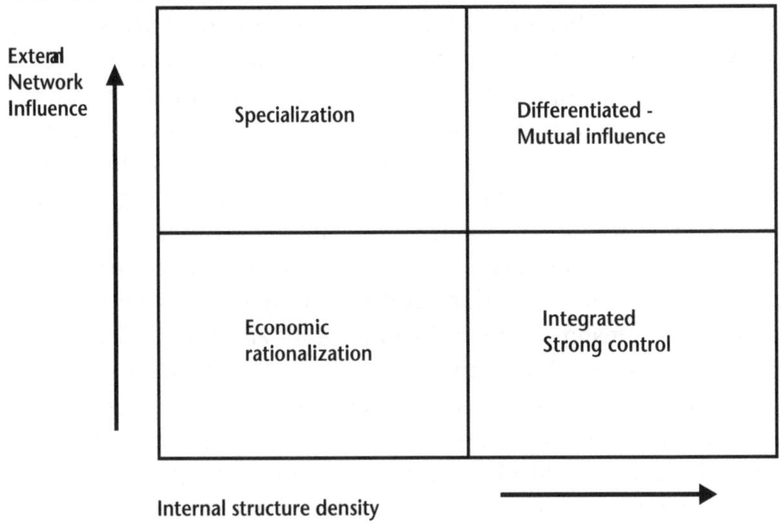

Source: Nohria and Ghoshal (1997)

complexity and unique resources are low, the corporation and the supply chain follow the economic logic of economies of scale and scope for efficient production. With strong local resources, subsidiaries join federations with substantial autonomy within the multinational corporation. With complex environments and weaker local resources, the parent dominates in a global organization. When both complexity and resources are high, management must balance the organization through integration.

Organizational solutions

The supply chain adds complexity through its relationships beyond corporate boundaries. The structure of the supply chain itself becomes extended to a point where it becomes difficult to manage as a single entity. Markets involve traditional relationships in which companies in different environments can deal with each other even with differing mechanisms of contracts and trade. The supply chain, however, often requires integration, forcing management to deal with the internal operations of affiliates and external partners in cooperation and collaboration within differing cultural contexts. Even organizational units within the corporation often behave as if they are in a market relationship, negotiating over transfer prices and resources.

The global supply chain is both complex and extended in space and organization. There is little relevant guidance other than personal experience as preparation. Pressures on management tend towards fragmentation. Perceiving the full network is difficult, especially in operating detail. The supply chain may require decisions that are counterintuitive in the context of a single unit.

Meeting changing market demands within a fixed set of production facilities requires agility in production changeovers. Strategic options apart from the factory itself can reduce lead time. Surviving garment manufacturers in the United States use market proximity as a competitive advantage to achieve fast flexible response despite the higher costs of production. Capacity fluctuations can be met through redundant capacity within the production network. Other alternatives are to move final production closer to the market, even though it may still lie outside national market boundaries.

The Maquiladora plants of northern Mexico are there for that reason.

Organizational solutions are not always clearly evident. Lateral management may be the closest solution. Strategy could be guided, at least to a point, through matrix organizations that manage headquarters-subsidiary relationships, with the addition of product dimensions. Matrix organizations build conflict into the organization as they add process on top of functional areas. Other solutions treat each product group as separate enterprises; the parent becomes a holding company controlling only financial and other overhead resources (Pasternack & Visscio, 1998). Adding an additional product dimension takes the conflict one step further.

The problem has led to new forms, such as heterarchy, proposed by Hedlund (1994) that we previously noted in Chapter 8. In effect, it is a multidimensional matrix with further conflicts and often unworkable as a formal long-term organizational structure. It also diffuses responsibility for decisions. A temporary solution of task-oriented teams may often work better, created to achieve specific solutions and then dissolved afterwards.

Leadership is especially difficult with complexity and the span of activities. The ability to perceive problems is difficult, because of their variety, cultural divisions among partners and the sheer complexity of selecting from multiple options. Leadership begins with a global mindset (Jeannet 2000). The central vision should set direction and establish key relationships. The supply chain structure must match the global strategy of the transnational company. Operating control may still be local (Braithwaite & Christopher 1991; O'Laughlin et al. 1993). Some elements of control may even be delegated to external partners. The management focus is on system design and coordination, with authority delegated to operating management, both inside and outside of the corporation.

International logistics

International logistics is the forgotten child of the global supply chain. In discussion of international production, there has been little discussion of logistics, even though inventory, transportation and communication are the enabling elements in establishing global production networks (Fawcett & Closs 1993).

International logistics in concept is no different than the domestic variety. It involves movement, inventory and coordination. The problem in discussing international logistics management is the country-specific and region-specific nature of the context. Figure 11.7 presents a general description of the process. However, the geographic convergence taking place elsewhere in transnational companies also affects logistics. Managers can go too far in trying to adapt to local situations. Regional groupings are not always as logical as product groupings (Zuprod 1996). Consider these scenarios:

- A European manufacturer moves products across borders by truck inside the European Union without delays with only the documentation necessary to identify the shipment to the carrier and the receiver of the goods.
- A United States shipper to the European Union must document the shipment for the carriers' bills of lading and the ultimate receiver for customs to assess duty and apply any regulations, ship via truck to a port, possibly for consolidation by freight forwarder or non-vessel operator into a container. This container is carried by ocean carrier to a port in the European Union where the shipment is offloaded, subjected to potential inspection, cus-

Figure 11.7. The International Logistics Channel

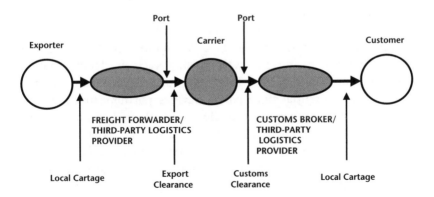

toms duty and any restrictions on entry, loaded on a truck and then delivered to the customer.

- Another United States shipper also documents the shipment for the carrier using domestic bills of lading and the international airbill and for customs authorities and the receiver. The shipment goes by truck, possibly by an independent carrier, to an airport, transported by air to the destination city. It is precleared by automated customs and delivered to a customer, also by truck, by a carrier designated by the receiving freight forwarder.

These describe typical procedures used in international trade. They have patterns that differ by geography more than by their local orientations. Managing documentation is a key element in international logistics. In the past it has been a manual operation. More recently, shippers, carriers and governments are automating information recording and processing to reduce cost and increase the speed of the transaction.

Every transfer point is a source of potential loss of control or delay. Transfers also increase handling costs. Routings play a pivotal role in avoiding transfers, especially to carriers with whom the shipper has had no dealings. The complexity of international shipping has required the development of intermediaries: international freight forwarders, international express companies, non-vessel operator common carriers, third-party logistics providers and export trading companies (Thomchick & Rosenbaum 1984) to manage the process, often contracting with other parties such as brokers, forwarders and carriers. Intermediaries are changing their functions. Some forwarders have been absorbed into formerly quasi-governmental postal organizations, such as the acquisition of Danzas, a Swiss forwarder, by Deutsche Post, the German Post Office.

Third-party logistics providers now offer services beyond transport, order processing and warehousing such as documentation and managing relations with local customs officials. Many companies will ask potential third-party logistics partners to enter new markets with them to provide services that other parties in the supply chain cannot perform. Third-party logistics providers and international freight forwarders appear to be combining functions to provide more complete services such as coordinating movements, managing customs and documentation requirements and even coordinating supply chains. Other institutions provide functions specific to individual countries. One example is the use of public warehouses in Latin America for financing inventories.

Managing lead time is crucial. It means not only transport time, but also customs clearance and coordination delays. Variations in lead time significantly affect cost through the need to manage inventory. One simulation study of the relationship between a computer manufacturer in California and its Singapore subsidiary showed that market fluctuation was more important than supply disruption. Lead times from Singapore were too long for response without use of air cargo or inventory close to markets.

Customs barriers shape the supply chain. Customs processes become more complex with the expansion of supply chain networks and the need for consolidation and routing for movement across national boundaries (Heaver 1992). The international express companies have found that differences among national and regional tariffs have become a significant problem that requires solution. The process itself becomes a major source of delay, although pre-clearance of shipments before they actually arrive is now an accepted practice in many countries for small shipments and for others by negotiation. The trend has been to shift from physical inspection to information monitoring and, more recently, to certifying processes of self-administration by shippers and intermediaries (Appels & Struye de Swielande 1998). At the least, responsibility for record-keeping and compliance is shifting to shippers (Jones Carr & Crum 1995). Customs clearance is moving towards centralized control rather than processing at the borders or clearance at the first point of entry as into the European Union. Competition among gateways is leading to pressures to simplify and standardize customs processes by the use of technology.

As for duties, the basis of calculation can vary by country and product, although they are normally based on cost, insurance and freight valuation. The magnitude of duties in comparison to transport costs makes them highly significant. Tariff duties can be designed to encourage industries such as automobile assembly by posing high differentials between automobiles and component parts. When components are imported and finished products are exported, drawbacks are sometimes used to refund duty charges for components that do not enter local markets.

Non-tariff barriers parallel customs tariffs in influence. These result from political and economic pressures and negotiations and result in quotas, prohibitions, local content rules, difficult inspection processes and other means to limit or keep out products that compete with local industry or create political problems.

Developing economies present special problems. In many countries, there is almost a complete lack of information available outside the country. Fawcett et al. (1997), writing about logistics and the Maquiladora firms that involve United States-bound production in Mexico, stress the importance of strategic planning and information in developing logistics capabilities to support manufacturing. Another study of the Maquiladora firms stressed the importance of supplier integration, especially in information sharing, supplier relations and agility in responding to routings and delays (Stank & Lackey 1997). The experience of United States firms in China indicated that the greatest barriers were finding responsive transport carriers and suppliers (Carter et al. 1997).

Free trade zones and export-processing zones are a way for communities to attract industry and avoid tariffs, unless the goods are imported into the host country for consumption (Ferguson 1985; Tansuhaj & Jackson 1989). A specific location in a community is established as a foreign zone inside the borders of the host country. Materials are brought in, stored or converted into products and exported. This can also be applied to finished products that are stored within the zone. They have not entered the domestic market and therefore do not pay duty. Products that are sold in the domestic market cross the border and do pay duty. These actions avoid payment of customs duty until close to the time of sale. Customs duties can be a significant cost, and avoiding payment until the last possible moment can reduce the financial costs of holding inventory by significant amounts.

Concluding comments

The supply chain is caught in a convergence between international and domestic business. The differences are real but diminishing, a result of the combined impacts of government policies, information technology and transportation. The three provide management with the ability to coordinate strategy and operations across geographic barriers as global systems.

The transnational corporation provides an initial perspective. Global products will dominate world markets, and competition forces a quest for efficiency. The roles of national subsidiaries in most global supply chains are shifting from the local operations of the multinational corporation to the globally integrated production and distribution operations of the transnational corporation. Continual change becomes the defining constant. The transnational company model that stresses internalized production is not sufficient by itself to describe the new model of global organization. Geography in the sense of information transfer is no longer a technical problem. Information technology now enables one organization to coordinate with the operations of another, even around the globe. Culture still presents a hurdle, but there is a question of how much the world will need to adapt to the mold of e-mail, Internet and graphic information transfer.

Logistics, the transfer of physical material and products, still serves as a limit to globalization. Operations are very much specific to countries, regions and interregional movements. The problems of managing international supply chain operations are also specific to individual industries and regions, making it hard to generalize. Each must be examined on its own merits. Choices of mode of transport, routings and even the carrier are determined by supply chain choices, determining source and receiver. However, logistics also serves as a constraint on supply chain structure, especially in the case of locating facilities for low cost or market proximity.

Illustrative case

Li & Fung

»We can make private-label brands for retailers who were too small for them before« (Fellman 2000). William Fung, grandson of the founder and president of the Hong Kong trading company that bears his name, made this statement at the start of a new Internet venture. Li & Fung will organize and manage supply chains over the Internet for smaller retail chains that are not large enough to manage the process for themselves. They will combine orders to achieve economies of scale in production and distribution operations. A typical example is a polo shirt, made of cotton from the United States, knitted and dyed in China and sewn in Bangladesh. This shirt could be customized by adding logo and side vents, and changing collars, all managed through Li & Fung's own proprietary software.

Observers note that Li & Fung demonstrate that supply chain management is a distinct core competency, apart from the products and services that flow through it. It is better known to large companies with supply chains that it has managed than with smaller retailers. Further at the time of writing, many Internet B2B businesses have failed, emphasizing the risks of the venture. However, they now supply private label merchandise for major retail chains in the United States and Europe.

He stated, »We are not being transformed into an Internet company.« (Jacob 2000, p. 10) His brother Victor, the chairman, describes it as an »information node« connecting 600 customers to thousands of factories in 32 countries. Their competitive advantage evolved from trading relationships as exporters from China threatened by narrow profit margins in the 1970s. They literally remade the company through long-term relationships with a network of suppliers, a concept that they called »dispersed manufacturing« (Magretta 1998). This worldwide network enables Li & Fung to supply United States markets for example, avoiding regional trade barriers such as the North American Free Trade Agreement through suppliers in Mexico.

The 1994 annual report of the Asian Development Bank (1995) notes a trend to manufacturing across borders. »[It] represents a new form of cooperation that differs significantly from conventional arms-length trade. [It] engages participants in a vertically integrated production structure crossing national borders, benefiting all of them.« Victor Leung describes his business: »I'm creating products that did not exist before, a product that is made from Korean yarn, Taiwanese dye and accessories from China, all sewn together in Thailand« (Tanzier 1999).

When a retailer orders garments, Li & Fung orders the yarn, reserves production capacity at weaving mills and arranges production. This would take place within a 4 to 5 weeks so that the retailer can determine whether the sales trend is positive before committing to full production. In addition, they offer product development, raw material sourcing, production planning and management, quality assurance, export documentation, shipping consolidation, managing customs and market import quotas (http://www.lifung.com; Tanzier 2000). Organizing the process is aided by optimization techniques to balance price, production lead times and quality subject to constraints such as shipping costs and labor rates. Victor Fung stated: »We're not asking which country can do the best job overall. Instead, we're pulling apart the value chain and optimizing each step and we're doing it globally« (Magretta 1998, p. 106).

A 1996 article emphasized the strategic direction of Li & Fung, to move up the supply chain, from production alone toward both product development and marketing. Acquisitions have enabled it to broaden its supply base from Chinese firms in Southeast Asia to India and later to the Western Hemisphere. They now operate through 48 sales offices in 32 countries. Victor Fung has been quoted as saying:

»Value adding is the challenge facing Hong Kong and other maturing economies of Asia. The future of Asia doesn't lie in trimming production costs, but in its ability to upgrade its infrastructure and expertise so that can move up the value-added chain in world trade.« (via http://web3.asia1.com.sg/timesnet/data/ab/docs/ab0914.html)

12. Strategic modeling and location

»... information and the mechanisms for delivering it are the
glue that holds together the structure of businesses.«
(Evans & Wurster 2000, p. 10)

Models are essential for planning the supply chain (Figure 12.1). Potential actions have uncertain outcomes. Environments are turbulent. There are too many potentially actionable variables. The only prescription where there are no guidelines for managers is to experiment (Brown & Eisenhardt 1998), testing variables to see what happens. Models are a selective representation of reality; they provide a means to experiment, without endangering the organization. Models also have a subjective dimension. As Schrage (2000) points out, we shape our models and they shape our perceptions.

Models have several uses in supply chain management:

- to test alternative courses of action
- to determine optimal policies
- to predict future events
- to communicate concepts and relationships
- to determine optimal location choices.

Testing alternative actions through the use of models is a form of »what if?«. Selecting parameters for change makes it possible to explore the impact of decisions before they are made. In some cases and with specific forms of modeling, certain relationships can be optimized within the system. It may also be possible to predict when future events will occur, if not in time but under certain identifiable conditions. Models also provide a means to communicate. Because model parameters can be changed, it is possible to express concepts and relationships through the structure of the model. By expressing the outcomes in precise terms, it may also be possible to

Figure 12.1. Supply Chain Modeling

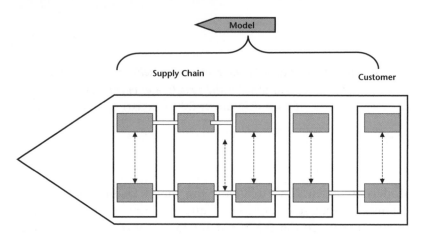

identify who will be affected and how, enabling negotiation to proceed with greater understanding of the consequences.

In some respects, models can be better than information systems at conveying relationships among variables. They encourage experimentation to discover and learn what issues and variables are salient. Schrage (2000, p. 136) notes: »Consumers of innovation discover – rather than know – what new products and services they need.«

Models are also useful in location and system analysis. When a specific processing site is added to a supply chain, how does it affect the system as a whole and what is the impact on existing facilities? The basic assumptions behind most models are oriented towards cost. The world, however, is becoming »dematerialized«. The cost of transport becomes less important in the world of the »new economy«. This transformed economy calls for new forms of modeling that will incorporate new variables. The problem is that we are not sure which variables are important, how they should be measured and how to incorporate them into our modeling frameworks.

Modeling plays a new role with the expanding use of information technology. Modeling becomes a form of strategic introspection, except that a model becomes an explicit prototype that externalizes the thought and encourages collaboration. Models may be even better in establishing and maintaining relationships than they are in transmitting information. The ubiquity of spreadsheets as a foundation of modeling has promoted a new culture of give-and-take, of recognizing trade-offs and joint problem solutions. Models become politically important. Schrage (2000, p. 136) notes: »A model decoupled from politics is little more than an intellectual exercise.« In short, models bring a new transparency to expressions of thought, a vehicle to communicate and a vehicle to relate different parts of the organization to each other.

This chapter is divided into four parts: location analysis, simulation modeling, optimization and planning models and a perspective on future development. The overall purpose is to establish the role of strategic models in supply chain management and fit modeling into a general management view, without becoming involved in the technical aspects of model development.

Location analysis

It may seem strange to combine location and models in a single discussion. However, the location problem lends itself to systematic evaluations that are augmented with the use of models. Management presents several obstacles:

- There appears to be little direct consideration of the supply chain in corporate location decisions.
- Decisions focus on single locations rather than the network as a whole.
- Data collection for systematic analysis often appears to be overwhelming.

The concepts behind location analysis have also changed. Most of the standard models from economic geographers involve transport costs and weight. In a »weightless« economy, the bulk resources that once dominated location analysis are no longer the major issue. Further, differences in cost between sea transport and other forms of transport on a world scene distort simple solutions.

Today, industries are »footloose,« drawn by markets, resources (principally low labor costs) and access to knowledge. As products rise in value relative to their weight, transport costs become a smaller part of product value. With the declining costs and increasing access to telecommunication, the physical movement costs are not as important as they were once. More important is reduction of total cycle time, for response to changing markets, flexibility in meeting changing demands and reduced pipeline inventories.

Another factor is agglomeration, also described as clustering (Porter 1998). Specific industries often develop by building a critical mass within a given area. Examples include Silicon Valley and other clusters of the electronics industry in the United States; software programming in Bangalore, India, leather footwear and ceramic tiles in northern Italy; and machine tools and automobiles in Stuttgart, Germany. This mass allows more casual contact between personnel, a common labor pool and specialized infrastructures of banks, transport carriers, educational institutions and other support institutions. How they start is subject to conjecture. In the case of Silicon Valley, it was Stanford University and the initial start-up companies that were closely identified with it (Saxenian 1994).

Country selection

In the evaluation of any particular site, there are a variety of elements to consider: cost versus response time; infrastructure and its performance; the quality and availability of human resources; public inducements for investment; the structure of tariffs and duties, which are often designed to encourage specific activities; non-tariff barriers of quotas; overly zealous inspections; and restrictive trade agreements. Political stability can be a question. Regional trade areas often present external barriers to encourage internal investment.

The ultimate choice often falls on »soft analysis« and management perception. Location analysis has been a neglected area, despite its overbearing importance in the mind of the decision-maker. Risk becomes pre-eminent because failure also makes the organization vulnerable.

Location site selection with qualitative data[15]

Most modeling efforts rely on quantitative methods and data. There are, however, many situations where choices must be made at least in part using qualitative data. Analytic hierarchy processing, developed by Saaty (1980), can establish choice preferences based on multiple criteria regardless of whether the data are quantitative or qualitative.

Investment by global corporations in overseas operations typifies problems with mixed quantitative and qualitative characteristics. Much of the evaluation is subjective, such as the political climates, whereas other elements, such as wage rates, are quantitative. Quantitative approaches focus on financial feasibility and comparative costs. However, these are too narrow to reflect the complexity of the decision. Other factors such as the quality of the labor force, infrastructure and political stability can become even more important. The procedure does not produce an objective selection for all managers but a choice based on subjective factors and weights for each individual decision-maker.

The core of the analytical hierarchy processing model is a systematic rank-ordered inventory of decision criteria, whether quantitative or not. These are used in evaluating individual sites using a procedure that recognizes a hierarchy of importance for these criteria, from broad decision elements at the top to more specific elements as we descend further into the decision. The procedure differs from standard checklists in that these elements have a relative importance for each alternative. The method uses a series of pairwise comparisons between criteria and between decision alternatives, reflecting human decision characteristics of trade-offs and relative value scales. It is currently available as a software package, Expert Choice.

Case: location decision of a software center

A software center is to be chosen from four candidate sites: Dublin, Bangalore, Moscow and Austin, Texas. Although wage rates for programmers are an obvious criterion, others that are equally important would be more subjective. In this particular problem, there were seven major potential decision elements. These were not all

---

15. This section was written by Ashok Chandrashekar, IBM Corporation.

equally important; the weights were determined through the analytical hierarchy processing program:

- the political climate
- macroeconomic factors
- the market
- the efficiency of public administration
- operations and infrastructure
- human resources
- natural resources.

Below this level were 33 items at a secondary level that were selected to capture the full set of factors in the site selection decision. It is important to point out that these lists are arbitrary on the part of the user.

Two of these primary factors were selected for this demonstration: the political climate and human resources. For the political climate, five secondary factors were also selected:

- the nature of the political regime
- social stability
- territorial stability
- the stability of the institutional framework
- the quality of community relations.

The others were human resource factors, usually critical in an international site selection:

- the supply of skilled labor
- the quality of labor relations
- the availability of technical or managerial talent
- the cultural and linguistic compatibility with the parent firm's corporate culture
- the attractiveness of the local environments for expatriates and dependents
- wage levels and social costs

Data can be either subjective or statistical data available from both government and nongovernmental sources. The pairwise procedure for subjective evaluations for the full set of elements would be daunting for most users. The use of statistical data is a more feasible process.

A summary of the procedure

Executives were asked to evaluate the relative importance of these secondary factors. For example, political climate is composed of issues such as institutional, territorial and sociological stability, nature of the political regime and community relations. It is difficult for most managers to set weights directly for each criterion, that is, allocate a weight of 0.2 to the stability of the institutional framework and so on. The analytical hierarchy process gets around this by asking the manager to compare two criteria at a time. For example on a scale of 1 to 9, the manager is asked to rate institutional stability versus territorial stability. Specifically, the manager is asked to decide how much more important institutional stability is than territorial stability. One manager may say that institutional stability is 5 times more important than territorial stability. On the other hand, a manager in a mining organization may prefer territorial stability compared with institutional stability. The preferences are situation specific.

Similar comparisons are made for each pair: that is, institutional stability is compared with all the criteria for that category, including territorial stability, sociological stability etc. Then the next criterion (territorial stability) is again compared on the same scale of 1 to 9 with the remaining criteria. When all comparisons are done, matrix algebra is used to come up with composite rankings. The Expert Choice software does all the matrix manipulation, and the final weights are generated. For example, Table 12.1 shows the weights for the political climate.

Table 12.1. Criteria weights for the political climate

Stability of the institutional framework	0.449
Territorial stability	0.218
Sociological stability	0.191
Nature of the political regime	0.071
Community relations	0.070

Two points should be emphasized here. First, there should be some consistency, though complete consistency is not required. Let us say a manager says that institutional stability is twice as important as territorial stability and that territorial stability is twice as important as sociological stability. Although analytical hierarchy processing is flexible enough to accommodate a manager who decides that institutional stability is three times as important as sociological stability, it would be totally inconsistent for the manager to say that sociological stability is more important than territorial stability.

The second issue to be emphasized is that these judgments made at one point in time are based on the circumstances relevant at that time. The weights may change at different time or under different circumstances. For human resources, the executive's judgments resulted in these weights (Table 12.2):

Table 12.2. Criteria weights for human resources

Supply of technical and managerial talent	0.347
Attractiveness for key personnel	0.242
Supply of skilled labor	0.131
Magnitude of the cultural gap	0.100
Language compatibility	0.079
Wage levels and social costs	0.068
Labor relations	0.033

Similar comparisons are made for each site for each category. A manager is asked to compare the four sites for wage levels and social costs on a pairwise basis. For example, the manager may decide that Moscow is five times more preferable for wage levels only when compared with Dublin, assuming that we do not know actual wage data. The rankings for the different sites are shown in Table 12.3.

Table 12.3. Preference weights for wage levels and social costs

Rank	Site	Preference Weight
1	Moscow	0.614
2	Bangalore	0.231
3	Dublin	0.106
4	Austin	0.049

The preference weights are multiplied by the criteria weights and summed to arrive at the overall rank order and preference weights for the alternative sites, shown in Table 12.4.

Table 12.4. Overall preference weights for site selection

Rank	Site	Preference Weight
1	Austin	0.434
2	Dublin	0.329
3	Bangalore	0.142
4	Moscow	0.095

Note the reverse order in the overall preference weights. Wages are the only advantages of Bangalore and Moscow as locations. Technical and managerial talent had a much higher criterion weighting.

Using objective data

Previously, we used pairwise comparisons. However, in some cases actual data are available and should be used if possible. Assume that typical annual salaries in the four cities for software programmers are as follows:

Austin   USD 60,000
Dublin   USD 37,500
Moscow   USD 12,000
Bangalore   USD   8,500

These data can be converted into a series of preferences. However, the data must be inverted so the highest salary becomes the least and lowest salary the most attractive. One way of doing this is to divide the salaries. For example, Bangalore is 7.05 time more preferable than Austin (60,000/8500). The resulting preference weights are shown in Table 12.5, and these can be multiple by the criterion weight.

In other areas, hard data can substitute for subjective interpretation. For example, a proxy for skilled labor and the availability of technical and managerial talent is the ratio of research and devel-

Table 12.5. Preference weights using salary as a proxy for wage levels and social costs

Rank	Site	Preference Weight
1	Bangalore	0.482
2	Moscow	0.341
3	Dublin	0.109
4	Austin	0.068

opment scientists and technicians per 1000 people, published in United Nations data. There are obvious pitfalls in using data without interpretation, but with background knowledge, it can reduce the selection problem. Further reduction is possible by using models that combine some of these indicators to provide composite scores.

Simulation models

In general, there are two basic approaches to logistics modeling for supply chain modeling: a) simulation and b) optimization and planning. Simulation models are mathematical descriptions of operations or problems. They can be simple or developed in detail. The simulation is only a description of an operation at one particular time or for a specified time period, operating under one set of parameter estimates. The do not provide »best« answers, only one answer at a time, reflecting a particular set of numerical assumption values. It is possible by successive runs to move towards better solutions, but an optimal result cannot be guaranteed.

The power of a simulation to identify a problem is demonstrated in a case study by David Levy (1995). A computer company in the United States sourced products from Singapore. The focus was specifically on product flow: looking at the impact of supply chain disruptions on demand fulfillment and inventory over distance. The model assumes a set of decision rules and linkages. Demand, production and deliveries from suppliers fluctuated. The model evolved dynamically. The previous month was a starting-point for

Table 12.6. Sourcing options for a Singapore plant

	Production for sale this month	Production for sale next month
Vendors ship in 1 month	Version 1 United States assembly, responsive vendors	Version 2 Singapore assembly, responsive vendors
Vendors ship in 2 months	Version 3 United States assembly, slow vendors	Version 4 Singapore assembly, slow vendors

Source: Levy (1995, p. 350)

operations in the next month. Each run had a sequence of 36 months. Four different scenarios were used (Table 12.6).

These were considered as the principal options available to the computer company; air freight was too expensive for the product. Although the logistics costs of sourcing from Singapore were an additional cost, production costs normally would more than offset them under stable conditions. His conclusions were that demand instability or long lead times alone were not the difficulty, but the combination of demand disruptions and long lead times were the problem.

A second set of runs compared supply chain disruptions with sales forecast volatility. Forecasting was the basis for production, inventory and vendor orders. Supply chain disruptions over time tended to smooth, but demand as measured by forecast errors did not. This came as a surprise to management, which shifted production offshore as soon as it had stabilized, when demand was the major source of instability.

This example demonstrates a use for simulation modeling in evaluating the effects of uncertainty, in this case time variability. Figure 12.2 portrays several different sources of variability in the supply chain. Production schedules and transit times are subject to time delays that can significantly affect cost through the need for inventory buffers and customer service through the inability to meet delivery schedules. Demand uncertainty is another factor that adds cost and adds potential havoc to the system. Part of the problem can be relieved through better forecast management, capturing early sales data and careful analysis (Fisher et al. 2000). Another

Figure 12.2. Modeling Uncertainty

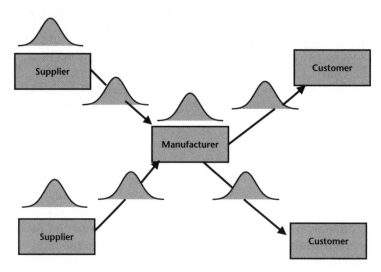

part can be reduced through faster supply chain and order cycle times. Simulation provides the ability to assess potential actions in advance of their implementation.

Financial considerations

Many governments use subsidies, tariffs and taxation to encourage exports from their own industries. The effects are not always visible without analysis. Consider the following hypothetical but still realistic example (Nelson & Toledano 1979).

Global Enterprises, headquartered in Gamma, has two potential sources of supply: one in country Alpha, the other in Beta. Procurement requires 2500 units. Production costs per unit are USD 7.20 in Alpha and 8.00 in Beta. A standard gross profit margin of 25% over production cost is used to calculate an internal transfer price from the new source to the parent company. Corporate income taxes are set at rates of 45% for Alpha, 35% for Beta and 52% for Gamma. Freight costs are USD 1.50 per unit from Alpha and USD 3.00 from Beta. The product transfer price is USD 9.00 from Alpha and USD 10.00 from Beta. The analysis in Table 12.7

Table 12.7. Landed Price Comparition.
Source based on landed price in USD

	Alpha	Beta
Production cost	22,500	25,000
Transportation cost	3,750	7,500
CIF price in Gamma	26,250	32,500
Duty in Gamma	2,100	2,600
Landed price in Gamma	28,350	35,100

compares landed costs (total cost delivered to Global in Gamma after calculating all taxes, subsidies, transfer prices and transportation costs).

If Global were to buy based on costs (or in open markets) without any benefit of special financing arrangements, the obvious choice would be Alpha. Beta could subsidize the sale through an export profit incentive to make the price competitive.

Global could also establish wholly owned subsidiaries in either country and handle the whole transfer internally without external financial influences. With these incentives, the situation changes. Following the transfer prices and incentives shown in Table 12.8, the calculations ultimately provide higher profit using Beta. Prices based on a higher production cost base show a higher profit because of the higher price based on cost. Beta adds USD 7500 in export profit incentives (USD 3 per unit) to establish a much higher profit for Beta. Beta's income tax is much higher, resulting in a higher landed cost from Beta and lower profit. Gamma's income tax is lower because of the higher landed cost, but the net profit from the entire transaction including profit from Beta is higher.

The example illustrates the role of financial incentives in selecting sites or suppliers for international product movements. There are also other influences:

- labor cost based on location and union contracts;
- capital availability from local sources or from outside sources such as aid programs;
- capital cost based on incentive rates and ease of transfer among the parties to the investment;

Table 12.8. Financial Aspects of Foreign Plant Location.
Sourcing based on financial considerations in USD

Transfer price	22,500	25,000
Production cost	18,000	20,000
Transfer profit	2,250	5,000
Export profit incentives	0	7,500
Profit	4,500	12,500
Income tax	2,025	4,375
Net profit to produce	2,475	8,125
Revenue in Gamma	37,500	37,500
Landed cost in Gamma	28,350	35,100
Profit	9,150	2,400
Tax in Gamma	4,757	1,248
Net profit in Gamma	4,392	1,152
Net profit to Global	6,867	9,277

- tax rates that differ not only between countries but also for particular incentives;
- tax benefits, including depreciation schedules and other treatment of assets; and
- resource access, including infrastructure as well as physical materials.

The important measure is cost, not price. Costs reflect activities and financial advantage. They can be shifted between locations and stages of production. Pricing for location analysis is arbitrary, because prices define where taxes should be paid.

Optimization and planning models

Optimization models in supply chain management are usually associated with large-scale networks, although they are also employed in more focused applications such as production scheduling and vehicle routing. We are focusing here on supply chain network applications.

Designing and managing the supply chain requires the evaluation of system changes before they are implemented. The supply chain has a large number of potential trade-offs, over many variables and many different states. Planners require a comprehensive view to ask »what if« questions. Planning for supply chain management involves two stages: the corporate plan and the supply chain plan (Rushton & Saw 1992). Corporate planning becomes the basis for supply chain planning and strategy development. At the same time, supply chain planning should contribute to corporate planning. The initial stages of the supply chain plan establishes the decision environment: external elements of supply structure, markets, country and regional constraints including exchange rates, customs duty, transport capability and capacity, options in information technology and internal elements of production capacity, customer service policies and corporate organization. It should also identify objectives, product characteristics and sourcing constraints.

These elements become the basis for quantitative strategy planning models to evaluate strategic options. The role of these models is to provide a rational basis for developing and evaluating strategic options. The analyst, in effect, has a dialogue with the model. A good planning model represents enough features of the situation to permit the planner to investigate alternatives and to test their sensitivity to underlying assumptions. To use models well, however, managers should have a general understanding of how models are developed, their relationships, as well as the problem setting. Models should be used to gain insight into the problem and possibly to narrow choices. Although outputs may indicate solutions, the results should be balanced by judgments that assume familiarity with the methods.

The dilemma of supply chain planning lies in defining the scope of any proposed model. Scope determines the extent of the model. It means the extent, how many stages in a complex supply process should be included and the level of detail necessary to shape the direction of the system. Few models have the capacity to span both production and distribution networks within a single structure. Further, no model can be sufficiently comprehensive to replace other more detailed planning models and processes within the supply chain.

The methods of optimization modeling

Optimization modeling is a set of variations of linear programming. The intent here is to describe applications in network optimization. In a supply chain context, the models offer solutions for routing shipments from factories or other supply points to customers. There are three classes of these programs in particular to introduce here: the transportation problem, the transshipment problem and mixed integer linear programming. The transportation problem assigns routes to shipments from factories to customers, minimizing transport and production costs and taking into account customer demands and factory capacities. The transshipment model is a simple extension of the transportation problem to deal with three-stage systems such as factory to distribution center to customers, answering the question of which factory should be uses to route to which distribution center to which customer. Again, it takes into account capacities and demands and minimizes the total cost.

The network problem must be formulated in a particular mathematical structure that restricts many solutions to approximations and narrowly defined problem formulations. For practical purposes, all variables must be linear. To keep computation within reasonable limits, movements must be simplified to a limited number of products, often treated as a single commodity. Within that structure, the model will provide an optimal or a close-to-optimal solution. Optimizing models indicate potential decisions, but failing that, their optimizing behavior provides a basis for comparing different network designs. It also becomes a benchmark for comparing runs where some of the assumptions have been changed.

The transportation problem model has been applied to the expansion of manufacturing plants and breweries. Note that all transport costs are linear. Variable production costs can be included but are assumed to be proportional to output: they are also linear. Fixed costs cannot be included because they result in non-linear production cost functions. Some methods using successive iterations can be used, however, to overcome this linearity constraint. Notice that the transportation problem can only handle cost minimization. Other variables such as transit time must be treated separately, although they can be handled by the same problem formulation.

The transportation problem handles management questions about relatively simple supply chains. What about more multifaceted chains involving more than one level of production or routing from production through distribution centers or transshipment points to market?

In the transshipment problem, the number of potential routings is much larger because of the greater number of possible combinations; the number of calculations can become quite large. The formulation is also more practical, reflecting a more realistic context. An oil company used the model to route products over a combination of river barges and oil pipelines. A major automobile manufacturer used it to assign component production to factories and route output to the next stage within a global production system.

There is a further development in mixed integer linear programming methods. It is now a significant method of network analysis and planning for supply chains. Transportation and transshipment problems can solve transportation routing or other problems that can be formulated within their particular framework, including production scheduling. However, there are other more complex problems, such as selecting possible sites to route products to distribution center to customer. Each site has different costs and capacities, and only a subset can be chosen. The solutions utilize mixed integer linear programming and have received more interest and application because they handle this higher level of complexity.

A typical but simple problem is a set of possible factory locations supplying a set of customers. The actual number of sites is less than the number of possible locations. There must be an objective function to minimize facility and transportation costs. As in other linear programming models, the model must specify the flows from factories to customers, taking into account customer demands, factory and other capacity. There must also be an additional equation to specify whether or not a particular factory is included within the network. The model can deal with fixed facility costs as well as variable production and transportation costs.

A typical problem may have a set of possible locations such as factories or distribution centers, but only a subset of these can be used. Goods are shipped from each combination of sites to the set of customers (or first to intermediate points and then to customers if combined with a transshipment model). The combination of the factory (fixed) cost and the variable production and transportation costs determine the cost. In the end, the solution finds the set of sites that produce the lowest total cost.

Development of planning models for the global supply chain

Vidal & Goetschalckx (1997) have reviewed the development of mixed integer linear programming models. Many problems discussed above have been overcome, but models of the global supply chain are more difficult to solve because of the combinatorial possibilities. Some problems have not been completely resolved, as the scale of the problem becomes larger, with a need by users to incorporate customer service and unique requests. Computational methods have now reached a point, however, that models are available to handle capacity constraints that were not feasible before.

Global supply chain modeling presents new challenges. Possibly the most defining published paper was by Cohen et al. (1989). The model deals with three levels: suppliers, plants and markets. It covers a planning horizon of 12 quarters for multiple products (outputs) and material (inputs). The firm buys at the given local price in each resource market. Minimum and maximum demands are deterministic and differentiated by product, market and time period. Supplier contracts include cost, duration and volume. There are economies of scale in production and materials procurement. Transfer prices are used between factories and markets. Tariffs are charged for transfers of both materials and products. There is also provision for local content restriction. Corporate income tax is paid in each country of operation. Both plant locations and their capacities are fixed in advance, but plants can be chosen for individual products.

This model is also limited in that it does not include intermediate products and interplant shipments, or distribution centers in the distribution system. There is no provision for inventory; supply and demand are matched in each time period. Competitive actions and national product design differences are ignored.

The model determines which suppliers will be used. Which products will be produced in each plant, the volume of output for these products for each plant, product flows from which plants to which markets and the volume of material flows from which vendor to which plant?

The international components are supply contracts designating the length of the contract, both fixed and variable costs and minimal and maximum shipment volumes. Exchange rates utilize one standard currency, with all cash flows designated in this currency, but multiple exchange-rate factors will be used. Costs and prices are designated in the following notation. Economies of scale are represented by using artificial products corresponding to different outputs. Local content rules in some countries require a minimum expenditure on production and materials based on sales within the country.

Profits are defined for each plant, market and for the firm as a whole. The first equations below do not take into account currency or tax factors. Profit for the firm in standardized currency is revenue less inbound procurement, transport and tariffs, less production costs, less fixed supplier contracts calculated in standardized currency. Cash flows are charged in currencies of the source country. Product mix variables are eliminated because they are determined by the inbound and outbound flows. The firm's after-tax profit function is the sum of specific profit in each country. Transfer prices between countries now become important.

In supply contracts, selection of vendor contracts opens a »time window« during which a plant can source from one specific vendor. The bill of materials governs actual material flow. Inventory is cleared every period; plant output equals total shipments as market demand (in units) Outbound flows are constrained by volume limits. The currency flows generated by shipments from plants to markets may be also be constrained.

There are two types of constraints on production capacity based on 1) overall product mix capacity and 2) individual item capacity. For local content, there is a requirement to spend a fraction of sales revenue in the country where the good was manufactured.

A solution process
Given a set of products, markets and infrastructure, the model develops a medium-term plan through an international manufactur-

ing strategy, a set of supply contracts and market volume allocations. The model is solvable in concept through a mixed integer
non-linear program (Lawrence & Pasternack 1998).

The authors raise another issue: how to implement a plan developed from this model. They recognize the difficulty of managing a
complex international network over time and suggest an incentive
structure to encourage decentralized decisions to make adjustments for short-term reality.

Application

Digital Equipment Corporation (DEC) reported on the development and use of a global supply chain model based on mixed integer linear programming (Arntzen et al. 1995). This model specifies
a vendor-production-distribution network and minimizes either
cost or weighted cumulative production and distribution times,
subject to estimated demand, local content, offset trade and joint
capacity for multiple products, supply chains and time periods. It is
reported to have saved over USD 100 million.

The model was developed to answer a need for guidance in re-
structuring the corporation after a disastrous financial loss. The
previous corporate supply chain structure had been successful during a period when mid-size computers were in demand. The
change to a PC environment led to emphasis on the core encouraged outsourcing of major components and required less manufacturing capacity. The redesign began with rationalizing its supply
and distribution network and re-engineering business processes.
The global supply chain model was developed as part of the renovation to answer specific questions such as:

- How many plants would DEC need?
- Where would individual products be produced?
- The value of tax havens for location?
- How many distribution centers and their location?
- How should cost be balanced against total cycle time in manu-
  facturing and distribution?
- Which suppliers should supply which plant?

The global supply chain model addressed problems that included
multiple products, facilities, production stages, time periods and

transportation modes. It could balance cost against time. It also included international issues of customs duty, local content and offset trade. The time dimension was included along with cost, using weighted activity time, the sum of processing times for each segment multiplied by the number of units processed. The global supply chain model minimized a combination of total cost and activity, subject to constraints of meeting customer demand, controlling inventories and assigning vendors to individual production facilities.

It has been used to evaluate the entire supply chain for major businesses and for the company as a whole. In a typical application, the model would find an optimal solution. Management would then hold one element, such as a particular plant as fixed within the system. The model would be used for a large number of runs. It has been used to rationalize the manufacturing base from 33 to 12 plants and to design a parts services system that could be integrated with manufacturing and a distribution system for the Americas. The global model allowed analysis of multistage operations across levels within individual supply chains. It permitted the analysis of specific international issues such as customs duty and duty drawbacks.

Modeling uncertainty within global supply chain programming models is a further development. Although most models have been deterministic in orientation, the problems often include random elements. Vidal & Goetschalckx (2000, p. 112) have presented a demonstration model that takes into account the effect of variation, changing demand, variable lead times and variable lead times on total system cost and configuration. They observed that, with changes in their test parameters, configuration of the system varied considerably, even though changes in total system cost were small. They observed, »The value of [mixed integer linear programming] models is that they provide fast sensitivity analysis based on optimization of the system under different conditions. Obtaining these new optimal solutions without using [mixed integer linear programming] is nearly impossible.«

Perspective

The Hewlett-Packard experience

Hewlett-Packard has been a prime user of supply chain models. In fact, they have probably published more about their use of supply chain models than has any other corporation. Lee & Billington (1993) identify four areas and a fifth from another paper (Billington & Davis 1992) where these models have been eminently useful:

- inventory and service benchmarking to establish reference points for strategic action;
- operational planning and control to test processes and procedures;
- what-if analysis for strategic experimentation;
- supply chain design to establish close-to-optimal configurations; and
- a vehicle for communication to top management to express concepts in tangible form.

Hewlett-Packard established the Strategic Planning and Modeling Group (SPAM) in 1988. It introduced quantitative methods into management strategy. The first effort was the Bubble Model, which analyzed individual plant sites as combinations of fixed and variable costs following a structure using activity-based costing, to estimate the total cost of different production scenarios. It considers four cost categories: build, linkage, logistics and implementation. Build costs include both direct and overhead costs that establish economies of scale. Although it uses programming methods, this particular model was used to aid management decision, not to provide an optimizing solution.

A later model, SPAM, captured uncertainties that had not been included in the original Bubble Model. the development of this model stressed preliminary understanding of the problem before the actual model development. Although the method was not specified, it appears to use simulation.

This led to the development of a further model, the Worldwide Inventory Network Optimizer. The central concept is that output volume determines inbound inventory. Delays upstream will reduce output downstream. Although the method is again not specified in the literature, it appears from the writing to be a complex simulation. The Worldwide Inventory Network Optimizer has now evolved into the Supply Chain Analysis Tool.

In the course of developing and using these models, Hewlett-Packard arrived at two concepts: the importance of uncertainty in the supply chain (Davis 1993) and the efficiency frontier (Lee & Billington 1995). Uncertainty arises from supplier performance, the manufacturing process and distribution. The two are related through the amount of inventory necessary to protect the chain and the customer against risk created by uncertainty, reflected in the efficiency frontier.

The efficiency frontier is a curve plotting the relationship between finished goods inventory and the customer order fill rate, given current demand, process and supply conditions (Figure 12.3). It has been used successfully at several divisions of the company, identifying uncertainties within the system. Further work by SPAM has led to studies of

- relocating facilities within the United States and Europe;
- product design for supply chain management;
- determining the location of postponed customization;
- examining supply chain relationships and inventory beyond corporate boundaries to include suppliers, sales force and dealers; and

Figure 12.3. The Efficiency Frontier

- expansion to broader perspectives by marketing and finance on the supply chain, principally through a forecasting project called flap (forecasting, logistics and planning).

Over time, the focus shifted from production to distribution to customers.

A management science laboratory

One major hurdle is making management science methods easily available to supply chain management. One solution is to create models that are both useful and easy to construct. Slats et al. (1995, p. 14) note: »The objective of a logistic laboratory is to provide a set of logistic models and sub-models and means to quickly build logistic models based on optimization, heuristics and/or simulation.« The laboratory would encourage experimentation to test both present and possible configurations against changes in market conditions, infrastructure, information impairment and management concepts.

In their logistic laboratory, tasks would begin with market assessment, establishing the physical configuration of the system and designing the control system. There would then be experimentation by the use of models to evaluate possible options in a riskless setting. Slats et al. cite two models that have been developed in Europe to implement this concept: distribution planning support system and TASTE.

The distribution planning support system is built around an integrated support framework. A network problem is disaggregated into smaller parts for ease of analysis. It then subjects the problem to three descending levels of optimization exercises for physical configuration (such as distribution centers), deployment of resources (such as inventory) and flow rates (such as delivery frequencies), followed by a fourth level for operations where TASTE is employed.

TASTE is a simulation package. It includes a collection of components: distribution centers, control units and customers. The user selects and applies these components in a graphic system design. The TASTE interpreter provides the ability to execute the system.

Executing the system provides the ability to test and modify proposed solutions.

The programming perspective

Geoffrion & Powers (1995) noted several factors that have changed the use of programming models in logistics and therefore in supply chain management:

- the price-to-performance ratio of telecommunications;
- the decentralization of corporate information technology that relieved stand-alone applications;
- the growth of EDI and automated identification; and
- the shift of optimization installations from mainframe to PCs.

The algorithms have also evolved. First came non-optimizing cost calculators for evaluating system designs. Then heuristic methods came, incorporating model features and conserving then scarce computing resources, but were unsatisfactory because they did not produce results that could be used for benchmarking. Next, linear programming on a case-by-case basis was used in many applications, even though it often took multiple runs to compare alternatives. Mixed integer linear programming became an attractive method but was discouraging to use because of the need to incorporate it in application-specific software. Improvements in algorithms enabled larger models to be solved with available resources. Geoffrion & Powers note, however, that all of the methods above are still in use, propelled by the broadly available increases in computational power, a reluctance by users to shift mixed integer linear programming software from mainframe to desktop PCs, discomfort with sophisticated models and memory of failures to achieve optimization on previous models. Data collection and preparation presents the bulk of the workload.

A complete system combining data management with an optimizer and user presentation software has been sold as an integrated program, SAILS (Strategic Analysis of Integrated Logistics Systems). It presents scenario generation, menus for report selection, the capability to build complete models from publicly available databases and the ability to compare runs with a base scenario. Clients have reported uses of SAILS that far exceed the initial conception planned for the program, including production allocations, distribution, reverse logistics and the use of »focused factories«.

The future appears to reside in expanding telecommunication and better algorithms. Pressure from users for more sophistication continues unabated. Continuing expansion in the numbers of users that perform local analysis will add further motivation.

Concluding comments

Models will always be with us. There appears to be no better way to understand the problems of the supply chain than by formulating a model structure and testing the variables contained within it. The ubiquity of computing resources makes potential for use very high. Supply chain managers can be more effective if they understand and use models to develop and test their decisions.

At the same time, models have limits. There are too many »soft« areas in supply chain management to rely on models alone to indicate direction. At best, they lay out choices based on their own structure and process. They may leave out important variables that cannot be quantified. They may imply organizational relationships that do not exist. In short, they must be used with caution.

The stumbling block of the past was data. The development of IT and specifically XML and ERP makes data more accessible. Geoffrion & Powers project more efficient algorithms. This combined with the great expansion in computing power makes models more accessible. At the least, they provide a powerful tool for communicating.

STRATEGY

13. Strategy of the supply chain

*»Every two or three years, supply chain design gets
reinvented. And that's okay. That's what growth is all
about.«*
Hugh Aitken, Sun Microsystems,
quoted in Bovet & Martha (2000, p. 243)

Is there a clear appreciation of strategy for the supply chain? In a
survey of logistics strategy, Clinton & Closs (1997) found little consistency among responding firms and concluded that the concept of
strategy was »promising« but not conclusive. For the supply chain,
there is little agreement on perspective or scope. Bechtel & Jayaram
(1997) identify four distinct approaches:

- functional chain awareness, emphasizing the span of functional
  activities within the supply chain;
- linkage and logistics, establishing the role of logistics operations
  as the connector between activities;
- an information orientation, underscoring the role of information
  in enabling the supply chain to coordinate activities; and
- integration, stressing the need to manage the supply chain to act
  as a single unified process.

Other discussions emphasize relationships, value-adding activities,
the supply chain as a demand pipeline, systems thinking, total quality management, process engineering, modeling and cost analysis.
Strategies depend on the particular emphasis. Under these conditions, there is little chance for consensus. Figure 13.1 shows the objective, if not the solution.

The scope of activities within the supply chain has also been
widely debated, as we have noted in Chapter 1. Although we prefer
the comprehensive »dirt-to-dirt« view of Cooper et al. (1997),

Figure 13.1. Supply Chain Strategy

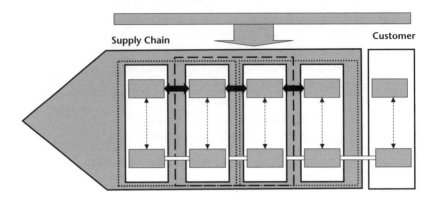

much of the management discussion focuses at most on connections to immediate customers and first-tier suppliers.

There is also a shift towards the customer as decision-maker. The conceptual foundation of the supply chain, the Value Chain of Michael Porter (1980, 1985), points to the customer as responding rather than initiating action. This, however, does not match the general marketing orientation of business towards the customer. Two advocates argue that the customer initiates the chain of decisions within the supply chain. Hines (1996a) proposes the Value Stream, where the system pulls orders from the customer, rather than pushing it towards the market. Kalakota & Robinson (1999) similarly discuss electronic commerce, tracing the order from customer to production and procurement through the Internet.

We discuss strategy at two levels. This chapter deals with the internal options of the supply chain. The next chapter considers the interaction of the supply chain and corporate strategy. This immediate discussion is oriented to the model of Chapter 1: activity structure, operational processes and organizational relationships. Identifying activities and locating them within organizational units becomes the first step. We then look at processes as a single system. Finally, we establish the underlying interorganizational relationships for supply chain operations.

Supply chain management as a competitive weapon

The market determines objectives for the supply chain, captured in the title of Blackwell's (1997) book, *From Mind to Market*. The supply chain in some cases can create competitive advantage through superior design and performance. At the least, a well-functioning supply chain is necessary for corporate survival.

- The first requirement is to fill orders rapidly and reliably.
- The second is to demonstrate flexibility in matching customer requirements.
- The third is to perform efficiently, because the ability of customers to search for the lowest price is now enhanced by the Web.
- We might also add a fourth: short time-to-market, introducing product development as a further dimension of the supply chain.

The conflict between speed and flexibility in serving customers versus efficiency introduce opposing resource requirements. In some cases, changes in production processes and product modularity can provide solutions. Under most circumstances, managing this conflict becomes the essence of supply chain strategy.

What is known about the supply chain?

The supply chain has specific characteristics that shape strategy:

- a customer orientation
- a chain of activities across organizational boundaries
- performance dominated by time
- a global orientation
- driven by information
- complex systemic links
- lateral management processes
- a scope of activities that varies by individual perception.

Customer orientation becomes a seldom achieved ideal. In some cases, the customers, such as retailers, are only intermediate and their interpretation of demand is reflected in forecasts and actual orders. Supplying customers involves a chain of activities performed both within and outside the dominant organization, requiring managing both customer and supplier relationships. Performance takes place through a »pipeline« dominated by time, to produce, process orders and to hold inventory. The global dimension involves not only the physical parameters of time and space but a highly complex environment involving currency exchange, political issues and differing cultures and infrastructures. The system is activated, coordinated and in some cases jointly planned through the information system. All these links create an interdependent system. Each organization faces its own unique environment, limited information and operating restrictions that can lead to problems with unintended consequences. Finally, the scope of the supply chain is too broad for one manager but must rely on local decisions and lateral coordination.

Objectives can be grouped in three categories:

- service to customers
- low operating costs
- minimize assets.

They become the strategic balance, where no single objective dominates to the exclusion of the others. Service to customers must initiate any discussion of supply chain strategy. The costs of production, distribution, procurement, transport and other services are secondary. The third includes both physical facilities and inventory. How they are resolved depends on the market and the political skills of the supply chain manager.

The strategic model

The model of strategy of the supply chain has three components: structure, process and relationships. Each offers specific actions. Structure deals with the choice of partners, defining activities and locating them inside organizations. It influences strategy in two ways. First and most immediate is how it affects the supply chain itself, in process actions and the organizational relationships required. Second is its interaction with corporate strategy, affecting the nature of the economic environment and the options available. Processes involve the sequence of activities, the paths through which information and products flow. They are probably the major available source of change. They provide the ability to respond to the objectives of supply chain management. Relationships define the connections between organizations. They include not only information links and transactions but the willingness to coordinate operations, share information and other resources and contribute to the management of the supply chain as a whole.

Structure

Strategy in structure involves several issues: 1) the core and outsourcing, 2) developing structure and 3) customization and postponement.

The core and outsourcing
Business is moving towards holding only core competencies, the areas where it holds a competitive advantage. Other activities are outsourced to other parties. This trend favors the development of the supply chain to link activities in separate organizations as an integral unit. The motivation, on the one hand, is a desire for efficiency and superior performance through specialization Hamel & Prahalad 1994), and on the other, to increase returns to capital, using assets without owning them.

Yhe trend becomes reinforced access (Rifkin 2000). The enabling factor is the increasing capacity of information technology to transmit and process complex communication and coordinate across organizational boundaries regardless of physical separation. In some cases, the lack of ownership presents a risk that partners may change allegiance or that competitors will also be able to access the same resources. Logistics service providers, production and distribution are areas for direct service suppliers. Functional areas such as information systems, procurement and even supply chain management itself are now being outsourced.

Outsourcing requires negotiation and coordination. There is a problem of ensuring quality of performance. Outsourcing tends towards standardization and production at a basic level, losing the ability to differentiate in contracted services. On the other hand, it offers the opportunity to create partnerships as teams, utilizing their specialized insights for joint creative efforts. It also sets the stage for process.

Building structure
Developing the supply chain structure involves a series of steps:

1. Determine activity requirements to match the objectives of the supply chain.
2. Analyze the cost structures of these activities to establish potential economies of scale, scope and specialization.
3. Determine the optimal configuration of these activities in sequences and possible combinations in terms of market response and cost.
4. Define the core competencies of the firm in terms of their ability to achieve competitive advantage.
5. Identify and select organizations and their subcontractor organizations with the capability to manage these activities.
6. Negotiate with candidate firms to manage activities in logical groups to serve the supply chain as a whole.
7. Determine the organizational requirements for coordination, measurement and control.
8. Determine the forms of coordination that participating organizations will use, including management teams and information technology.

The first three steps define the tasks. The product and its related supply process determine activities. The choice of service or cost minimization objectives forces differences in activities. The service objectives and cost structures of individual activities dictate location and whether economies of scale or scope are relevant. Using activities as modular building blocks permits them to be shifted and be combined with other activities for more effective response and lower costs. These steps provide the functional organization of the supply chain.

Steps 4, 5 and 6 determine the organizational »ownership« of these activities. The key is to identify the core of competitive advantage, an area of ambiguity. The core itself has two definitions. The first includes the activities that have a superior ability to compete. The second includes tasks requiring critical coordination such as information system design, or product development may be included within the lead organization boundaries.

Steps 7 and 8 prescribe the management tasks. Negotiation defines firm boundaries for both the lead and partner firms. The task, the technical characteristics of the organization and negotiation determine the needs and the extent and the means of coordination.

There is a difference between working with an established supply chain versus designing a new supply chain. In an ongoing supply chain, these activities are already established within partner organizations. Configuration then involves shifting activities and evaluating and possibly replacing partners. These steps create a new supply chain organization.

There are also differences between stable supply chains where partners have been long-term associates and flexible supply chains where partners change in response to different products and customers. Partnerships in this setting activated in response to particular requirements becoming inactive again after the project is finished.

Customization and postponement
Customers now demand more product variety, to the point of individual product and service combinations. This has led to the concept of mass customization, in which product and service features are configured to individual customers (Pine 1993). Commands for differences in service can be easily transmitted as information between physical locations, to be interpreted and modified by computers and sent as instructions for particular actions or procedures. However, it also requires coordination between organizations that may be more difficult in practice.

Configuring individual products to match customers involves a different set of issues and options. The degree of adaptation is determined by the order penetration point (Figure 13.2): how far the order proceeds through the supply chain towards the source of supply (Sharman 1984). Information on individual orders enters the supply chain and progresses backward through the chain. Whether

Figure 13.2. The Decoupling Point in the Firm

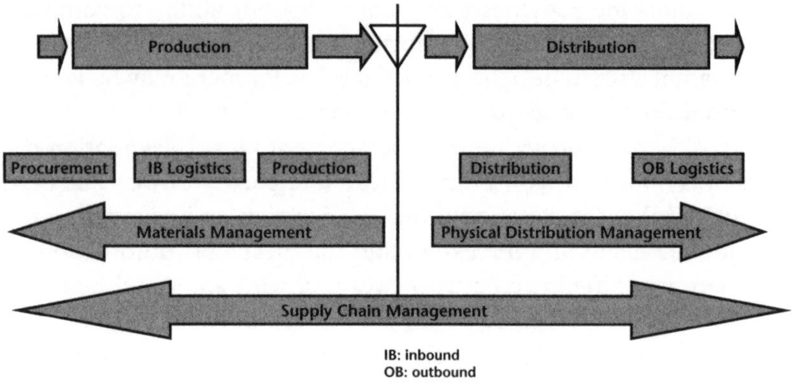

it stays in this form or is aggregated as it moves through distribution, manufacturing supplier component selection and design determines the degree of product customization.

These concepts are closely related to two others: product modularity and postponement. Modularity determines the range of product choices by establishing the possible combinations of components within a given product. Customers are guided to make choices within predetermined limits that become a strategic decision within the supply chain. In effect, the degree of modular product design is a choice in marketing strategy of how far to adapt to individual customer preference. Modularity allows product components to take advantage of economies of scale in production but to be combined with others at a later stage, after the customer order arrives. Some products such as computers are more modular in production than others.

Postponement delays actions until the last possible moment (Pagh & Cooper 1998). This is the direct opposite of holding inventory as a form of speculation that products will be sold (Bucklin 1965). Postponement can involve both products and services. For products, postponement delays final product completion until the order arrives. Completion actions can include final assembly, labeling, packing accessory items or packaging. One structural issue is whether the product should be finished at the factory or at some point closer to the customer such as a distribution center, or even at the facility of a third-party logistics provider. Another is further back in the supply chain, whether the supplier should hold or even produce components on demand before they enter into the production line. In effect, the customer order pulls the product and its components.

The order penetration point becomes a dividing line. On the one side is customer preference and market segmentation, expressed through inventory of finished product variety and multiple service options. Products are produced to order as a pull system, in preference to forecasting. Individual products are difficult to forecast because demands often show high variability. On the other side is a flow of components built according to an overall forecast in anticipation of demand as a push system. Demand variability is reduced because components serve aggregate demand rather than individual products.

As a concept, it is similar to the Mintzberg-Lampel stages of customization described in Chapter 10. Some orders will be matched at a location close to the customer, even at retail for accessories and minor changes. Other orders would go to a distribution center equipped to make more substantial changes such as packag-

Figure 13.3. Decoupling points in the Supply Chain

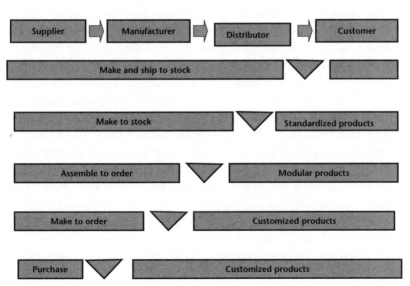

ing or even configuration. More fundamental product changes would be carried by orders to the factory. The orders for some products would involve suppliers for customized components. Finally, completely customized orders would penetrate the entire system. The range is shown in Figure 13.3.

The order penetration point is the bridge between the supply chain as a production system and the demand chain as an order fulfillment system (Hoekstra & Romme 1992). It raises issues within the supply chain about how far backward in supply customer orders should be carried and, conversely, how far forward towards the customer common components should be carried. On the one side, it stresses individual customer orders. On the other, it emphasizes production efficiency and standard processes. The strategic balance is the solution to the problem of trading off product and service variety against higher inventory costs.

Process

One strategic choice is whether the system should anticipate or respond to demand. Systems that anticipate or lead demand will push products towards the market using forecasting tools as a guide. As production-oriented systems, they have lower manufacturing costs because they produce for inventory at a higher cost of inventory and less flexibility in meeting demand. Systems that respond to demand have higher costs because they must be flexible in production and distribution.

Closs et al. (1998) developed a simulation model of a supply chain to study the issue. The model included a supplier, manufacturer, an intermediate distributor to two retailers and direct distribution to a third. An anticipatory »push« system uses inventory and forecasting to provide customer service. A responsive system operates by having market demand »pull« inventory through the system. The issues revolve around whether the responsive system provides better customer service and operates at lower cost because of superior inventory management. The simulation clearly indicated that responsive systems provide better service. Inventory costs, however, were equivocal between the two alternatives. The most significant reductions were at the retail level, favoring responsive systems. Responsive systems have a price: the cost of implementation and the effort to develop relationships.

Time and cost are the critical dimensions of supply chain process strategy. The time dimension includes service through order cycle time and the ability to respond through flexible response (Stalk 1990). It also determines the cost of inventory through the length of the total material flow cycle. In this section, we examine two aspects of time management: time delays and their impact on the performance of the supply chain process.

Process delays
Every process has a combination of productive time when value is added to the object of the process, material and products, and idle or non-productive time when material waits before the next stage of processing (Figure 13.4). Waiting time delays can occur for economic reasons such as the accumulation of batch quantities for production or for transport. The principle is the economics of minimizing production set-ups because of fixed costs. Another is the cost of handling and moving a single shipment through a transport system in distribution. The opposing ideal is a batch quantity of one unit. The trade-off is the cost of delay in inventory holding costs and loss of flexibility, versus the fixed costs involved in a production changeover or a transport schedule.

Potential delays in a supply chain are possible in the sequence of production, waiting for processing stages and in distribution, waiting for warehouse and terminal operations to take place and building quantities for truckload shipments. It is not unusual to experience value-adding processing time as low as 10% of the total elapsed time, the »logistics cover« (Braithwaite & Christopher 1991).

There are many ways to reduce total time in manufacturing such as parallel component production, cellular production, reducing changeover times and simplified production design. Flexible manufacturing also reduces waiting time because it reduces the need for finished product inventories. Distribution waiting time can be reduced by reducing inventory, consolidating processes such as shipments or using express services. In a procurement network, di-

Figure 13.4. Delays in the Supply Chain

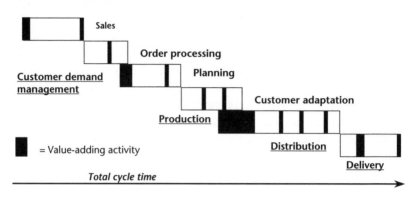

rect coordination of suppliers' and customers' production schedules also eliminates inventory.

The order fulfillment cycle exposes the order to a large number
of sources of delay, beginning with order acquisition, followed by
inventory management to protect against forecasting errors. It is also caught by delays from batching in production scheduling, followed by delays in shipment to distribution centers and then to intermediate and final customers. Solutions begin with direct customer orders into the system. They are further improved by adopt-
ing customer collaboration techniques to improve forecasts and introducing real-time production scheduling and flow-through distribution using cross-docking at distribution centers and direct store
and even home delivery.

Variation in time performance is another source of time delay
(Davis 1993). Variation in arrival times at the next stage or variation in processing time must be covered by inventory to maintain
material flow through the system. However, inventory means product that is not undergoing a value-changing process. Gaining control over variation is a step towards precise coordination leading to
improved response and reduced inventory cost (Figure 13.5).

Every supply chain offers different opportunities. Modeling
techniques using simulation provide an opportunity to test process
changes before introducing them into actual supply chains, to experiment with the future at minimum risk.

Figure 13.5. Variation in the Supply Chain

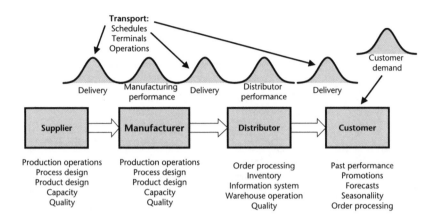

System characteristics

A supply chain system involves physical nodal points (stages such as factories and distribution centers) and information and product flows. Within this system, time dimensions characterize operations for product movement, facility capacity and information processing and similar parameters. The management system also involves decision rules for inventory reorder disciplines, forecasting and forecasting accuracy, customer priorities and resource allocation. This system must also contend with unpredictable events of rapid changes in demand, supply disruptions and failures of partner performance and computer systems, to name a few.

Much of the development of system concepts in business comes from the supply chain or its predecessors. The most widely quoted is a simulation model by Forrester (1961) shown in Figure 13.6. In this model, a small increase of 10% in retail sales passed through a series of stages: distributor, factory warehouse and factory. Each stage operated with a standard inventory reorder point discipline. Inventory would be consumed until it dropped below a pre-designated reorder point, releasing a replenishment order to the next stage where the process was repeated. Orders were the only source of information about demand available to each succeeding stage. This resulted in strong fluctuation in demand, increasing in ampli-

Figure 13.6. Dynamic Behavior in the Supply Chain.
The Forrester Model

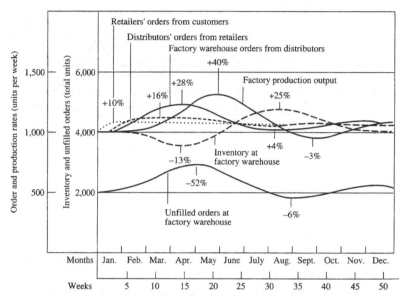

Source: Forrester (1961)

tude as replenishment orders went up the chain. To meet this apparent surge in demand, the factory instituted overtime production, soon followed by lay-offs as inventory was replenished downstream. The model demonstrates the perils of using standard decision rules unsupervised by human judgment. The concept of the Industrial Dynamics model has also been used to demonstrate the dilemma of managers who must make stocking decisions without benefit of information other than actual orders, as in the well-known »beer game« (Senge 1990).

Further experimentation has focused on designing better information networks (Towill et al. 1992). These internally induced demand oscillations are reduced as information is shared across the supply chain. Fluctuation can be dampened almost completely if demand at the point of final sale is transmitted instantaneously to manufacturing and distribution.

Lee et al. (1997) have provided empirical verification, calling it

»the bullwhip effect«. Their discussion points out that the problem extends beyond the timing of demand data release. Distortions entering in through data errors also contributes to the problem of misreading the market.

There is a message: a conventional set of decision rules creates unstable demand perceptions throughout the supply chain. Solutions encompass changes in both physical processes and information systems.

Physical solutions include:

• Reducing order quantities: this increases the frequency of ordering, thus increasing and smoothing the amount of information as it flows backward towards supply.
• Reducing processing times: inventory levels are determined by both demand and lead time. As processing times (and other components of lead time such as transit time from one stage to another) are reduced, inventory levels and order quantities can also be reduced.
• Eliminating stages in the channel: the channel becomes more stable as sources of delay are eliminated. Manufacturer-to-retailer channels reduce uncertainty over the original channel configuration.
• Producing to order: this becomes an ideal situation, pulling the order through the system. This solution is parallel to a shift in the order penetration point. No finished product inventory is held within the system, although as we have noted early, there may be component inventory that is produced to forecast.

Information solutions include:

• Improving forecasting: this reduces inventory in the channel by adding another source of information to the channel system. Ultimately it might lead to other methods of inventory control.
• Using DRP: this is tied to the accuracy of the forecast. It provides a formal planning structure for inventories downstream of production.
• Making demand information visible to the entire chain: sharing demand data allows all members to plan realistically without lags.

Figure 13.7. The P/D Ratio

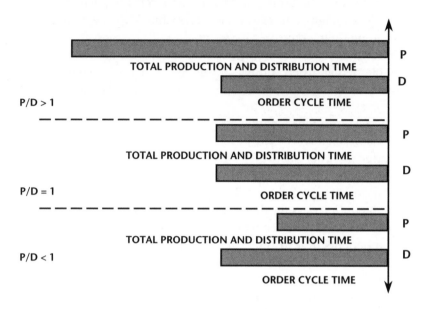

The relationship between production cycle and order cycle

The relationship of the order cycle and production times indicates how much flexibility the chain has to respond to demand changes. Figure 13.7 describes this condition. P designates the production cycle and D the order cycle. Visualize three situations:

P/D > 1. Production time is longer than the order cycle time. Thus, there is no flexibility possible. Products are manufactured and distributed to match a forecast of demand.

P/D = 1. Production time and order cycle time are equal. There is probably little flexibility in this relationship either. Random delays will weaken customer service.

P/D < 1. Production time is shorter than the order cycle time. This situation is ideal for flexibility and encourages make-to-order systems.

The ratio can be influenced by redefining the order cycle to match production. This, however, may not be a feasible solution in the face of competition that can deliver in shorter order cycles. An alternative lies in postponement and product modularity. Assembling products to order reduces P by relying on modular components. It becomes in effect a P/D < 1 situation. However, it must be supported by a component system that maintains a reliable supply in anticipation of orders.

Unintended consequences

Systems often have unintended consequences in chaotic behavior (Wilding 1998). Roughly defined, chaos is random behavior within a deterministic system. It is generated by fixed rules, excluding chance. Chaos is predictable within limits, but specific patterns of chaotic behavior are not repeated. This becomes especially significant for systems with automated processes.

Supply chains are non-linear systems with feedback loops. Operating processes lead to decisions that influence the environments in which they operate. The system then reacts once more with a changing environment requiring further decisions. Inventory stockouts affect customer service, which, in turn, affects decisions about carrying inventory.

Chaotic systems have five defining characteristics:
- They are sensitive to their initial starting conditions. Small deviations from an accurate value amplify until the results become unpredictable. Stable systems suddenly become unstable.
- Even chaotic systems can exhibit stability under certain conditions. Although they never repeat the same patterns, they may continue with the same behavior or settle into stable behavior patterns.
- Chaotic systems produce similar but not identical patterns. Systems will gravitate towards stable behavior
- Chaotic systems can only be understood through the interactions of their components. This argues against optimizing individual components.
- Chaotic systems can produce unstable results even with simple calculations.

To demonstrate these effects on the supply chain, Wilding (1998) used a simulation model with a factory, two stages of warehousing and a customer. He concludes that 1) dramatic changes generated by the system itself occur unexpectedly, 2) short-term forecasts are possible but long-term planning is difficult, 3) supply chains do not achieve equilibrium but are vulnerable to small disturbances, 4) the supply chain must be considered as a complete system, not as a set of optimized components and 5) chaos can be reduced by communicating demand information as far upstream as possible.

This suggests that package automated software will not produce results free from error. The danger for practical systems is that they are evaluated over too short a time period. Control systems such as ERP can become unstable and unpredictable.

The supply chain as a social system

Supply chain management is more than a series of decision rules and software; it also includes human interactions. Supply chain system modeling through simulation can incorporate representations of these interactions in parallel to decision rules. Towill (1996, p. 23) notes that: »Industrial Dynamics is concerned with problem solving in living systems which bring together machines, people and organizations.« This recognizes the role of managers in organizing thought and experience into purposeful decisions. The system created by human interaction is known as soft systems methodology (Checkland & Scholes 1990). It becomes a system of logic-based inquiry involving six elements:

- customers and beneficiaries
- actors (managers) who perform transactions and processes
- the transforming transactions and processes
- a global perspective on the supply chain as a whole
- the owners as managers of the supply chain
- the environment of the supply chain.

The core of the system is a combination of the global perspective, transactions and processes. The system is evaluated by three criteria: efficacy (does it work?), efficiency and effectiveness. It emphasizes a learning process for managers. The process of knowledge is giving meaning to data as an inquiring process. Managers have a purpose in defining the supply chain as a functioning system. However, it interacts with its environment to create a larger system in which the interactions may not be recognized. One example close to many managers' hearts is the power structure of their organizations, determining the scope of possible actions, or the willingness of customers to respond to change.

Towill (1996) and his associates have used Industrial Dynamics modeling, combining hard systems and social systems to apply feedback and control engineering to the supply chain. Modeling brings increased insight and better use of resources to improve specific problems in operations performance. It relies on management perceptions of the real world to develop influence diagrams to map managers' understanding. The conceptual model is then developed with business objectives, analysis of both inputs and outputs to formulate block diagrams. Modeling options in simulation and control theory are added to create the model. Applications have included identifying problems in process re-engineering, establishing the validity of proposed changes in control systems, predicting future behavior with proposed changes and benchmarking proposed strategies.

Interorganizational relationships

Organizational cooperation and integration become the foundation for both structure and process. The strategic imperative is to develop lateral coordination across organizational boundaries (Schary 1998). It becomes the biggest challenge to strategy, as organizations tend to look inside for guidance. They develop their own cultures and motivations.

The principal vehicle is establishing trust among supply chain partners. This reduces risk and enables interdependence. It is prerequisite for sharing data, facilities and other resources. However, it is also difficult to create. As Doney & Cannon (1997) have described it, trust is perceived as credibility and commitment to joint gain. It comes through experience in dealing with joint transactions of expanding scope and establishing personal contact with individual members of the other organization. It culminates in open sharing of data, joint decisions and allocation of tasks. Classical contractual relations are not always adequate in a turbulent world. Relational contracting binding the parties to unforeseen but joint problem solutions may be more appropriate.

The supply chain is usually perceived as a lead firm, linked either directly or through distributors to customers, with a supporting chain of dependent suppliers. In several industries, suppliers are gaining in status and power. Intel dominates personal computer supply chains through its technology in processor chips, determining the timing of new models across the industry. Observers of the world automobile industry such as Bhattacharya et al. (1996), Hines (1994) and Lamming (1993) note the rising power of suppliers compared with the car assemblers. How power will evolve or be shared is open for questioning.

Organizational devices for interorganizational management are difficult to prescribe in an age of changing management structures. Traditional forms such as matrix organizations as a formal team structure create one set of problems as they solve another. Interfunctional and interorganizational teams have been offered as one solution in procurement (Laseter 1998). Virtual teams connected electronically are another (Schrage 1995).

The significance of the problem is underscored by this comment:

»... We have yet to establish an effective network where suppliers, customers and specialists -spread across the globe can collaborate with each other in a meaningful way.«

»The biggest stumbling block in the entire process lies in the interfaces of these individual functions ...«

»Today we are nowhere close to achieving such seamless integration. It will take many more virtual technologies and some real years before the immaterial world materializes.«

Letter to *The Economist*, August 9, 1997

Management issues

Shareholder value

How does supply chain strategy contribute to financial gains? The most significant measure for the corporation is shareholder value. Shareholder value is the financial value created for shareholders by the companies in which they invest. Christopher & Ryals (1999, p. 2) note that shareholder value can be measured either by internal measures or by market-based external measures. The most well-known internal measure is economic value added. Economic value added is defined as operating profit less the cost of capital. Market-based external measures focus on market value added, the total market capitalization of the company less the total capital invested. The problem for the supply chain is how to maximize shareholder value collectively for the partners in the chain beyond the corporation. The conventional approaches are growth in revenue, reduction in operating cost, more efficient use of fixed capital and more efficient use of working capital (Christopher & Ryals 1999).

There is no conceptual problem with sharing increases in revenues as they are passed through the supply chain as payment for services or materials. They will be allocated through negotiation and established bargaining positions.

Cost reductions, however, are different. The question leads to decisions about how they are to be shared, a task for negotiation. They include:

- reduced costs of input materials;
- reduced costs for services;
- higher efficiency within processes;
- higher efficiency in the use of facilities such as economies of scale or scope;
- more effective coordination processes to match demand to inventory or production capacity;
- redesign of the supply chain to combine, shift or eliminate processing stages;
- reductions in cycle time to reduce working capital requirements;
- management of customs duties and other trade restrictions through product form and production location; and

- management of demand (and supply) to reduce fluctuation in demand and supply.

Fixed capital assets also present problems. When individual companies in the chain emphasize core competencies, they are shifting asset ownership to other partners. When one company gains through higher returns on its own assets, a partner may face potential loss – unless they can achieve high utilization and efficiency through operations and services for other supply chains. In the computer industry, companies such as Hewlett-Packard shift production to subcontracting manufacturing companies such as Flextronics or Solectron, who operate with thin margins of profit. For these subcontractors, profitability lies with high utilization of their facilities, implying connections to other manufacturers and profit allocation. Ultimately, however, supply chain management must be concerned with returns on the entire base of assets for the supply chain. The financial health of suppliers and their financial returns are important to long-term motivation and the survival of the relationships.

The global supply chain presents other challenges. Firms develop global chains in part to take advantage of lower costs. However, much of the savings may be lost through payment of customs duties designed to encourage local manufacturing or protect local industry. They penalize complete products compared with those requiring additional manufacture, such as assembled cars versus kits of components. Some locations have designated tariff provisions enabling them to export into specific regions such as the EU, Mercosur or NAFTA. Not taking advantage of these provisions adds cost, placing the supply chain at a disadvantage in the market.

The most subtle cost-reducing action is to reduce fluctuation in the market. We have seen how decision rules can create internal disturbance to the supply chain system. Customers generate fluctuation through their own ordering patterns. This may be reduced by changing ordering procedures or capturing information at the point of sale or use. Marketing actions increase fluctuation through special offers. Procter & Gamble moved to stable pricing for precisely this reason, to reduce fluctuating demand patterns. In supply, movement towards lot sizes from suppliers and production that match the demand off-take can reduce fluctuation and hence the need for peak capacity.

Time is essential to managing cash flow. This is generally referred to as the cash-to-cash cycle, from investment in materials to realized sale in the final market. Reducing cycle time reduces the need for cash to finance supply chain processes. It is possible by balancing terms to offer customer credit terms shorter than those offered by suppliers so that operations can be financed on borrowed money. The entire pipeline of inventory also requires financing. Shortening queues and operations has a payoff in less capital required. In the supply chain context, however, each firm manages its own cash flow. However, this is a cost element and subject of negotiation in buyer-seller relations. Faster processing times equate to less cash requirements and lower costs and prices. In concept, it could push financing up the supply chain as customers move inventory faster than their suppliers' credit terms.

Information technology

IT is the most important element in supply chain strategy. The guiding principle is that it is easier to send information than the physical product or even to engage in personal contact. For manufacturing supply chains, IT encourages localized production networks. Information includes design, production and supply coordination. It also supports group interaction on design. The real changes may be less obvious: the substitution of computer-aided design for physical prototypes, such as the use of a computer-based aircraft mockup instead of the physical representation that has been used in previous design efforts. Inventories can be controlled more closely through monitoring of actual product demand.

The movement towards Web-based software has implications for competition among supply chains. Companies of any size can take advantage of pre-installed software such as ERP or other software, only having to adapt operations to the program. At the same time, Web-based software is standardized. It offers little opportunity for unique applications, leading to potential loss of competitive advantage in processes. For the supply chain, competitive advantage becomes competitive necessity. Advantage then comes through internal elements, such as data management or physical operations.

IT has opened the door to specialized supply chains tied to specific industries. It now offers a possibility of finer division to subsector chains not tied to economies of scale. One supply chain may be able to dominate in a narrow field and, by its customer relations, to keep competitors away, because the cost of entry may be higher than the potential rewards.

There is a debate about the value of e-mail and other forms of telecommunication versus personal contact. The value of personal contact rides on the context of personal engagement. For the supply chain, the debate is especially important because it asks the question of whether a supply chain can be managed entirely by an electronic network. This has made the supply chain possible. Can it create flexible virtual supply networks that change rapidly, without personal interaction?

Concluding comments

There does not appear to be a clear strategy for the supply chain at present. This is partly a result of the inability to come to a consensus about the scope of supply chain operations. The predisposition is to begin with a restricted view, possibly looking towards future expansion. There are also problems of boundaries between the initiating concept of the Value Chain, involving demand-creating activities of marketing and sales, and the supply chain, which takes in customer orders, configures products and delivers.

The concepts discussed here are general and disconnected. We have offered the tripartite structure-process-relationship framework as a means to organize thinking. Structure emphasizes a general process of physical flow, connecting both core and outsourced activities together in a system. Process recognizes the flow in more detail. Strategy involves both time and system. Compressing time becomes a virtue, freeing the system to be flexible in meeting customer variety. Supply chains are systems, and processes establish the initial linkages. However, systems have behaviors that surprise and require caution in design. Relationships are essential to the supply chain because activities are part of organizations. Organizations must be tied to each other beyond the market to achieve a coordinated effort.

Financial issues by themselves have not been the center of discussion for supply chains focused on operational issues. Yet the purpose of the supply chain is to achieve profitable results. Any future strategy discussion must take these issues directly into account.

IT is no longer separate but an integral part of the supply chain. We observe the multitude of pragmatic applications. We have not integrated IT well into supply chain strategy. Perhaps the pace of change is too fast. One thing is certain: it will influence the future of the supply chain more than any other factor.

14. The supply chain and corporate strategy

»We are again in the early days of a new corporate form. The business web, as it is in the modern enterprise, is perhaps not quite as revolutionary as its predecessor. But the evidence suggests that it differs enough to demand new ways of thinking, behaving and being.«
(Tapscott et al. 2000, p. 248)

Integrated supply chain management is a new way of doing business. While it has roots in the past, its development has come through information technology. The customer is now the central focus. The information content of products is increasing as we move towards a weightless world. Outsourcing has become widely accepted practice as corporations concentrate on core advantages. Integrated supply chain management recognizes the need to interact with customers and suppliers. It gains worldwide perspective through the pursuit of global supply and markets and the ease of transport. It is also a process in evolution, redefining itself and the business units that collaborate to deliver the end product.

There is little question of the importance of supply chains to the corporations that organize them. Treacy & Wiersema (1993) emphasize the three basic components of corporate strategies: demand creation, product development and operations. However, operations as competitive advantage have suffered from ambiguity. Only recently has management recognized their contribution. Now supply chains are acknowledged as major contributors to corporate success. The relation between the supply chain and the corporation is emphasized in Figure 14.1. Corporations are expected to have strategies. Is this also true for supply chains?

The purpose of this chapter is to explore this relationship be-

Figure 14.1. The Supply Chain and Corporate Strategy

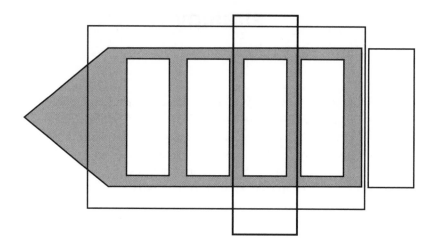

tween supply chains and their parent organizations and point towards the future direction of this relationship. We also want to define where competitive advantage lies. The first section describes
the new competition: supply chains rather than firms in competition with each other. We then point to the revolution within the
supply chain brought about through the Web by comparing the
Web to the »traditional« supply chain discussed thus far. The next
section takes the supply chain as a strategic focus, to examine how
it contributes to strategy. This discussion includes both a model for
the new corporate configuration and how corporate strategy applies
to the supply chain. Finally, we discuss the search for competitive
advantage.

A new concept of competition

The supply chain offers a new form of competition that goes beyond corporate boundaries but also reinforces the position of the
corporation. The key question is: does corporate strategy shape the
direction of the supply chain or does the supply chain determine
corporate strategy? On the one hand, some companies were con-
ceived in the beginning with a supply chain in mind: Nike, Cisco

and Benetton, to name a few. Others have arrived later at decisions to outsource major parts of their supply system to outside organizations: General Motors and Hewlett-Packard. Still others have decided on corporate strategie, then adapting their supply chains. Gillette began with shavers and personal grooming products and found that it could also distribute other low-value but high-volume items, leading to acquisition of companies that now supply major parts of their product lines.

Corporate strategy has come under close scrutiny in recent years (cf. Mintzberg et al. 1998). The concept and its usefulness in setting organizational direction are open to debate. There are several distinct modes of thought, with unique orientations. In one way, strategy crystallizes thought. It defines the organization, sets direction and provides a focus for action. At the same time, it oversimplifies complex problems, reducing ambiguity and suppressing information. It may provide guidelines, but it also reduces creativity. It sets direction, which is necessary with limited resources, but it may also miss opportunities.

The supply chain changes the strategic perspective. First, there are more participants, each acting with varying degrees of autonomy and influence. Partners with their own resources and goals can offer new ideas and capabilities. Their own unique competitive and resource environments influence individual strategies. Potentially they provide advantages of specialization, expertise and flexibility, while sharing risk and reward. A large part of supply chain strategy focuses on how to make the supply chain work cohesively as a managed system, with motivation, joint planning and execution and control.

The supply chain: the fundamental unit for strategy

Economists and corporate strategists now recognize the strategic implications of the supply chain. One school regards the supply chain as an extension of logistics, with the additional interaction of suppliers (Houlihan 1986; Cooper & Ellram 1993). Another discusses flexible specialization, within industrial districts such as the Emilia Romagna area of Italy and later Silicon Valley (Piori & Sabel 1983; Best 1990; Saxenian 1994) and the experience of one company, Benetton (Jarillo 1993; Harrison 1994). The underlying theme is that small enterprises could become linked business systems to produce and deliver a single product to market. Even more holistic views are the ecosystem presented by Moore (1996), the clock-speed competition by Fine (1998) the concept of lean production (Womack et al. 1991; Womack & Jones 1996); examination of the power of multinational corporations through their supply chains (Harrison 1994); and the Value Stream (Hines 1994, 1996a). A fourth is evolving through the Internet and focusing on flexible connections and the customer (Tapscott et al. 2000; Bovet & Martha 2000; Kalakota & Robinson 1999).

The holistic approach to the supply chain presents the supply chain as an integral organization. Best (1990) builds on these early approaches to emphasize economic competition between supply chains. Moore (1996) examines the supply chain from an ecological perspective. Womack & Jones (1996) took the lessons of Japanese automobile production and combined them under the term »lean thinking«. It strove to take waste out of production through an ongoing process of improving efficiency and eliminating waste through a combined system of production and distribution. Brandenberger & Nalebuff (1996) focus on pairs of relationships, describing the mixture of competition and cooperation from a game-theory perspective. Fine (1998) emphasizes the changing supply chain structure as a repeating cycle of fragmentation and integration. Many writers describe supply chains as networks, with strong interconnections and interdependence, leading to systemic behavior (Forrester 1961; Senge 1990; Mason-Jones et al. 1997). All these views have legitimacy, but they are difficult to combine under the umbrella of a single concept.

Of these perspectives, we discuss three here: ecosystem, clock-speed and the Value Stream. They are selected because of the diversity of their viewpoints.

Business ecology

Moore's (1996) holistic view of supply chains uses a biological model to describe the supply chain as an integral operating unit, a business ecological system. It is a network of the lead firm, its customers' and suppliers' contributions and processes, co-evolving and adapting to a changing environment and an »opportunity environment« of unmet customer needs and technologies. Through core capabilities, it presents a total experience to the customer, generating profits to sustain a process of innovation, leadership and ecosystem support.

There is an evolution of stages within an industry:

- pioneering, where the lead firm links capabilities to create value propositions that offer advantages over the competition;
- expanding to build critical mass within a market, take advantage economies of scale and consolidate the structure of the chain;
- establishing authority to stabilize chain relationships; however, at this point, the chain becomes vulnerable to outside firms; and
- renewal or death becomes the decision in response to external threats.

The most important themes are the need for collaboration beyond the boundaries of the firm and to recognize that the ecosystem or supply chain goes through a cycle of competition normally associated with individual firms. The long-term view of the car industry provides one example. The automobile evolved with elemental beginnings to become a complex industry. The United States car industry evolved from expanding markets to market maturity and was then threatened by Japanese competition. It has since struggled to recover, but in a new form – as supply chains – trying to adapt to a changing environment.

Clockspeed

Fine (1998) argues that structure is the key to both supply chains and corporate strategy. The choice of suppliers determines not only the direction for the future but also which capabilities become important for competitive advantage. Capability, however, can be temporary. Supply chain structure can change rapidly, depending on the industry. Some industries such as computers go through rapid evolution, driven by the pace of their technologies. Others, notably aerospace, change at a slower pace. Even though technology is changing here also, the rate of change is not so pronounced. Fine (1998) describes a cycle of transition from vertically integrated to fragmented supply chains and back again. The forces of change propelling the supply chain from internal ownership to an outsourced structure stem from 1) increasing competition, 2) products becoming almost undifferentiated commodities, 3) the entry of niche competitors and 4) the inability of organizations to respond to rapid change. When companies are in competitive markets, they tend to subcontract activities that can be performed equally well on the outside. When companies have unique new technologies, they will integrate to capture profits and control their future direction. These companies seek to combine the new elements with other subsystems to create more value for the customer.

Fine argues that:

»... a company's real core capability – the inner core, if you will – lies in the ability to design and manage the supply chain in order to gain advantage, albeit temporary, in a market where competitive forces may change at lightning speed.« (Fine 1998, p. 76)

There are two characteristics of supply chains:

- amplification of demand volatility (the Forrester effect), which increases as demand moves upstream, such as the variation in demand through internal order disciplines and the industry demand cycle; and
- amplification of time volatility, which increases as products move towards the market, such as the rate of change of products as they move from material and component levels through final product to final user.

Together these characteristics argue for short, direct channels with high interdependence, especially in industries with rapid rates of change. Strategy begins with mapping the chain to identify supply chain members and their characteristics: clockspeed (rate of change), the driving factors and profitability. Supply chain management involves not only product design but also process engineering and supply chain organization. The supply chain involves what to outsource with which suppliers. This decision determines the balance of dependence between independence and dependence on suppliers.

Value Stream

The Value Stream (Hines 1994; Hines et al. 1998) emphasizes process. Its roots are in 1) process engineering, 2) lean production originally developed by the MIT motor vehicle project (Womack et al. 1990) and later applied to business in general (Womack & Jones 1996) and 3) the Value Chain of Michael Porter (1985). Although Hines used the Value Stream primarily to develop procurement strategy, it provides a concept for the supply chain as a whole. Lean production can be summarized in a statement that it describes a system that uses less of all inputs to create a system that responds to consumer choices (Hines 1996a). The stress is on customer response, integrated processes, organizational relationships and an orientation towards product customization.

The essential management-oriented characteristics are:

- It is customer-driven.
- It is organized around a product line rather than functions.
- It is managed through teams on a basis of work flow, not through hierarchy.
- Information is freely exchanged, including a real and transparent cost structure.
- Responsibility is assigned to the lowest possible level.
- Relations with employees, suppliers and customers are based on mutual obligations.

Porter's Value Chain is a push model, with product flow towards the final customer. Responding to customers, however, requires a reverse-pull orientation. Hines calls it the integrated materials value pipeline (Figure 14.2). Customers ultimately define the final output, through either direct signals or the market. Customer decisions flow towards supply: from product configuration through marketing and distribution to production and procurement. Prod-

Figure 14.2. The Value Stream

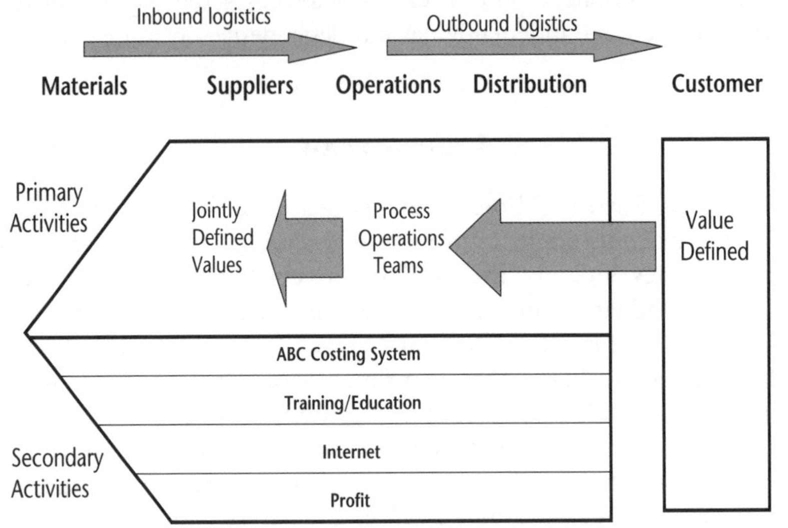

Source: Adapted from Hines (1996b)

uct flow towards the customer fulfills customer orders and preferences.

As strategy, mapping begins with the company mission, customers and the strategic direction of supply chain partners through key
processes. Processes are either customer-oriented or not. Customer-oriented processes interact directly with customers, as the essential center of the supply chain. Non-customary processes, supplier
integration, information systems and human resources management support these key processes. Strategic concerns are then determined through specific value-stream processes.

The supply chain environment as a strategic focus

Several interdependent elements currently shape the Web-based
supply chain: 1) strategic direction, 2) the structural change of core
outsourcing, 3) information and interdependence and 4) globalization.

Strategic direction

The shift from efficiency to value creation permeates current thinking in the supply chain. Economies of scale and scope may still be important, but there are stronger priorities to increase value through meeting customer needs. This reflects a shift in orientation from products as objects to customers as enduring relationships. The supply chain then must emphasize customer satisfaction and loyalty. The customer focus accumulates experience beyond individual products but develops a succession of services that become important in distinguishing one competitor from another. This is a moving target; the current state of the supply chain may provide temporary advantage, but permanent advantage comes through a continuous learning process to create and deliver products and services to meet changing customer requirements.

Core and outsourcing

Management perspectives in general are shifting from internal control to external partnership relations. They provide strengths through specialization, flexibility in resources and capacity. It becomes advantageous to shift fixed costs and assets to other parties, although both must be absorbed through other supply chain costs and pricing agreements. There are also disadvantages. On the one hand, it may be easier to direct change within the conventional organization. On the other hand, lateral transactions even within the same organization can often be as difficult as dealing with the market. Managing external organizations must contend with differing cultures and practices, technical problems, management perceptions and motivations. Ultimately, however, outsourcing allows organizations to focus their collective energies on the most advantageous resources where the profit potential is highest.

Information

Supply chains are also complex systems of information flows and analysis focused around directing a physical flow. Evans & Wurster

(2000, p. 10) note that »... Information and the mechanisms for delivering it are the glue that holds together the structure of businesses«. Conflict is inherent in a system where the economics of information differs from the economics of physical things. These flows are separate and follow their own logic. Information has a potentially wide reach and the ability to increase scale almost without cost, whereas the physical network is constrained by the economies of scale and scope for individual processes. At the same time, collaboration requires a depth of communication that also limits the number of supply chain partners.

The expanding role of information creates a change in perspective:

- The economics of information establishes different networks for data and information than for physical products.
- Information is easier to move than physical products.
- An increasing proportion of products and services have information content as the source of value for individual customers.
- The ease of communication of information makes it easier to outsource and manage activities that are not part of the strategic core of the supply chain.
- Information opens the structure of the supply chain to collaboration with networks of partner organizations.
- Information serves customers directly. It also changes the nature of intermediaries between supply activities and the customer.

Information also becomes embedded as a major value-adding component within products, in addition to the services bundled with them as part of the value proposition to customers. As information adds value, it also makes the supply chain more flexible because higher value-to-weight reduces the proportion of cost of transportation in the total product cost.

Globalization

Globalization involves markets, production and the global infrastructure. Globalization at this point is on an irreversible course. The most significant markets are for global products. Competitors in a global economy must meet each other in every major market. Avoiding markets invites competitors to use them to subsidize other markets. Competition for the global production base also requires supply chains to seek the most efficient or most sophisticated sources of supply. The net result is to introduce another layer of complexity in production and distribution: governmental regulation, customs charges and trade restrictions and national and regional infrastructures of transport, banking and telecommunication. Overseas production is driven by both a search for efficiency and market access.

At the same time, there are facilitating trends that make global operations easier. Telecommunication is now moving to global standards and technologies that depend less on local infrastructure. The transportation industry is also becoming global and specialized: express companies, regional carriers, ocean container systems and third-party logistics service providers simplify the movement of products and materials.

The old and the new

The divide between »traditional« or Web-based supply chains signifies the changes now taking place. Tradition in supply chains does not run deep; they are in constant evolution, responding to new technological capabilities and customer requirements. The Web, however, brings abrupt change in both strategy and operations. Evolution has taken us through an expanding scope of operations, the development of computer-based information systems and the creation of new institutions, notably third-party logistics and lean production systems.

Whether the Web is the major event as it is being heralded cannot be settled at this date. However, it offers dramatically new direction and we will consider it in that light. It is important to note, however, that some of the major themes of Web-based supply chains are rooted in current practice. We may also note the frequently cited examples of the new wave of supply chains: Dell and Cisco. Dell sells primarily over the Web or telephone, receiving and configuring orders, sending information to suppliers for carefully orchestrated production and delivery. Cisco also receives most of its orders over the Web, configures and sends them to one or more of 37 manufacturing plants, of which it only owns three; the rest are subcontracted.

Nike, a pre-Web company, subcontracts its production and distribution to external contractors. In the past, Nike operated on the basis of 6-month product order cycles, though they have begun to add direct order and replenishment.

The traditional supply chain

The most comprehensive contemporary description is that of the Council of Logistics Management report, *Twenty-First Century Logistics* (Bowersox et al. 1999), which summarized results from a previous survey of world-class logistics conducted in 1995 (Bowersox et al. 1995). The study emphasized the role of the supply chain in integrating customer requirements into the supply chain. It further discussed the continuing problem of integration across functional boundaries and the further step of strategic alignment with partners. Alignment includes links to connect operations, supplier management and financial considerations. The study raised issues in information technology, but the intent was to establish current practice rather than to project future development.

The general characteristics of traditional supply chains include stable relations with partners and that they will remain part of a common system over extended periods of time. This probably characterizes most supply chain operations today. In contrast is the development of the virtual supply chain, in which partners are oriented to specific projects and supply networks change rapidly to meet different needs (Chandrashekar & Schary 1999). Partners change rapidly as product needs change.

As a pre-Web supply chain, Alcatel manufactured build-to-order, highly expensive and sophisticated digital telephone switches, which were individually configured to meet the unique requirements of each telephone system customer. Alcatel developed a pool of more than 200 suppliers, although only a few were employed on any single product unit. They developed a highly flexible production system, one that serves as a prototype.

The Web-based supply chain

More than in even traditional supply chains, information drives the Web-based network. The Web provides the vehicle, with ease of connection, sufficient bandwidth for complex communication and direct interaction. The Web integrates the supply chain into a larger, more complete business process. The names for this new form vary, such as the Value Net (Bovet & Martha 2000), the e-Web (Tapscott et al. 2000) or the now familiar Value Chain (Porter 1985). Regardless of the name, the point is clear. The supply chain must create value for the customer and with the customer as an active participant. This shift in focus forces reorganization of the entire supply process.

The Web emphasizes two strategic elements in combination: marketing and operations. Marketing within the Web includes the customer-facing activities of attracting customers into long-term relationships, taking in orders, configuring products and delivery. It engages the customer in decisions about design and delivery of the product, the operations of the supply chain and the accompanying services. Responding to the need for flexibility accelerates the trend towards a strategic core with an outsourcing structure.

Communication is not the only element, although the Web makes coordination vastly easier. Products now have embedded information content, adding value without significant change in physical dimensions of weight and cube. This makes transport costs less significant, while increasing the cost of inventory. Further, it adds flexibility in sourcing, producing and delivery, changing the nature of supply options.

The marketing orientation

In the Web-based supply chain, separating supply from marketing becomes difficult. Selecting customers is a key first step, identifying only those that the supply chain can serve profitably. The second step is to create the value proposition, the bundle of product and services to meet these needs. More than the physical product alone, the value proposition describes the total experience of ordering, delivery and post-sale support. Ultimately, many supply chains are moving towards a build-to-order profile and away from mass production of standardized products. Dell Computer and Gateway

Computer serve as prototypes of Web-based supply. Even the car industry is beginning to follow this pattern, although not yet to the same degree.

Marketing holds a defining role in this new scenario, with two important shifts in perspective. First is the change in orientation from cost to value. The second is the shift from the physical product to the customer's value experience. The role of marketing in the supply chain focuses on delivering the customer experience at any location at any time. More than ever before, control has shifted to the customer as the source of revenue and direction. Interactive communication as a dialogue of options and preferences is replacing one-way promotion.

Procurement and distribution shift towards direct delivery or to new institutions and practices, some of which are also Web-based. Older bricks and mortar organizations are augmented or replaced by e-commerce. New intermediaries such as e-procurement networks take on roles with new capabilities such as price discovery and coordination of delivery. Third-party logistics providers perform tasks that were formerly performed by distributors or even manufacturers.

One developing innovation lies in automobile sales over the Web. The most immediate practice is for consumers to search dealerships for availability and price. The next step is pooled inventories in varieties of configurations available on a regional basis. The ultimate step, now practiced in Japan and selected factories in North America, is to build cars directly to customer order. The role of the car dealership must be redefined, although their future as an institution is not yet clear.

Pricing also takes on a new role. The auction basis for business-to business or business-to-consumer networks have destroyed the ability of firms to set prices for customers. Profit margins based on products alone are drastically reduced. Products become commodified, losing competitive advantage; the search now turns to the service »wrap« (Bovet & Martha 2000), the complete set of product, product- and customer-related services: the value proposition. The market sets prices, with compensation for additional services. This forces the search for competitive advantage to customer service and the supporting elements of the supply chain. Matching and customizing customer product and service requirements become the tools of competitive advantage in the age of the Web-based supply network.

Operations in the Web-based supply chain
The new ease of communication influences both supply chain structure and process. It adds strength to the momentum for core and outsourcing decisions. The ability to send complex signals expands the ability of management to coordinate processes and product designs. E-commerce embraces more than the supply chain.

In general, there are five different member types (Tapscott et al. 2000):

- customers, which now take on an interactive role with their suppliers;
- context providers, which manage the interface between customers and the supply chain;
- content providers, which coordinate and participate in procurement, production and distribution in the supply chain;
- commerce service providers, which perform banking and other financial services; and
- infrastructure providers, which provide the immediate infrastructure of communication, transport, industry standards and similar direct support activities.

In general, the context provider is the organizer. However, the collaborative nature of the Web-based supply chain ultimately results in power sharing, in which suppliers collaborate in product development and decision-making in the extended enterprise.

The physical Web-based supply chain does not differ significantly from »traditional« chains in appearance. Some of the same themes reappear, such as the sequence from material to information and service-enhanced products. However, their extension and the new characteristics enabled by the Web expands possibilities for the supply chain. Following the strategic framework of structure, process and interorganizational relations, some of these dimensions can be identified. All can be found as examples in current supply chains.

Structure will change:

- customization – expanding to match needs for product variety through postponement and channel assembly;
- disaggregation – the outsourcing of activities to other organizations;
- control over customer touch points – necessary to maintain connections to the customer;
- flight from assets – increasing stockholder value by shifting activities to other parties;
- scalability – the ability to change the size of operations to meet demands;
- flexibility – the ability to switch supply chain members as product demands change;
- costs – change from fine-tuning present operations to new structures.

Processes will be:

- standardized among partners;
- interconnected for direct communication between stages;
- coordinated for seamless product movement between stages; and
- Web-resident rather than client-resident software.

Interorganizational relations involve:

- open communication across the Web to all partners;
- focus and involvement by all supply chain members with the final customer;
- development of trust, including sharing operating data and costs;
- investment by partners in organizational relations;
- governance through Web-based partnerships, setting rules and standards;
- development of knowledge management across the supply chain with a common culture based on self-interest.

The effect of these changes is to open the supply chain to new forms of enterprise that can meet the specialized needs of individual niche markets, move rapidly in response to opportunity and operate without a need for economies of scale. The scalability argument applies directly to the information system. The physical product system may be limited by capacity and economies of scale. Compromise may be necessary between the two, or failing that, to keep these systems entirely separate. Evans & Wurster (2000, p. 19) note that »traditional business models become deeply vulnerable wherever the compromise between the two sets of economics suppresses value«. Breaking the connection raises the possibility of new forms of supply chain organization.

Interaction with the customer provides the basis for organizational design and process. It also creates a potential for latent networks of suppliers and service providers to be called for specific projects. The need for direct personal interorganizational contact as opposed to electronic communication that will be necessary has yet to be determined.

The Web creates a need for network connections. Tapscott et al. (2000) have identified five different Web forms:

- *Agoras* – exchange sites where buyers and sellers come together. Business-to-business exchange has been the strongest part of the Internet to date, although business-to-consumer exchange is growing rapidly and holds promise for the future.
- *Aggregators* – where e-commerce merchants bring assortments together for sale, offering choice to buyers at both industry and consumer levels. W.W. Grainger offers an on-line catalog of more than 200,000 maintenance, repair and operations supplies to business buyers. Amazon offers more than 2 million book titles.
- *Value chains* – the supply chain with a Web site for customers to order and interact with the supply chain. A value chain includes more than the original product flow activities of the supply chain of production, procurement and distribution but also marketing.
- *Alliances* – these tend to be formal partnerships usually undertaken for development of technologies and products.
- *Distributors* – these are networks for the movement of products (and services). They would include transport and logistics service companies in their role of product movement and data networks for the movement of information.

The supply chain includes several of these forms, although the Value Chain retains the primary emphasis. Upstream agoras are used actively in procurement, and the supply chain may feed downstream agoras in distribution. It may also rely on aggregators, upstream for supplies of non-strategic items and downstream for market outlets as in resellers such as Amazon. Distributors enable the actual movement of products and may establish their own supply chains. Alliances in the sense above are only relevant by defining the supply chain to include research and development.

For the supply chain, none of this differs materially from current concepts and practice. The Web emphasizes the orientation towards customers, rapid changes in structure and organizational alignment with narrowing scope of activities. By stressing broader systems than corporate boundaries, the supply chain changes the nature of business. By overcoming economies of scale, the Web-based supply chain extends the range of competition from rivalries largely confined to giant organizations to include smaller, more nimble organizations.

The new element is the emergence of business-to-business (B2B) networks on the Web. They promise lower prices and possibly of equal importance, lower transaction costs. Thus far they have been oriented towards specific industries and purchasing behavior. Kaplan & Sawhney (2000) have developed a classification system that divides procurement sites into systematic versus spot purchasing. The one uses contracts and continued relationships. The other deals with spot markets. They also separate production material and components from operating supplies (maintenance, repair and operations items). As a new form of intermediary, they are still evolving as institutions. From the standpoint of the supply chain, they offer new forms of procurement. Similar networks are emerging for transport and specialized logistics processes for individual products.

Applying corporate strategy

How do models of corporate strategy contribute to understanding supply chain strategy? Mintzberg et al. (1998) identify several different schools of corporate strategy. A supply chain can proceed through a deliberate *a priori* design, establishing outsourcing partners and relationships prior to operation. However, projecting plans very far into the future is difficult because of the nature of the supply chain as a system and changes in the supply chain environment, both for the chain as a whole and within the chain. Successful planned strategies appear to be rare. Most strategies evolve from accumulated decisions, shaped by reaction to the environment, from individual innovation and other unanticipated factors. These can be considered as *emergent* strategies and characterize much of supply chain strategy.

Entrepreneurship is the vision of the leader, and the task is to gain acceptance throughout the supply chain. It is useful for motivation but must continually adapt to change. *Power* and especially *resource-based* strategy have obvious relevance and are explored later. *Cultural* strategies define interorganizational relationships. Mintzberg et al. (1998, p. 272) suggest without providing overall guidance that »While the combination of two firms may make sense from a 'rational' product or market point of view, the less apparent cultural differences may derail the union.«

Environmental strategies make the corporation into an organism that reacts to external influences but fails to provide direction in their absence. *Configuration* describes process development that dictates specific types of strategy. Moore (1996), for example, identifies stages of technology development, identifying the importance of »operational excellence« only in the later stage of product adoption.

We focus on the application of three additional strategies: 1) *positioning*, made popular by Michael Porter (1980, 1985, 1990), 2) *resource-based* strategies and 3) *organizational learning*. The purpose is not to select a single strategic viewpoint but to use all three to help in defining a strategy for the supply chain.

Positioning

Positioning is a framework for analysis. It uses economic analysis to establish frameworks by industry for strategic action. Porter has contributed a) the now-familiar Value Chain and Value System (Porter 1985), b) five forces affecting the corporate position (Porter

1980) and c) the Diamond (Porter 1990) that ties the location of economic activity to particular country locations. His arguments are especially relevant to global business.

The Value Chain (Figure 14.3) is the process by which each stage in the supply chain adds value to product flow. Strategic moves within the supply chain can change the proportion of value added within each stage and thereby the division of profits. It is influenced by shifts in product design and service. A move by one semiconductor manufacturer (such as National Semiconductor) to integrate more functions on a single chip changes the role of other stages further downstream because their contributions to the final product must also change.

The five forces refer to the positioning of the company within a series of individual country markets that determine strategic choices (Figure 14.3). First is its position relative to customers, whether it is the dominant supplier, measured in market share. A second is its position relative to competitors in overall market share as an indicator of market power. Third is its position as buyer, a customer of other companies, reflecting its ability to dominate resource markets, measured by its share of purchases. A fourth is its position relative to substitute products. The fifth is the threat of new entrants that might dislodge it from the market, possibly with a new supply chain. The five act both on the supply chain as a whole as well as on individual members.

A supply chain faces a market for its collective output. It draws resources from within the chain, and members sell to other members. The five forces also identify the rivalries within the supply chain. Positioning relative to both buyer and customer is internal. It is less conclusive in dealing with the external relations of the supply chain as a whole. The supply chain itself is subject to external competitive threats from all sides. Every stage carries its own positioning, and the collective outcome is not automatically determined. It also fails to recognize other, non-economic forces such as power, organizational cultures, internal and often intangible resources and the dynamics of change within the supply chain.

The Diamond (Figure 14.4) describes geographic factors influencing competitive advantage for individual countries. Each country has unique characteristics: special factors that favor certain types of industry. They include demand in the home market to en-

Figure 14.3. Porter's Five Forces

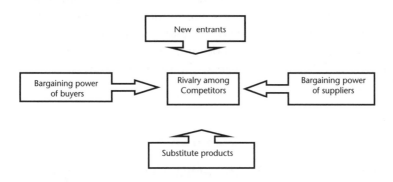

courage product development, supporting industries including infrastructure, local resource pools such as skilled or low-cost labor, clustering of related industries and the adaptation of industries in response to these factors as well as the supplier structure (Porter 1990). Porter uses these factors to explain the development of particular industries in specific locations, such as watch-making and pharmaceuticals in Switzerland, greenhouse growing of flowers and pot plants in the Netherlands and insulin and enzymes in Denmark.

Figure 14.4. Porter's »Diamond«

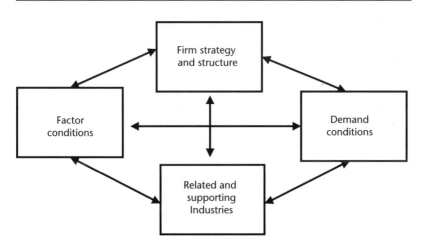

Mintzberg et al. (1998) criticize Porter's positioning as analytical rather than dynamic. It fails to recognize that strategy must deal with organizational response to continuously evolving markets. It freezes corporate strategy and, by analogy, the supply chain at one particular point in time. It does not link position directly to performance. Other views recognize the value of power, resources and learning.

Power

Power deals with influence within and between organizations more than with external environmental factors such as technology and global politics. Power plays an essential role within the supply chain. Organizations, as coalitions of members with diverging interests, have conflicts over the use of scarce resources. These can be resolved through negotiation, leading to emergent strategies and collective decisions. Culture can be a major obstacle to power, especially in international settings, because it expresses dominant values. It can create a climate of resistance to decisions and organizational clashes, especially important for organizational networks.

Organizational culture offers two possible orientations. Resource-based strategy exploits and develops corporate assets. The supply chain expands the resource base through organizational alliances and strategic sourcing.

The other is the use of dynamic capabilities, using intangibles and with a cultural stress on continuous learning. The two converge if we accept that the learning climate itself becomes a strategic resource.

Power becomes a political process to ensure that the strongest members influence the final direction, while providing a vehicle for other viewpoints. Successful uses of power can stimulate change through acceptance in the face of organizational resistance. This applies both to interfunctional relationships and between member organizations. Externally, power is manifested through cooperation between organizations, collective strategies, alliances and strategic sourcing. As suppliers and customers gain power, power relations gain in importance.

Resource-Based Strategies

The general theme of Resource-Based Strategy is suggested by Stalk et al. (1992). Competing as a process focuses on differential advantage and market power. Power stems from control over resources. Operations utilize resources to execute processes.

The firm seeks profit using its own unique resources (Figure 14.5). These can be both tangible and intangible and include:

• input factors from the market;
• assets owned or controlled by the firm; and
• capabilities, skills, knowledge and assets exercised through organizations.

The difference between assets and capabilities is the difference between »having« and »doing«. Capabilities are valuable only if they are enhanced through use. In the context of the supply chain, firms subcontract in the market for resources that become assets to utilize in production and delivery systems. The driving force is the search for capabilities that provide sustainable competitive advantage. Maximizing profit for the supply chain comes through matching customer requirements while minimizing the use of assets.

Figure 14.5. Resource-based Strategy

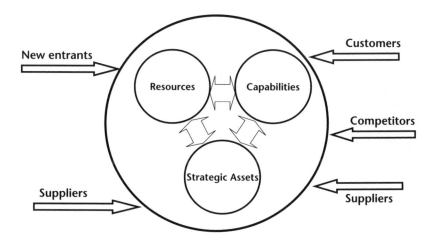

The process of development of a resource-based strategy proceeds through three stages:

Resources → capabilities → competencies

The underlying argument is that firms have resources that become organized as capabilities, the ability to perform operations at least equal to the performance of competitors, »world class«. When these capabilities are superior to those of competitors, they become competencies. Olavarrieta & Ellinger (1997) argue that logistics (and supply chain) processes provide potential for competitive advantage. The inputs, apart from unique products, are available to competitors. Production capacity, transportation, software and other tangible elements can be copied, reproduced or are available in the market. The market ultimately copies even unique products.

The task of enterprise managers is to balance functional activities of the firm, capabilities and competencies against the needs of customers (Hatten & Rosenthal 1999). For the supply chain must be added interorganizational relations. Their model provides a framework to establish an alignment across functions, processes and relationships. This applies to both present customers and potential markets. Thus, it aids both current analysis and strategic thinking.

The dominant structural characteristic of the supply chain is the network of activities that take place around product and material flow across organizational boundaries. The fluidity of the supply chain makes individual activity skills available to competitors. The key to superior performance becomes the ability to organize and coordinate these activities. This is beyond specific supply chain features but is a collective skill that must be created in the organization as a whole. The most critical issue appears to be interorganizational cooperation, the development of strategic alliances, partner relations and sourcing. This requires adaptive efforts on both sides. Although other issues such as specifying processes or software development are also important, they will fail if organizational relationships have not been developed. Further, this becomes an ongoing process, adapting to and anticipating changes in the supply chain environment.

Only the intangible elements of management skills, organizational structure, processes and relationships provide sustainable advantage. They cannot be copied perfectly and often require skills and experience that are only built up in organizations over long periods of time. These can become the real core competencies of the supply chain. The Li and Fung case at the end of Chapter 11 describes a company that provides this skill. When these skills successful, they embrace the ability to define customer requirements, select collaborating partners, design and coordinate complex processes more rapidly than competitors at low cost. Only to the extent that competitors cannot follow readily do skills become competencies.

The implied question is how can they become a sustainable and unique advantage in competition (Hedlund 1994; Nonaka & Takeuchi 1995). In a directly applicable setting, Manheim & Medina (1999) point out that anything that can be set out as procedure or software can be copied, and initial advantages are likely to be short-lived. Competitive advantage comes through a learning process in which the path to achieving competence is not clear, difficult to copy and described as »causal ambiguity«.

Organizational learning

The preceding discussion has pointed towards knowledge and learning as the ultimate path to operational strategy. Organizational learning becomes perhaps the only resource that is a source of competitive advantage. As Dodgson (1993, p. 377) notes:

> »... the ways firms hold, supplement and organize knowledge and routines around their activities and within their cultures and adapt and develop organizational efficiency by improving the use of the broad skills of their workforces«.

In the view of Mintzberg et al. (1998, pp. 208-209): »Given a turbulent environment, the collective system learns how to adapt. Learning creates sense-making that ultimately becomes strategy. However, the process requires management guidance to provide focus and structure.«

Cumulative knowledge and understanding are difficult to emulate, and the path itself is often difficult to describe, even for participants, or as Lindblom (1959) called it, »the science of muddling through«. The definition of the learning organization describes the firm not only as a processor of information but as a continuous process for developing a locus of competencies (Cohendet et al. 1999). The emphasis is on organizing and disseminating information to change operations. This also falls into the category of emergent strategies.

Organizational learning takes place at three levels (Argyris & Schön 1978) (Figure 14.6).

- Learning to do a process better has been named single-loop learning. If an order fulfillment process is improved through more efficient procedures, this becomes learning within a limited scope. Learning takes place within the bounds of an identified framework under one set of assumptions. This first loop creates few difficulties in the organization because the underlying assumptions and objectives are not questioned, only how to achieve them.
- When the process and its assumptions are re-examined, it becomes double-loop learning. This second stage essentially seeks to change the system. Redesigning the system, changing the time parameters and stages of the system constitutes double-loop learning. It creates more organizational difficulties because questioning the assumptions may lead to reorganization and changes in roles within the organization.
- A third level, deutero learning, becomes more profound (Nevis et al 1995). Management changes the cultural climate of the organization to encourage the learning process within the organization; it becomes »learning to learn«. This requires a shift in management values towards experimentation, encouragement of new initiatives and tolerance for failed efforts and mistakes.

Knowledge can be divided into explicit and implicit categories. Explicit knowledge becomes formal procedures, software and other tangible expressions. Examples would include ERP and supply chain management software. This is transferable between individu-

Figure 14.6. Organizational Learning

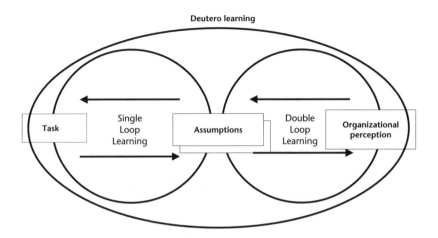

als and organizations. It offers little competitive advantage because competitors can follow the same precise path.

Implicit knowledge is difficult to express and can be characterized as »learning by doing«. Companies that adopt ERP systems follow specified procedures. However, making them operational may require insights that are not evident without direct experience.

A learning-based organization has both to acquire and disseminate information (Figure 14.7). Learning generally involves intuiting, interpreting and disseminating information. The process can utilize the four stages of knowledge processing, »the dynamic spiral« (Nonaka & Takeuchi 1995).

Knowledge creation follows a path through four stages from acquiring to exploitation:
- *Socialization.* This stage converts tacit (implicit) knowledge held within the organization to others, also in tacit form through demonstration and experience. This information is usually local in origin.
- *Externalization.* This stage converts tacit information into codified (explicit) information so that it can be disseminated to other parts of the organization.

- *Combination.* This is conversion of one form of codified knowledge to another form of codified knowledge, as in a shift from manual procedure to software.
- *Internalization.* Knowledge is now converted from codified form to new tacit forms. One example would be the example earlier in which the explicit knowledge of ERP becomes internal to the organization and users learn how to interpret the interfaces of the system.

The supply chain raises specific issues in transferring learning across organizations. The first is the problem of the transfer itself, across boundaries and cultures. How can learning become a common denominator of the supply chain? The combination of organizational cultures, differing histories, procedures and data systems make transference difficult.

Following a sequence of knowledge acquisition, distribution and interpretation, Balasubramanian (2000) suggests a role for information systems. A wide set of collection technologies feeds into a database. Information can distributed through collaborative hypermedia (electronic multimedia), including text, graphics, video and audio over the Web. The richer the media, the greater the ease of understanding.

A second issue is appropriation of knowledge by partners (Larsson et al. 1998). Although the argument is primarily focused on

Figure 14.7. The Path of Organizational Learning

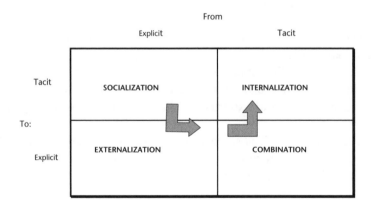

technological issues, it could be applied in other operations as well. Suppliers developing technologies for one supply chain may also apply to other applications in other competing supply chains. In other cases, it is willingly shared with competitors, as the Toyota-General Motors joint venture in NUMMI, the automobile assembly plant in California, demonstrates. The motivation may be political: to diffuse potential antagonism. However, the implicit knowledge embedded in the Toyota Production System may still be difficult to copy.

The learning process becomes a competitive advantage, perhaps the most lasting of all. Manheim & Medina (1999) argue, following Hedlund (1994), that software and other documented knowledge is explicit and can be emulated by competitors. The most potent form of learning is tacit knowledge, difficult to transmit except through experience.

In a later paper, Manheim & Medina (1999, p. 115) emphasize the role of patterns in problem-solving, decisions and work. They serve as guides to ways to how individuals or groups think or act. They name the process cognitive informatics: the use of knowledge about how people think or act to design information technology support that enhances their capabilities. They should therefore be retained in a knowledge management system that can provide these patterns as needed. Mintzberg et al. (1998, p. 209) suggest that strategy appears first as patterns, later become plans and then guides to behavior.

The realism of supply chain strategy

What is known about the supply chain as strategy? First, it is a major process that, in one sense, is larger than the individual processes for any member firm. It must answer to one overriding objective: satisfying the ultimate customer. Second, as a process it performs operations through linked activities. These links may involve several media in combination such as the Web and direct contact. They connect subprocesses that perform the work of the chain. Third, activities are »owned« by individual organizations that ultimately have a stake in the process as a whole. Supply chain strategy therefore ultimately depends on managing interorganizational relations.

Figure 14.8. The Supply Chain and its Environment

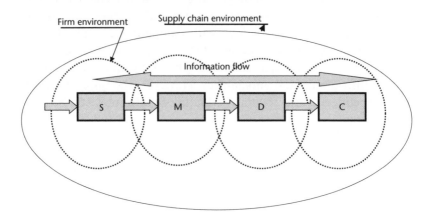

The role of the supply chain is enhanced by the trend to core and outsourcing. The chain is therefore a process of activities managed by specialist organizations, with a tighter focus for the lead organization, but also more collaboration with external units, where coordination becomes critical. Global networks extend the reach of the supply chain, introducing more organizations with supply, market and environmental issues (Figure 14.8). The problems of coordination involve matching both technology and organizations.

In a world of rapid change in markets, technology and environment, supply chain strategy often dictates temporary networks: partnerships of necessarily short duration. The supply chain organization must evolve with the market, to meet new customer requirements for more product variety and services. The essential element of strategy is recognizing the opportunity created through technology to create and deliver new products and services, while adapting to social and resource environment pressures. Networks become virtual, fluid arrangements that last only as long as partners create value within the chain.

Supply chain strategy becomes the cumulative effect of operating decisions shaped by management vision. The role of the manager in a supply chain setting is different from the role in other organizations. The emphasis is to set general direction, negotiate and manage interorganizational relations. This is also limited by the manager's span of knowledge, bounded rationality that forces reliance on other managers. The crucial element in management is the role of the integrator. Lawrence & Lorsch (1977) noted many years ago that integrators achieve their own goals through other organizations. Their greatest skills are in persuasion and group leadership. This is probably the constant element in strategy.

Managing relationships is a shift in orientation from a purely logistical perspective. Logistics management developed decision rules for traditional transportation-inventory trade-offs in conventional logistics and interfunctional processes. In that sense the supply chain extends the logistics concept. Supply chain strategy, however, has further scope for action: to design the process, select and manage supply chain partners and to become involved with broader activities of product design and conservation of resources.

There are also limits to action. The first is developing a common vision with broad acceptance. The second is managing complexity within the system. Learning as an organizational process becomes crucial to practice. No strategy is complete; it will always be undergoing change. The third is accommodating the dynamic elements of the environment. All strategies are temporary. Supply chains require a meta-strategy, planning in advance for change and adaptation to a world with multiple dimensions in flux.

Strategy starts with the architect. It emerges through delegated or negotiated authority to become a collective decision. Strategy takes on definable form through the triad of the supply chain: structure, process and organizational relations. It is shaped in turn by the dynamics of markets, environments and information technology, and in particular, e-commerce, which casts a broad shadow over business in general.

APPENDIX

Case studies

B&O – an example of supply chain management

Bang & Olufsen (B&O) is an internationally known producer of audio and television equipment known for high quality, advanced design and perfect functionality. In 1998, B&O had a turnover of approximately DKK 3.1 billion, of which almost 25% came locally from Denmark. B&O has about 2600 employees. Sales take place through 12 national sales companies that are 100% owned by B&O as well as through a number of independent agents. There are about 2150 dealers in 40 countries, although approximately 90% of B&O's sales take place in Europe. They provide an example of a niche marketer, producing on a make-and-ship-to-order basis.

B&O's supply chain

B&O has probably come closer than any other company in Denmark in implementing supply chain management, both backward toward suppliers and forward to the ultimate end users, the consumers. B&O does not use the term supply chain management to describe the process. However, the principles used to obtain a better integration and coordination in the total supply chain are identical. Figure B.1 schematically illustrates the current supply chain. Many significant changes have taken place within the last decade, both internally and for customers, suppliers and transporters. In the following, we briefly describe the most important changes and their consequences.

In 1987, B&O launched a large logistics project with the aim of increasing B&O's earnings by:

- increasing the level of service for customers
- reducing the capital tied up in warehouse stocks.

Figure B.1. Bang & Olufsen's Supply Chain

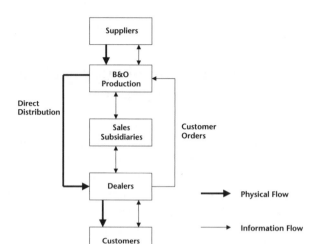

The project was carried out internally through seminars and cours-es and a handbook for all employees to inform them of the project, its objectives and the process of change.

Distribution system

B&O's dealers can be categorized by sales volume, the B&O share, product merchandising, training, service, and the level of sales pro-motion activities. This resulted in a two-tier dealer network:

- B1 dealers: dealers who deal exclusively with B&O products, with standardized store layouts, training requirements, compu-ter systems and customer service; and
- C/D/E dealers: individual stores, specialty shops within other more general stores, and chain stores that also offer other brands and have not presented standardized store layouts.

B&O strives to develop its retail network but emphasizes the high end of the dealer segment, the new B1 stores, named Match-Point stores. To these stores, B&O offers a number of consultant and sys-tem services such as a system for product configuration and price determination in which software determines cables, contacts, and other components necessary for customer-specified systems and their cost. Orders from the Match-Point stores go directly from the dealers to B&O's central customer center in Denmark. Orders from other stores are processed through country sales subsidiaries. B&O has committed itself to provide Match-Point stores with a particularly high level of service.

In 1989, B&O carried out sweeping changes in European distribution. Previously, distribution took place from a central warehouse in Struer, Denmark to warehouses in each of the 12 national subsidiaries. Goods were then distributed to dealers. From 1989 to 1993, B&O gradually moved toward direct distribution from factories in Denmark to some 2500 dealers in Europe. At the same time, warehouses of the national subsidiaries were closed.

Direct distribution provided a number of advantages. Finished products in stock were reduced by approximately two thirds. Eliminating warehouses resulted in savings in personnel, storage and handling costs and capital investment. Transport costs did not rise as a consequence of direct distribution, because of a change in transport policy. Previously, national sales companies controlled the transport. Centralized transport provided direct movement to dealers utilizing a hub-and-spoke system, minimizing delays en route and making the transport system comparable to a production process.

Increased competition and liberalization in the European transport market also resulted in falling prices. B&O negotiated better transport agreements by concentrating its movements in the hands of a few companies. Transport agreements have a duration of 1 year with 3-month notification prior to cancellation. Current partnership agreements typically extend over 2 or 3 years.

Direct distribution was expanded in 1993 to include spare parts. In the beginning, agreements were made with air freight companies and national distribution, but in 1995 B&O shifted to a single courier, DHL. B&O now prints DHL's bar codes on product packages. Using EDI and bar codes, delivery information is now sent electronically to be printed on address labels. Bar codes use the same system for each country, replacing nine different systems. DHL can track and trace and produce proof of delivery for individual shipments. The bar codes also contain information about product specifications and return addresses.

The partnership agreement has also improved the quality of transport operations, since B&O has placed demands on quality that exceed the normal supplier requirements. For example, this applies to special requirements for handling products, documentation and performance. For spare parts, transport costs today are the same as before 1993, but transit times for delivery have been reduced from more than 48 to 24 hours. The change to direct distribution resulted in a one-time saving in 1993 of about DKK 30 million from reduction in storage costs and warehouse personnel. Sales companies previously carried between 2500 and 6000 spare parts with an average turnover ratio of about once per year. Today, B&O holds approximately 19,000 parts in Struer. The large number is necessary because B&O will guarantee and provide material support for products for service periods from 10 to 12 years, depending on the specific product.

B&O is planning to extend its supply chain links directly to consumers, the end-user. Direct delivery to the customer provides advantages in cost and susceptibility to damage, especially for heavy television sets and speakers. Delivery will proceed directly from Struer to end-users instead of via the dealers. A convenient time of delivery will be arranged for the customer, and the dealer will unpack, install and test the system.

Production

B&O has factories in Struer and Skive. The production is divided among an assembly factory, a mechanical components factory (which produces aluminum and plastic elements and other components) and an electronics factory that attaches the print boards. In addition, there are telephone, plastic and assembly plants. This last produces the insulin NovoPen for Novo Nordisk, among other things. The last two are part of B&O Telecom A/S and B&O Medicom A/S, which aim to implement and develop new business areas within telecommunications and medicine, based on B&O's areas of core expertise.

Production lead time has been greatly reduced. Assembly is order-controlled and based on dealer orders, which are sent through the sales companies directly into the production planning. The goal of the logistics system is that 98% of the orders are to be delivered by the agreed delivery time. In addition, 85% of all final orders for goods must be delivered in Europe within 5 days. With regard to spare parts, 85% of the orders for these are to be delivered in Europe within 24 hours, 98% in 48 hours and the rest at the agreed time.

Supplier agreements

In 1993, B&O introduced a new purchasing strategy in which the company would take a more active position utilizing new trends in procurement, namely reducing the supplier base and outsourcing that part of the production process that is not a part of B&O's core competence. B&O reduced the number of suppliers, from 800 to now about 240 in the period from 1990 to 1998. Previously, B&O was oriented to produce almost everything in-house. Today, a number of standard tasks are left to suppliers, including casting large plastic elements, initial forming of metal components and wire production, leaving B&O now to concentrate on its core expertise. The core applies to aluminum finishing and surface treatment. The mechanical components department concentrates its efforts on the core areas of advanced plastic molding, aluminum, and chemical and mechanical finishing and surface treatment.

B&O has increased its cooperation with key suppliers through partnership agreements. Cooperation is based on development of mutual trust. In cooperation with the suppliers, B&O continuously strives to improve all functional areas and to eliminate all unprofitable activities. Both sides share cost and capacity data, and the suppliers are considered as de facto members of the B&O organization. Multiple lines of communication have developed among the partners themselves. In addition to the conventional path of communication between sales staff and buyers, B&O's production personnel themselves have contact with suppliers' technicians, including quality control. Supplier employees take part in courses given within B&O. Development personnel from B&O monitors supply processes.

Suppliers in partnership have access to B&O's production plans and B&O's materials requirements for specific planning periods.

The supplier is allowed to see for at least 1 year ahead what B&O expects to produce. Mutual objectives and policies have been set for inventory and the speed of response to orders. Suppliers are responsible for stock arrangement and monitoring stock levels. Supplier agreements normally mean that B&O commits itself to schedules that take into account completing the products within the suppliers' lead times, including its own process times. B&O's obligations to the supplier extend to orders approved for production. For special components with long lead times, B&O make special agreements with suppliers because uncertainty increases as the time frame is extended.

Every supplier is systematically evaluated. Each year, structured supplier evaluations and quality audits are carried out to monitor supplier performance. Evaluation includes organization and management, finance, technology, logistics, quality control and information systems. Logistics is important, both internally and for suppliers, focusing on these elements:

- flexibility
- quality
- flexible ordering
- delivery time.

B&O considers flexibility to be an important competitive parameter, utilizing order size and minimizing delivery time. Deliveries should match requirements at agreed times and quantities accompanied by necessary documentation.

B&O requires electronic connection with suppliers to transfer drawings, documentation and payments. Suppliers should have the greatest influence possible on planning and ordering and are furnished routinely with production plans based on forecast information. Alternatively, the supplier can access forecasts through the EDI system. In 1999, B&O installed SAP R/3, opening new possibilities for supplier on-line connection through the Internet. With this connection, key suppliers can see forecasts and the daily needs.

Receipts are not monitored on goods from suppliers without problems during the previous five deliveries. Most goods are first stocked without receipt documentation. These goods go directly to assembly. Small errors within tolerances found in assembly are monitored and reported routinely to the supplier. The system cannot manage synchronized deliveries at this time. Thus, buffer stocks are necessary before assembly. Large and expensive elements go directly to assembly without being put into stock. Picture tubes, cabinets and packing boxes are delivered once or twice a day, and stocks cover only from a half to a whole day's production. Direct contact is made with suppliers to resolve serious errors...

Cooperation between B&O, Kaiserplast and WBL

The triad of B&O, Kaiserplast and WBL demonstrates the close cooperation with suppliers (Figure B.2). Kaiserplast supplies pressure die cast plastic components. WBL produces molds for Kaiserplast's injection molding machines. Kaiserplast has delivered injection-molded components to B&O for many years, but only as a supplier of production capacity in competition with other injection molding producers. Pressure die cast products manufacturers utilized bids from different makers of molds and tools in their own bidding processes. The result was that Kaiserplast and WBL committed time and effort without the certainty of orders.

In 1997, B&O made a partnership agreement with Kaiserplast. At the same time, Kaiserplast took over some of B&O's injection molding machines and some of B&O's employees from the closed section. The new cooperation resulted in a significant change in the relationship. From being a periodic supplier of standard components to ensure that B&O's full capacity was utilized, Kaiserplast has now become an integral part of B&O's production process. Technicians from Kaiserplast were involved in product development and invited to internal B&O seminars with many joint meetings before the partnership agreement and during the start-up phase.

Close cooperation between B&O and Kaiserplast has also influenced relationships with the tool and mold producer WBL. Whereas in the past, B&O and Kaiserplast had only occasionally used WBL as a supplier, the relationship changed to frequent contact, where B&O, Kaiserplast and WBL now developed new molds and tools in close cooperation. The advantage of the triangular relationship was that, instead of consuming resources to bid on projects,

*Figure B.2. Triad between B&O, a Key Supplier and a Supplier of
Tools and Molds*

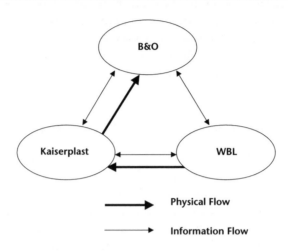

the partners could now concentrate on the production process, improving quality and efficiency.

Summary

B&O introduced supply chain management gradually in stages. Beginning in 1987, B&O had a vision of how to organize the logistics
system to assure fast and effective supply to end-users. That vision
has been more or less maintained, although it has been modified by
competition, information technology, supplier relations and the
transport market. In the last decade, B&O has carried out significant changes in the total supply chain:

- internally optimizing production processes and changing from
  production for inventory to production controlled by customer
  orders;
- closing subsidiary warehouses , replaced by direct distribution
  to dealers;
- outsourcing production of standard items to suppliers;

- implementing partnership agreements with key suppliers and transport companies;
- expanding the network of dedicated B&O stores;
- facilitating on-line orders from dealers directly to production planning; and
- installing SAP R/3, intranet, extranet and Internet.

The accumulated effect of these changes has created a flexible and effective supply chain. The long, hard journey was rewarded in 1996 with the Danish Logistics Award and in 2000 with the European Supply Chain Excellence.

Cisco Systems

As one of the most successful and most highly capitalized information technology companies in the world, California-based Cisco Systems, founded in 1984, had revenues of USD 18.9 billion (fiscal year 2000), earnings of USD 2.7 billion and more than 23,000 employees worldwide. It has played a dominant role in successive waves of Internet innovation, from routers to packet switches and currently to optical networks. The company has grown both through internal product development and through an aggressive acquisition program.

Cisco's current products encompass a broad range of networking solutions including routers, LAN and WAN switches for communication via the Internet, Web site management tools, network management software and Internet appliances. Cisco's services also include customer services for network design, implementation, maintenance, and support. The common platform that ties these products and services together is Cisco's IOS™ software.

Cisco's products are sold in more than 115 countries, 69% in the Americas, 25% in Europe and the Middle East and 14% in Japan and other Asian and Western Pacific countries. Customers range from multinational corporations to small and medium-sized companies in three target markets: large organizations, service providers and small and medium-sized businesses. The products are sold through several channels including in-house sales force, distributors, value-added resellers and large system integrators. About 90% of revenues are generated through the Internet.

Cisco has been a pioneer in computer-based supply chain development, beginning with an untried Oracle ERP software installation in 1995 that introduced many problems but has now become an advanced, fully functioning system. Implementing its virtual supply chain has reduced inventory by 45% over the past 6 years and time-to-market by up to 12 weeks. Virtual manufacturing has saved more than USD 175 million in operating costs (Cisco 2000, p. 12). Cisco also provides new partners with a quick-start kit to provide immediate and secure access to the Web site.

Cisco re-engineers its supply chain

In the mid-1990s, Cisco encountered problems because of uncontrolled high growth rates. The supply chain costs were unacceptably high, sales increased by 100% per year and product life cycles were continuing to shorten. At the same time, customers' demands for reliability, flexibility and speed were rapidly increasing. To keep pace, Cisco radically re-engineered its business processes from design and forecasting to procurement, production, distribution and customer relationships. The primary goals were to serve customers better, cope with large growth rates in sales, personnel and product proliferation and reduce costs. Key areas for improvements included product testing, supplier relationships, new product introduction and fulfillment capability.

The Cisco Connection Online (CCO), placed in operation in 1997, has become one of the most prominent developments for customers. It provides a wide variety of information to customers and receives customer queries about orders and service. The Cisco Marketplace, a site on the CCO, allows customers to place orders both for direct customers and resellers and check order status. It also permits direct downloading of software, replacing distribution of CDs delivered by couriers. By 1998, CCO brought in 65% of total revenue. The site also saved Cisco USD 250 million in information services.

Outsourcing to suppliers

Bunnell (2000, p. 146) commented that »what Cisco does best is running a corporation of networked engineers, marketers, programmers, sales people and technicians who build and sell equipment«. Early in its corporate life, Cisco management decided that suppliers could add more value than Cisco in manufacturing and Cisco would concentrate on its core: strategy, engineering, design, marketing and customer service, letting other companies build the equipment. This arrangement provides flexibility necessary to keep pace with networking developments. Subcontractors who act as if they were part of the Cisco Corporation produce about 70% to 80% of revenue, much of which may never physically enter company facilities.

Cisco has created a single company out of its supplier network, through an extranet connecting to suppliers and customers. Orders may go directly suppliers without filtering through the parent company. This saves processing, inventory and delivery costs, in addition to reducing manufacturing costs compared with producing its own hardware products. Customers configure their own orders on CCO. The order is then routed through an order entry and scheduling database that seeks the first available production time slot to match the order promise date. The order is translated into parts orders for subcontractors and parts distributors. Half of the orders with their build-to-order information go directly to contractors, using off-the-shelf components cataloged on a specialized CCO site, the Manufacturing Connection Online (MCO). Subcontractors are in effect the Cisco factory.

Subcontractors may also collaborate with Cisco and each other on design changes, even to the point of creating new products locally. They may buy parts from other suppliers. A new product information base disseminates design information to engineers working on the project. Suppliers use the CCO ERP system for their own production systems. They also receive a 12-month updated forecast once a week. Subassemblies are built to forecast and supplied to all product lines.

One of the interesting features of Cisco's supply chain is the use of distributors. Normally distributors are a last or intermediate stage on the way to customers. Here their role is first to be a supply source for suppliers to meet production orders, but second, to compete against suppliers in supplying Cisco itself. Both distributors and suppliers seek to increase their share of value added. This rivalry, however, does not jeopardize their positions within the Cisco supply chain.

In the 1990s, Cisco's purchasing process has evolved through four distinct stages of transformation (Laseter 1998):

- managing transactions
- focusing on costs
- sharing risk
- transferring knowledge.

The first stage of transformation reflected an arm's-length approach, with most purchasing accomplished through transaction-oriented competitive bidding.

The second stage developed a strong, stable supply base, seeking to keep product development and production costs within acceptable limits. Cost models were developed to identify and understand suppliers' cost drivers and risks in partnering with Cisco.

The third stage balanced known risk against potential reward, leading to changes in the structure of supplier relationships. With short product life cycles, profit implications from product shortages are high. Time – the ability to execute new products and change quickly – becomes critical. Cisco wanted to reward suppliers who would meet its aggressive product delivery targets with higher supplier margins or long-term contracts.

The fourth stage focuses on transferring knowledge from Cisco to selected suppliers, so that they can use Cisco's information and intellectual capital for their own development. This becomes an investment of human capital and information systems in key suppliers.

Today, based on published figures, Cisco has about 37 contract manufacturers worldwide. Five of these contract manufacturers are responsible for nearly 60% of final assembly and testing, and 100% of basic production. In total, 14 global manufacturing sites are linked via Cisco's extranet. The only plants directly owned and managed by Cisco retain production of the most complex products. Low- to mid-end products are outsourced.

Celestica is a supplier to Cisco, with over 18,000 employees around the world. Celestica provides services of design, production, testing and general supply chain management. It plays an important role in the Cisco supply chain, developing and producing high technology products. Marvin McGee, Executive Vice-President of Celestica states: »Our role with Cisco is a global one. If Cisco needs to ramp up manufacturing abroad, Celestica can supply products, services and know-how virtually anywhere in the world« (Ansley 2000).

Production is organized in a tier-network of contract manufactures, with system suppliers as the first tier and component suppliers as the second tier. Products flow from first and second-tier suppliers without traditional documentation and notification. The contract manufacturers produce to a daily production plan, derived from a single shared long-term forecast. Cisco designs the production methods and monitors operations at its partners 24 hours a day. Finished products are moved either to Cisco or directly to customers. Suppliers are automatically paid upon receipt.

Logistics operations

The logistics operations of Cisco have been dramatically transformed since 1997. On-line supply automation reduced inventory positions from stockpiling to cover delays and errors by making real-time information available on sales requests and current inventory levels. Cisco's own inventory was reduced by 45%.

In the United States, Cisco has now decided to outsource shipping and warehousing activities to FedEx. All Cisco-operated warehouses will be replaced within a transition period of 5 years. Redwood Logistics was named to provide back-end factory transport and inventory support for the United States and Mexico.

The European distribution network presented a difficult logistics problem. More than 100 carriers were involved in shipping to European customers. Cisco reduced the number of carriers to three, supervised by UPS Worldwide Logistics. Shipments to Europe now go through a European logistics center in Best, the Netherlands. UPS Worldwide Logistics operates and manages Cisco's European supply chain. Customers have a single point of contact and Cisco can track products to their destination on a real-time basis. They can also promise customers a time-definite delivery throughout Europe within 5 to 8 days.

Part of the Cisco supply chain strategy is to outsource anything not considered as a Cisco core competency while retaining strict control over logistics service providers. The second is to manage manufacturing and logistics completely through electronic networks. Newly acquired firms are integrated into the system as quickly as possible.

Cisco's chairman John Chambers has called the Cisco approach global virtual manufacturing. It involves establishing manufacturing plants and relationships with contract manufacturers across the world. In the case of Cisco, it has been Taiwan where they have been able to collaborate with local partners. Virtual manufacturing itself is a revolutionary concept. The Internet is pivotal and integrated into the center of manufacturing processes. Manufacturing itself becomes a service that may be subcontracted to another manufacturer that becomes a virtual partner in a network supply chain. The flexibility of virtual manufacturing offers three advantages: rapid product development, rapid response and scalability.

Coloplast A/S[16]

Coloplast is a Danish company founded in 1957 by Aage Louis-Hansen to supply surgical products. It is still run and controlled by his family. The company has undergone rapid expansion in recent years in sales, profit and employment. Annual net turnover for 1998/1999 was about DKK 3 billion (USD 400 million) with dominant market shares in several local markets. During the last decade, the net turnover has nearly quadrupled. The Coloplast group has set an objective of achieving turnover exceeding DKK 6 billion by 2005 and to maintain a profit margin of 15%. The turnover objective will be achieved through organic growth and acquisition of new business. The number of employees has reached about 3300, nearly half of them in Denmark. The company conducts 97% of its business outside Denmark.

---

16. This case study is based on the *Coloplast Annual Report 1998/99*, *Coloplast Environmental Statement 1998/99* and the Coloplast Web site at http://www.coloplast.dk.

Coloplast exemplifies a small company operating within a highly specialized market, serving multinational markets. They have expanded not only in sales but also in the complexity of production and distribution. The number of products in the product line is growing even faster than sales. There is an implicit question in this case about how long this supply chain can continue in its present form, given its internal complexity and pressures from the marketplace.

Mission

The Coloplast Mission is the foundation of the company's activities. It includes the following statement:

»Throughout the world we wish to be perceived as dependable providers of consumable products and services. Our customers are healthcare professionals and users. Our primary concern is to improve the quality of life of individuals suffering from a disabling condition.

We respond quickly to market needs to ensure the highest level of customer satisfaction. We strive to offer preferred product ranges based on innovation, advanced technology and cost-effectiveness«.

Organization

Coloplast has six business areas:

* ostomy care
* continence care
* wound care
* skin care
* breast care
* consumer products.

The first five business areas are organized in product divisions. In 1995 consumer products was transferred to a subsidiary company, which sells personal care products to consumers through retail stores. Each division is responsible for its product development, marketing, production and logistics function.

Logistics

The logistics departments in each division operate parallel to each other, but their activities are coordinated through a corporate logistics department, which was established in 1996. It was formed because of a need for inter-division coordination.

Each department is responsible for operations activities in its division, including capacity planning, materials management, production planning and delivery to national sales subsidiaries. Direct functional responsibilities include the data systems at their production plants because most of the data supports logistics functions. Coloplast also has a central information systems department responsible for corporate development of information technology, including management information systems within the sales companies. Coloplast uses standard software whenever possible. Individual plants may deviate, but their software is not supported.

The corporate logistics department requires that the systems and the methods used in each division be developed according to corporate standards and that the logistics performance be comparable but also utilize special abilities and competence in the organization and in each individual. The framework agreements with the suppliers are made within each division, but the company has instituted a concept of »lead buyers« in which a purchasing manager from one division can enter into a purchasing agreement on behalf of the other departments. It is important to keep the competence in purchasing within each division because this competence is also needed for product development. Organizationally, the corporate logistics department reports to the corporate logistics manager, who is also logistics manager at Ostomy Care, and who then reports to the plant manager.

Sales and marketing

Sales and marketing is organized geographically, with one division managing European subsidiary sales companies, one division for the United States and a third one for overseas and distributor markets, including Australia and Japan.

The sales organization becomes an important strength of Coloplast. Coloplast has 16 wholly owned subsidiary sales companies serving most major European markets, the United States, Australia, China, Canada, Argentina and Japan. They sell directly to hospitals, who are their major customers, and to smaller customers through medical supply distributors. These subsidiaries are responsible for all sales and distribution activity within the countries where they operate, including marketing plans, channeling and customer selection, sales force management, pricing and promotion. They participate jointly, however, with the logistics department in each division to control distribution inventories. For other countries, products are distributed through sales offices and distributors supplied directly from the factories. The distribution channels are shown in Figure C.1.

Distribution system

Coloplast has 16 subsidiaries, including Denmark. National stocks are allocated to their respective markets and cannot be transferred to other markets because instruction manuals and packaging is printed in specific languages.

A few subsidiary companies have outsourced their warehousing to a third-party operator, as is the case in the Netherlands and Belgium. Most subsidiary companies still have their own warehouse facilities, however. In the future, the traditional warehousing and distribution activities related to finished products could be outsourced. However, Coloplast will continue to distribute customized products.

Coloplast has analyzed the distribution structure in Europe and has concluded that a decentralized warehouse structure is better than a centralized or regionalized one. One important reason for this is that the products differ by country. The close integration between marketing and distribution will also be lost if centralized. One of Coloplast's largest competitors has chosen a centralized distribution structure in Europe, resulting in poor delivery service and low motivation within their national sales companies.

Another contributing factor for Coloplast to maintain its decentralized structure is that the traditional distribution chain may be weakened in the future by direct distribution, which will mean Coloplast would take over more of the distributors' activities. This has happened in a number of countries because Coloplast is able to ensure delivery of small quantities with high precision. The distribution of Coloplast products is relatively complex compared with conventional distribution. In principle, a new distribution channel is opened the moment a patient enters surgery for ostomy and Coloplast products are used. Many small shipments are sent to end-users. In England, the distributor chain is about to disappear and Coloplast delivers directly to end-users. Thus, the subsidiary acts as a central distribution center. Direct distribution becomes a major factor in competition because Coloplast gains substantial market information by doing so.

The product is only a part of the service package today. Customer service, education, patient care and other factors also play an important role. In England there are home care companies that attend to this problem. If Coloplast does not develop direct delivery of services, it runs the risk of becoming a supplier itself to a service provider. In England Coloplast has established a company that handles the patients' prescriptions, the financial accounts with the country, instructions and the product.

Distributors have reduced the stocks of Coloplast products with Coloplast's increased assurance and frequency of delivery. They used to carry 2 to 4 weeks of stocks but now are almost down to zero stocks on some products, relying on rapid service from Coloplast.

The shipping department in Coloplast is responsible for negotiating freight rates with carriers for all plants. For 5 years Coloplast has centralized negotiations of transport contracts with carriers. Before, distribution to the sales subsidiaries was split among a variety of carriers, using only short-term contracts. Now, shipments are concentrated on four carriers. The shipping department mainly serves the 16 sales subsidiaries, while the agents and distributors normally buy FOB, arranging for the transport themselves. Distribution from the sales subsidiaries to customers is still the responsibility of the national sales companies.

The advantages of centralizing the transport decisions are reductions in:

* the workload of negotiating freight rates
* the actual freight rates
* the problems of dealing with various currencies.

Normally, freight contracts are negotiated for a 2-year period. When the contracts are renewed, other selected carriers can also participate in the bidding.

The value density of Coloplast's products is fairly high, which means that the transport cost is not the highest priority when choosing a carrier. Consistency, regular service and a personal network of offices and reliable agents become more important.

Movements are primarily by motor carrier within Europe, by ocean container to Japan, Australia and the United States, with occasional air freight shipments to meet specific needs. Overseas shipments are consolidated from the plants before shipment. Shipments are made once per week to each sales company, without regard to shipment size. Shipments within Europe are not consolidated from the four production plants but go directly from each plant to the sales companies. Normally, Coloplast does not use combined transport (swap-body) within Europe, but occasionally will ship to Italy on swap-bodies.

From a logistics perspective, sales companies and distributors are important links because they hold all finished product inventories and share control of stock levels. They set inventory target levels, but the logistics departments control the inventory stock levels. Their major customers (hospitals) usually hold only limited stocks and thus depend directly on Coloplast for fast and reliable delivery.

Production

Coloplast has five plants in Denmark and two in the United States after the acquisition of Amoena Corporation in 1994 (breast prostheses, special textiles and bras for mastectomized women) and

Figure C.1. Distribution Channels in Coloplast

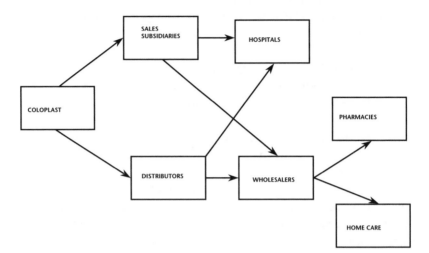

Sween Corporation in 1995 (skin care products). The two plants in the United States have satellite factories in Alabama and Costa Rica. Coloplast has also recently established production in China. In addition, Coloplast has 85% of the equity in Amoena GmbH in Germany, a world leader within external silicone prostheses. Combining Amoena's competence in silicone technology with Coloplast's competence in skin adhesives has enabled the production of breast prostheses that meet a variety of requirements for end-users. Coloplast has adopted a Japanese concept, kaizen, »small systematic improvements«. Throughput time in production has been reduced from an average of 7 to 8 hours to 2 hours. Production is driven only by orders. There is no factory-held finished product inventory; the only inventory is that held for shipment.

High-quality products are important to Coloplast. The company's slogan »We won't let you down« implies that the customers can always rely on the functional reliability of their products. Coloplast products are sold based on high quality and performance, not on price.

Although Coloplast has a central quality control department that inspects all incoming materials; the employees maintain essential quality control during the production process. In 1994, Coloplast's procedures of quality certification were reviewed for the new

European standard EN 46001 certificate. Coloplast was therefore in a position to CE-mark all its products from 1995, 3 years before it was mandatory according to the EU Medical Device Directive. The EN 46001 certification was reconfirmed in 1997. In 1996 Coloplast was awarded the Danish Quality Prize.

The production equipment is specialized, designed and constructed by Coloplast in cooperation with external suppliers. This provides competitive advantage, but it also creates problems in production operations, because new machinery is in prototype development even when used in production, requiring frequent alterations during early production runs.

Product development is essential for Coloplast; roughly 5% of the net turnover and 20% of the white-collar employees are dedicated to research and development. Technology developed in one product group is often transferred to another. For example, technology developed for adhesives for ostomy bags has been utilized in developing other products.

The production planning system

Until 1990, each sales company used its own monthly sales plan as a basis for production planning and delivery. The lead time from the product divisions to the sales companies was about 10 weeks. The long lead time created problems in forecasting, sales orders and fluctuating production scheduling requirements that exceeded capacity. This in turn resulted in wide deviations between open orders for production and actual sales figures reported by the sales companies. Each order was considered independently, regardless of its effect on other orders. While one order was being produced, other orders had to wait in queues. The result was uneven production, fluctuating with the timing of order placement. The sales companies then had to hold extra inventory to allow for these fluctuations. The »bullwhip« effect is illustrated in Figure C.2.

A new concept, closed loop distribution, was introduced in 1990. The sales subsidiaries now cooperate with each individual logistics unit to determine specific inventory level for each country. The logistics department supports sales subsidiaries with finished products based on the agreed service levels. The closed loop distribution system carries current inventory status by SKU on local computers and is electronically transferred via EDI to the corporate

Figure C.2.　The »bullwhip« effect

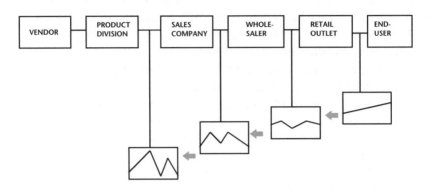

computer, providing open access to information about inventory levels of each product for each sales subsidiary. In addition, sales subsidiaries report sales data every month. Total inventory was not reduced by the closed loop distribution system. However, these products comprise 70-80% of sales but only about 40% of inventory costs. Other products account for the remaining 60% of inventory. The target level for average inventory at sales subsidiaries is 6 to 7 weeks in order to ensure high service levels.

For some divisions, nearly 90% of products are included in the closed loop distribution system, but only about 50% for other divisions. The excluded products are a combination of many low-volume products and a large proportion of sales through distributors and agents.

New products are not placed on closed loop distribution. They do not take up much production capacity in the initial stages and sales are difficult to estimate. Normally, introducing new products involves test marketing in one country first and then introducing them through an international rollout 6 months later.

Production is scheduled once a week. Production planning follows these steps:

- Production capacity is allocated to non-closed-loop distribution orders.
- The capacity requirements for non-closed-loop distribution products and critical closed-loop distribution products are calculated in relation to bottlenecks in the production system.

- A closed-loop distribution index is calculated for the remaining products. Based on these indexes, it is determined which orders are going to be produced under the assumption that all products should have the same inventory level in relation to the weekly consumption. Coloplast refers to this principle as equal run out.
- Closed-loop distribution products with a critical inventory index are entered into the production plan.

The equal run out principle implies that if there is a shortage of capacity, all subsidiary companies should empty their stocks at approximately the same time. The calculation is based on a priority index, the relationship between actual stocks, including in-transit goods, and preferred levels.

Priority index = (the actual stock/the preferred stock) × 100

This index is applied to allocate scarce capacity. The subsidiary company with the lowest index gets the first allocation. Afterwards the calculation is repeated and the next subsidiary company, which now has the lowest index, gets the next allocation, and so forth. The capacity profile is calculated for approximately 6 months ahead. When the capacity is permanently set, the materials to be purchased can easily be determined. Once a week, the forecast for every subsidiary company is recalculated. The warehouses of the subsidiary companies serve provide a safety buffer. Measurements of capacity are taken regularly to determine whether extra shifts are necessary to maintain stock levels. Each subsidiary company has its own warehouse, although eventually Coloplast will take over the ownership. although inventory management is already centralized.

The total number of package SKUs is about 10,000, increasing from about 3,000. A package SKU can be defined, for example, as a product dedicated to one specific country. If the same product is dedicated to another country, it becomes a new SKU.

About 800 different products are controlled individually in the production process. As a rule of thumb, the number of product variations is also increased by a factor of 10 every time a new generation of products is introduced on the market. The first assortment of plastic bags had 100 product variations and three levels of depth in the bill of materials, identifying the options in product package variations. The next generation had an assortment of 1300 and five levels in the bill of materials. The last generation (Assure and Alterna products) had 2500 product variations and a depth of seven in the bill of materials. Thus, the monitoring task has become increasingly complex, further enhanced by the fact that previous generations are still produced in full scale.

In the next generation of products, fewer will be produced to cover a wider consumer range. The aim of production planning is to manage these variations through product rationalization. This should introduce significant savings from both economies of scale and a production learning effect.

Supplier relationships

Purchasing is also decentralized. However, for some key suppliers, demand is combined into total frame orders. Most external suppliers provide only raw materials, although others are used for their unique research and development capabilities. Coloplast utilizes single sourcing for most raw materials. Normally, frame orders are negotiated to cover a 15-month period but are revised every quarter. Individual production orders are called within the frame order. The majority of suppliers are located in Denmark, with others in Sweden, the Netherlands, the United Kingdom, Germany and Japan.

The number of significant suppliers is about 110 – a figure that has not changed in recent years. One consequence of CEN certification is that Coloplast's suppliers must be certified. There are many quality and environmental demands on the suppliers. Coloplast's materials requirements determine the choice of suppliers. This explains why the supplier base has remained unchanged. Changing suppliers is a lengthy process because a new supplier is required to undergo test and approval processes to meet CEN standards, and this becomes a barrier to switching.

Coloplast has conducted a risk profile analysis of its suppliers based on 3 factors:

- the ability to deliver
- the willingness to deliver
- the existence of other alternatives.

The worst possible situation is when the supplier's ability and willingness to deliver is low and there are no alternative suppliers. The willingness and the ability to deliver are each weighted at 25%, while the existence of other alternatives account for 50%. If a supplier has a low aggregate score in the risk profile analysis, Coloplast will actively seek other suppliers.

In general, geography is not critical for selecting suppliers. However, for some services such as product sterilization, it is important that the supplier locations be close. The same is true for the purchase of large-volume products such as, corrugated boxes and other forms of packaging, where Danish suppliers are preferred.

Coloplast would like to outsource materials management by giving the suppliers information on the expected sales and on-going production plans. The supplier would take responsibility for Coloplast's materials. The suppliers are, however, not particularly interested in taking over this function. This may be because the supplier's sales staff do not have adequate knowledge of production processes. Coloplast is a low-volume customer to many of these suppliers, making them therefore reluctant to provide these services.

There are a few situations where there is close cooperation, as in the case of Smith & Nephew and Uni-Plast, and there are possibilities for handing over this responsibility. Coloplast already has a consignment agreement with Smith & Nephew, which leads to automatic replenishment. Coloplast has also established Kanban systems with suppliers of injection molds and packaging materials.

Coloplast follows its suppliers' performance closely in terms of delivery and quality complaints. Supplier scores are posted on both a green board and a red board in the logistics department. A red board posting is a call to action. As a new initiative Coloplast has sent employees to a supplier with quality problems to work within the supplier's production system for a week. Direct contact makes it easier to explain problems and creates a stronger bond with the supplier.

The future

Coloplast expects increased pressure in the future for higher cost-effectiveness. Competition will increase and the market for continence products may stagnate because of more efficient surgery.

Health care reforms in some major markets may also have a negative impact on the market.

Today, manufacturing of products is concentrated in Denmark. In 1994 Coloplast acquired the Amoena Corporation in the United States, a company with a leading position in breast forms and related appliances. In 1995 Coloplast acquired another company based in the United States, Sween Corporation, which produced skin care products. With these acquisitions, Coloplast has developed a strong basis for future development in North America.

Coloplast has been conscious of increasing environmental pressures from legislation, public authorities and the public in general. Coloplast's products are »single-use products«, the basic material used is PVC and the amount of packaging materials utilized is relatively large. Therefore, Coloplast is sensitive to environmental criticism.

In 1997 Coloplast's five Danish plants were environmentally certified, complying with BS 7750 and ISO 14001. The environmental activities are decentralized to the product divisions but supported by a central environmental department to ensure the development of competence, system observance and development as well as reporting.

Coloplast performs »cradle-to-grave« analysis to evaluate the environmental impact of the products over the entire product life cycle. The use of PVC and phthalates in the products is especially under scrutiny. Another issue is whether to change products from single-use to multi-use or recyclable. Assessment of the environmental impact has been integrated into the development of new products and processes. Since 1996/1997, Coloplast has published a verified environmental statement.

In the future, EDI will play a major role in the communications with the major suppliers and customers. Currently, it has only limited use. Thus, Coloplast has EDI connections with a few suppliers. The national sales subsidiary in Norway communicates directly with hospitals using it.

Coloplast is beginning to implement a bar code system through the whole supply chain, from raw materials to transportation of finished products because of the large volume of data. Shop orders in production are controlled by bar code. Lot numbering ensures production control. In the future the use of electronic data interchange and EAN bar coding will be further extended.

Dell Computer

The Dell business model is heralded as the prototype of future business. It consists of two parts: Dell Direct and Internet-based operations.

In the Dell Direct model, the computer is not manufactured until the order is received. While this sounds like a make-to-order system, it differs because the make-to-order system holds component and material inventory, but Dell Direct uses inventory ordered from suppliers at the time that the customer orders. This reduces holding work-in-process inventory, limits cash outflow and the costs of excess and obsolete inventory. It also avoids the accompanying depreciation of finished product inventory value from competitors' actions to reduce their own inventories that ultimately destroys profit margins for the industry. This is a critical problem in an industry where technology generates extremely short product life cycles.

Processing speed and inventory velocity dominate the supply chain. Inventory reduction begins in the design stage, using parts in common throughout the product line whenever possible, reducing the number of stock-keeping units and combinations of components. It continues with close management of the transition between product generations so that production is not saddled with obsolete inventory.

The Dell Internet Model uses the Web site for customer-direct orders, allowing them to configure their computers in the order. This provides a sense of where the market is heading in specific preferences. This process is aided by the modularity of the computer, so that common industry standards allow complete components to be interchanged. The process is automated so that human resource requirements can be reduced substantially. The process has worked for both individual customers and organizations. The order process allows customers to configure and price their own orders, and track their orders through production to shipment and by connecting links to delivery. The approach was that part of the Dell information system should be available to customers. The major difficulty in this change has been getting customers to adapt. Michael Dell described it: »Driving change in your own organization is hard enough; driving change in other organizations is nearly impossible« (Dell 1999, p. 97).

Dell's relationships with suppliers are also a pioneering effort. Dell has worked closely with key suppliers to reduce quality defects to the point that the monitor supplier delivers directly to customers without inspections by Dell. This supplier receives order information as it is released for production and ships via a third-party logistics provider who performs merge-in-transit so that the monitor is delivered with the rest of the order.

Dell relies heavily on outsourcing, coordinated through a Web-based communication system. Order lead times are short – 4 to 5 days in some cases – and inventories are low, in some cases measured in hours. Suppliers feed nine factories in five geographical, areas replenishing inventories as they are used. Suppliers do not have to be concerned about inventory buildup. Inventory and replenishment needs are communicated regularly, even hourly to some vendors. Suppliers deliver enough inventory from locally sited warehouses to factories for the next two hours of production.

Michael Dell sent an e-mail to Dell's supply chain group about why they weren't »eating their own dog food« (Rocks 2000a), meaning that they were not using the Web for internal operations as the company used it for sales and customer orders. This triggered a change from manual coordination through phone, fax or e-mail to direct electronic connection. Return on capital has increased over an 8-year period from 30% to 290% (Rocks 2000a). Thirty to forty suppliers account for 90% of purchases through the Web. The Web also provides immediate visibility over demand and the capacity to share inventory and quality data, forecasts and future plans. Nypro, a major supplier manufacturing plastic components, anticipates cutting inventory by 70% – from 2 weeks to 3 days (Rocks 2000b). This level of coordination would not have been possible without capitalizing on the use of information.

Suppliers sometimes participate in research and development partnerships, even to the point that Dell relies on them completely for specific development efforts. One task is to link suppliers to customer requirements who place orders and register problems through the Direct Model. Problems in the case of monitor controls were fixed by joint effort between Dell and its supplier after the supplier understood the problem. Transmitting information has been heavily stressed. Direct and immediate communication with suppliers is important, connecting teams on the same project regardless of location. Demand drives the process, rather than supply. Real time provides an advantage in anticipating just-in-time delivery.

Michael Dell summed up their orientation in a recent interview:

»Some of the simplest lessons are that you can use information to replace physical assets. Information is a whole lot easier to manage than physical assets. The other lesson is that you can deliver entirely new products and services if you use customer information as opposed to trying to guess what will sell. Demand drives supply rather than supply driving demand. We can be a whole lot more responsive to the demand signal.« (Rock 2000a)

References

Abernathy, F.H., J.T. Dunlop, J.H. Hammond & D. Weil (1999): *A Stitch in Time*. New York: Oxford University Press.

Abrahamsson, M. (1993): Daily Direct Distribution. *International Journal of Logistics Management 4*(2): 75-84.

Abrahamsson, M. & S. Brege (1997): Structural Changes in the Supply Chain. *International Journal of Logistics Management 8*(1): 35-44.

Abrahamsson, M., S. Brege & A. Norrman (1998): Distribution channel re-engineering – organizational separation of the distribution and sales functions in the European market. *Transport Logistics 1*(4): 237-249.

Adler, P.S., B. Goldoftas & D.I. Levine (1999): Flexibility versus Efficiency? A Case Study of Model Changeovers in the Toyota Production System. *Organizational Science 10*(January-February 1999): 43-68.

Andrews, P.P. & J. Hahn (1998): Transforming Supply Chains into Value Webs. *Strategy & Leadership 26*(3): 6-11.

Ansari, A. & B. Modarress (1992): *Just in Time Purchasing*. New York: The Free Press.

Ansley, M. (2000): Virtual Manufacturing. *CMA Management 74*(1): 31-35.

Appels, T. & H. Struye de Swielande (1998): Rolling Back the Frontiers: the Customs Clearance Revolution. *International Journal of Logistics Management 9*(No. 1): 111-118.

Argyris, C. & D. Schön (1978): *Organizational Learning: a Theory of Action Perspective*. Reading, MA: Addison-Wesley.

Arntzen, B.C., G.C. Brown, T.P. Harrison & L.L. Trafton (1995): Global Supply Chain Management at Digital Equipment Corporation. *Interfaces 25*(January-February): 69-93.

Ashkenas, R., D. Ulrich, T. Jick & S. Kerr (1998): *The Boundaryless Organization*. San Francisco: Jossey-Bass.

Asian Development Bank (1995): *Annual Report of the Bank 1994*. Manila: Asian Development Bank.

Bade, D.J. & J.K. Mueller (1999): New for the Millennium: 4PL. *Transportation & Distribution* (February): 78-80.

Bagchi, P.K. (1989): Carrier Selection: the Analytic Hierarchy Process. *Logistics and Transportation Review* 25(1): 63-73.

Bagchi, P.K. (1996): Role of Benchmarking as a Competitive Strategy: the Logistics Experience. *International Journal of Physical Distribution and Logistics Management* 26(2): 4-22.

Bagchi, P.K. & T. Skjøtt-Larsen (1995): European Logistics in Transition: Some Insights. *International Journal of Logistics Management,* 6 (2): 11-24.

Bagchi, P.K. & H. Virum (1998a): Logistical Alliances: Trends and Prospects in Integrated Europe. *Journal of Business Logistics* 19(1): 191-213.

Bagchi, P.K. & H. Virum (1998b): European Logistics Alliances: A Management Model. *International Journal of Logistics Management* 7(1): 93-108.

Bailey, P. & D. Farmer (1990): *Purchasing Principles and Management.* London: Pitman.

Balasubramanian, B. (2000): *Organizational Learning and Information Systems.* http://www.epapyrus.com (June 24) 11 pp.

Banfield, E. (1999): *Harnessing Value in the Supply Chain: Strategic Sourcing in Action.* New York: John Wiley.

Barney, J. (1999): How a Firm's Capabilities Affect Boundary Decisions. *Sloan Management Review* 40(3): 137-148.

Barney, J.B. & M.H. Hansen (1994): Trustworthiness as a Source of Competitive Advantage. *Strategic Management Journal* 15: 175-190.

Barron, K. (2000): Logistics in Brown. *Forbes* (January 10): 78-83.

Bartlett, C.A. & S. Ghoshal (1996): Beyond Strategic Planning to Organizational Learning: Lifeblood of the Individualized Corporation. *Strategy and Leadership* (January/February): 14-19.

Bechtel, C. & J. Jayaram (1997): Supply Chain Management: a Strategic Perspective. *International Journal of Logistics Management* 8(1): 15-34.

Bensaou, M. (1999): Portfolios of Buyer-Supplier Relationships. *Sloan Management Review* 40(4): 35-44.

Bensaou, M. & E. Anderson (1999): Buyer-Supplier Relations in Industrial Markets: When Do Buyers Risk Making Idiosyncratic Investments? *Organization Science* 10(4): 460-481.

Berglund, M., P. van Laarhoven, G. Sharman & S. Wandel (1999): Third-party Logistics: Is There a Future? *International Journal of Logistics Management 10*(1): 59-70.

Best, M.H. (1990): *The New Competition.* Cambridge, MA: Harvard University Press.

Bhattacharya, A.K., J. Jina & A.D. Walton (1996): A new perspective in manufacturing systems design: turbulence management and rapid re-invention. *International Journal of Technology Management 12*(2): 144-163.

Billington, C.A. & T.C. Davis (1992): Manufacturing Strategy Analysis: Models and Practice. *Omega International Journal of Management Science 20*(5/6): 587-595.

Bingham, J.E. & P.S. Pezzini (1990): Systems Design for International Logistics. *International Journal of Technology Management 5*(4): 472-479.

Blackman, D.A. (1999): The Milkman Returns. *Wall Street Journal (North American Edition)* (December 15): B1-B6.

Blackwell, R. (1997): *From Mind to Market: Reinventing the Retail Supply Chain.* New York: HarperBusiness.

Blumberg, D.F. (1999): Strategic Examination of Reverse Logistics and Repair Service, Requirements, Needs, Market Size and Opportunities. *Journal of Business Logistics 20*(2): 141-157.

Boer, H. (1994): Flexible Manufacturing Systems. In J. Storey (ed.) *New Wave Manufacturing Strategies.* London: Chapman: 80-102.

Bovet, D. & J. Martha (2000): *Value Nets – Breaking the Supply Chain to Unlock Hidden Profits.* New York: John Wiley & Sons.

Bowersox, D.J., D.J. Closs & T.P. Stank (1995): *21st Century Logistics.* Oak Brook, IL: Council of Logistics Management.

Bowersox, D.J., D.J. Closs & T.P. Stank (1999): *Twenty First Century Logistics: Making Supply Chain Integration a Reality.* Oak Brook, IL: Council of Logistics Management.

Braithwaite, A. & M. Christopher (1991): Managing the Global Pipeline. *International Journal of Logistics Management 2*(2): 55-62.

Brandenberger, A.M. & B.J. Nalebuff (1996): *Co-opetition.* Boston: Harvard Business School Press.

Brandes, H. (1995): Strategic Changes in Purchasing. *European Journal of Purchasing and Supply Management 1*(2): 77-87.

Bressler, S.E. & C.E. Grantham (2000): *Communities of Commerce*. New York: McGraw-Hill.

Brewer, P.C. & T.W. Speh (2000): Using the Balanced Scorecard to Measure Supply Chain Performance. *Journal of Business Logistics 21*(1): 75-93.

Brown, J.S. & P. Duguid (1998): *The Social Life of Information*. Boston, MA: Harvard Business School Press.

Bryan, L., J. Frazer, J. Oppenheim & W. Rall (1999): *The Race for the World*. Boston: Harvard Business School Press.

Bucklin, L.P. (1960): The Economic Structure of Channels of Distribution. In M.L. Bell (ed.): *Marketing, a Maturing Discipline*. Chicago: American Marketing Association: 379-385.

Bucklin, L.P. (1965): Postponement, Speculation and the Structure of Distribution Channels. *Journal of Marketing Research 2* (February): 26-31. Reprinted in B.E. Mallen (ed.) *The Marketing Channel: A Conceptual Viewpoint*. New York: John Wiley, 1968: 68.

Bunnell, D. (2000): *The Cisco Connection*. New York: Wiley.

Business Week (1997): Can Honda Build a World Car? *Business Week* (October 8): 100-108.

Business Week (1998): The New Trailblazers. *Business Week* (April 6): 88.

Business Week (1999). Sweatshops: No More Excuses. *Business Week* (November 8): 104.

Carter, C.R. & L.M. Ellram (1998): Reverse Logistics: A Review of the Literature and Framework for Future Investigation. *Journal of Business Logistics 9*(1): 85-102.

Carter, J.R. & S.K. Vickery (1989): Currency Exchange Rates: their Impact on Global Sourcing. *Journal of Purchasing and Materials Management 25*(Fall 1989): 19-25.

Carter, J.R., J.N. Pearson & L. Peng (1997): Logistics Barriers to International Operations. *Journal of Business Logistics 18*(2): 129-145.

Chandrashekar, A. & P. Schary (1999): Toward the Virtual Supply Chain. *International Journal of Logistics Management 10*(2): 27-40.

Checkland, P. & J. Scholes (1990*)*: *Soft Systems Methodology in Action*. Chichester: Wiley.

Christiansen, P.E. (2000): Vendor-managed Logistics. *Logistics Solutions 2*(2): 10-13.

Christopher, M. & H. Peck (1997): Managing Logistics in Fashion Markets. *International Journal of Logistics Management 8*(2): 63-74.

Christopher, M. & L. Ryals (1999): Supply Chain Strategy: Its Impact on Shareholder Value. *International Journal of Logistics Management 10*(1): 1-10.

Cisco (2000): *Cisco Fact Sheet* via www.cisco.com (accessed November 6, 2000).

Clinton, S.R. & D.J. Closs (1997): Logistics Strategy: Does it Exist? *Journal of Business Logistics 18*(1): 19-44.

Clark, K.B. & T. Fujimoto (1991): *Product Development Performance – Strategy, Organization, and Management in the World Auto Industry.* Boston: Harvard Business School Press.

Closs, D.J., A.S. Roath, T.J. Goldsby, J.A. Eckert & S.M. Swartz (1998): Empirical Comparison of Anticipatory and Response-based Supply Chain Strategies. *International Journal of Logistics Management 9*(2): 21-34.

Coase, R.H. (1937): The nature of the firm. *Economica 4*: 386-405.

Cohen, M.A., M. Fisher & R. Jaikumar (1989): International Manufacturing and Distribution Networks: a Normative Model Framework. In K. Ferdows (ed.) *Managing International Manufacturing.* Amsterdam: North-Holland: 67-93.

Cohendet, P., F. Kern, B. Mehmanpazir & F. Munier (1999): Knowledge Creation, Competence Creation and Integrated Networks in Globalized Firms. *Cambridge Journal of Economics*: *23*(1999): 225-241.

Cokins, G. (1996): *Activity Based Cost Management: Making It Work.* New York: McGraw-Hill.

Cokins, G. (1999): *Understanding Activity Based Costing and Supply Chain Management.* www.ascet.com (September 27).

Collins, P. & B. Reynolds (1995): Re-engineering a European Supply-Chain. *Logistics Focus 3*(2): 2-6.

Cooke, J.A. (1998): VMI: Very Mixed Impact? *Logistics Management* (December): 51-53.

Cooper, M. & L. Ellram (1993): Characteristics of Supply Chain Management and its Implications for Purchasing and Logistics Strategy. *International Journal of Logistics Management* 4(2): 13-24.

Cooper, R. & R.S. Kaplan (1999): The Promise – and Peril – of Integrated Cost Systems. *Harvard Business Review* 76(July-August): 109-119.

Cooper, M.C., D.M. Lambert & J.D. Pagh (1997): Supply Chain Management: More Than a New Name for Logistics. *International Journal of Logistics Management* 8(1): 1-14.

Copacino, W.C. (1996): Moving beyond ECR to »ECR Plus«. *Logistics Management* (June): 74-75.

Cox, A. (1996): Relational competence and strategic procurement management. *European Journal of Purchasing and Supply Management* 2(1): 57-70.

Cox, K.R. (ed.) (1997): *Spaces of Globalization: Reasserting the Power of the Local.* New York: Guilford Press: 19-44.

Coyle, D. (1997): *Weightless World.* Cambridge, MA: MIT Press.

Custom Manufacturing – Nike Model Shows Web's Limitations (1999): http://www.individual.com (December 7, 1999): 2 p.

Daugherty, P.J., Droge, C. & R. Germain (1994): Benchmarking Logistics in Manufacturing Firms. *International Journal of Logistics Management* 5(1): 9-18.

Davenport, T.H. (1993): *Process Innovation – Reengineering Work through Information Technology.* Boston: Harvard Business School Press.

Davenport, T.W. (1998): Putting the Enterprise into the Enterprise System. *Harvard Business Review* 76(August/September): 121-131.

Davidow, W.H. & M.S. Malone (1992): *The Virtual Corporation.* New York: HarperBusiness.

Davis, T.C. (1993): Effective Supply Chain Management. *Sloan Management Review* 35(Summer): 35-46.

Day, G.S. (1999): *The Market Driven Organization.* New York: The Free Press.

Day, J. (2000): *They Do More than Carry the Load* (January 12): via www.individual.com: 7 p.

Dell, M. (1999): *Direct from Dell.* New York: Harper Business.

Dertouzos, M.L. (1997): *What Will Be – How the New World of Information Will Change Our Lives.* London: Piatkus.

De Toni, A. & G. Nassimbeni (2000): Just-in-Time Purchasing: an Empirical Study of Operational Practices. *Omega: International Journal of Management Science 28*: 631-651.

Dizard, W. (1997): *Meganet – How the Global Communications Network Will Connect Everyone on Earth.* Boulder, CO: Westview Press.

Dodgson, M. (1993): Organizational Learning: a Review of Some Literatures. *Organizational Studies 14*(3): 375-394.

Doherty, K. (1998): How Far to Supply Chain Paradise? *Food Logistics* (September): 23-31.

Doney, P.M. & J.P. Cannon (1997): An Examination of Trust in Buyer-Seller Relationships. *Journal of Marketing 61*(April): 35-51.

Drucker, T. (1989): Beyond the Information Revolution. *The Atlantic Monthly* (October): 47-55.

Du Bois, F.L., B. Toyne & M.D. Oliff (1993): International Manufacturing Strategies of U.S. Multinationals: a Conceptual Framework Based on a Four-Industry Study. *Journal of International Business Studies* (Second Quarter): 307-332.

Dunning, J.H. (1993): *The Globalization of Business.* New York: Routledge.

Dupuis, M. & Prime, N. (1996): Business Distance and Global Retailing: a Model for Analysis of Key Success/Failure Factors. *International Journal of Retail and Distribution Management 24*(11): 30-38.

Dvorak, R.E. & F. van Paaschen (1996): Retail Logistics: One Size Does Not Fit All. *McKinsey Quarterly* October(2): 120-129.

Dyer, J.H. (1997): Effective Interfirm Collaboration: How Firms Minimize Transaction Costs and Maximize Transaction Value. *Strategic Management Journal 18*(7): 535-556.

Eisenhardt, K.M. & S.L. Brown (1998): Competing on the Edge: Strategy as Structured Chaos. *Long Range Planning 31*(5): 786-789.

Ellram, L.M. (1995): Total Cost of Ownership. *International Journal of Physical Distribution and Logistics Management 25*(8): 4-23.

Ellram, L.M. & A.B. Maltz (1995): The Use of Total Cost of Ownership Concepts to Model the Outsourcing Decision. *International Journal of Logistics Management 6*(2): 55-66.

Ellram, L.M. & S.P. Siferd (1993): Purchasing: the Cornerstone of the Total Cost of Ownership Concept. *Journal of Business Logistics 14*(1): 163-184.

Emerging Markets Offer Fertile Ground ... (1999). http://www.individual.com (November 19, 1999), 3 p.

Engström, T., D. Jonsson & B. Johansson (1996): Alternatives to Line Assembly: Some Swedish Examples. *International Journal of Industrial Ergonomics 17*: 235-245.

Evans, G.N., D.R. Towill & M.M. Naim (1995): Business Process Re-engineering of the Supply Chain. *Production Planning and Control 6*(3): 227-237.

Evans, P. & T.K. Wurster (2000): *Blown to Bits.* Boston: Harvard Business School Press.

Ewing, J. & M. Johnston (1999): This Smart Car's not so Dumb. *Business Week* September 20: 22.

Fawcett, S.E. & D.J. Closs (1993): Coordinated Global Manufacturing, the Manufacturing Interface and Firm Performance. *Journal of Business Logistics 14*(2): 1-25.

Fawcett, S., L.L. Stanley & S.R. Smith (1997): Developing a Logistics Capability to Improve the Performance of International Operations. *Journal of Business Logistics 18*(2): 101-127.

Feitzinger, E. & H.L. Lee (1997): Mass Customization at Hewlett-Packard: the Power of Postponement. *Harvard Business Review 75*(January-February): 116-121.

Fellman, J. (2000): Li & Fung, Old-Economy Middleman, Sees Web Gold. *International Herald Tribune* (August 17).

Ferdows, K. (2000): Making the Most of Foreign Factories. In J.E. Garten (ed.) *World View.* Boston: Harvard Business Review Press: 143-165.

Ferguson, W. (1985): Foreign Trade Zones: a Resource for Materials Managers. *Journal of Purchasing and Materials Management* (Winter): 21-27.

Fernie, J. (1999): The Internationalization of the Retail Supply Chain. In J. Fernie & L. Sparks (ed.) *Logistics and Retail Management.* London: Kogan Page.

Fine, C. (1998): *Clockspeed.* New York, HarperCollins.

Fisher, M.L., A. Raman & A.S. McClelland (2000): Rocket Science Retailing Is Almost Here: Are You Ready?. *Harvard Business Review 78*(4): 115-124.

Florida, R. & M. Kenney (1993): *Beyond Mass Production: the Japanese System and its Transfer to the U.S.* New York: Oxford University Press.

Ford, D. (ed.) (1997): *Understanding Business Markets.* 2nd edn. London: The Dryden Press.

Forrester, J. (1961): *Industrial Dynamics.* Boston MA: MIT Press.

Forsyth, G. (1999): Modal Shift. *American Shipper* (August): 28-31.

Forsyth, G. (2000a): The Logistics of E-commerce: Are We Ready for the Online Retail Supply Chain? *American Shipper 42*(January): 13-20.

Forsyth, G. (2000b): Who's Who in E-Commerce. *American Shipper 42*(September): 34-55.

Foster, T.A. (1999a): 3Pls serve up supply chain innovation. *Logistics Management & Distribution Report 38*(11): 65-68.

Foster, T.A. (1999b): In Europe, 3PLs Rule. *Logistics Management* October: 49-56.

Foster, T.A. (1999c): Who's in Charge around Here? *Logistics Management & Distribution Report,* 38(6): 61-67.

Fox, M. (1998): Presentation for Manugistics at the Council of Logistics Management Annual Meeting, Orlando, FL.

Franke, U. (1999): TheVirtual Web as a New Entrepreneurial Approach to Network Organizations. *Entrepreneurship and Regional Development 11*: 203-229.

Franza, V. (1998): Streamlining the Channel. *Industrial Distribution* (September): *73*(2): via http//web4 infotrac.Galegroup.com.

Freyssenet, M. (1998): »Reflective Production«: an Alternative to Mass Production and Lean Production? *Economic and Industrial Democracy 19*(1): 91-117.

Frook, J.E. (1998): Linking the Supply Chain with the Cash Register. *Internet Week* (April 6, 1998): http://www.techweb.com (April 6): 7p.

Frook, J.E. (1998): Linking the Supply Chain with the Cash Register. *Internet Week* (April 6, 1998): http://www.techweb.com (April 6): 7 p.

Gadde, L.-E. & H. Haakansson (1994): The Changing Role of Purchasing: Reconsidering Three Strategic Issues. *European Journal of Purchasing and Supply Management 1*(1): 27-35.

Gadde, L.-E. & I. Snehota (2000): Making the Most of Supplier Relationships. *Industrial Marketing Management 29*: 305-316.

Galbraith, J.R. (1977): *Organizational Design*. Reading, MA: Addison-Wesley.

Galbraith, J.R. (1994): *Competing with Flexible Lateral Organizations*. Reading, MA: Addison-Wesley.

Gallop, N. (1998): The right time for rail? *Logistics Europe 6*(6): 26-30.

Garrison, R.H. & E.W. Noreen (1997): *Managerial Accounting*. 8th edn. Chicago: Irwin: Chapter 8.

Gattorna, J. (ed.) (1998): *Strategic Supply Chain Alignment*. London: Gower Press: chapter 27.

Geoffrion, A.M. & R.F. Powers (1995): Twenty Years of Strategic Distribution System Design. *Interfaces 25*(September-October): 105-127.

Gereffi, G. & M. Korzeniewics (ed.) (1994): *Commodity Chains and Global Capitalism*. Westport, CT: Greenwood Press.

Ghosh, A.K. & M.C. Cooper (1997): Managers' Perceptions of NAFTA. *International Journal of Logistics Management 8*(1): 33-46.

Ghoshal, S. & P. Moran (1996): Bad for Practice: a Critique of the Transaction Cost Theory. *Academy of Management Review 21*(1): 13-47.

Gilder, G. (2000): *Telecoms*. New York: The Free Press.

Gilmour, P. (1999): Benchmarking Supply Chain Operations. *International Journal of Physical Distribution and Logistics Management 29*(4): 259-266.

Greene, A. (1999): Two Faces of Mass Customization. *Manufacturing Systems* (March): 48f.

Griffiths, J., R. Bennett & E. Crooks (2000): Carmaker's Euro Moves Turns Screw on Ministers, *Financial Times* (August 11): 8.

Gulati, R. (1998): Alliances and Networks. *Strategic Management Journal, 19*: 293-317.

Gunasekaran, A. (1999a): Agile Manufacturing: Enablers and an Implementation Framework. *International Journal of Production Research 36*(6): 1223-1247.

Gunasekaran, A. (1999b): Just-in-time Purchasing: an Investigation for Research and Applications. *International Journal of Production Economics 59*(1-3): 77-84.

Gupta, A., I.J. Chen & D. Chiang (1997): Determining Organizational Structure Choices in Advanced Manufacturing Technology Management. *Omega, International Journal of Management Science 25*(5): 511-521.

Haakansson, H. & J. Johanson (1990): Formal and Informal Cooperation Strategies. In D. Ford (ed.) *Understanding Business Markets*. London: Academic Press.

Haakansson, H. & I. Snehota (ed.): (1995): *Developing Relationships in Business Networks*. London: Routledge.

Halliburton, C. & R. Hünerberg (1993): Pan-European Marketing – Myth or Reality? *Journal of International Marketing* (3): 79-89.

Hamel, G. & C.K. Prahalad (1994): *Competing for the Future*. Boston, MA: Harvard School Press.

Hammer, M. (1996): *Beyond Reengineering – How the Process-centered Organization is Changing Our Work and Our Lives*. New York: HarperBusiness.

Handfield, R.B. & E.L. Nichols, Jr. (1999): *Introduction to Supply Chain Management*. Englewood Cliffs, NJ: Prentice Hall.

Harland, C.M. (1996): Supply Chain Management: Relationships, Chains and Networks. *British Journal of Management 7*(March, Special Issue): 63-80.

Harrison, B. (1994): *Lean and Mean*. New York: Basic Books.

Hasnet, B. (1998): Integrated International Production and Non-market Activity. *Journal of Economic Issues 32*(June): 333-340.

Hastings, P. (1999): Buyer Beware. *Logistics Europe* (April): 32-37.

Hatten, K.J. & S.R. Rosenthal (1999): Managing the Process-centered Enterprise. *Long Range Planning 32*(3): 293-310.

Haugland, S.A. & K. Groenhaug (1995): Authority and Trust in Network Relationships. In Haakansson, H. & I. Snehota (ed.) *Developing Relationships in Business Networks*. London: Routledge.

Heaver, T.D. (1992): The Role of Customs Administration in the Structure and Efficiency of International Logistics: an International Comparison. *International Journal of Logistics Management* 3(1): 63-72.

Hedberg, B., Göran D., J. Hansson & N.G. Olve (1997): The Virtual Organization and Beyond. *Chichester: Wiley.*

Hedlund, G. (1994): A Model of Knowledge Management and the N-Form Corporation. *Strategic Management Journal 15*: 73-90.

Helper, S. (1993): An Exit-Voice Analysis of Supplier Relations: The Case of the US Automobile Industry. In Grabher, G. (ed.) *The Embedded Firm on the Socioeconomics of Industrial Networks.* London: Routledge.

Hertz, S. (1998): Domino Effects in International Networks. *Journal of Business-to-Business Marketing 5*(3): 3-31.

Hill, M. (1994): Computer Integrated Manufacturing: Elements and Totality. In J. Storey (ed.) *New Wave Manufacturing Strategies.* London: Chapman: 122-150.

Hines, P. (1994): *Creating World Class Suppliers.* London: Pitman Publishing.

Hines, P. (1995): Network Sourcing: a Hybrid Approach. *International Journal of Purchasing and Materials Management 31*(2): 18-24.

Hines, P. (1996a): Network Sourcing in Japan. *International Journal of Logistics Management 7*(1): 13-28.

Hines, P. (1996b): Purchasing for Lean Production: the New Strategic Agenda. *International Journal of Purchasing and Materials Management 32*(1): 2-10.

Hines, P., Rich, J. Bicheno, D. Brunt, D. Taylor, C. Butterworth & J. Sullivant (1998): Value Stream Management. *International Journal of Logistics Management 9*(1): 25-42.

Hoekstra, S. & J. Romme (1992): *Integral Logistic Structures.* London: McGraw-Hill.

Holmström, J. (1998): Business Process Innovation in the Supply Chain – a Case Study of Implementing Vendor Managed Inventory. *European Journal of Purchasing & Supply Management 4*(2-3): 127-131.

Horowitz, R. (1996): Mixed Results from ECR. *Traffic World* (October 21): 30.

Houlihan, J.B. (1986): International Supply Chain Management. *International Journal of Physical Distribution and Materials Management 15*(1): 22-38.

Hsuan, J. (1999): Impacts of Supplier-Buyer Relationships on Modularization in New Product Development. *European Journal of Purchasing and Supply Management 5*: 197-209.

i2 Technologies (2000): *Trade Matrix™ Solutions Overview.* via www.i2.com (September).

Information Week (1999). Globalization. *Information Week* (January 18): 39-48.

Internet-based Supply Chain Collaboration Delivers Early Rewards ... (1998). Newswire via http://www.newspage.com (October 6): 4 p.

Jacob, R. (2000): Old Values in a Click. *Financial Times* (August 1): 10.

Jarillo, J.C. (1993): *Strategic Networks.* London: Butterworth Heinemann.

Jarillo, J.C. & J.I. Martinez (1994): Benetton S.p.A. – Italy. In Jenster, P.V. & J.C. Jarillo (ed.) *Internationalizing the Medium-sized Firm.* Copenhagen: Copenhagen Business School Press.

Jarillo, J.C. & H.H. Stevenson (1991): Co-operative Strategies – the Payoffs and the Pitfalls. *Long Range Planning 24*(1): 64-74.

Jeannet, J.-P. (2000): *Managing with a Global Mindset.* London: Financial Times.

Johnson, H.T. & R.S. Kaplan (1987). *Relevance Lost.* Boston: Harvard Business School Press.

Johnson, J.R. (2000): RFID Gets the Green Light. *Warehouse Management* (May 2000): 28-29.

Jones, T. (1998): Reverse Logistics – Bringing the Product Back. Taking It Into the Future. In J. Gattorna (ed.) *Strategic Supply Chain Alignment: Best Practice in Supply Chain Management.* Aldershot: Gower Publishing.

Jones Carr, C.M. & M.R. Crum (1995): The U.S. Customs Modernization and Informed Compliance Act: Implications for the Logistics Pipeline. *International Journal of Logistics Management 6*(2): 67-81.

Joyce, W.E., V.E. McGee & J.W. Slocum (1997): Designing Lateral Organizations: an Analysis of the Benefits, Costs, and Enablers of Nonhierarchical Organizational Forms. *Decision Science 28*(1): 1-25.

Juga, J. (1996): *Changing Logistics Organization.* Turku: Turku School of Economics and Business Administration (Publications of the Turku School of Economics and Business Administration/Series A-7).

Kalakota, R. & M. Robinson (1999): *E-business – Roadmap for Success.* Reading, MA: Addison Wesley Longman.

Kaplan, R.S. & D.P. Norton (1996): *The Balanced Scorecard.* Boston, MA: Harvard Business School Press.

Kaplan, S. & M. Sawhney (2000): E-Hubs: the New B2B Marketplaces. *Harvard Business Review 78*(May-June): 97-103.

Kay, R. (2000): New Wireless Technology Promises Smarter Packages. *Computerworld* (April 24): 64.

Ketelhöhn, W. (1993): An Interview with Aldo Palmeri of Benetton: the Early Growth Years. *European Management Journal 11*(3): 321-331.

Kidd, P.T. (1994): *Agile Manufacturing: Forging New Frontiers.* Wokingham, UK: Addison-Wesley.

Knight, P. (1998): Global Manufacturing: the Nike Story Is Just Good Business. *Vital Speeches of the Day* (August 12): 637-640.

Knight, P. (2000): A Forum for Improving Globalisation. *Financial Times* (August 1): 13.

Knill, B. (1997): How Efficient Is Efficient Consumer Response? *Material Handling Engineering* (July): SCMW: 13-15.

Kogut, B. (1984): Normative Observations on the International Value Chain and Strategic Groups. *Journal of International Business Studies 15*(Fall): 151-68.

Kogut, B. (1985): Designing Global Strategies: Comparative and Competitive Value-added Chains. *Sloan Management Review 2*(Summer): 15-27.

Kogut, B. (1989): Research Notes and Communications: a Note on Global Strategies. *Strategic Management Journal 10*: 383-389.

Korten, D.C. (1995): *When Corporations Rule the World.* San Francisco: Berrett-Kohler.

Kotzab H. (1999): Improving Supply Chain Performance by Efficient Consumer Response? A Critical Comparison of Existing ECR Approaches. *Journal of Business and Industrial Marketing* 14(5/6): 364-377.

Kraljic, P. (1983): Purchasing Must Become Supply Management. *Harvard Business Review 61*: 109-117.

Krause, D.R., R.B. Handfield & T.V. Scannell (1998): An Empirical Investigation of Supplier Development: Reactive and Strategic Processes. *Journal of Operations Management 17*(1): 39-58.

Kroon, L. & G. Vrijens (1995): Returnable Containers: an Example of Reverse Logistics. *International Journal of Logistics Management 25*(2): 56-69.

Kulkarni, S. (1996): A Supply Side Strategy. *Journal of Business Strategy 17*(5): 17-21.

Kurt Salmon Associates (1993): *Efficient Consumer Response. Enhancing Consumer Value in the Grocery Industry.* Washington, DC: Kurt Salmon Associates.

LaLonde, B.J. & T.L. Pohlen (1996): Issues in Supply Chain Costing. *International Journal of Logistics Management 7*(1): 1-12.

Lambert, D.M., M.C. Cooper & J.D. Pagh (1998): Supply Chain Management: Implementation Issues and Research Opportunities. *International Journal of Logistics Management 9*(2): 1-18.

Lamming, R. (1993): *Beyond Partnership.* Englewood Cliffs, NJ: Prentice-Hall.

Lamming, R. & J. Hampson (1996): The Environment as a Supply Chain Management Issue. *British Journal of Management 7*(Special Issue): 45-62.

Lampel, J. & H. Mintzberg (1996): Customizing Customization. *Sloan Management Review 38*(1): 21-30.

Larsson, R., L. Bennington, K. Henriksson & J. Sparks (1998): The Organizational Dilemma: Collective Knowledge Development in Alliances. *Organization Science: 9*(May-June): 285-305.

Laseter, T.M. (1998): *Balanced Sourcing – Cooperation and Competition in Supplier Relationships.* San Francisco: Jossey-Bass.

Lawrence, P.R. & J.W. Lorsch (1967): *Organization and Environment.* Homewood, IL: Irwin.

Lawrence, P.R. & J.W. Lorsch (1977): New Management Job: the Integrator. *Harvard Business Review 55*(November-December): 142-151.

Lawrence, J.A. Jr. & B.A. Pasternack (1998): *Applied Management Science – a Computer-integrated Approach for Decision Making.* New York: John Wiley & Sons.

Lee, H.L. & C.A. Billington (1993): Material Management in De-centralized Supply Chains. *Operations Research 41*(September-October 1993): 835-847.

Lee, H.L. & C.A. Billington (1995): The Evolution of Supply-Chain Management Models and Practice at Hewlett-Packard. *Interfaces 25*(5): 42-64.

Lee, H.L., C. Billington, & B. Carey (1993): Hewlett-Packard Gains Control Of Inventory and Service through Design for Lo-calization. *Interfaces 23*(July-August 1993): 1-11.

Lee, H.L., V. Padmanabhan & S. Whang (1997): The Bullwhip Ef-fect in Supply Chains. *Sloan Management Review 38*(3): 93-102.

Levitt, T. (1986): The Globalization of Markets. In *The Marketing Imagination.* New York: The Free Press: 20-49.

Levy, D.L. (1995): Sourcing and Supply Chain Instability. *Journal of International Business Studies 26*(2): 343-360.

Liberatore, M.J. & T. Miller (1998): A Framework for Integrating Activity-based Costing and the Balanced Scorecard in the Lo-gistics Strategy Development and Monitoring Process. *Journal of Business Logistics 19*(2): 131-154.

Lieb, R.C. & H.L. Randall (1996): A Comparison of the Use of Third-Party Logistics Services by Large American Manufactur-ers, 1991, 1994, and 1995. *Journal of Business Logistics 17*(1): 305-320.

Lindblom, C.E. (1959): The science of muddling through. *Public Administration Review 19*: 79-88.

Lipis, L.J., R. Villars, D. Byron & V. Turner (2000): *Putting Mar-kets into Place: an E-marketplace Definition and Forecast.* http://www.idc.com.

Love, P.E.D. & A. Gunasekaran (1997): Process Reengineering: a Review of Enablers. *International Journal of Production Economics 50*(2,3): 183-197.

MacKenzie, D. (1999): Case Study, *Cargovision,* April: 3.

Magill, P. (2000): Outsourcing Logistics. The Transition to 4th Party Partnerships in Europe. *Financial Times, Retail & Consum-er.*

Magretta, J. (1998): Fast, Global and Entrepeneurial: Supply Chain Management, Hong Kong Style. *Harvard Business Review* 76(September-October): 103-114.

Mair, A.J. (1994): *Honda's Global Local Corporation.* New York, NY: St. Martin's Press.

Mair, A.J. (1997): Strategic Localization: the Myth of the Postnational Enterprise. In K.J. Cox (ed.) *Spaces of Globalization: Reasserting the Power of the Local.* New York: Guilford: 64-88.

Maister, D.H. (1976): Centralization of Inventories and the Square Root Law. *International Journal of Physical Distribution* 6(3): 124-134.

Mallen, B.E. (1973): Functional Spinoff: a Key to Anticipating Change in Distribution Structure. *Journal of Marketing 37*(July): 18-25.

Manheim, M.I. & B.M.V. Medina (1999): Beyond Supply Chain Integration: Opportunities for Competitive Advantage. In D. Waters (ed.) *Global Logistics and Distribution Planning.* 3rd edn. London: Kogan Page.

Mannheim, M.L. (1994): Beyond the Logistics Pipeline: Opportunities for Competitive Advantage. In J.C. Cooper (ed.) *Logistics and Distribution Planning.* 2nd edn. London: Kogan Page: 62-97.

Martin, A. (1994): *Infopartnering – the Ultimate Strategy for Achieving Efficient Consumer Response.* Essex Junction, VT: Oliver Wright Publications.

Maruca, R.F. (1994): The Right Way to Go Global: an Interview with Whirlpool CEO David Whitman. *Harvard Business Review* 72(2): 134-146.

Mason-Jones, R., M.H. Naim & D.R. Towill (1997): The Impact of Pipeline Control on Supply Chain Dynamics. *International Journal of Logistics Management* 9(2): 47-62.

Mather, H. (1992): Design for Logistics – the Next Challenge for Designers. *Production and Inventory Control 25*(4th quarter): 7-10.

Mazel, J. (1999): Supplier Selection and Management Report. *Management Library, Newsletter,* September.

McCutcheon, D.M., A.S. Raturi & J.R. Meredith (1994): The Customization-Responsiveness Squeeze. *Sloan Management Review 35*(2): 89-99.

McGrath, M.E. & R.W. Hoole (1992): Manufacturing's New Economies of Scale. *Harvard Business Review 70*(May-June): 94-102.

McMillan, J. (1990): Managing Suppliers: Incentive Systems in Japanese and U.S. Industry. *California Management Review 32*(4): 38-58.

Methé, D. (1991): *Technological Competition in Global Industries.* New York: Global Books.

Miles, R.E. & C. Snow (1992): Causes of Failure in Network Organizations. *California Management Review 34*(4): 53-72.

Mintzberg, H. & J. Lampel (1996): Customizing Customization. *Sloan Management Review 38*(Fall): 21-31.

Mintzberg H. & L. van der Heyden (1999): Organigraphs: Drawing How Companies Really Work. *Harvard Business Review 77*(September-October): 87-94.

Mintzberg, H., B. Ahlstrand & J. Lampel (1998): *Strategic Safari.* New York: The Free Press.

Modern Materials Handling (2000): WMS in a New Light: 67-77.

Monahan, A. (1998): Deconstructing Information Walls: the Impact of the European Data Directive on U.S. Businesses. *Law and Policy in International Business 29*(Winter): 275-296.

Moore, J.F. (1996): *The Death of Competition.* New York: HarperBusiness.

Morgan, B.W. (1998): *Strategy and Enterprise Value in the Relationship Economy.* New York: Van Nostrand Reinhold.

Murphy, P.R., R.F. Poist & C.D. Braunschweig (1995): Role and Relevance of Logistics to Corporate Environmentalism: an Empirical Assessment. *International Journal of Physical Distribution and Logistics Management 25*(2): 5-19.

Nadler, D.A. & M.L. Tushman (1998): *Competing by Design.* New York: Oxford University Press.

Nelson, P.T. & G. Toledano (1979): Challenge for International Logistics. *Journal of Business Logistics 2*(1): 14-21.

Nelson, R.R. & S.G. Winter (1982): *An Evolutionary Theory of Economic Change.* Cambridge, MA: Belknap Harvard.

Nevis, E.C., DiBella, A.J., & Gould, J.M. (1995): Understanding Organizations as Learning Systems. *Sloan Management Review 36*(2): 73-85.

Nohria, N. & S. Ghoshal (1997): *The Differentiated Network*. San Francisco: Jossey-Bass.

Nonaka, I. & H. Takeuchi (1995): *The Knowledge-creating Company*. New York: Oxford.

Noorderhaven, N.G. (1995): Transaction, Interaction, Institutionalization: Toward a Dynamic Theory of Hybrid Governance. *Scandinavian Journal of Management 11*(1): 43-55.

O'Hara-Devereaux, M. & R. Johansen (1994): *Global Work: Bridging Distance, Culture and Time*. San Francisco: Jossey-Bass.

O'Laughlin, K.A., J. Cooper & E. Cabocel (1993): *Reconfiguring European Logistics Systems*. Oak Brook, IL: Council of Logistics Management.

Ohmae, K. (1985): *Triad Power: the Coming Shape of Global Competition*. New York: the Free Press.

Ohmae, K. (1999): *The Borderless World*. Revised edn. New York: HarperBusiness.

Ohno, T. (1988): *The Toyota Production System*. Cambridge, MA: Productivity Press.

Olavarrieta, S. & A.E. Ellinger (1997): Resource-based Theory and Strategic Logistics Research. *International Journal of Physical Distribution and Logistics Management 27*(9/10): 559-587.

Olsen, R.F. & L.M. Ellram (1997): A Portfolio Approach to Supplier Relationships. *Industrial Marketing Management 26*(2): 101-113.

Pagh, J.D. & M.C. Cooper (1998): Postponement and Speculation Strategies: How to Choose the Right Strategy. *Journal of Business Logistics 19*(2): 13-33.

Pasternack, B.A. & A.J. Viscio (1998): *The Centerless Corporation*. New York: Simon and Schuster.

Patel, J. (2000): *UPS Delivers E-Billing Strategy*. Via www.individual.com (June 13): 3 p.

Perry, M., A.S. Sohal & P. Rumpf (1999): Quick Response Supply Chain Alliances in the Australian Textiles, Clothing and Footwear Industry. *International Journal of Production Economics 62*: 119-132.

Picard, J. (1983): Physical Distribution Organization in Multinationals: the Position of Authority. *International Journal of Physical Distribution and Materials Management 13*(1): 20-32.

Pine, B.J. (1993): *Mass Customization: the New Frontier in Business Competition.* Boston: Harvard Business School Press.

Piore, M. & C.F. Sabel (1983): *The Second Industrial Divide.* New York: Basic Books.

Plock, S. (1997): The Internet, Java and the Auto Industry. *Automotive Manufacturing & Production 109*(1): 60-62.

Pohlen, T.L. & B.J. LaLonde (1994): Implementing Activity-Based Costing (ABC): in Logistics. *Journal of Business Logistics 15*(2): 1-24.

Poirier, C.C. & S.E. Reiter (1996): *Supply Chain Optimization.* San Francisco: Berrett-Koehler.

Porter, M.E. (1980): *Competitive Strategy.* New York: Free Press.

Porter, M.E. (1985): *Competitive Advantage.* New York: Free Press.

Porter, M.E. (1990): *The Competitive Advantage of Nations.* New York: The Free Press.

Porter, M.E. (1991): Towards a Dynamic Theory of Strategy. *Strategic Management Journal 12*: 95-117.

Porter, M.E. (1998): Clusters and the New Economics of Competition. *Harvard Business Review 76*(November/December): 77-90.

Prahalad, C.K. & G. Hamel (1990): The Core Competence of the Corporation. *Harvard Business Review 68*(3): 79-91.

Prahalad, C.K. & V. Ramaswamy & M.S. Krishnan (2000): Consumer Centricity. *Informationweek* April 10: 67-76.

PricewaterhouseCoopers (1999): *Information and Technology in the Supply Chain. Making Technology Pay.* London: Euromoney Institutional Investor.

PricewaterhouseCoopers (2000): *Information and Technology in the Supply Chain. E-supply Chain: Revolution or E-volution?* London: Euromoney Institutional Investor.

Pringle, M. (1998): Channel Assembly: Evolution, Revolution or Who Cares? *Computer Technology Review 18*(January): 18.

Procknow, S. (1999): *Bridging the Gap.* Industrial Distribution (March): 128.

Quinn, J.B. (1999): Strategic Outsourcing: Leveraging Knowledge Capabilities. *Sloan Management Review 40*(4): 9-21.

Quinn, J.B. & F.G. Hilmer (1994): Strategic Outsourcing. *Sloan Management Review 35*(Summer): 43-55.

Rangan, S. (1998): Do Multinationals Operate Flexibly? Theory and Evidence. *Journal of International Business Studies 29*(Winter): 217-237.

Richardson, J. (1993): Parallel Sourcing and Supplier Performance in the Japanese Automobile Industry. *Strategic Management Journal 14*: 339-350.

Rifkin, J. (2000): *The Age of Access.* New York: Putnam.

Ring, P.S. & A.H. Van de Ven (1994): Developmental Processes of Co-operative Interorganizational Relationships. *Academy of Management Review 19*(1): 90-118.

Rocks, D. (2000a): The Internet Wasn't a Disruption for Dell. *Business Week Online* (September 7): 3 p.

Rocks, D. (2000b): Dell's Second Revolution. *Business Week Online* (September 18): 2 p.

Rogers, D.S. & R.S. Tibben-Lembke (1998): *Going Backwards: Reverse Logistics Trends and Practices.* Reno NV: Reverse Logistics Executive Council.

Rogers, M. (1997): Bridging the Gap between IT and Marketing. *PC Week* (December 8): 88. Via http://web4 infotrac.Galegroup.com.

Rovizzi, L. & D. Thompson (1992): Fitting Company Strategy to Industry Structure: a Strategic Audit of the Rise of Benetton and Stefanel. *Business Strategy Review* (Autumn): 73-79.

Rushton, A. & R. Saw (1992): A Methodology for Logistics Strategy Planning. *International Journal of Logistics Management 3*(1): 46-62.

Saaty, T.L. (1980): *Analytic Hierarchy Process, Planning, Priority Setting, Resource Allocation.* New York: McGraw-Hill.

Sabbagh, K. (1996): *21ˢᵗ Century Jet.* New York: Scribner.

Sako, M. (1992): *Prices, Quality and Trust – Inter-firm Relations in Britain and Japan.* Cambridge, UK: Cambridge University Press.

Sako, M. (1996): Supplier Relationships and Innovation. In M. Dodgson & R. Rothwell (ed.) *The Handbook of Industrial Innovation.* Cheltenham: Edward Elgar.

Sanchez, R. (1999): Modular Architecture in the Marketing Process. *Journal of Marketing 63*(Special Issue): 92-111.

Savage, C.M. (1990): *Fifth Generation Management.* Boston: Digital Press.

Saxenian, A. (1994): *Regional Advantage: Culture and Competition in Silicon Valley and Route 128.* Cambridge, MA: Harvard University Press.

Schary, P.B. (1998): Strategic Dimensions of the Supply Chain. *Transport Logistics 1*(3): 155-66.

Schrage, M. (1995): *No More Teams! Mastering the Dynamics of Creative Collaboration.* New York: Century Doubleday.

Schrage, M. (2000): *Serious Play.* Boston: Harvard Business School Press.

Sender, I. (1998): Microplanning Jeanswear for the Masses. *Chain Store Age Executive with Shopping Center Age 74*(January): 60 (2): via http//web4 infotrac.Galegroup.com.

Senge, P.M. (1990): *The Fifth Discipline.* New York: Doubleday.

Shank, J.K. & V. Govindarajan (1993): *Strategic Cost Management.* New York: The Free Press.

Sharman, G. (1984). The Rediscovery of Logistics. *Harvard Business Review 62*(September-October 1984): 104-109.

Sharp, J.M., Z. Irani & S. Desai (1999): Working towards Agile Manufacturing in the UK Industry. *International Journal of Production Economics 62*: 155-169.

Shi, Y. & M. Gregory (1998): International Manufacturing Networks to Develop Global Competitive Capabilities. *Journal of Operations Management 16*: 195-214.

Shingo, S. (1987*): Non-stock Production.* Cambridge, MA: Productivity Press.

Sink, H.L. & C.J. Langley (1997): A Managerial Framework for the Acquisition of Third-party Logistics Services. *Journal of Business Logistics 18*(2): 163-189.

Skjøtt-Larsen, T. (1999): Interorganisational Relations from a Supply Chain Management Point of View. *Logistic Management 1*(2): 96-108.

Skjøtt-Larsen, T. (2000): Third-party Logistics – from an Interorganizational Point of View. *International Journal of Physical Distribution and Logistics Management 30*(2): 112-127.

Slats, P.J., B. Bhola, J.J.M. Evers & G. Dijkhuizen (1995): Logistic Chain Modeling. *European Journal of Operational Research 87*: 1-20.

Slywotzky, A.J. (2000): The Age of the Choiceboard. *Harvard Business Review 78*(January-February): 40-41.

Souza, C. (2000): *RossettaNet Members Cast First Stones*. Via www. individual.com (October 18).

Spear, S. & H.K. Bowen (1999): Decoding the DNA of the Toyota Production System. *Harvard Business Review 77*(September-October): 97-106.

Spendolini, M.J. (1992): *The Benchmarking Book*. New York: AMACOM.

Stalk, G. (1990): *Competing against Time*. New York: Collier Mac-Millan.

Stalk, G.H., P. Evans & L.E. Shulman (1992): Competing on Capabilities. *Harvard Business Review 70*(March-April): 57-69.

Stallkamp, T.T. (2000): *Chrysler's Leap of Faith: Redefining the Supplier Relationship*, www.manufacturing.net/scl/scmr (December 21, 2000).

Stank, T.P. & C.W. Lackey (1997): Enhancing Performance through Logistical Capabilities in Mexican Maquiladora Firms. *Journal of Business Logistics 81*(1): 91-124.

Stigler, G.J. (1951): The Division of Labor Is Limited by the Extent of the Market. *Journal of Political Economy 59*(June): 185-193.

Stock, J. (1998): *Development and Implementation of Reverse Logistics Programs*. Oak Brook, IL: Council of Logistics Management.

Stonehill, A.I., N. Ravn & K. Dullum (1982): Management of Foreign Exchange Economic Exposure. In Gerndahl, G. (ed.) *International Financial Management*. Stockholm: Norstedts.

Storper, M. (1997): Territories, Flows and Hierarchies in the Global Economy. In K.J. Cox (ed.) *Spaces of Globalization: Reasserting the Power of the Local*. New York: Guilford: 19-44.

Supply-Chain Council (1997): *Supply Chain Operations Reference Model – Release 2.0* (August 1): via http://www.supply-chain.org): 106-115.

Supply-Chain Council (no date a): *Supply-Chain Operations Reference Model – Overview of SCOR Version 3.0*. Pittsburgh, PA: Supply-Chain Council.

Supply-Chain Council (no date b): *Supply-Chain Operations Reference Model – Overview of SCOR Version 4.0*. Pittsburgh, PA: Supply-Chain Council.

Sweeny, M.T. (1994): A Methodology for the Strategic Management of International Manufacturing and Sourcing. *International Journal of Logistics Management* 5(1): 55-65.

Tadjer, R. (1998): *Internetweek* April 13: 40.

Tansuhaj, P.S. & G.C. Jackson (1989): Foreign Trade Zones: a Comparative Analysis of Users and Non-users. *Journal of Business Logistics* 10(1): 15-30.

Tanzier, A. (1999): Stitches in Time. *Forbes 164*(September 6): 118, 3p.

Tapscott, D. (1995): *The Digital Economy*. New York: McGraw-Hill.

Tapscott, D. & A. Caston (1993): *Paradigm Shift*. New York: McGraw-Hill.

Tapscott, D., D. Ticoll & A. Lowry (2000): *Digital Capital – Harnesssing the Power of Business Webs*. London: Nicholas Brealey Publishing.

Taylor, D. & D. Brunt (2001): *Manufacturing Operations and Supply Chain Management. The LEAN Approach*. London: Thomson Learning.

Taylor, P. (1999): Internet Reshapes World Computing. *Financial Times* (November 3): Information Technology Section p. 1.

The Economist (1998): After the PC. *The Economist* (September 12): 79-82.

The Economist (2000a). Distribution Dilemmas (February 26) via www.economist.com.

The Economist (2000b): Asian Capitalism: the End of Tycoons. *The Economist* (April 29, 2000): 67-69.

The Economist (2000c): Smarting (September 16): 73-74.

The United Nations Global Compact and SA8000 (2000). http://www.cepaa.org/global_compact.htm (December 21, 2000).

Thomchick, E.A. & L. Rosenbaum (1984): The Role of U.S. Export Trading Companies in International Logistics. *Journal of Business Logistics* 5(2): 85-127.

Thompson, J.D. (1967): *Organizations in Action*. New York: McGraw-Hill.

Toth, M. (1998): What's Up with ECR? *Progressive Grocer* (December): 8 via http//web4 infotrac.Galegroup.com.

Towill, D.R., M.M. Naim & J. Wikner (1992): Industrial Dynamics Simulation Models in the Design of Supply Chains. *International Journal of Physical Distribution and Logistics Management* 22(5): 3-14.

Towill, D.R. (1996): Industrial Dynamics Modeling of Supply Chains. *International Journal of Physical Distribution and Logistics Management* 26(2): 23-42.

Trading Partners Unite – New Standard Takes Guesswork out of Supply-Chain [Management] (1998). (February 26) 3 p. via http://www.newspage.com.

Treacy, M. & F. Wiersma (1993): Customer Intimacy and other Value Disciplines. *Harvard Business Review 71*(January-February): 84-93.

Trunk, C. (2000): WMS in Business-to-Business E-commerce. *Material Handling Management* (May): 52-55.

UNCTAD (1993): *World Investment Report* 1993. New York: United Nations.

UNCTAD (1999): *World Investment Report* 1999. New York: United Nations.

Van Damme, D.A., & F.L.A. van der Zon (1999): Activity Based Costing and Decision Support. *International Journal of Logistics Management*: 10(1): 71-82.

Van Hoek, R. (1998): Reconfiguring the Supply Chain to Implement Postponed Manufacturing. *International Journal of Logistics Management* 9(1): 95-110.

Van Hoek, R. (1999): From Reversed Logistics to Green Supply Chains. *Supply Chain Management* 5(3): 129-134.

Van Hoek, R.I. & H.A.M. Weken (1998a): How Modular Production Can Contribute to Integration in Inbound and Outbound Logistics. *International Journal of Logistics: Research and Applications* 1(1): 39-56.

Van Hoek, R.I. & H.A.M. Weken (1998b): The Impact of Modular Production on the Dynamics of Supply Chains. *International Journal of Logistics Management* 9(2): 35-50.

Van Hoek, R.I. & H.A.M. Weken (2000): *Smart (Car): and Smart Logistics*. Oak Brook, IL: Council for Logistics Management.

Van Hoek, R., E. Pelen & H.R. Commandeur 3rd (1999): Achieving Mass Customization through Postponement: a Study of International Changes. *Journal of Market Focused Management* pp. 353-368.

Vantine, J.G. & C. Marra (1997): Logistics Challenges and Opportunities in Mercosur. *International Journal of Logistics Management* 8(1): 55-66.

Vickery, S.K., J.R. Carter & M. D'Itri (1992): A Bayesian Approach to Managing Foreign Exchange in International Sourcing. *Production and Inventory Management Journal* 30(Third Quarter): 15-20.

VICS (1998a): *The CPFR Process Model.* Via http://www.cpfr.org 3 p.

VICS (1998b): *Corporate Values: a Shift toward Collaboration.* Via http://www.cpfr.org 2 p.

VICS (1998c): *The Organizational Shift: Changing to a Consumer-centric, Inter-enterprise Orientation.* Via http://www.cpfr.org 3 p.

Vidal, C.J. & M. Goetschalckx (1997): Strategic Production-Distribution Models: a Critical Review with Emphasis on Global Supply Chain Models. *European Journal of Operations Research 98*: 1-11.

Vidal, C.J. & M. Goetschalckx (2000): Modeling the Effect of Uncertainties on Global Logistics Systems. *Journal of Business Logistics 21*(1): 95-120.

Violino, B. (2000): *UPS Sketches Broad E-commerce Agenda* (May 9): via www.individual.com: 9 p.

Vizard, T. & K. Bull (1998): Selling Seibel. *Info World* (November 30): via http://www.infoworld.com 5 p.

Vos, B. & E. Van de Berg (1996): Assessing International Allocation Strategies. *International Journal of Logistics Management* 7(2): 69-84.

Wall Street Journal (2000): Parts Shortages Hamper Electronics Makers (July 7): B5.

Waller, D.G., R.L. D'Avanzo & D.M. Lambert (1995): *Supply Chain Directions for a New North America.* Oak Brook, IL: Council of Logistics Management.

Waller, M., M.E. Johnson & T. Davis (1999): Vendor-managed Inventory in the Retail Supply Chain. *Journal of Business Logistics 20*(1): 183-203.

Webb, L. (1997): Unpicking the eco-rules for packaging. *Pulp & Paper International (PPI): 39*(10): 53-59.

Whiteoak, P. (1994): The Realities of Quick Response in the Grocery Sector: a Supplier Viewpoint. *International Journal of Physical Distribution and Logistics Management 24*(10): 33-39.

Wilding, R.D. (1998): Chaos Theory: Implications for Supply Chain Management. *International Journal of Logistics Management 9*(1): 43-56.

Williamson, O.E. (1975): *Markets and Hierarchies: Analysis and Antitrust Implications.* London: The Free Press.

Williamson, O.E. (1985): *The Economic Institutions of Capitalism: Firms, Markets, Relational Contracting.* New York: The Free Press.

Williamson, O.E. (1993): Calculativeness, Trust, and Economic Organization. *Journal of Law and Economics 36*(April): 453-486.

Williamson, O.E. (1996): *The Mechanisms of Governance.* Oxford: Oxford University Press.

Womack, J.P. & D.T. Jones (1996): *Lean Thinking: Banish Waste and Create Wealth in your Corporation.* New York: Simon & Schuster.

Womack, J.P., D.T. Jones & D. Roos (1990): *The Machine that Changed the World.* New York: HarperBooks.

Wu, H.-J. & Dunn, S.C. (1995): Environmentally Responsible Logistics Systems. *International Journal of Physical Distribution & Logistics Management 25*(2): 20-39.

Yeung, H.W. (1997): Business Networks and Transnational Operations: a Study of Hong Kong Firms in the ASEAN Region. *Economic Geography 73*(January): 1-25.

Yusuf, Y.Y., M. Sarhadi & A. Gunekaran (1999): Agile Manufacturing: the Drives, Concepts and Attributes. *International Journal of Production Economics 62*: 33-43.

Zajac, E. & C.P. Olsen (1993): From Transaction Cost to Transactional Value of Interorganizational Strategies. *Journal of Management Studies 30*(1): 131-145.

Zuprod, J. (1996): How Important Is Local Culture to Global Logistics? *Transportation and Distribution* (December): 61-63.

Index